DATE DUE			
ILCSO 10-12-92			
GAYLORD			PRINTED IN U.S.A.

REVIEW 7

REVIEW

Volume 7   1985

Edited by

James O. Hoge and James L. W. West III

University Press of Virginia
Charlottesville

THE UNIVERSITY PRESS OF VIRGINIA
Copyright © 1985 by the Rector and Visitors
of the University of Virginia

This journal is a member of (CELJ) the Conference of Editors of Learned Journals

First published 1985

ISSN 0190-3233
ISBN 0-8139-1076-5

Printed in the United States of America

Major funding for *Review* is provided by the generous gifts of Mr. and Mrs. Henry J. Dekker, Mr. and Mrs. J. S. Hill, and Mr. and Mrs. Adger S. Johnson to the Virginia Tech Foundation. Additional support is provided by the *Review* Association, a group of major universities which support the aims and purposes of the series. Member universities are as follows:

>City College of New York
>Columbia University
>University of Colorado
>Duke University
>Harvard University
>University of Minnesota
>Pennsylvania State University
>University of Virginia

Contents

Whim-whams and Flim-flams: 1
The Oxford University Press Edition of *Tristram Shandy*
  by Melvyn New
     Review of Laurence Sterne, *Tristram Shandy*, ed. Ian Campell Ross

Moral-Historical-Critical-Poststructural: Approaches   19
and Assumptions in Recent Shakespearean Scholarship
  by Mary Beth Rose
     Review of Jonathan Dollimore, *Radical Tragedy*; Stephen Booth, King Lear, Macbeth, *Indefinition, and Tragedy*; James L. Calderwood, *To Be and Not to Be: Negation and Metadrama in* Hamlet; Robert Rentoul Reed, Jr., *Crime and God's Judgment in Shakespeare*; C. G. Thayer, *Shakespearean Politics: Government and Misgovernment in the Great Histories*; Robert S. Miola, *Shakespeare's Rome*; Sarup Singh, *Family Relationships in Shakespeare and the Restoration Comedy of Manners*

Subject and Object in Henry James   43
  by Ruth Bernard Yeazell
     Review of Paul B Armstrong, *The Phenomenology of Henry James*; Stuart Hutchinson, *Henry James: An American as Modernist*; William W. Stowe, *Balzac, James, and the Realistic Novel*

Looking for Coherence in the Later Eighteenth Century   57
  by Leopold Damrosch, Jr.
     Review of Frederic V. Bogel, *Literature and Insubstantiality in Later Eighteenth-Century England*

Romanticism through the Mind of Hazlitt 65
   by Jeffrey C. Robinson
      Review of John Kinnaird, *William Hazlitt: Critic of Power*;
      David Bromwich, *Hazlitt: The Mind of a Critic*

Advancing toward Chaos in New Stevens Criticism 77
   by Barbara M. Fisher
      Review of David M. La Guardia, *Advance on Chaos: The Sanctifying Imagination of Wallace Stevens*; Leonora Woodman, *Stanza My Stone: Wallace Stevens and the Hermetic Tradition*

Five Versions of Milton at Horton 89
   by Richard S. Ide
      Review of A. N. Wilson, *The Life of John Milton*; Maryann Cale McGuire, *Milton's Puritan Masque*; Richard Helgerson, *Self-Crowned Laureates: Spenser, Jonson, Milton, and the Literary System*; John Guillory, *Poetic Authority: Spenser, Milton, and Literary History*; William Kerrigan, *The Sacred Complex: On the Psychogenesis of Paradise Lost*

Aesthetic Sensibility and the Idea of the Imagination 113
in America
   By Robert F. Lucid
      Review of Louis J. Budd, *Our Mark Twain: The Making of His Public Personality*; John Raeburn, *Fame Became of Him: Hemingway as Public Writer*

Ruth apRoberts, Matthew Arnold, and God 119
   by David J. DeLaura
      Review of Ruth apRoberts, *Arnold and God*

Emily Dickinson: The Poet as Experienced Virgin   145
   by Jerome Loving
      Review of William H. Shurr, *The Marriage of Emily Dickinson: A Study of the Fascicles*; Vivian R. Pollak, *Emily Dickinson: The Anxiety of Gender*

On Measuring Shakespeare's Theatre   153
   by William H. Allison
      Review of John Orrell, *The Quest for Shakespeare's Globe*

W. B. Yeats: A Commentary on the *New Commentary*   163
   by Richard J. Finneran
      Review of A. Norman Jeffares, *A New Commentary on The Poems of W. B. Yeats*

H. L. Mencken and the Harlem Renaissance   191
   by Fred Hobson
      Review of Charles Scruggs, *The Sage in Harlem: H. L. Mencken and the Black Writers of the 1920s*

Failed Splendor: Edward Brunner's Remaking   197
of *The Bridge*
   by L. S. Dembo
      Review of Edward Brunner, *Splendid Failure: Hart Crane and the Making of* The Bridge

Nightmare to Daydream to Art   207
   by Arnold B. Fox
      Review of Andrew Wright, *Anthony Trollope: Dream and Art*

Approaches to Biography: Two Studies of H.D.   215
   by Fred D. Crawford
      Review of Barbara Guest, *Herself Defined: The Poet H.D. and Her World*

Truth and Fiction: Carlyle Edited and Re-edited   239
   by Rodger L. Tarr
      Review of *Carlyle's Latter-Day Pamphlets*, ed. Michael K. Goldberg and Jules P. Seigel; *The Correspondence of Thomas Carlyle and John Ruskin*, ed. George Allan Cate; Fred Kaplan, *Thomas Carlyle, a Biography*

The Story of a Lie: A Sequel to *A Sequel*   259
   by William E. Fredeman
      Review of John Carter and Graham Pollard, *An Enquiry into the Nature of Certain Nineteenth Century Pamphlets*, 2d ed.; Nicolas Barker and John Collins, *A Sequel to* An Enquiry into the Nature of Certain Nineteenth Century Pamphlets

How Substantial Was Robert Browning?   297
   by John Maynard
      Review of Jacob Korg, *Browning and Italy*; Clyde de L. Ryals, *Becoming Brwoning: The Poems and Plays of Robert Browning*

The Message in the Novels: 305
Walker Percy and the Critics
   by Veronica A. Makowsky
      Review of Martin Luschei, *The Sovereign Wayfarer: Walker Percy's Diagnosis of the Malaise*; Robert Coles, *Walker Percy: An American Search*; Panthea Reid Broughton, ed., *The Art of Walker Percy: Stratagems for Being*; Jac Tharpe, ed., *Walker Percy: Art and Ethics*; Jac Tharpe, *Walker Percy*;

Lewis Baker, *The Percys of Mississippi: Politics and Literature in the New South*

Waste Land Indeed: Eliot in Our Time   329
  by Ruth Z. Temple
    Review of Charles Tomlinson, *Poetry and Metamorphosis*; Ronald Bush, *T. S. Eliot: A Study in Character and Style*; David Spurr, *Conflicts in Consciousness: T. S. Eliot's Poetry and Criticism*; Caroline Behr, *T. S. Eliot: A Chronology of His Life and Works*; Michael Grant, ed., *T. S. Eliot: The Critical Heritage*; Robert H. Canary, *T. S. Eliot: The Poet and His Critics*; David Ned Tobin, *The Presence of the Past: T. S. Eliot's Victorian Inheritance*

Contributors   347

Editorial Board

Felicia Bonaparte
City College, CUNY

Jerome H. Buckley
Harvard University

Paul Connolly
Yeshiva University

A. S. G. Edwards
University of Victoria

Ian Jack
Cambridge University

Robert Kellogg
University of Virginia

James R. Kincaid
University of Colorado

Cecil Y. Lang
University of Virginia

James B. Meriwether
University of South Carolina

Hershel Parker
University of Delaware

Martin Roth
University of Minnesota

George Stade
Columbia University

John L. Sharpe III
Duke University

G. Thomas Tanselle
John Simon Guggenheim Memorial Foundation

Stanley Weintraub
Pennsylvania State University

Whim-whams and Flim-flams: The Oxford University Press Edition of *Tristram Shandy*

Melvyn New

Laurence Sterne, *Tristram Shandy*, ed. Ian Campbell Ross. Oxford: The Clarendon Press, Oxford University Press, 1983. xxix, 595 pp.

Several years ago, in concluding my review of Richard Wendorf and Charles Ryskamp's *The Works of William Collins*, published by Oxford University Press (1979), I suggested that editors and publishers (commercial and scholarly) needed to come "to some working arrangement concerning the multitude of editions presently being produced."[1] It seems appropriate, therefore, to begin this review of Ian Campbell Ross's edition of *Tristram Shandy* with a somewhat stronger suggestion: editors and publishers (commercial and scholarly) need to come to some working arrangement concerning the *integrity* of their enterprise, the relationship between scholarship and profit.

In advertising this edition, Oxford University Press uses the term "scholarly edition"[2] and indeed from Oxford we expect no less. Perhaps I am not aware of some new definition of "scholarly," but if the word still means that Professor Ross mastered the scholarship necessary to produce an edition of *Tristram Shandy* different in kind and quality from the textbook editions of James A. Work (Odyssey Press, 1940), Ian Watt (Houghton Mifflin, 1965), Graham Petrie (Penguin, 1967), or Howard Anderson (Norton, 1980), then the claim is false advertising. In the dust-cover blurb we are told that Ross provides "fresh and detailed explanatory notes"; in a 1983 Oxford University Press catalogue we are told that "full explanatory notes" are included. In truth, the notes are clearly derivative from Work's edition, by way of Petrie. There is hardly one single indication of independent research. Forty-three years of intervening scholarship, if we can believe these notes, have not only produced scant new insights or explanations unavailable in Work, they have not even produced new questions. In short, despite the $55.00 price of the hardcover edition, and despite its being advertised as 640 pages (or 625 or 630 pages, depending upon which advertisement one reads), this edition is of no more value than the Oxford World Classics paperback textbook edition (1983) of 595 pages selling for $4.95. Indeed, the two are identical, except for the size of the page and the type.

Moreover, both publisher and editor seem to be aware of the scholarly and economic culpability of their enterprise, an admission I find lurking behind their puffing the edition as "the first single-volume edition to take as copy-text for volumes I and II the York edition, now established as pre-dating the London edition" (jacket blurb). What an odd statement this is—unless both editor and publisher are aware that a "scholarly edition" of *Tristram Shandy* had been published in *two* volumes in 1978, five years before the Oxford edition. It is this edition that Ross either used to establish his own text (and he does cite it in his selected bibliography) without giving adequate credit—or did not use, in which case his claim that he is a "scholarly" editor is highly suspect.

Let me speak directly to the point. There is in print one "scholarly" edition of the text of *Tristram Shandy*, published by the University of Florida Press in 1978; it is published in two volumes, and at the end of the second contains an introduction to the text's composition and publication, nineteen pages of textual notes, a list of emendations, an historical collation, a bibliography of life-time editions, and additional appendices dealing with specific textual problems. Volume III of this edition was published in 1984; it contains some 500 pages of notes to *Tristram Shandy* (and yet its editors would not speak of "full" explanations), along with an introduction to the problems and issues involved in annotating Sterne, an appendix of military terms, and a selected index of authors cited. To be sure, since I am the general editor of the Florida edition of Sterne's *Works*, and a co-editor of the three-volume edition of

Whim-whams and Flim-flams

Tristram Shandy, I have a vested interest in making a claim for the Florida edition—and in the polite world of scholarship it is considered bad manners to express a view where self-interest is concerned. This will be, unfortunately, an impolite review. The Oxford *Tristram Shandy* is a textbook edition, worth at most $4.95. Its text is better than those of other textbook editions, since it comes after the work of Kenneth Monkman and myself, but for students the differences are of minimal significance.[3] Its notes are no improvement over James Work's in 1940. Its introduction is mundane.

For students, Work's edition, with footnotes rather than backnotes, remains my first choice. Watt's edition, also with footnotes, has a more useful introduction than Work's, but its text, despite the gesture toward some collation, is disappointing—of course, Watt did not have Monkman's and my work to rely upon. The Penguin edition two years later was quite unnecessary in view of Work's and Watt's still being in print, although Christopher Ricks has written a pleasant introduction. The 1980 Norton edition has a quite unreliable text, notes carelessly derived from Work and Watt, and a selection of critical essays chosen, I assume, by lottery; that on its cover it is labelled a "Critical Edition" and "an Authoritative Text" simply suggests that in the world of textbook salesmanship "critical" and "authoritative" and "scholarly" have lost their old-fashioned associations with integrity. Into this situation—best summarized by saying that since 1940 no significant improvement has been made to Work's fine textbook edition—Oxford offers its "scholarly" edition, not only for the textbook price of $4.95, but at the scholarly price of $55.00. As a textbook, it ranks third or fourth out of the five annotated texts now available at student prices; as anything more, I can only suggest that if any library has paid $55.00 for this volume, basing its purchase on the Oxford University Press imprint or on its advertisements, that library ought to sue for breach of promise. What is sad to contemplate indeed, in this day of ever-rising book prices and diminishing library resources, is that many libraries, using the convenience of standing orders, did waste $55.00 for this book—which is, of course, precisely what Oxford University Press was counting on. I am afraid that what is good for business may not always be good for the cause of scholarship.

The text of the Oxford *Tristram Shandy* is indeed based on the correct copy-texts,[4] and is an accurate transcription as far as I have been willing to determine. Ross gives no indication that he collated multiple copies of each text to make certain he did not have a variant state; he either had great faith in his capacity to choose a copy without press variants or he allowed the Florida edition to relieve him of this particular "scholarly" anxiety. That he might know about such minutiae as states and variants is suggested by his note to the dedication to Volume I, in which he calls attention to two states and indicates that he is using the "second, corrected state."[5] The Florida edition had also noted the two states (II: 844), as follows:

State 1   **State 2**

well wisher   *Well-wisher*
Fellow-Subject∧   *Fellow-Subject,*

Unfortunately, what the Florida edition calls State 1, Ross decided to call State 2, and vice versa. Perhaps the Florida editors are wrong, but surely in that case a "scholarly" edition ought to explain the error. Why does the absence of a hyphen and a comma indicate a "second, corrected state" rather than an "uncorrected" first state? Does Ross really have evidence of priority between these states? Or is it possible, given the lack of explanation, that he simply confused his notes from the Florida edition?

Ross also notes that the dedication to Volume IX exists in two states, information again available either through his unrecorded collations of multiple copies of Volume IX, or in the textual note to the Florida edition (II: 862). These two instances of variant states are the only evidence of textual collation in the notes of the Oxford *Tristram Shandy*. Only a handful of other variant readings are made note of in any fashion, despite the fact that Ross emends his copy-text on numerous occasions. For example, Ross alters "nicity" to "nicety" (p. 18), "gentlemen" to "gentleman" (p. 19), "likwise" to "likewise" (p. 22), and "and" to "or" (p. 23), all second edition

Whim-whams and Flim-flams 5

readings, and readings accepted by the Florida edition and listed in Apendix Two (List of Emendations), II: 863. Ross does not call attention to any of them, nor to his changes in punctuation on pages 32, 37, and 42.[6] They too are changes accepted into the Florida text, as noted in the List of Emendations. On page 56 Ross emends the copy-text reading "come cast away" to "comes cast away," an interesting emendation that modern editors before the Florida edition have not made; the emendation is explained in the Florida edition in the textual note to 77.26 (II: 845). On the other hand, Ross keeps the copy-text reading of *Aldergate-street* (p. 57), despite the fact that no such street exists, while a John Beale did indeed have a printing establishment on the well-known *Aldersgate-street*, as explained in the Florida edition's textual note to 79.18 (II: 845-46). The change was made in the second edition.

Ross has given us only the barest few clues about the rationale behind his process of editing. In his "Note on the Text" he informs us that he has corrected "obvious errors"—a license of dubious "scholarly" value. He then informs us that the copy-text has been "followed for accidentals" though "substantial [sic?] emendations from later editions in which Sterne took an interest have generally been incorporated" (p. xxv). What this ratonale produces, as evidenced by the emendations already noted, is what we might best call an "unprincipled" text ("——Here are two senses, cried *Eugenius* . . . pointing with the fore finger of his right hand to the word *Crevice* . . ." [I: 258]). Why is *"Aldergate-street"* not an "obvious" error, especially since it is corrected in the second edition? Or in Volume II, why is *"Cochorn"* (p. 73) not altered to *"Coehorn,"* when the *"c"* is so clearly a compositorial error in a name Sterne obviously was familiar with? Or why is "radical moister" retained on the same page, when Sterne has "radical moisture" on the nineteen other occasions of its use in *Tristram Shandy*? Ross would seem to have a conservative policy of emendation here, and yet, in addition to those changes I noted in the first volume, we might ask why "diversons" is silently corrected to "diversions" (p. 72), "slopped" to "sloped" (p. 78) or *"Alquise"* to *"Alquife"* (p. 122) in the second volume? Why would "whimisical" (p. 115) be retained (it is corrected in the second edition), but "diversons" need correcting? This is part of the difficulty of pretending to a "scholarly" text when one has simply not done the work required to produce one.

We can approach the problem of the Oxford text from a somewhat different direction. In Volume II there is a passage rendered in the copy-text and in Ross's edition as follows: "but it was a little hard to male-treat him after, and plunder him after he was laid in his grave" (p. 113). This was emended in the Florida edition, following Work's suggested reading, to "male-treat him before, and plunder him after . . ." (I: 167), and the alteration is explained in a textual note (II: 848) as well as recorded in the List of Emendations. Is it really no longer a part of scholarship, not to say of "scholarly" editing, to explain your difference with a previous "scholarly" editor, if you decide his emendation is incorrect? Surely some exchange of views is still a part of the scholarly enterprise. Ross had access to the Florida edition and cites it in his bibliography. Did he not like this emendation? Did he think it too liberal? Foolish? "Unscholarly"? Did he think about it at all?

I do not want to pursue Ross's text much further. What is apparent throughout, I believe, is a rather random emendation of the text, without record and without very much reason that I can determine. At times spellings are corrected, at times not, at times punctuation is altered, at times not, at times proper names are corrected, at times not, at times changes from the second edition are admitted into the text, at times not. Through it all, Ross keeps the reader in the dark as to precisely what editorial principles he espouses; and keeps this particular reader in especial suspense over the question of the relationship of his text to the Florida text. My final determination is that it barely matters. If Ross did not use the Florida text he most certainly should not have allowed Oxford University Press to call his work "scholarly"; if he did use it, he should have established more clearly his relationship to it, not to say dependence upon it.

In Volume IV, Sterne has a nonsense footnote that contains, among other puzzles of the copy-text, the phrase "Bar e Jas." In an essay published in 1976 in *Studies in Bibliography* Norman Fry and I provided almost certainly Sterne's source for much of the note, as well as a suggestion for emending "Bar e Jas" to "Bar & Jas."[7] The point is miniscule, I am certain, but after all what do "scholarly" editors do if not pursue the minutiae of a text? A "scholarly" editor might certainly *disagree* with our emendation, but I do not think he is free to *ignore* it, most especially if his work is going to be advertised as a "scholarly edition." Indeed, Sterne's foreign language borrowings are an especial burden for any editor and I set forth some principles for dealing with them in both the *SB* essay and an earlier one in *PBSA*.[8] These are not obscure journals, yet Ross blithely ignores both articles—as indeed he ignores almost entirely the scholarship on Sterne since Work's edition in 1940.

Because of his "careful" collation of texts—or because Kenneth Monkman called attention to them in 1970—Ross does show an awareness of several sentences added in the second edition of Volume V—though he deals most strangely with them. The first edition reads:

The *Danes*, an' please your honour, quoth the corporal, who were on the left at the siege of *Limerick*, were all auxiliaries.———And very good ones, said my uncle *Toby*.—But the auxiliaries, *Trim*, my brother is talking about,—I conceive to be different things.———

The version of the second edition (and of the Florida edition, I: 485) is different:

The *Danes*, an' please your honour, quoth the corporal, who were on the left at the siege of *Limerick*, were all auxiliaries.———And very good ones, said my uncle *Toby*.—And your honour roul'd with them, captains with captains.—Very well, said the corporal.—But the auxiliaries, my brother is talking about, answered by uncle*Toby*—I conceive to be different things.———

Ross seems to have liked the two new sentences, but not the rewritten third sentence that forms part of the paragraph, and so emends the passage creatively:

The *Danes*, an' please your honour, quoth the corporal, who were on the left at the siege of *Limerick*, were all auxiliaries.———And very good ones, said my uncle *Toby*.—And your honour roul'd with them, captains with captains.—Very well, said the corporal.—But the auxiliaries, *Trim*, my brother is talking about,—I conceive to be different things.—— [p. 323]

Walter Shandy with his penknife could not have acted more cavalierly with his text.

If we turn now to the "full" and "fresh" annotations of the Oxford edition, we shall again be sorely disappointed. I want to begin this examination by quoting the tribute I paid to James Work's edition in my introduction to Volume III of the Florida *Tristram Shandy*, the volume of annotations:

> There have been several annotated textbook editions of *Tristram* prior to this scholarly edition. The best by far is that by James Aiken Work, first published in 1940. Work's annotations are primarily of a historical and pedagogical nature: he identifies historical and contemporary personages mentioned by Sterne, defines "difficult" and foreign words and phrases, and elucidates allusions that a modern student audience could not be expected to grasp. He also identifies, but almost always by citation alone, some of Sterne's major borrowings, particularly those from Rabelais, Burton, and Montaigne. So thorough is his identification of persons that we have chosen to quote his notes directly, whenever we are unable to improve on them. That we should be compelled to write "Alfonso Tostado (c. 1400-1455) was a famous theological author in Spain" to avoid Work's "an eminent Spanish theologian and author" seems an exercise in futility. . . . Our admiration for Work's edition is great, as should be evident in the notes, so that those few occasions where we have discovered him to be in error should not be taken as anything more than the particular errors they are. Few if any eighteenth-century authors have been better served in being made available to a general reading audience than Sterne has been in James Work's edition of *Tristram Shandy*. [III:30]

To a very great extent, the notes of the Oxford edition (and, to be fair, of the Riverside, Penguin, and Norton editions as well) are little more than re-*Works*, if I might. When these editions limit their pretensions to that of student textbooks, little harm is done, except perhaps to the cash flow of the Odyssey Press. But to suggest that after forty years of incessant scholarly activity we know nothing more about *Tristram Shandy* than Work did in 1940, and to make that suggestion in a "scholarly

Whim-whams and Flim-flams

edition" or a "critical edition"—that is culpable.

I could not possibly address all the shortcomings of Ross's annotations, but will provide instead merely a sample sufficient to justify my harsh judgment. I begin with a brief history of the annotation of a rather simple passage in Volume I:

> My way is ever to point out to the curious, different tracts of investigation, to come at the first springs of the events I tell;—not with a pedantic *Fescue*,—or in the decisive Manner of *Tacitus*, who outwits himself and his reader . . . . [I: 74]

Work's annotation is, I believe, a good, solid note for a student edition: "Cornelius Tacitus (c. 55-c. 120), a Roman historian, whose style, proverbial for its brevity, is occasionally obscure and affected, and whose interpretation of actions appears sometimes to be over-subtilized" (p. 66, n. 4) Notice, however, how the idea of "over-subtilized" interpretation is lost in Watt's rewriting of the note in 1965: "Occasional obscurities result from the laconic brevity of this Roman historian's style" (p. 50, n. 7). Petrie seems to have had Watt in mind: "Referring to the elliptical and often obscure style of the Roman historian" (p. 621). Anderson in 1980 is not very different: "Tacitus was an ancient Roman historian whose style is sometimes so concise that his meaning becomes unclear" (p. 47, n. 7). And finally, the "scholarly" Ross: "Cornelius Tacitus (*c.* 56-*c.* 120), Roman orator and historian, and exponent of a literary style admired for its compactness but at times criticized as elliptical" (p. 548). I have two problems with this brief history: (1) if the four editors could add nothing to Work, it surely would have been better to have quoted him directly rather than to work so hard to rephrase him; and (2) it seems to me that the annotators after Work all followed the wrong path in stressing Tacitus' brevity, when Sterne seems so clearly to be alluding to the "over-subtilizing" of action that is Work's second observation; after all, the subject of the passage in *Tristram Shandy* is not obscurity or brevity but motive-mongering. And indeed, a little research into the eighteenth-century context uncovers almost precisely the view of Tacitus held by Sterne. Richard Steele, in *Spectator* 202, excuses himself for falling, like Tacitus, "into Observations upon [a trivial incident] which were too great for the Occasion" and ascribing it "to Causes which had nothing to do towards it." Donald F. Bond's annotation is particularly illuminating: "Rapin (*Reflections upon History*, chap. vii) notes that Tacitus is always seeing stratagem and policy where they do not exist. 'Policy is the Universal Motive: the Clue that unravels all Transactions....' "[9]

Another example of a lack of scholarship is suggested by that passage in Volume II where Walter and Toby are left standing "like *Brutus* and *Cassius* at the close of the scene making up their accounts" (I: 134). Work refers to Shakespeare's *Julius Caesar*, IV.ii.52, "at which point, according to eighteenth century stage directions, all save Brutus and Cassius *exeunt*" (p. 116, n. 1). Watt, Anderson, and Ross all offer the same citation (Petrie has no note), and I have no quarrel with them, except to be puzzled by the fact that an equally obvious allusion to the play one page earlier is not annotated, namely Walter's comment to Toby to "forgive, I pray thee, this rash humour which my mother gave me." Surely Sterne has *Julius Caesar*, IV.iii.119-21, in mind: "Cas. Have not you love enough to bear with me, / When that rash humor which my mother gave me / Makes me forgetful?" It is not that I expect an editor to recover every allusion in his text (not even in an edition promising "full" explanation), but simply that I am suspicious when three editors after Work are familiar enough with *Julius Caesar* to spot the allusion to IV.ii.52, but not the one to a passage within 120 lines of it. One almost suspects that their citations were taken from the Work edition.

Another borrowing from Shakespeare occurs early in Volume I, where Yorick's downfall is predicted in words echoing those Shakespeare assigns, ironically enough, to Cardinal Wolsey in *Henry VIII* (III.ii.355-57): "The third day comes a frost, a killing frost, / And when he thinks, good easy man, full surely / His greatness is a-ripening, nips his root...." *Tristram Shandy*'s version is as follows: "that when he thought, good easy man! full surely preferment was o'ripening--they had smote his root..." (I: 33). The borrowing was first noted by Watt (p. 23, n. 5) and appropriated by Anderson, but it is not cited in the "full" notes of the Oxford edition. Even were we to assume that for some reason or another Ross decided the echo was not an echo, should he not, again as a "scholarly" editor, indicate that previous annotators have been misled? The fact is, of course, that Ross never looked at the Watt or Anderson editions in compiling his notes. He was busy with Work and Petrie, to be sure, but in this particular instance neither had recorded the borrowing.

This is hardly the only borrowing missed by Ross's "full" annotations. However, what disturbs me is not, I repeat, that an editor misses borrowings, but that Ross's "full" and "fresh" annotations add so little of substance to Work's findings forty-three years earlier—and, indeed, that some valid annotations are dropped. In I.xii, for example, there is an entire passage in italics (*"When to gratify a private appetite . . . to offer it up with"* [I: 32]), that Work (p. 29, n. 2) correctly identified as a paraphrase from Thomas Tenison's introduction to his *Genuine Remains of Sr. Francis Bacon* (the identification was actually first made by John Ferriar, Sterne's first "annotator" at the end of the eighteenth century); Ross ignores the borrowing. Or again, in Volume II, when Tristram launches into his discussion concerning the causes of obscurity, Ross omits a specific reference to the *Essay Concerning Human Understanding*, II.29.3, cited by Work (p. 85, n. 1). He does cite chapter and verse for the Locke borrowing in Volume III (Chapter 18) on duration, although not Jean-Claude Sallés important qualification of the debt published in 1955;[10] and for the discussion of wit and judgment two chapters later he cites the *Essay*, but gives no indication at all of the important long tradition of opposition to Locke on his separation of wit and judgment. One might not expect such a detail in a textbook edition, but surely a "scholarly" edition owes us something at this point in *Tristram Shandy* besides the geographical location of *"Angermania"* and *"Ingria"* (p. 560). Ross's annotations suggest a strange set of priorities in determining what exactly a reader might need in order to understand Sterne's work. It is therefore to be expected, I suppose, that when Tristram discusses at length the nature of property (III.34), with an example directly from Locke's *Two Treatises of Government*, that Ross will remain silent—despite Work's having pointed the way forty-three years earlier (p. 221, n. 1). This preponderant inconsistency throughout the entire set of notes is terribly damaging to Ross's credibility as a "scholarly" annotator. Indeed, the notes inspire no confidence at all that Ross read Chambers or Locke, Rabelais or Burton, Sterne's sermons or letters, in preparation for annotating *Tristram Shandy*. He did, however, read Work's and Petrie's annotations—carelessly.

Since we have arrived at the third volume, I will dwell on it a bit further, because within a few of its pages we can find the sort of annotating that prevails in the Oxford edition, beginning with Ross's identification of *"All is not gain that is got into the purse"* (I: 256) as a "proverbial expression" (p. 562). One hesitates to argue with so astute an observation, except to say that it seems rather lonesome without similarly identifying the phrase "crush'd his nose . . . as flat as a pancake" a few pages earlier (I: 253) or "saving the mark" (I: 260) a few pages later, not to mention "turn up trumps" "old dogs . . . learning new tricks" and "take up cudgels" in the pages immediately following. In short, *Tristram Shandy*'s prose is so replete with proverbial phrases that pointing out one among the hundred or more is surely an exercise of both futility and capriciousness. A scholarly editor would try to point out as many as he possibly could catch; Ross annotates only this single instance.

But, indeed, capriciousness defines the entire enterprise. Ephraim Chambers's *Cyclopaedia*, for example, is recognized as the source for Sterne's chapter on bridges (Chapter 25), but not for the list of engines of war in the previous chapter, or for the definition of "nose" a few chapters later (I: 262). In the note on bridges, Ross follows Work so closely that he too omits the dates for the Marquis de l'Hôpital while providing those for Bernouilli, even though both men are named in the same sentence (p. 562; Work, p. 213, n. 3). Ross recognizes Chambers as the source for Sterne's error *"Des Eaux"* (I: 263), but does not cite W. G. Day's essay in 1970 which first pointed out the debt.[11] I perhaps do not know what to expect from a "scholarly" edition, but I do wonder that Ross can pillage that small part of the scholarship he gives evidence of having read without assigning credit by way of citation. Of course, what Ross has *not* read seems an equal negligence. He does

Whim-whams and Flim-flams

not seem to know, for example, another essay by Day on Sterne and Ozell (1972) which should be brought to bear on Chapter 35; Ross identifies Bruscambille and Paraeus and Bouchet, but without noting the very convincing argument by Day that Sterne found these names and the contents of his entire discussion at this point in Chapter 40 of the first volume of Ozell's edition of Rabelais.[12] Work's note (p. 229, n. 3) on the changes Walter makes to Erasmus' text is omitted, although it seems to me highly useful and quite probably correct. Here as elsewhere the omission seems the result of carelessness rather than choice. Ross does accept Work's note on the "*Savoyard's* box" (a "hurdy gurdy" p. 214, n. 1), as do Watt, Petrie, and Anderson, despite the fact that the more likely definition is "raree-show box," since Walter is imagined to be "peeping" into it (I: 252). "Pantoufles" (I: 222) is annotated, but not "trunk-hose" (I: 218), or "pumps" (I: 221), or "jack-boots" (I: 241), the latter being particularly worth noting as a probable pun on Lord Bute. The phrasing of the mention of Cardinal Alberoni (I: 250) is from N. Tindal's continuation of Paul de Rapin-Thoyras's *History of England*, as pointed out by Theodore Baird in 1936.[13] Inexplicably, to my mind, Work never made use of Baird's essay, nor does he cite Tindal in his notes, despite the fact that Sterne copied many sentences verbatim in his description of battles and the demolition of Dunkirk. Why subsequent editors have followed Work's lead in not incorporating Tindal into the list of authors most in evidence in *Tristram Shandy* remains a mystery to me.

The notes to Volume IV show much the same blend of inconsistency and error. *Ex mero motu* is defined as "from mere impulse" (p. 565), but in context it clearly has the meaning "of his own accord"—"since the stranger *ex mero motu* had confessed . . ." (I: 309). The term occurs in royal correspondence, as Chambers informs us, to signify that the king acts "of his own will and motion" and not under duress or misinformation. "Butter'd buns" (I: 302) is correctly annotated, but if one is going to annotate bawdy expressions, why not comment on "Rever. J. Tubal" and "J. Scrudr." in Sterne's nonsense note (I: 310) or on "doubled the cape" on page 313? That Work comments only on "butter'd buns" may *explain* Ross's doing so, but hardly *excuses* what is more and more evidently the pattern of annotation in this "scholarly" edition. Why is a word like "stamina" not annotated (I: 306), since no one today uses it quite like Sterne and his age did: "in the very first stamina and rudiments of its formation . . ."? Why is Sterne's borrowing his definition of death from Chambers not pointed out (I: 309); or his sentence on the "School of Athens" by Raphael (I: 333) not traced to a sentence by Jonathan Richardson the Younger, as convincingly pointed out by R. F. Brissenden in 1964?[14] Why are Sterne's self-borrowings from his sermons on pages 332 and 350 not noted? The allusion to Longinus in the passage on Diana's temple (I: 337) is not explained; "radical heat" (I: 354) is not defined, although "radical moister," we remember, had been defined earlier. Of the borrowing from Montaigne in Chapter 15, Ross writes that Sterne "paraphrases, at times inaccurately" (p. 568). Sterne quotes accurately, I think, but brings two separated passages together to produce an effect quite different from Montaigne's original intention. It would have been useful in "full" annotations to provide the borrowed passages—but that is one thing the Oxford "scholarly" edition is unwilling to do in any instance, having an eye, probably, on the cost of paper. The extent of Sterne's use of other texts in creating his own, surely one of the primary interests of any "scholarly" annotator, cannot even be guessed at until we are able to put his borrowed passages alongside his sources in some systematic manner.

Of the mention of a "bishop" in Chapter 20, Ross concludes that "this reference brought about a permanent break" (p. 568) between Warburton and Sterne. I know of no evidence for this assertion. The note on the Duke of Ormond (p. 569) does not mention Ormond's central role in bringing about the Treaty of Utrecht, certainly a major event in *Tristram Shandy*. That "Homenas" was to be the central character of Sterne's "Rabelaisian Fragment" is not noted. But perhaps the most indicative "scholarly" note in Volume IV is Ross's annotation of Sterne's invocation of Pope Leo the III (I: 389): "Leo III (d. 816) did not make any significant statement concerning baptism, unlike Innocent III (1160-1216) of whom Sterne was perhaps thinking" (p. 570). We have here a sense of penetrating

Whim-whams and Flim-flams 15

scholarship, the learned annotator digging into the papal archives to discover Sterne's error. Anderson demonstrates equal scholarship: "Probably Innocent III" (p. 230, n. 2) is his pithy summary of many years of research. That both Anderson and Ross are copying Work is nowhere acknowledged in their notes, though perhaps not unexpectedly, Work did happen to make the same point in 1940: "There is an important pronouncement regarding the intention of the priest in baptism, in a decree of Innocent III; I have been unable to discover anything of the sort in Leo III" (p. 327, n. 2). But what interests me even more than this less than innocent appropriation of Pope Innocent III, is that the annotation contributes so little to our understanding of Sterne, who, like Anderson and Ross in this case, was always more interested in a show of scholarship than in the thing itself. His entire discussion at this point is lifted from a note to Rabelais, as pointed out by W. G. Day in 1972.[15] Had Sterne bothered to pursue Rabelais' citation to the *Corpus Juris Canonici* he would have discovered (as Work also notes) that Pope Zachary and not Pope Leo III was responsible for the decree under question, but Sterne seems to have resisted doing research and fell upon Innocent III instead, quite probably at random. However, even if he did pick him because of a particular decree, is not the fact that the entire discussion is borrowed from the pages of Rabelais really the information Sterne's reader should have? Ross makes no mention of it.

There is nothing to be gained by continuing volume by volume through Ross's annotations to *Tristram Shandy*. Each volume's notes would tell the same story: minimal new research and maximal borrowing from James Work. The information presented is accurate enough (one does wonder about the note to "Hermitage and Cotê roti" [II: 623] as "vineyards *in* the Rhône" [p. 588; my italics]), but it is the accuracy primarily of Work some forty-three years ago. Certainly its annotations are no better than Work's—indeed, they are no better than Petrie's, which were published without the misleading fanfares of "scholarly," "full," and "fresh," not to mention a $55.00 price tag.[16] What we have here, without a shadow of a doubt, is a fifth student textbook edition of *Tristram Shandy*, with annotations determined forty-three years ago to be appropriate to the needs of a student encountering *Tristram Shandy* for the first time. As such, it competes with Petrie's Penguin edition especially, since in format and annotation it is most like it. Any other claims are false, misleading, culpable—and to use the term "scholarly" to describe it is to be reminded of Tristram's own sharp insight into comparable worth: " ☞ A dwarf who brings a standard along with him to measure his own size—take my word, is a dwarf in more articles than one . . ." (I: 375).

It is rumored that Ross will next undertake a biography of Sterne for Oxford University Press, despite Arthur Cash's fine recent biography.[17] If this is indeed true I would suggest that he read Cash more carefully than heretofore in order to avoid the embarrassment of copying what he does not understand. Without doubt, given my shandean taste for absurdity, my favorite note in Ross's collection is that for "whim-wham": "A whim-wham was not only a plaything but also a legal term in a document relating to the licensing of midwives, called a faculty" (p. 542). This piece of nonsense, based upon a borrowing from Cash (who is, of course, not cited) is actually a misreading of the following passage from *Early and Middle Years*: "But if Sterne intended to erase all identifying clues, he neglected one. The lawyer, Didius, was immediately recognized as Dr Francis Topham. The clue is contained in that incident in which Didius 'coax'd many of the old licensed [midwives] in the neighbourhood, to open their faculties afresh, in order to have this whim-wham of his inserted'. The whim-wham referred to so ambiguously is only a legal phrase, in a document called a 'faculty', giving the midwife her office along with all its 'rights, members, and appurtenances whatsoever' . . . ."[18] Granted that the grammar of this sentence is somewhat confusing, it is nonetheless readily apparent that what is meant is that with the phrase "whim-wham" Sterne is alluding to the legal phrase "rights, members, and appurtenances whatsoever," and not that "whim-wham" was a term heard around the Inns of Court in the eighteenth century. Rabelais could have taught Ross what the term obviously meant to Sterne, given the context, namely, "whim-whams, men's pissing tools," as the translators have succinctly put it.[19] On the other hand, I believe Ross could have taught Rabelais something about what "flim-flam" might mean to Sterneans of the twentieth century, namely, "the Oxford University Press's scholarly edition of *Tristram Shandy*." Or as Tristram would have put it, the entire enterprise amounts to nothing more than a "cock and bull" story.

Notes

1. *Eighteenth-Century Studies*, 15 (1982), p. 362.

2. For example, in *PMLA*, 98 (1983), p. 950.

3. Kenneth Monkman, "The Bibliography of the Early Editions of *Tristram Shandy*," *Library*, 25 (1970), pp. 11-39.

4. One speaks of copy-texts to acknowledge the serial nature of publication of the nine volumes of *Tristram Shandy* between 1759 and 1767.

5. Page 542. Unless otherwise indicated, quotations from *Tristram Shandy* will be from the Florida edition, cited by volume and page number. Quotations from the Oxford edition will be cited in the text.

6. I.e., reconcile. *to* reconcile: (p. 32)
    weakness!∧ *to* weakness!" (p. 37)
    him;" *to* him;∧ (p. 37)
    child, *to* child. (p. 42)

7. Melvyn New and Norman Fry, "Some Borrowings in *Tristram Shandy*: The Textual Problem," *Studies in Bibliography*, 29 (1976), pp. 324-26; see also the Florida edition of *Tristram Shandy*, textual note to 310.20ff. (II: 852-53).

8. Melvyn New, "*Tristram Shandy* and Heinrich van Deventer's *Observations*," *PBSA*, 69 (1975), pp. 84-90.

9. *The Spectator*, ed. Donald F. Bond (Oxford: Clarendon Press, 1965), II: 291; cf. the note to 74.7-8 in the Florida edition of *Tristram Shandy*, III: 110.

10. Jean-Claude Sallé, "A Source of Sterne's Conception of Time," *Review of English Studies*, n.s. 6 (1955), pp. 180-82.

11. W. G. Day, "A Note on Sterne: 'Des Eaux,' " *Notes & Queries*, 215 (1970), p. 303.

12. W. G. Day, "Sterne and Ozell," *English Studies*, 53 (1972), pp. 434-36. Day demonstrates that Sterne used the translation by Thomas Urquhart and Peter Motteux, with notes by John Ozell. This is the work I refer to herein simply as "Rabelais."

13. Theodore Baird, "The Time-Scheme of *Tristram Shandy* and a Source," *PMLA*, 51 (1936), p. 815, n. 68.

14. R. F. Brissenden, "Sterne and Painting," in *Of Books and Humankind*, ed. John Butt (London: Routledge and Kegan Paul, 1964), pp. 97-98.

15. "Sterne and Ozell," p. 435.

16. It is noteworthy that Oxford University Press, despite the $55.00 cost, has not included the two Hogarth illustrations that most scholars would consider legitimate parts of the text of *Tristram Shandy*; and that the marbled page is printed in black and white, rather than in color. The paperback edition has on its cover an entertaining illustration of Toby and Trim by Bunbury, produced after Sterne's death and rather gratuitous in the absence of the Hogarth illustrations. Nevertheless, it seems to me to make the $4.95 version a useful corrective to Tobyphiles.

17. Arthur H. Cash, *Laurence Sterne: The Early and Middle Years* (London: Metheun, 1975).

18. Cash, p. 289.

19. Rabelais, IV.32.

Moral-Historical-Critical-Poststructural: Approaches and Assumptions in Recent Shakespearean Scholarship

Mary Beth Rose

Jonathan Dollimore. *Radical Tragedy: Religion, Ideology and Power in the Drama of Shakespeare and His Contemporaries.* Chicago: University of Chicago Press, 1984. 312 pp.

Stephen Booth. King Lear, Macbeth, *Indefinition, and Tragedy.* New Haven: Yale University Press, 1983. xi, 183 pp.

James L. Calderwood. *To Be and Not To Be: Negation and Metadrama in* Hamlet. New York: Columbia University Press, 1983. xvi, 222 pp.

Robert Rentoul Reed, Jr. *Crime and God's Judgment in Shakespeare.* Lexington: University Press of Kentucky, 1984. 225 pp.

C. G. Thayer. *Shakespearean Politics: Government and Misgovernment in the Great Histories.* Athens: Ohio University Press, 1983. x, 190 pp.

Robert S. Miola. *Shakespeare's Rome.* Cambridge: Cambridge University Press, 1983. xii, 133 pp.

Sarup Singh. *Family Relationships in Shakespeare and the Restoration Comedy of Manners.* Delhi: Oxford University Press, 1983. x, 233 pp.

Shakespeare occupies a unique, indeed an unchallenged position at the center of Anglo-American culture, both lay and academic. Since the late seventeenth century, when his merits were first elaborated systematically in literary criticism, his vast artistic eminence and his crucial function as seer, as commentator on our morals, emotions, and traditions, gradually have become institutionalized. The Shakespearean canon as text and performance increasingly has provided a cultural nexus, where moral, literary, and artistic assumptions can be articulated and from which they can be inferred. Taken as a whole, Shakespearean commentary in its various forms has become one of the significant arenas in which the struggle to determine meaning and define value takes place. In Shakespearean discourse much is therefore at stake.

Twentieth-century scholarship about Shakespeare has created many different approaches to the subject which, while they often overlap in a single study, are nevertheless relatively well distinguished one from another. Editors and bibliographers penetrate the mysteries of the text. Historical scholars trace the transmission of literary tradition by focusing on Shakespeare's sources and open new possibilities for interpretation by examining the context in which the plays and poems were written. Heirs of the new criticism draw meanings (often ironic and ambivalent) from the text considered as a discrete verbal entity and investigate the relationship between the values elicited and dramatic forms. Those interested in Shakespeare as theater treat the plays as performances and excavate and reconstruct the conditions at the Globe. Plays and poems are further illuminated from diverse theoretical perspectives, including, for example, theology, psychoanalysis, feminism, deconstruction, and imaginative, often interdisciplinary, combinations of these perspectives or of the methods described above.

Despite their eclecticism and diversity, all of these approaches assume without question not only the immense artistic superiority but also the cultural authority and centrality of Shakespeare. These ideas seem in no danger of losing their power; yet many of the assumptions that flowed placidly from them in the past have begun to be sharply, even severely scrutinized. Whatever one's opinion of feminist, deconstructive, and new historical research, critics who take these approaches have reassessed a number of once unexamined postulates of Shakespearean scholarship, often simply by asking new questions. This skepticism about traditional assumptions (to be discussed below) has called into question particularly those aspects of traditional approaches that are concerned with interpretation, the establishment of meaning. Whether one celebrates or laments the self-consciousness generated by this scrutiny, it remains one of the most interesting developments of recent Shakespearean scholarship, and it cannot be ignored. In discussing the seven books under review here, I will of course consider them as separate texts but will also assess them in relation to this development.

Jonathan Dollimore's *Radical Tragedy: Religion, Ideology and Power in the Drama of Shakespeare and His Contemporaries* is one of the most important books that has appeared recently. Treating Shakespeare as one of a number of writers in the English Renaissance theater, Dollimore is to my knowledge the first critic to subject the whole tradition of Jacobean tragedy to an extended poststructuralist critique. His analysis is always trenchant, bold, and sweeping. He seeks first to define as idealistic and ahistorical the terms in which the whole body of Anglo-American criticism of the drama has been couched; next to deconstruct these terms by exposing the ideology on which they are based as resigned and self-interested; and third to offer an alternative vision which, rooted in a clearly defined materialist perspective, better serves the cause of history, realism, and the plays themselves.

Acknowledging the kinship between his work and the new historical research that has been reassessing Renaissance literature in the context of its (often subversive) relation to political and religious power, Dollimore articulates his goals: "In recent years it has become increasingly apparent that this was a drama which undermined religious orthodoxy. My aim is to show that its challenge in this respect generates other, equally important subversive preoccupations—namely, a critique of ideology, the demystification of political and power relations and the decentring of man." Emerging from the interaction between these concerns was a radical social and political realism characterizing plays as diverse as Shakespeare's *Coriolanus* and Webster's *The White Devil* (pp. 4-5). Dollimore argues that modern Anglo-American literary criticism of

Renaissance drama has dealt until recent years almost exclusively with "aesthetic and ideological conceptions of order, integration, equilibrium, and so on . . . a perspective which sees universal and orthodox truth conveyed in and through formal coherence" (pp. 5, 63). This critical tradition stems partly from a distorted emphasis on the idealistic rather than the skeptical intellectual configurations of the Renaissance, on the conservative visions of divinely sanctioned social and political hierarchy propagated by Christian humanism and the Tudor-Stuart monarchies, rather than on the equally important and complicated reactions that arose to challenge that orthodoxy. This "modern obsession with a *telos* of harmonic integration" (p. 5) found its most succinct scholarly formulation in E. M. W. Tillyard's well-known "Elizabethan world picture," which the drama has been presumed to embody. Dollimore acknowledges that "the view that Shakespeare and his contemporaries adhered to the tenets of the so-called Elizabethan world picture has long been discredited" (p. 6). However, he finds equally distorting the opposite claim that this ideology—in which "the divine plan in-formed the universe generally and society particularly, being manifested in Order and Degree"—survived only as a medieval anachronism. Believing that the Elizabethan world picture did indeed persist vitally into the Renaissance, he sets out to determine "an adequate conception of [the dramatists'] . . . actual relationship to it" (p. 6).

Aiming to rectify distortions and re-place emphases, this book's most exciting promise is to provide a new, because newly balanced, picture of the interrelations among the complex forces that comprise society and literature. Dollimore's first task is to clear out and clear up the old terms and ideas that he perceives to be clouding the view. His major targets are such concepts as Christian providentialism, a dominant, orthodox conception which posited "the idea of purpose and order teleologically incoded both in the universe generally and in the identity of things in particular" (p. 102); and a series of assumptions that he sums up collectively as "essentialism," a set of idealistic intellectual traditions that places "man" at the center of a universal scheme in which "he" exists as a "unitary subject integrated internally as a consequence of being integrated into the cosmic design" (p. 39). Essentialist thinking therefore privileges values like autonomy and transcendence, which idealize the individual as an entity separate from society and history. By simultaneously viewing suffering as inevitable and the autonomous individual as potentially capable of transcending suffering, essentialist ideology tends to muffle any questioning of the existing social order, however oppressive it might be.

As these arguments indicate, Dollimore's positions are firmly rooted in a Marxist/materialist perspective, which he very clearly defines as the view that "ideology has a material existence—that is, the system of beliefs which constitutes ideology is built into cultural practices and social institutions" (p. 18). Rather than positing an unalterable universal order in which "man" is central, a materialist conception of ideology perceives "a decentring of man and a corresponding emphasis on the extent to which subjectivity was to be socially identified" (p. 155). One of Dollimore's major premises is that the relation of Jacobean tragedy to the orthodox essentialist ideologies of the Renaissance is primarily one of subversion, as an "emergent" culture challenges a dominant one (p. 7). Consequently, Jacobean tragedy delivers an assault on Christian humanism while at the same time beginning to concern itself with social and political realism (p. 39).

Dollimore's effort to establish his arguments theoretically and historically forms the strongest part of this book. With great erudition and confident grasp, he sweeps over intellectual history, drawing freely on Medieval, Renaissance, Romantic, and twentieth-century thinkers in his attempt to reinterpret the past in terms of the present and the future. Inevitably some of this journey passes through familiar terrain, as advocations of providentialism are contrasted with Renaissance decay theory, for example, or the orthodox ideology of such thinkers as Hooker and Davies is contrasted with the skeptical interrogations of Bacon, Machiavelli, and Montaigne. However, Dollimore's excursions are always useful, such as his brief review of Augustinian and Thomistic views of the human soul (pp. 161-62); often they are brightly original, such as his analysis of the ways in which Calvinist ideas of evil and human responsibility can be deconstructed from the contradictions within them, rather than from their confrontation with competing views (pp. 103-06; 168).

Equally compelling is Dollimore's reassessment of the relevance of Renaissance literary theory to the drama. He makes a distinction between "idealist mimesis," in which, following the tradition of didacticism, dramatic conventions imitate the providential workings of divine order, and "realist mimesis," which shows the drama "rapidly progressing as a form with empirical, historical and contemporary emphases" (p. 71). By tracing an unresolved tension between these two conceptions in the literary theory of Sidney, Bacon, and Fulke Greville, Dollimore demonstrates the ways in which this theory provides a striking example of competing conceptions of the real in the Renaissance. Arguing that the drama presents a similar focus for the struggle among distinctive visions of reality, Dollimore successfully defeats the received view that Renaissance drama and Renaissance literary theory have little direct relation to one another.

This intelligent, well-developed argument, linking the drama and literary theory in conceptual and rhetorical terms, brings us to Dollimore's analyses of the plays themselves. Quoting Raymond Williams with approval on competing conceptions of the real, he offers the idea that Jacobean tragedies dramatize visions of complexity: " 'What in the history of thought may be seen as a confusion or an overlapping is often the precise moment of the dramatic impulse, since it is because the meaning and the experiences are uncertain and complex that the dramatic mode is more powerful' " (p. 91). This is a promising, flexible premise from which to illuminate Renaissance dramatic texts; but Dollimore's analyses of specific plays are neither as convincing nor as powerful as his theories about them.

Part of the problem stems from too rigid an emphasis on the relation between literature and power as one of subversion and dominance and a corresponding insistence that the primary concern of many of the tragedies is the socio-political struggle between innocence and the evils of power (p. 122). When too literally pursued, these positions lead Dollimore to a selectivity and distrust of the aesthetic that often weaken his arguments unnecessarily.

For example, in a brief and decidedly unsatisfactory discussion of censorship, he argues that this ideologically-motivated suppression was "designed to predetermine the nature of all drama" (p. 22). Yet although he quotes certain contemporary expressions of anxiety about the theater as a source of disorder, he neither demonstrates, nor cites studies that demonstrate, the nature and/or extent of this censorship. Nor does he deal with the complicating, although by no means necessarily opposing factor that the theater was both loved and encouraged by the Elizabethan and the Jacobean courts. From the non-established premise that "*Pace* Astrophel, these writers wrote looking not into their hearts but over their shoulders" (p. 24), he argues that certain formal configurations that can be viewed as embodiments of orthodox ideology are merely evasions of censorship, aesthetic disguises adapted by the poets to escape the punishment of power for their actual, subversive aim of offering a radical critique of social relations (p. 28). Therefore, although "Jacobean tragedy does often effect some kind of closure, it is usually a perfunctory rather than a profound reassertion of order. . . . We may feel that such closure was a kind of condition for subversive thought to be foregrounded at all" (p. 60). The skeptical "spirit" of, for example, *The Revenger's Tragedy* belies its literal adherence to "the letter of providentialist orthodoxy and, perhaps, of censorship" (p. 140). Similarly, the "providentialist gloss" in the Argument of *Sejanus* may well have been dictated by expediency, as may the last act's "crude attempt to interpret history according to this same providentialist justice" (p. 134). Finally, tragic death is itself an aesthetic evasion that, by "mystifying closure" rather than emphasizing irony and dislocation, "works to evade tragic insight" (p. 50).

From the point of view of the author's intention, which is Dollimore's point of view in these passages, why should the Argument and the last act of *Sejanus*, no matter how crudely integrated, be assigned less truth value than the rest of the play? Why should the fact of death in tragedy be granted less centrality than the fact of social injustice? The answers to these questions lie in Dollimore's theory of history—and of Renaissance drama as part of that history— as a series of dialectical relationships leading inexorably toward social change. His theory incorporates a view of dramatic form as a secondary superstructure imposed on a primary subversive meaning in order to outwit power. This suspicion of the aesthetic as a "front" often renders Dollimore's interpretations overly selective and, as a result, unconvincing.

The analysis of *King Lear* is a case in point. Arguing that *Lear* decenters man "in order to make visible social process and its forms of ideological misrecognition" (p. 191), Dollimore contends that *Lear* is "above all, a play about power, property and inheritance" (p. 197), rather than about human dignity, endurance, transcendence, and/or redemption, as Christian and humanist critics have argued. Discussing Edmund's "revolutionary skepticism," Dollimore inquires, "Are we to assume that Edmund is simply evil and therefore so is his philosophy? I want to argue that we need not" (p. 198).

This emphasis on the political and social concerns of the play is undoubtedly important, but in de-emphasizing Edmund's villainy Dollimore ignores crucial factors such as fluctuations in the response of the audience, which after some initial attraction to Edmund's wit and bravado, sides emphatically against him. Dollimore therefore underestimates the tremendous power of sympathy for Lear, Gloucester, and Cordelia that works against our acceptance of Edmund's point of view and complicates the tragic intention of the play beyond the materialist vs. idealist configuration that preoccupies him. If one asks instead why Shakespeare made Edmund's values— resting on merit rather than birth—villainous in light of the fact of the rising commercial classes in Jacobean England, one might reveal Shakespeare's tragic vision as nostalgic and conservative rather than revolutionary and skeptical. Such an interpretation would augment rather than undermine the historicism of Dollimore's central thesis and his goal of revealing the drama in its "actual relation" to the Elizabethan world picture.

As his interpretation of Edmund indicates, Dollimore tends to accept the dislocated point of view of the disillusioned malcontent figures in Jacobean tragedy (Enobarbus, Edmund, Flamineo, Vindice) as the most real. This emphasis leads to some fascinating insights, such as the ways in which these figures live in the "social moment," wholly dependent upon the society that they see through and despise. Depicting the malcontent as the representative, oracular figure in Jacobean tragedy is a good strategy in many cases: *The White Devil*, for example, or *The Revenger's Tragedy*. Yet the emphasis seems distorted when the claim, as it does, encompasses the entire tragic tradition. Dollimore's emphases on social and political realism could just as easily, and perhaps with less distortion, have led to an examination of satire, both dramatic and non-dramatic. The fact that *Troilus and Cressida*, only arguably a tragedy, is one of the first plays he turns to, helps make the point.

Given Dollimore's considerable erudition and grasp, along with his mistrust of the function of dramatic form, one feels he could make his case just as well by surveying Renaissance literature and intellectual history as a whole, rather than settling on a single genre. As the emphases in this essay indicate, Dollimore's analyses of individual plays are not as memorable as his theories. Partly this discrepancy stems from the occasional heavy-handedness of repetitive prose that does him a disservice by turning his trenchant analytical skepticism into a kind of complacent chant.

Nevertheless, the contemplation of Jacobean tragedy is obviously what led Dollimore to produce this book, which, with its far-reaching implications and bold intelligence, enriches our criticism and expands its potential. If his interpretations of individual plays are weak, that is because his real interest lies not in the concrete details of particular texts but in a view of literary criticism that is passionately *engagé*. In the long last chapter, discussion of Jacobean tragedy simply drops out, dissolving into a pointed critique of modernism in which the individualistic idealism of the likes of Coleridge, A. C. Bradley, D. H. Lawrence, T. S. Eliot, and F. R. Leavis is rejected as self-serving, ahistorical, and naive. Dollimore makes the intriguing argument that the idealization of individualism, autonomy, and transcendence involves a projection into the Renaissance of post-enlightenment values. His connection of the "essentialist" emphasis on universality with an often unwittingly racist oblivion to cultural difference also provides a needed corrective to the smug parochialism that characterizes criticism of Shakespeare at its worst. But as his last few pages make clear, Dollimore's purpose is not simply a skeptical interrogation of traditional claims, an everlasting "no" to the idea of meaning. He aims at a more positive vision, a replacement of meaning with meaning which is nothing less than "an alternative conception of the relations between history, society and subjectivity. . . . It is a radical alternative which, in the context of materialist analysis, helps vindicate certain objectives: not essence but potential, not the human condition but cultural difference, not destiny but collectively identified goals" (p. 271).

Two other books by major Shakespearean scholars are also concerned with reassessing tragedy. In King Lear, Macbeth, *Indefinition, and Tragedy* Stephen Booth writes: "The search for a definition of tragedy has been the most persistent and widespread of all nonreligious quests for definition" (p. 81). Booth characterizes his new contribution to this critical odyssey as the time-honored task of accounting for the greatness of works of art: specifically, of *King Lear* and *Macbeth,* and by implication, of Shakespearean tragedy in general. Basing his analysis solidly in the dynamics of audience response, Booth argues that tragedy emanates from the fact of indefinition, by which he means inconclusiveness, the lack of certain identity, and the denial of limits. Secondly, he "propounds the related idea that literary works we call tragedies have their value as enabling actions by which we are made capable, temporarily, of enduring manifestations of the fact that nothing in human experience is or can be definite" (p. ix). These propositions are elaborated in the two close readings of *Lear* and *Macbeth* that form the crux of this book. Booth applies patient, meticulous insight to the concrete verbal texture of each play, connecting its highly intricate fluctuations with equally fluid and subtle changes in audience response.

In his interpretation of *King Lear,* Booth focuses on the facts of indefinition and uncertainty as the central experiences of the play, tracing "indefiniteness manifested in such things as failure to conclude, failure to reach an expected kind of conclusion, failure of characters to abide by the common-law rules for their generic types, and awkward interaction between set speeches or stock verbal formulas and situations that do not fit them" (p. 63). Like a Beethoven symphony, *Lear* promises to end and then doesn't (e.g., the ceremonial trial-by-combat between Edgar and Edmund has the feel of dramatic conclusion, the triumph of virtue); offers seemingly simple, uniform assertions which are in fact multiple and complex (e.g., "and my poor fool is hanged" brings to mind both Lear's fool and Cordelia, and "makes two distinct and yet inseparable statements. Our minds are for a moment firmly fixed in two places at once" [p. 331]); seems to present stability and certainty of identification and then undermines them (e.g., our opinion of Gloucester changes numerous times throughout the play; Albany fights both for and against Cordelia and Lear). Through his thorough grasp of detail, Booth lovingly dissects the verbal texture of the play, demonstrating the infinite, almost invisible care with which its ironies, ambiguities, and paradoxes have been interwoven in order subtly to compel us to abandon our faith in the comfortable categories by which we arrange our daily lives.

The *Lear* essay is rich with elaborated examples of this process. One of my favorites is Booth's unraveling of the hostile encounter between Kent and Oswald (II.ii) which lands Kent in the stocks. Although our knowledge of the two characters would seem to lead us to love Kent and hate Oswald ("no henchman of Goneril gets any sympathy from us" [p. 51]), Shakespeare does not generate such a simplistic, automatic response. As Booth explains, Kent begins picking on Oswald who, guilty of no present wrong, protests his innocence in a friendly and forthcoming manner: "Oswald's *local* innocence of any crime to justify an attack on him makes our delight in his humiliation less easy to revel in than we would like" (p. 52). Booth shows the parallels between the construction of this incident and the complexity of our reactions to, for example, the virtuous Edgar's smugness, the villainous Edmund's attractiveness, the virtuous Cordelia's self-righteousness.

In his essay on *Macbeth*, Booth systematically elaborates his idea that Shakespearean tragedy is an achievement of its audience. Like Dollimore, Booth bases his theory on a distinction (emanating from Plato) between the aesthetic and the real. With its lack of security and lack of discernible, absolute truth, "real" life, Booth argues, does not conform to the coherent patterns asserted by art. Yet, he continues, we live our lives complacently hiding from the fact of infinite contradiction and uncertainty, avoiding in our ordinary experience inconsistencies that, if faced, would "put our minds in panic" (p. 117).

Like Dollimore, then, Booth resists the notion of permanent, absolute truth and contrasts the impermanence and inconsistency of "real" life with the formal coherence of art. Yet for Dollimore the aesthetic is an evasion, a mask cloaking the actual subversive function of Renaissance tragedy as an agent of historical change. For Booth the aesthetic, with its ability to evoke and contain contradiction, allows us to experience from a distance tragic facts that would otherwise be too terrifying to confront. Tragedy is the most valuable form of drama, more valuable than comedy because of its superior grasp of the "real," or the fact of indefinition that for Booth constitutes the real (p. 77). If, by giving form to formlessness, tragic drama denies and subverts tragic insight, it also renders that (repressed) insight accessible, providing "an effectively miraculous experience of practical paradox" (p. 114). Conferring upon us the power to comprehend, "dramatic tragedy is an enabling act" that inspires us with gratitude (p. 114). While for Dollimore the message of tragedy retains a politically necessary aesthetic disguise, the disguise of formal coherence, for Booth tragic form redeems itself from the lie of fiction by its therapeutic value.

Like all theories, this one is arguable. First, although Booth does well on his own defining the complex fluidity of what he construes as the real, his arguments would be augmented if he demonstrated some awareness of recent criticism that has tackled similar issues. Booth's implicit method involves holding all factors constant but the fluctuations of the text, a method that frees him to engage in the approaches of the new criticism. But other factors crucial to this theory—e.g., audience response, assumptions of what constitutes the real—could also be subjected to the same rigorous exploration that the texts receive. For example, throughout his book Booth assumes a uniformity of audience response to the smallest details as well as to the most sweeping movements of the plays, an assumption that denies their complexity. Moreover, we do not all complacently avoid recognizing inconsistency; many of us are aware that our lives are riddled with it and do not necessarily panic at the fact. Indeed what Booth sees as a source of discomfort, danger, and dismay—the limitlessness, uncertainty, and infinite possibilities which subvert our orthodoxies—Dollimore sees as a vision of liberation and a source of salvation. However, where Dollimore moves away from the texts entirely, Booth returns to them. His mode of analysis, convincingly entrenched in the concrete, not only illuminates overlooked aspects of the plays; it also draws our attention to the dynamics of audience response as a crux of the experience of tragedy. By first investigating and then idealizing the moral and psychological functions of tragic form, Booth reminds us of the unique role that tragedy can play in our lives.

In *To Be and Not To Be: Negation and Metadrama in* Hamlet, James L. Calderwood is also concerned with the tragic paradox of meaningful meaninglessness. Unlike Dollimore and like Booth, he concentrates on the thicket of the text, focusing on the ways in which wordplay, soliloquy, scene, and structure interact with the conventions of genre and the facts of theatrical performance to create "metadramatic" meaning. Unlike Booth and like Dollimore, he grapples with poststructuralist poetics as a way of assessing current methods of literary criticism. In contrast to both Dollimore and Booth, Calderwood does not aim at a definitive view of Shakespearean tragedy; rather, he focuses solely on *Hamlet* and states his goal as follows: "I am interested in exploring the kinds of dramatic indirection, duplicity, and reversibility in the play that make it not only possible but likely that critics will arrive at such apparently incompatible positions" (p. xv).

As Calderwood explains, he has benefited a good deal from deconstructionist theory, particularly Derrida's insistence on the absence of ultimate meaning and the need to abandon a metaphysics of "presence," that wrongly assumes the existence of an objective, unmediated reality, which it is possible to comprehend. He adds, "In the absence of such a world, and of any 'transcendental signified' above or behind it, what remains is what our symbolic systems project through the creative free play of fashioning fiction" (p. 190). But in working through *Hamlet*, Calderwood also works through deconstruction to reassert the existence of meaning in Shakespearean tragedy.

Calderwood argues that *Hamlet* involves a process of achieving identity that proceeds through separation and isolation to an ultimate fusion of public and private, individual and collective, past and present, tradition and innovation, fictional and real. This process occurs on the verbal level of wordplay, the level of action within the drama, and the level of interaction between playwright and play, actors and spectators. The journey begins with rejection and negativity: Hamlet Jr. must separate himself from Hamlet Sr., along with his "schoolboy conceptions of a world of received values and determinate meanings" and his "dream of primal unity in which things with the same names are the same" (pp. 190, 195), just as Shakespeare must separate his play from the *Ur-Hamlet* and other plays in the revenge-tragedy genre. Similarly, the theatrical self-reflexivity of *Hamlet*, with its plays within plays, forces the spectator fully to distinguish theatrical illusion as created fiction or risk identification with the obtuse Polonius.

Through a complex analysis in which he includes discussion of, for example, naming and negation (non-action, non-revenge) in *Hamlet*, Calderwood demonstrates that the negativity in the play becomes a necessary step in the process of reintegration. That is, separation and isolation are the means of achieving individuality that, not becoming paralyzed by its distinction, recognizes itself as both separate and conjoined. This process is dramatized when Hamlet leaps into Ophelia's grave. Shouting "This is I / Hamlet the Dane!" he acknowledges both his own irreplaceable singularity and the commonness of death (thus, to be *and* not to be). As Calderwood writes, "This verbal affirmation of an identity that is both individual and generic, that acknowledges both difference and similarity, is confirmed in action when he kills the King both for himself and his father. At the same point Shakespeare, having established the individuality of his play, its metadramatic difference, acknowledges at last its generic nature as well by completing its revenge form. Thus, out of the negative, the positive; out of not-being, being; and out of inaction, action. Similarly, out of deconstruction, reconstruction" (p. 194).

Presented in a series of short chapters, Calderwood's book comprises an attempt to avoid systemization and offers its ideas informally as small nuggets of insight that are sometimes rather slight. Occasionally these delicate trees block the view of the forest. But the openness and intelligence with which Calderwood confronts the often impenetrable abstractions of deconstruction and unravels them concretely must be cause for gratitude. Moreover, his responsive absorption of these ideas makes his analysis of *Hamlet* convincing and lends wider implications to this interpretation. Like Dollimore, Calderwood senses the need not to reject the radical implications of deconstruction but to move beyond their polarizing negativity. That deconstruction constitutes a step toward a more comprehensive intellectual synthesis is a refreshing idea, an idea that lets in the air.

Together the three books on tragedy by Dollimore, Booth, and Calderwood raise all the issues that have begun to preoccupy Shakespearean scholarship: the difficulty of distinguishing and determining poetic meaning; the attempt to reassess the complex relations among literature, society, and history; and the need to scrutinize traditional values previously accepted without question. Given these concerns, it is striking to encounter two books that, focusing primarily on Shakespeare's history plays, betray neither self-consciousness nor skepticism about the values they so straightforwardly and wholeheartedly advocate.

Robert Rentoul Reed, Jr.'s *Crime and God's Judgment in Shakespeare* attempts to mold the first and second tetralogies, along with *Hamlet* and *Macbeth*, to the tenets of the Old Testament doctrine of God's vengeance. Not only does Reed never perceive or question the variety and complexity of views "in Shakespeare's time"; he seeks to establish a strict, uniform, almost literal providentialism—"the doctrine that recognizes God as both the Judge and the Avenger and yet ascribes to a human agent the execution of God's judgment"—as an all-encompassing system of meaning that accounts for the unity of these plays (p. 203). In analyzing the two tetralogies Reed therefore makes much of passages like John of Gaunt's "God's is the quarrel... Let heaven revenge" in *Richard II*, unwinding what he perceives to be the accurate prophetic power of such remarks in explicating all the events of the drama. For the tragedies his arguments are slightly less predictable: God's purpose in *Hamlet* is to put Fortinbras on the throne of Denmark; the action of *Macbeth* unfolds as God reveals his ultimate design of freeing Scotland from an oppressive ruling class. Reed also perceives a reassuringly increasing awareness of providential intervention and God's grace progressively marking Shakespeare's plays: "The judgments of God, it would seem, as we find them in Shakespeare's plays, are properly to be evaluated in terms of their beneficent consequences . . . and not principally in terms of the act of judgment itself" (p. 198).

Reed's study will obviously be of primary interest to theological critics of Shakespeare, and it is these scholars with whom he enthusiastically, sometimes bitterly, debates. However, in raising the questions that interest him—Is the Ghost of Hamlet's father Christian or pagan, Catholic or Protestant? Are the witches who torment Macbeth primary demonic agents or merely the instruments of demons?—Reed often draws our attention to fascinating documents from Tudor / Stuart religious and occult literature. Throughout Reed explicitly clarifies his religious beliefs and makes no effort at detachment, which is not his goal. Yet he does attempt to ground his analysis in history. At these moments his simplistic ideas of the Middle Ages and Renaissance, manifested as a lack of awareness of the complexity and variety of the intellectual and religious climate (e.g., pp. 21, 163), become problematic. At times he conflates the Renaissance, Shakespeare, and the fictional events of the plays with a confusing lack of distinction that leaves the reader afloat in circular logic (e.g., pp. 125, 145). Once again, some awareness of recent historical research would have rendered his arguments more convincing. But perhaps Reed is not trying to persuade those of us not already participating in his particular scholarly conversation.

In *Shakespearean Politics: Government and Misgovernment in the Great Histories*, C. G. Thayer approaches the second tetralogy with views of history and politics directly opposite to Reed's. Where Reed sees the hand of God, Thayer sees human manipulation; where Reed looks back to the Middle Ages and Renaissance with nostalgia for what he perceives as the absence of materialistic sophistication and the greater self-reliance of these periods (Reed, pp. 73, 121, 163), Thayer looks back with some disdain at the barbarism, the "typically bloody-minded way of the sixteenth and seventeenth centuries" (p. 14). In short Thayer takes the Whig view, which perceives history as a steady progression away from the "regressive and outrageous" toward greater freedom and enlightenment (p. 12); his purpose is to demonstrate the ways in which the second tetralogy embodies this vision: "The whole movement of the great tetralogy is from injustice to justice. England is not punished for allowing Bolingbroke to depose Richard, not in this group of plays and not in the first tetralogy; it is rewarded, with strong efforts toward good government under King Henry IV and the final restoration of justice and a great national triumph under Henry V. The movement and the reward are rendered concrete in the wholly opposed figures of Richard II and Henry V" (p. 12).

Thayer proceeds to analyze each of the plays, charting a progressive journey away from the deluded Richard's "dangerous notions of divine right" toward the kingship of an idealized Henry V, "a man-centered kingship—with a king responsible to God but responsible also to his country and his countrymen" (p. 150). He presents his arguments more accessibly and to a potentially wider audience than does Reed. While Reed's book is repetitive, Thayer's is written in a chatty, congenial style that, if occasionally cloying, is very readable. Moreover, Thayer's study contains some interesting and convincing analysis, such as his discussion of Richard II's self-deception and his review of the conception of the King's two bodies, including the interesting idea that Shakespeare "neatly split" apart the notions of divine right and indefeasible hereditary right to the throne in his dramatization of kingship (p. 161).

Despite the virtues of this book, it is marred by excessive partisanship. Although Thayer seems at times to acknowledge dramatic complexity, his more characteristic response to the ambiguity he sees is an attempt to cancel it out. Thus, while recognizing that Bolingbroke usurps the throne, his desire as a critic is to champion that ambivalent figure and to bully the reader into taking sides: "The legitimacy of King Henry V is never an issue; nor for Shakespeare, is the legitimacy of King Henry IV" (p. 106). Indeed neither Thayer nor Reed seems willing to recognize the possibility that Shakespeare's plays could raise questions rather than answer them. The unskeptical enthusiasm of both critics for their opposing points of view reminds us of the ways in which Shakespearean scholarship becomes a projection of individual moral myths and personal spiritual allegories. Of course much recent scholarship has revealed the self-interest behind all intellectual argument, no matter how seemingly detached or sophisticated; but the lack of awareness of the contingency of their own moral assumptions makes the work of Reed and Thayer seem old-fashioned and naive.

Robert S. Miola's learned study *Shakespeare's Rome* is traditional in the best sense of that term. Taking what he calls an "organic approach to the problem of coherence" in Shakespeare's conception of Rome, Miola traces the ways in which the playwright's vision of the city evolved from *The Rape of Lucrece* and *Titus Andronicus* through the Plutarchan tragedies and *Cymbeline* (p. 15). In his analysis of these works Miola focuses on Shakespeare's changing use of his sources, the political motifs of invasion and rebellion, and the thematic implications of the Roman ideals of constancy, honor, and *pietas*—"the loving respect owed to family, country, and gods" (p. 17). He argues that as Shakespeare's career develops, his interpretations of Rome, with its life-denying and rigid emphases on heroic valor, become increasingly complex and critical. In *Cymbeline* the playwright's tragic conception of Rome at last gives way to the romance vision of a flexible, compassionate, and surviving Britain. Miola's argument reflects the view that Shakespeare's use of dramatic forms progressed along with his changing imaginative vision, in conjoined evolution from the lyric, comic and tragic to the final inclusive and harmonious generic vision of romance. The chronological exploration of Shakespeare's Rome makes an admirable case for this point of view. The conception as Miola has designed it is itself original, and his lucid erudition further strengthens his demonstrations.

The treatment of Shakespeare's use of his sources is particularly creative. As Miola explains, he is not seeking to discover direct sources "but to penetrate into the deep sources lying below the surface of the text" (p. 16). As a background to his analysis of Shakespeare's methods, he provides a brief but serviceable discussion of Elizabethan classicism, which he describes as "enthusiastically acquisitive and undiscriminating," an attitude that accounts for its ahistorical, eclectic character (p. 9). Although Miola draws on a wide range of ancient writers and their Renaissance interpreters, he focuses primarily on Virgil.

Miola demonstrates Shakespeare's transmutation of Virgil both within and among *Lucrece* and the plays. He shows, for example, that from his earliest Roman works (*Lucrece* and *Titus*), "Shakespeare depicts Roman destructiveness by focusing on the ironic disparity between intention and deed and by portraying Roman action as *impius*, as a flagrant violation of Vergilian *pietas*. Hence the recurring images of shattered families and perverted family relations" (p. 60). Citing Virgil's image of Aeneas carrying Anchises on his back from the flaming Troy, Miola shows how this tableau had provided a commonplace emblem of filial love for Renaissance humanists. He then unravels in a new light the bitter irony of Cassius's allusion to saving the drowning Caesar from the Tiber in *Julius Caesar* (pp. 112-15): "Despite Caesar's descent from Aeneas and his position as leader of state, he is seen here as a type of Anchises—weak, old, and troublesome. Cassius casts himself as a new Aeneas, one unwilling to shoulder the burden of the past, but destined with Brutus to found a new Rome. . . . He here replaces the articulated emblem of *pietas*, the image of the son saving his father, with the inarticulated emblem of *impietas*, the image of the son slaying the father" (pp. 83-85). In contrast, Shakespeare minimizes the emphasis on the destruction of family ties in *Antony and Cleopatra*, despite the insistence on this theme in Plutarch and Appian. Miola uses such discoveries both to underscore thematic points (in *Antony and Cleopatra*, Rome and its values begin to lose centrality as

Shakespeare presents his paradoxical view of the lovers) and to demonstrate the dramatist's growing independence in his use of sources, a development also apparent in the portrayal of Cleopatra as both Roman and un-Roman, Lavinia and Dido (pp. 160-61).

These are but a few examples in a book composed of solid, often eloquent, interpretations, but they should provide hints of the convincing way in which Miola combines historical and thematic analysis to demonstrate that Shakespeare's vision of Rome "evolved dynamically throughout his career" (p. 16). With his criticism of Rome's rigid, deathly obsession with Stoic military heroism growing increasingly severe, Shakespeare at last shows these values transcended in *Cymbeline,* when "British flexibility and humility overcome Roman constancy and honor" (p. 233).

As the title indicates, Sarup Singh's *Family Relationships in Shakespeare and the Restoration Comedy of Manners* shares with *Shakespeare's Rome* a concern for the playwright's conceptions of the family; but Singh approaches the topic from a broadly comparative point of view, placing Shakespeare's sexual values in historical context and contrasting them to the representation of family relationships in Restoration comedy. Dividing his study into "Parents and Children," "Crabbed Age and Youth," and "Husbands and Wives," Singh's method is first to survey Shakespeare's treatment of these topics and then to provide a complementary chapter on the comedy of manners. Singh sees in his subject "certain basic human relationships as determined or influenced by the problem of large social relations," and explains, "I see the situations in these plays more or less as I would see similar situations in life. Whether it is a legitimate critical approach or not, I find it very rewarding" (p. ix).

Although Singh's book will not present scholars interested in his subject with much in the way of new material or ideas, it is worth reading. His study is very useful as a compendium: for instance, if one wanted to consider the treatment of mothers in Shakespeare, the examples in this book present themselves readily as a group; and this is the case for the rest of the writer's categories as well. The study also contains many serviceable observations and includes a somewhat sketchy survey in which Singh reviews the rise of the nuclear family and the evolving conception of marriage as a contract in the seventeenth century, all of which he eventually brings to bear as a contrast between Shakespearean and Restoration drama.

Despite the disclaimer in which Singh discards analytic precision as a goal, grounding his interpretations solely in personal response, his analysis suffers from fuzziness of focus. Like Thayer, Singh wants to view history as progressive, a march toward greater freedom, and to make moral judgments on the literature based on this criterion: e.g., "It is only fair to conclude ... that in the area of domestic relationships, Restoration comedy registers a clear advance over Shakespeare" (p. 75). At the same time his thoughtfulness will not permit him to overlook different sides of issues. As a result he gives the impression of retreating from the complex implications of his own insights. Realizing, for example, that Elizabethan women had only two options, endurance and patience in marriage or living alone, he nevertheless insists that Shakespeare transcended his time in attempting to apply a "single standard" of sexual morality to his male and female characters (pp. 132-33).

Part of the problem stems, once again, from the lack of analytic distinctions. Although Singh is interested in demonstrating both discrepancies and continuities between Shakespeare's sexual values and those of Restoration comedy, he never mentions the treatment of these themes in Jacobean city comedy or in the Beaumont and Fletcher plays, both obvious links. Courtship and marriage are fused throughout his analysis of both eras, and the critical differences in women's positions are overlooked as a result: Rosalind and Desdemona, Beatrice and Imogen, Millamant and Mrs. Fainall, are not quite in the same boat. While Singh uses the earlier work of feminist scholars like Juliet Dusinberre, Carol Thomas Neely, Germaine Greer, and Coppélia Kahn, he shows no awareness of more recent scholarship on women, love, and marriage that would have enriched and deepened his arguments. An enhanced perspective might have prevented sentimental formulations such as that which appears when, referring to *The Way of the World*, he observes, "The emphasis here is clearly on the preservation of the nuclear family. In this family the husband may theoretically be the senior partner, but how does it matter if the wife is assured of his love and affection?" (p. 195). Singh's sensitivity and openness to a variety of literary and historical sources suggest that he would respond in an interested and interesting way to newer work, which perhaps has not yet come to his attention.[1]

In the serious treatment that Singh gives his subject matter, he frequently relies on feminist perspectives. Thus he raises issues that question traditional moral and critical assumptions. Yet, teetering on the brink of new insights, he often falls back on more familiar moral assumptions that deny those insights: the lack of an integrated critical perspective stems from oscillation between the traditional and the new. This book therefore brings us back to the challenges to traditional modes of analysis currently confronting Shakespearean scholarship.

The seven books under review draw unevenly on the growing body of recent scholarship that is attempting to reformulate issues crucial to the interpretation of Shakespeare. Given the voluminous diversity of Shakespearean commentary, any lack of awareness of recent research may seem inevitable. How should all the new scholarship be taken into account? To what extent should one critic's terms and assumptions be allowed to enter into another's analysis and possibly to transform the independent way in which questions are raised? Naturally some discussions are mutually exclusive: textual scholars need not consider the particular problems addressed by deconstructionists; source studies and bibliographies do not depend for their value on an awareness of the insights of feminism and the new historical research. But in their singularity as well as in their attachment to broader developments, the books considered in this essay do propel us to think about the ways in which the issues of Shakespearean discourse are being recast. Those critics who fail to address works that have a direct bearing on the issues they themselves have chosen to investigate have produced the less convincing and less helpful books. In contrast the stronger studies combine knowledge of traditional assumptions with awareness of innovative approaches, losing nothing in the way of individual perspective and orientation when they confront and assimilate the energy of new ideas.

Note

1. Among the many new books and articles about women, love, and sexuality in Renaissance England, three studies that come to mind are Arthur Kirsch, *Shakespeare and the Experience of Love* (Cambridge: Cambridge Univ. Press, 1981); Linda Bamber, *Comic Women, Tragic Men: A Study of Gender and Genre in Shakespeare* (Stanford: Stanford Univ. Press, 1982); and Irene G. Dash, *Wooing, Wedding, and Power: Women in Shakespeare's Plays* (New York: Columbia Univ. Press, 1981).

Subject and Object in Henry James

Ruth Bernard Yeazell

Paul B. Armstrong. *The Phenomenology of Henry James.* Chapel Hill: University of North Carolina Press, 1983. xiii, 242 pp.

Stuart Hutchinson. *Henry James: An American as Modernist.* London: Vision Press, 1982, and Totowa, N.J.: Barnes & Noble, 1983. 136 pp.

William W. Stowe. *Balzac, James, and the Realistic Novel.* Princeton: Princeton University Press, 1983. xviii, 203 pp.

In Virginia Woolf's *To the Lighthouse,* Lily Briscoe can never think of Mr. Ramsay's work without seeing clearly before her "a scrubbed kitchen table"—an image permanently conjured up for the artist by a conversation she once had with Andrew Ramsay, the philosopher's son: "She asked him what his father's books were about. 'Subject and object and the nature of reality,' Andrew had said. And when she said Heavens, she had no notion what that meant. 'Think of a kitchen table then,' he told her, 'when you're not there.' "[1] It is not hard to imagine that Henry James, an artist who was also the son and brother of philosophers, would have identified with both voices in this dialogue. Paul B. Armstrong, the author of the most successful of the three books under review here, goes still further, and argues for a "convergence between art and philosophy" in the novelist's own work: if Armstrong's Henry James is not exactly a philosopher himself, he joins his brother William as an "important American participant . . . in the phenomenological tradition" (p. vii). Neither of the other two critics makes such a formal claim to philosophy: Stuart Hutchinson is more concerned with James as a typically "American" writer, and William W. Stowe with his relations to Balzac and the European realistic novel. But all three books implicitly take as their central problem "subject and object and the nature of reality" in James's fiction.

The usual complaint about James, of course, is that he thinks away not the observer but the kitchen table—leaving his characters "suspended in the void," as Edith Wharton said of the principals in *The Golden Bowl*.[2] Stuart Hutchinson generally wishes to appreciate James rather than to complain of him, but his account of what is missing from the novelist's world has a familiar ring:

Why are his characters on the whole so stripped of resources? Why are they so deprived of the unscheming and untreacherous relations and friends, the instinctive pleasures, the jobs, the habits, the talents, the achievements, the good meals, that keep most of us going? Is it because James, so dedicated to the *art* of fiction, so inveterately a spectator at life's feast, knew terribly little about the adventures such things provide? Is this why most of his central characters are so exclusively (for many readers too exclusively) thrust in on their intensely private experience? [p. 42]

Hutchinson's principal answer to these rhetorical questions is that James's native country left him "unfurnished with structures of reality" (p. 15), and that he and the other major nineteenth-century American writers were perforce compelled to become "modernists," to anticipate the European as "fabricators, rather than imitators, of reality" (p. 7). Armstrong would in part agree: in an epilogue entitled "The Modernity of Henry James," he argues that James's treatment of consciousness "leads away from the conventions of realism toward the preoccupation with the processes of creating and construing meaning that is one hallmark of modern fiction" (p. 206). And even Stowe, who takes those conventions of realism as his subject and emphasizes a nineteenth- rather than a twentieth-century tradition, begins by declaring that Balzac and James "created the 'reality' they claimed to have discovered" (p. 3), and describes their texts as "conscious, literary constructions" that deliberately question and criticize the very processes of perception and representation (p. 171). But both

Armstrong and Stowe know that James is a mimetic artist as well as a self-conscious "fabricator," and that what Armstrong calls the "paradox of James's contradictory attitudes toward reality and interpretation" (p. 208) can partly be resolved by recognizing that mimesis itself is a far more complicated issue than Hutchinson seems to think. While Armstrong's is finally a more rigorous and intellectually satisfying book than Stowe's, they resemble one another in their sophisticated efforts to account for both Jamesian consciousness *and* the kitchen table. James's characters are not so deprived of "the good meals that keep most of us going" as Hutchinson imagines: Lambert Strether and Marie de Vionnet still enjoy an *"omelette aux tomates"* and a "bottle of straw-coloured Chablis" at their "delightful" left bank café—and even in *The Golden Bowl*, Father Mitchell twiddles his thumbs over his "satisfied stomach" in due appreciation of "the hand employed at Fawns for mayonnaise of salmon."[3]

Hutchinson insists that James is an American writer in order to liberate him from the Great Tradition—to "relieve" the late work especially from the "inappropriate demands made of it" by Leavis's readings (p. 79). The "traditional validities, which sustain *Emma* and *Middlemarch*, and which enable these novels to confirm realities the reader expects, are only superficially available to *The Portrait of a Lady*" (p. 25); and by the time of *The Golden Bowl*, "Maggie and Amerigo face the trial of the twentieth century never having been sustained by solidities and fulfilments formerly available" (p. 133). Since "nothing comes pre-packed in a sustaining historical and social shape to an American writer" (p. 59), James was forced to rely wholly on the artificial structures of his imagination: "How could he have a confident grip on what is real when, like all his compatriots, he had experienced the invention of nation [sic]?" (p. 112). Hutchinson suggests that Europeans would also soon lose their "confident grip" on the real, but that the accident of history granted the Americans a headstart. If such generalizations seem facile and overblown, they do have a respectable ancestry in Tocqueville's shrewd observations, and in James's own witty catalogue of all that was missing from Hawthorne's America. But the effort to replace the Great

Tradition with a modernism born of a naked America produces some rather heterogeneous literary relations:

> With its sense that its characters may wear only a mask of life, *What Maisie Knew* might have been *The Blithedale Romance* or *The Confidence Man* or *Huckleberry Finn* or *The Counterfeiters*. With its sense that its characters live as dispossessed spectators, it might have been all these other novels again or *The Mayor of Casterbridge* or *In Remembrance of Things Past,* both having many scenes in which characters gaze through windows at what they are separated from; it might too have been *The Waste Land*. . . . With its sense of the inevitable relativity of structures of meaning, *What Maisie Knew* relates again to any of the above works and even to *Ulysses*. . . . Last of all, with its sense that the central character remains uninitiated into final knowledge, *What Maisie Knew* might have been *The Trial.* [pp. 71-72]

Part of the trouble is that Hutchinson can see no alternative between a complacently naive realism and the modernist abyss. He dutifully sides with the party of doubt, but cannot quite abandon his own sturdy belief in "reality"—nor critically examine what it might mean. The "bleakest aspect" of James's fiction, according to Hutchinson, "is that his characters remain unblessed by the fellow feeling and intercourse which keep most of us going to the extent that any consciousness of masked dispossession disappears. We feel connected and real. Maisie, however, with all the other characters in the book and with so many other characters in James, remains essentially unconnected" (p. 73). "I have myself resources for personal and communal fulfilment such as James does not account for," he assures us elsewhere (pp. 113-14). One ironic effect of Hutchinson's exaggerated polarities is to make the great nineteenth-century English novelists themselves seem complacent and naive. Neither Jane Austen nor George Eliot accepts the conventions of her world as unquestioningly as he suggests. Nor is James's work quite so epistemologically and morally unstable. It is possible to recognize that all interpretation in *The Ambassadors* is limited and partial, for example, without believing that Sarah Pocock's view of Chad and Madame de

Subject and Object in James 47

Vionnet is "neither truer nor falser than anyone else's" in the novel (p. 88).

William Stowe can argue the Jamesian novel's affinities with nineteenth-century realism without ignoring its self-consciousness about interpretation because he has a more flexible and sophisticated idea of what realism itself entails. The novels of Balzac and James, he contends, aspire to the conditions both of representational painting and of music: they are "doubly mimetic, imitating in words both the surface of the world and the processes by which we relate things in the world one to another" (p. 56). Such art strives at once to render experience and "to render it intelligible" (p. 13). Borrowing the term from Lévi-Strauss, Stowe suggests that we approach a work of Balzac or James as a *"modèle réduit"*—a version of the phenomenal world which eliminates the inessential and the temporarily irrelevant in order to "render its subject more richly intelligible than it would be as a phenomenon in nature or in society, and at the same time to be richly intelligible itself" (p. 10). A novel that is "intelligible" in this sense does not necessarily have a final and unambiguous meaning, but it must invite the reader's active mental engagement: a *"modèle réduit"* is "a machine for thinking" (p. 11). Stowe's book does not propose a new definition of realism so much as a "pragmatic poetics of the mode" (p. xii), and in paired readings of *Le Père Goriot* and *The American*, *Illusions perdues* and *The Princess Casamassima*, *La Cousine Bette* and *The Wings of the Dove*, he sets out to examine how a half-dozen such "machines" actually work.

Stowe sensibly contends that the realistic novel must not be reduced either to "transparent reportage" (p. 171) or to "self-reflexive textuality" (p. 172). His concluding remarks warn against contemporary criticism's "sophisticated flight from the naive epistemological assumptions it associates with realism" (p. 172), and his book as a whole makes a welcome effort to show that the realism of Balzac and James is anything but naive. Yet *Balzac, James, and the Realistic Novel* is finally more attractive in its aims than its achievement. The idea of "systematic realism" for which Stowe argues never quite takes hold—perhaps because it depends on initially forcing the term "systematic" to perform an awkward triple service:

> The combination of these two tropes suggest [sic] a threefold definition of what might be called "systematic realism." James and Balzac both work methodically (systematically) to present a convincing picture of life in the world. Their realistic intentions naturally lead them to describe and analyze systems of behavior, communication, exploitation, and so on, that structure the world, and to rely . . . upon these systems to help structure their texts. . . . Finally, their desire to create literary analogues for life in the world leads them to elaborate textual systems . . . to reproduce something like the density and texture of experience and to involve the reader in an active process of reading and interpretation. [p. 8]

A similar affinity for forced triplets leads Stowe to divide his chosen texts according to whether they emphasize the process of interpretation (*Le Père Goriot, The American*), the process of representation (*Illusions perdues, The Princess Casamassima*) or a vision of "experience as drama" (*La Cousine Bette, The Wings of the Dove*). This third category hardly seems parallel to the other two, and would appear to have been much influenced by Peter Brooks's work on melodrama in the same novelists. Stowe's individual chapters often betray the strain of keeping the focus on his key terms, while simultaneously juggling with the three levels of "systematic realism": the discussion of *The Wings of the Dove*, for example, argues that the reader becomes "an interpreting spectator of three dramas on three different stages"—the "stage of the world," the "stages" of the characters' own consciousness, and "the stage of the text," on the last of which takes place "the drama of textuality" (pp. 130-31). Stowe does make a reasonable case for the centrality of interpretation in *Le Père Goriot* and *The American*, and by concentrating on the issue of representation in *The Princess Casamassima*, he arrives at a clever solution to the problem of that novel's notorious vagueness about anarchism: James's novel becomes not a failed representation of the political facts themselves, but a successful representation of his characters' own necessarily vague representations. "The conspirators . . . cultivate a mystifying form of reference which suggests that they know what they are talking about, hides their ignorance if they do not, and leaves the reader free to imagine the vast network of potential terrorists to which they refer" (pp. 86-87). But Stowe's comments about particular novels can often fall disappointingly flat, as when he calls Kate Croy "a creature of sincere loyalties and simple desires" (p. 143) or says that Merton Densher "may be slow, but he is not evil" (p. 161). One need not share Stuart Hutchinson's belief that all judgment in the later James is hopelessly relative to find such remarks inadequate to the epistemological and moral difficulties of the novelist's world.

In *The Phenomenology of Henry James*, Paul Armstrong argues that knowing and judging in James are necessarily both risky and incomplete, but that the world of his novels is not a nihilistic abyss. To read James as an existential phenomenologist is to understand that the structure of experience itself "provides a foundation that . . . allows us to discover and justify purposes and values to guide our lives. . . . Although nothing *beyond* experience guarantees our meanings and values, James and phenomenology discover *within* experience the basis for a purposeful existence" (p. 211). Armstrong intends his book to clarify the relations between consciousness and moral vision in James's novels as well as to introduce the major phenomenological thinkers to readers and critics of the novelist who are relatively unacquainted with contemporary philosophy. Those who agree with T. S. Eliot that James's was a mind too "fine" to be violated by an idea may resist Armstrong's persistent linking of the novelist with men like Heidegger, Husserl, Sartre and Merleu-Ponty—if not perhaps with William James. And even more sympathetic readers may be startled to learn, for example, that Isabel Archer "seems to agree with Heidegger" as well as with James himself when she tells Mrs. Touchett that everyone "should have a point of view" (p. 109). But a book that consistently emphasizes the unity of knowing and doing should be tested by the way in which it actually performs its task, and Armstrong's always thoughtful and often brilliant explications of James's texts more than justify the undertaking. Though Armstrong oddly fails to mention it, the unphilosophical reader should also recall that when Mrs. Touchett first arrives at Isabel's house in Albany, Isabel has been training her mind by sending it "trudging over the sandy plains of a history of German Thought."[4]

Even when he writes as a theorist, James does his own best thinking in narrative form. Armstrong knows this, and focuses his discussion of "The Art of Fiction" on its anecdote about the female English novelist whose momentary glimpse of a group of young French Protestants "seated at table round a finished meal" provided the sole "experience" out of which grew a successful tale of "the nature and way of life of the French Protestant youth."[5] The female novelist happens to have been Virginia Woolf's aunt, Anne Thackeray Ritchie, and Armstrong's treatment of this exemplary tale illuminates both James's own procedures as a writer and the way in which relations between subjects and objects determine the nature of reality in his fiction. As Armstrong observes, "Ritchie's distance from the group expresses symbolically the epistemological dilemma posed by the transcendence of any object to any perceiver. She glances at the gathering from the staircase and never even enters the room where the diners sit. She does not come into contact with them except through her impression" (p. 41). Like James himself when he characteristically refused to learn what "the fatal futility of Fact" had made of one of the "germs" of his novels, Ritchie takes her impression, but seeks no further acquaintance with the diners or their circumstances.[6] In part she bases her inspired guesswork about their life on her previous knowledge, as every perceiver does when he automatically extrapolates the sides of any object that are hidden from view. "She knew what youth was," James noted, "and what Protestantism; she also had the advantage of having seen what it was to be French, so that she converted these ideas into a concrete image and produced a reality."[7] But the brief impression has also its own "revelatory power" (p. 39). Drawing on Heidegger's explanation of how understanding is always "ahead of itself" (*sich vorweg*) and discloses "possibilities that explication then lays out thematically," Armstrong suggests that Ritchie's impression "projects her ahead of herself . . . to disclose possibilities about the pastor's household that she extrapolates from the scene before her with the help of her prior stores of knowledge. Her rendition of her impression is an explication of those possibilities—making explicit what she assumes to be implicit on the horizons of what she observes" (p. 40).

James offers this anecdote as an instructive account of the workings of the artist's imagination—and of the frequent disproportion between his apparent "experience" and his achievement. But phenomenology would suggest that the kind of imaginative knowing in which Ritchie engages is only a heightened version of all perception. As Armstrong argues, this is the way James's characters typically arrive at knowledge too—as when Isabel Archer's brief glimpse of an Osmond who sits while Madame Merle stands projects her "ahead of herself" and inspires her extended meditation on the nature of her marriage in *The Portrait of a Lady,* or when Maggie Verver's obscure impression of Amerigo's surprise at her waiting alone for him at home provides the germ that eventually grows into full knowledge of her husband's adultery. Of course such imaginative leaps remain hypothetical and liable to error; as the Prince later reminds Maggie when she confronts him with the circumstantial evidence of a shattered crystal bowl. "You're apparently drawing immense conclusions from very small matters."[8] Given the observer's inevitably limited point of view, she is always vulnerable to the discovery that the hidden side of the table does not form a smooth rectangle after all—or that her friend too has an "other side," like the new dimension of Kate Croy that Milly Theale senses when Densher returns from America: "It was fantastic, and Milly was aware of this; but the other side was what had, of a sudden, been turned straight toward her by the show of Mr. Densher's propinquity."[9] Again and again James's narratives turn on just such moments, when the hidden sides of people and situations suddenly disclose themselves, and the perceiver is forced to adjust his knowledge accordingly. So Chad and Marie de Vionnet float into view in *The Ambassadors* and inadvertently compel Strether to recognize what lies behind their "virtuous attachment." But to emphasize the vulnerability of perception is not to retreat into utter solipsism. The "real" is still confirmed, however tentatively, by the agreement of other people. Anne Ritchie "produced a reality," in James's terms, because her readers recognized in her tale what they believed to be the truth about young French

Protestants. Armstrong sums up "the paradoxical conclusion phenomenology has reached about the problematic relation between the Self and the Other": "Solipsism is inescapable but absurd; intersubjectivity is impossible but inevitable to some degree and attainable to a more considerable extent than most of us believe" (pp. 137-38).

Armstrong returns frequently to the Ritchie anecdote as a kind of phenomenological touchstone, but his subtle analysis of its implications is only one of many contributions he makes to our understanding of James's work. *The Phenomenology of Henry James* takes up "five major aspects of experience that, together, map James's understanding of human being—the 'impression' as a way of knowing, the imagination, freedom, personal relations, and the politics of the social world" (p. vii). Each chapter, with the exception of that on "The Art of Fiction," addresses one of these "aspects" and uses it to focus a reading of a particular Jamesian novel. The book opens with a discussion of the "impression" in *What Maisie Knew* and the analysis of "The Art of Fiction"; there follow chapters on *Roderick Hudson* and the imagination, *The Portrait of a Lady* and freedom, the Self and the Other in *The Golden Bowl*, and "the politics of experience" in *The Spoils of Poynton*. This organization can sometimes appear unduly schematic, but the book as a whole consistently emphasizes the interdependence of the questions it addresses, and for the most part its key terms seem to arise naturally from the novels themselves—as "freedom" does in *The Portrait of a Lady*, for example, or "care" in *The Golden Bowl*. By flexibly calling on a generous assortment of phenomenological thinkers as the occasion arises, Armstrong arrives at some stunning insights into his texts. The chapter on *Roderick Hudson*, for example, draws on the work of the relatively little-known Swiss psychiatrist Ludwig Binswanger, whose studies of "extravagant world-designs" help to clarify Roderick's grandiosity, his melodramatic shifts in mood and behavior. Binswanger's metaphoric term for such extravagance—"*Verstiegenheit*"—provides a splendid gloss on the novel's own metaphor of Roderick's fatally abrupt fall from an Alpine cliff: "*Verstiegenheit*," as Armstrong explains it, is "a term that defies translation because it compares the danger of rising upward too far and too fast on the wings of an overly active imagination with a danger of mountain climbing. If a mountaineer climbs too high and too far, he runs the risk of becoming '*verstiegen*'—that is, of getting stuck at a point from which he is less likely to descend safely than to plummet dizzily back to earth" (pp. 81-82). Armstrong's reading of the climactic scenes between Maggie Verver and Charlotte Stant in *The Golden Bowl* gains a similar impact from Sartre's analysis of the Self's conflict with the Other—especially from the Sartrean emphasis on the penetrating force of the gaze, and "the power that . . . comes from looking without the disturbance of being looked at" (p. 177).

Armstrong intends his interpretations of James's novels not so much to break new ground as to "help illuminate concerns already well established as important by the critical tradition" (p. 34), and in this he succeeds admirably. Isabel Archer's ambivalent longing for "freedom" is hardly a new issue in discussions of *The Portrait of a Lady*, for example, but Armstrong's analysis of the problem is both subtle and thorough. Though he argues—rightly, I believe—that Isabel's much-debated return to Osmond at the novel's close enacts a paradoxical kind of freedom ("Isabel freely consents to being bound and becomes free because bound" [p. 131]), he is wise enough to acknowledge that in representing the institution of marriage as a necessary social form, the ending betrays a partial failure of James's own imagination. And "like the limits of her attitude toward marriage . . . the flaws in Isabel's sexual understanding are undoubtedly to some extent James's too" (p. 133). Armstrong's effort to instruct the philosophically uninitiated can sometimes produce a certain repetitiousness and didacticism. And in pressing key terms like "care" (Heidegger's "*Sorge*"), his remarks can at other times sound unfortunately like the earnest clichés of contemporary psychology: Rowland Mallet will only succeed in his connection with Roderick Hudson if he manages to establish a "truly caring relationship," for example (p. 93). But these are minor flaws in a genuinely impressive book—and one that does much to answer what James called "the great question as to a poet or a novelist": "How does he feel about life? what, in the last analysis, is his philosophy?"[10] By linking the American novelist with a largely European tradition, *The Phenomenology of Henry James* is also a valuable piece of cultural criticism—though James himself might have preferred to think of it as a further act in an international drama.

That an English critic, Hutchinson, insists on liberating James from the Great Tradition and strenuously celebrates him as an American, while both Americans, Stowe and Armstrong, work to connect him to Europe, is an irony the novelist would have appreciated.

Notes

1. Virginia Woolf, *To the Lighthouse* (1927; rpt. London: Hogarth Press, 1967), p. 40.

2. "The characters in 'The Wings of the Dove' and 'The Golden Bowl' seem isolated in a Crookes tube for our inspection," Wharton wrote; "his stage was cleared like that of the Théâtre Français in the good old days when no chair or table was introduced that was not *relevant to the action* (a good rule for the stage, but an unnecessary embarrassment to fiction). Preoccupied by this, I one day said to him: 'What was your idea in suspending the four principal characters in "The Golden Bowl" in the void? What sort of life did they lead when they were not watching each other, and fencing with each other? Why have you stripped them of all the *human fringes* we necessarily trail after us through life?' " Edith Wharton, *A Backward Glance* (New York: Appleton-Century, 1934), pp. 190-91.

3. Henry James, *The Ambassadors* (1909; rpt. New York: Scribner's, 1971), VII, i; and *The Golden Bowl* (1909; rpt. New York: Scribner's, 1971), V, v. All quotations from James's novels are from the New York Edition and are cited by book and chapter numbers for the convenience of those with other editions.

4. Henry James, *The Portrait of a Lady* (1908; rpt. New York: Scribner's, 1971), I, iii.

5. Henry James, "The Art of Fiction" (1884), rpt. in *Henry James: The Future of the Novel*, ed. Leon Edel (New York: Vintage, 1956), p. 13.

6. Henry James, Preface to *The Spoils of Poynton* (1908); rpt. in *The Art of the Novel*, ed. Richard P. Blackmur (New York: Scribner's, 1934), p. 122.

7. James, "The Art of Fiction," p. 13.

8. James, *The Golden Bowl*, IV, x.

9. Henry James, *The Wings of the Dove* (1909; rpt. New York: Scribner's, 1970), IV, iii.

10. Henry James, "Ivan Turgénieff" (1874), rpt. in *French Poets and Novelists* (London: Macmillan, 1884), p. 243.

Looking for Coherence in the Later Eighteenth Century

Leopold Damrosch, Jr.

Fredric V. Bogel, *Literature and Insubstantiality in Later Eighteenth-Century England.* Princeton: Princeton University Press, 1984. xi, 226 pp.

Ever since the New Critics departed, the American academy has resolutely structured its interests by literary periods, and this has been a constant embarrassment for students of the later eighteenth century. Long ago there were two names for the half-century between the death of Pope and the birth of *Lyrical Ballads.* From one point of view it was the era of Pre-Romanticism; from an explicitly opposed point of view, it was the Age of Johnson (its usual name in college survey courses). The first viewpoint was openly teleological: Collins and Gray were born too soon for the blazing light of Romanticism, but like John the Baptist they were sent to bear witness of that light. The second viewpoint was openly reactionary: Johnson was the central figure of his "Age" and yet somehow he hated almost everything in it. "Sir, [Gray] was dull in company, dull in his closet, dull everywhere. He was dull in a new way, and that made many people think him GREAT." "All the business of the world is to be done in a new way; men are to be hanged in a new way; Tyburn itself is not safe from the fury of innovation."[1]

During the past decade new studies of Johnson (apart from biographies) have almost ceased to appear; his common-sense criticism and wisdom-literature moralism do not much interest the most recent critics. Attention has turned principally to the poets, inspired by Bate and by Frye on the "Age of Sensibility," with impressive results such as John Sitter's investigation of "literary loneliness."[2] In addition, Sterne's relocation of reality in a decentered consciousness has been greatly appealing, the self-revising Boswell of the journals has proved attractive, and the putative verities of the *Life of Johnson* have been placed interestingly under suspicion.[3] What one sees most clearly, in these recent studies, is the frustration of writers marooned between the confident Augustans and the confident Romantics. Yet there is surely something peculiar about a perspective that dismisses to the periphery such imposing figures as Johnson, Goldsmith (except for *The Deserted Village*), Gibbon, Smollett, and Burke.

Fredric Bogel, in *Literature and Insubstantiality in Later Eighteenth-Century England*, has written an invigorating book, deeply meditated and briskly argued, that proposes a striking hypothesis with which to see the period whole. Bogel believes that the Augustans were preoccupied with epistemology and their successors with ontology. It was no longer a question of how to know reality, but rather of how to endure the impoverished reality of a world bereft of a vertical or metaphysical dimension (the ghosts of Weber and Lukács hover somewhere behind this book). Bogel detects a double movement in writers' responses to this one-dimensional world: on the one hand, a new fascination with the phenomenological details of quotidian experience, but on the other hand, a bleak perception of experience as mean, hollow, and impoverished. Some individuals stress the former movement, some the latter, but most exhibit a combination of both, and they evolve various strategies (such as the palimpsest of successive "pasts" in Gray and Macpherson) by which to recharge experience with density and meaning. At the rhetorical level, fundamental tensions are reflected in contradictions or dilemmas which, unlike the Renaissance/Augustan paradoxes that harmonized *discordia* in a higher *concors*, refuse adamantly to be reconciled at all. "If the terms of paradox converge on an implied plenitude, those of dilemma strain away from a central vacuity that is the mere shadow or impress of a vanished and transcendent center" (p. 197). Whatever "substantiality" may have felt like to an earlier generation—Bogel admits that the concept is "almost distressingly roomy" (p. 68)—the period between Pope and Wordsworth is mired in "insubstantiality."

One may well entertain suspicions of this kind of hypothesis, but if so they are soon relieved by the clarity and intelligence with which Bogel deploys it. He confesses disarmingly to skepticism about schemes of periodization, and addresses individual works—to borrow his own phrase for eighteenth-century approaches to the past—with "an imaginative effort of great tentativeness and delicacy" (p. 134). His aim is not to stretch familiar texts on a Procrustean framework, but rather to use his hypothesis heuristically, defamiliarizing the texts by showing them in a new light. One wants to see what he will make of time-honored chestnuts, and he does not fail to produce them at apt moments: Gray's "Where ignorance is bliss," Johnson's "Observation with extensive view," Burke's "Art is man's nature." A number of canonical works are explored at length, sometimes with stunning results (the exposition of Burke's *Enquiry* is my favorite). But obscurer ones are adduced as well, and even when the reasons for their obscurity remain evident—Home's play *Douglas* perhaps dies on the operating table—they contribute to the plenitude that the exposition develops as it moves energetically forward.

One of Bogel's most admirable achievements is a graceful integration of earlier scholars' insights with his own, supporting his claims by showing their affinities with observations that others have made in very different contexts. He draws admirably on Bate on "satire manqué," Wimsatt on associationism and on Johnson's prose, Peter Gay on Hume, Lanham on rhetoric, Kenner on counterfeiting. And he displays as well a gift for the condensed phrase that illuminates a topic at one stroke: the "lucid pattern of earthly emptiness" in *The Vanity of Human Wishes* (p. 18), "the gradual dilation of *jeu d'esprit* into muted apocalyptic vision in Cowper's *Task*" (p. 24), "the ease with which a *hortus conclusus* may become a cul de sac" in Johnson's reflections on Edenic aspirations (p. 60), the "vast profound in which one falls from past to past" in Gray and Macpherson (p. 126).

The richest and fullest analyses are of Johnson and Burke, whose affinities are demonstrated at a deeper level than anyone has yet achieved, even while each is examined in his massive individualty. Burke's aesthetic and political philosophies are shown to emphasize "our immediate experience of the weight and power of things" (p. 150), and to do so by drastically revising traditional hierarchies of value. Perhaps one example may serve to illustrate the results that accrue, in which Bogel cites Burke's preference for "the cost of prejudice" over "naked reason," and then confronts it with a much-quoted quip of Tom Paine's that is usually taken as devastating to Burke.

> Such imagery is of course traditional, yet Burke does not use it in a traditional way. For clothing (and "habit"), the body, ornament and pleasing artifacts are, like circumstances, constitutive of their objects rather than superadded to them. When in *Rights of Man* Thomas Paine complained that Burke "pities the plumage, but forgets the dying bird," he assumed that Burke's imagery works in the traditional way (subordinating body to soul, external to internal, accident to essence, concrete to abstract) and that Burke's values, therefore, were simply inverted. One might more accurately say, however, that Burke pities the diseased limbs since they *are* the dying tree or that he pities the faded painting since it *is* the substantial form of an inspiration that without it would lack significant being. It is really Paine who is the traditional metaphysician in this encounter and Burke who, despite the apparent traditionalism of his appeal to history, develops his argument in terms of an untraditional system of values that permits the substantiality of artifice and fiction, illusion and prejudice, to displace the logicality of mere reason and the purity of mere abstraction. [pp. 122-23]

In the end, Bogel very nearly succeeds in making the later eighteenth century the Age of Johnson once again. He accomplishes this feat at some cost, by minimizing the metaphysical or vertical dimension in Johnson's thinking. Thus he emphasizes the poverty of experience in *The Vanity of Human Wishes* but has little to say about the poem's conclusion—identical with that of Boethius, who did not live in the Age of Sensibility—that a higher realm is capable of revaluing everything that happens in our disappointing world. But the dark side of Johnson has long been visible, ever since the work of Watkins and Bronson in the forties and of Bate in the fifties, and it is certainly amenable to Bogel's approach. What is most impressive is the way in which Bogel places Johnson's pessimism in a phenomenological context, expounding with welcome clarity his dual commitment to "general nature" and to the richness of sublunary experience, and showing how both of these emphases respond to deep currents in the age. The central Johnson of Bogel's pages is Boswell's Johnson, a figure whose unrivalled authenticity and presence are identified as the presiding theme of the *Life of Johnson*. Once again, familiar passages are made new: Bogel splendidly explicates Boswell's comparison of Johnson's temperament to "a warm West-Indian climate" (I myself have written foolishly about it); and William Gerard Hamilton's remark that "He has made a chasm, which not only nothing can fill up, but which nothing has a tendency to fill up" is made to seem virtually prophetic of Bogel's argument (pp. 186-87)).

As a device for opening up important aspects of later eighteenth-century experience, *Literature and Insubstantiality* is an unqualified success. Not since Price's "order and energy," twenty years ago, has anyone proposed so suggestive a structural pattern for helping us to see afresh what we had seen differently or never seen at all.[4] Whether this kind of interpretation can be wholly adequate or convincing is another matter, and doubts may legitimately be entertained even by admirers. What is being offered, really, is a "master code" of the kind Jameson describes, an interpretive structure which exists in the modern critic's imagination as much as it does in the original texts.[5] Saintsbury's peace of the Augustans, Bredvold's gloom of the Tory satirists, Bate's burden of the past and Bloom's anxiety of influence all reflect the contexts of their composition, and Bogel's book must do so too.

However firmly Bogel's chosen subjects eschewed metaphysics, his own approach is deeply metaphysical in the manner of Abrams's great *Natural Supernaturalism*.[6] Beyond that it is firmly psychological: the notion of insubstantiality owes much to R. D. Laing's account of schizoid experience, and the final chapter proposes a series of analogies between the writing of this period and Freud's theory of melancholia. This approach, subtle and generous though it is, tends to diminish those aspects of the period (if it is a "period") that are positive, aggressive, and outward-looking. Thus Bogel is excellent on the ways in which human actions in *Candide* "are drained of their ontological weight as well as of their moral significance" (p. 20), but he never mentions the militant Voltaire of the Calas affair and "Ecrasez l'infâme." And the ironies of *Candide* itself—like those in works by Diderot, Hume, and Gibbon—have a strongly positive and political component, the Enlightenment campaign against tyranny and superstition.

It may turn out that *Literature and Insubstantiality*, along with the work of many of the rest of us, is representative of a period of scholarship that was drawn particularly to metaphysical questions, and grounded these in a kind of psychological explanation. Texts, that is, have been considered as manifestations of divided consciousness, whether of the individual writer or of his age, and philosophical and psychological categories have been treated as mutually translatable.[7] Of late, however, the wind seems to be blowing in a different direction, with a renewed interest in sociohistorical contexts that scarcely appear in this book. Theorists like Jameson, Lentricchia and McGann offer themselves as heralds of an altogether different kind of master code, eighteenth-century versions of which are already appearing in studies of that eminently socialized form, the novel.[8] It is remarkable that Smollett is never once mentioned by Bogel; one would like to hear his views on the parallel versions of "reality" in *Humphry Clinker*, which rest upon a secure social foundation very different from the ontological abyss of the poets. Sterne is often invoked, but for some reason Bogel never enters into dialogue with the two most impressive studies of *Tristram Shandy*, Lanham's celebration of the positive aspects of life in a decentered world, and Swearingen's phenomenological account of consciousness as rooted in social being-with-others.[9] Similarly, Johnson's *Journey to the Western Islands* is examined for evidences of the irrecoverable past, rather than for its trenchant critique of a society in transition from feudal to "modern" ways. Gibbon's *Memoir* is discussed at length, but the *Decline and Fall* is only mentioned once, casually and in passing, and we hear nothing of the brilliant recreation of Indian culture by which Burke sought to expose the misdeeds, in a very real social and political world, of Warren Hastings and the East India Company.

Later Eighteenth Century 63

Even on the metaphysical level where Bogel is operating, one might point to signs of development rather than of anxiety and paralysis. However inadequate "Pre-Romanticism" was as a name for this period, there can be no doubt that it posed crucial questions which generated immensely original answers at the end of the century. Contradictions and dilemmas may have thwarted many of the writers whom Bogel considers, but they were soon to be profoundly reimagined in Kant's antinomies, Blake's contraries, and Coleridge's union of opposites. And as for the empirical realm, as opposed to the metaphysical, there was a good deal more to it than impoverishment. Even contradiction and dilemma, though doubtless insoluble in the ways Bogel describes, were frequently weapons in a polemic whose results were expected in the public world. Hume did hold that we can locate no secure center of consciousness, but this did not inhibit him from participating in the campaign against superstition; in the *Dialogues Concerning Natural Religion* (Part X) he advances not a dilemma but a trilemma, the famous objections of Epicurus to an omnipotent deity who is responsible for evil, and the trilemma is certainly intended to inspire a decisive conclusion. Tom Paine was unfair to Burke's metaphors, but perhaps he was not so unfair to Burke himself, since not everyone would agree that the monarchy is to the state as limbs are to a tree or paint to a painting. Burke did pity the plumage and forget the dying bird.

Notes

1. James Boswell, *Life of Johnson*, ed. G. B. Hill, rev. L. F. Powell (Oxford: Clarendon Press, 1964), II, 327 (28 March 1775); IV, 188 (1783).

2. Walter Jackson Bate, *The Burden of the Past and the English Poet* (Cambridge: Belknap Press, 1970); Northrop Frye, "Towards Defining an Age of Sensibility," in *Eighteenth-Century English Literature: Modern Essays in Criticism*, ed. James L. Clifford (New York: Oxford Univ. Press, 1959); John Sitter, *Literary Loneliness in Mid-Eighteenth-Century England* (Ithaca: Cornell Univ. Press, 1982).

3. On this last, see William C. Dowling, *Language and Logos in Boswell's "Life of Johnson"* (Princeton: Princeton Univ. Press, 1981).

4. Martin Price, *To the Place of Wisdom: Studies in Order and Energy from Dryden to Blake* (Garden City, N.J.: Doubleday, 1964).

5. See Fredric Jameson, *The Political Unconscious: Narrative as a Socially Symbolic Act* (Ithaca: Cornell Univ. Press, 1981).

6. M. H. Abrams, *Natural Supernaturalism: Tradition and Revolution in Romantic Literature* (New York: Norton, 1971).

7. This was my own procedure in *Symbol and Truth in Blake's Myth* (Princeton: Princeton Univ. Press, 1980). I do not mean in the least to repudiate the procedure, only to specify its limits.

8. Jameson, *The Political Unconscious*; Frank Lentricchia, *Criticism and Social Change* (Chicago: Univ. of Chicago Press, 1983); Jerome J. McGann, *The Romantic Ideology: A Critical Investigation* (Chicago: Univ. of Chicago Press, 1983). On the novel, see, for example, Terry Eagleton, *The Rape of Clarissa: Writing, Sexuality and Class Struggle In Samuel Richardson* (Minneapolis: Univ. of Minnesota Press, 1982), and Mary Poovey, *The Proper Lady and the Woman Writer: Ideology as Style in the Works of Mary Wollstonecraft, Mary Shelley, and Jane Austen* (Chicago: Univ. of Chicago Press, 1983).

9. Richard Lanham, Tristram Shandy: *The Games of Pleasure* (Berkeley: Univ. of California Press, 1973); James E. Swearingen, *Reflexivity in* Tristram Shandy: *An Essay in Phenomenological Criticism* (New Haven: Yale Univ. Press, 1977).

Romanticism through the Mind of Hazlitt

Jeffrey C. Robinson

John Kinnaird. *William Hazlitt: Critic of Power.* New York: Columbia University Press, 1978. xviii, 429 pp.

David Bromwich. *Hazlitt: The Mind of a Critic.* New York: Oxford University Press, 1983. xx, 450 pp.

At the end of a section in Milan Kundera's recent novel, *The Unbearable Lightness of Being,* Tereza, a soul worn down by the tensions of the 1968 Russian invasion of Czechoslovakia, suddenly discovers "a sense of beauty" in some fortuitous occurrences with her lover, and thinks: "It was the sense of beauty that cured her of her depression and imbued her with a new will to live." For Kundera, a novelist of lives warped or stunted by absolute totalitarian government, the sense of beauty does not—as it does, for example, for Keats—"overcome all other considerations." Rather it shows the opportunity that beauty grants for the recentering of the lost soul in order to encounter with greater buoyancy the alien threats of those with power. A major debate during the Romantic period flourished around the political status of that beauty emerging from the synthesizing, unifying, idealizing faculty of the human mind, the imagination; and Hazlitt was a central figure in the debate.

If it is too early to say that the essays and criticism of William Hazlitt are enjoying a renaissance in popularity, one can say with confidence that not coincidently do recent books on Hazlitt reinforce and contribute to a growing desire to understand what might be called the Romantic ideology of beauty. It is impossible to discuss Hazlitt intelligently without entering into a critique of Romanticism and of our received notions about it, for Hazlitt's preoccupation was with such a critique, a preoccupation that has rarely been taken seriously until recent times. The books by John Kinnaird and David Bromwich reviewed here take on in full stride the compelling importance and interest of Hazlitt.

"Beauty" became for the early generation of English Romantic poets the embodiment of a utopian vision of intimate communal relations or of secure individual solitude based upon love rather than power and situated in the country rather than in the city. Poetry took on the awesome burden of presenting this vision as, in effect, a replacement of the awkward fact of contemporary international politics (the dismayingly unrealized French Revolution, the Napoleonic aftermath, and England's war with France) and of the domestic repression of parties critical of the government. This direction for poetry was not new: since the middle of the eighteenth century, English poetry had sought to find value in solitude and beauty in what John Sitter has called a "flight from history." But the tumultuous history of the 1790s at home and abroad exacerbated and made more urgent the ideological tendencies of poetry, and Coleridge and Wordsworth brought their poetical genius in line with this need.

Coleridge's domestic blank-verse poems, *Lyrical Ballads* including *The Ancient Mariner*, and Wordsworth's then-unpublished *The Ruined Cottage*, *The Pedlar*, and the early version of the autobiographical *The Prelude* all establish the pre-eminence of "imagination" over reality, a faculty that often creates "beauty" by transforming reality into an idyll of itself. Beauty does not in this sense stand in relation to reality, particularly social and political reality, but is to be preferred. Perhaps paradigmatic of this process is *The Ruined Cottage*. Told by a pedlar to a poet, this is a narrative about the disintegration of a woman's mind and will manifest in the negligence of her child and property, leading to decay of the latter and death of both child and mother, a process triggered by depressed economic conditions caused partly by the war with France and causing the husband's permanent separation from and shattering of his family. But the story is told not to produce outrage at a society negligent and even hostile to its poor but rather to cultivate in the poet (and the reader) an elegiac perspective, a sensitivity to the tragedy of her life but a sensitivity born of the discovery of a fact deeper than the destruction of this woman's life, the fact of the permanence and eternal accessibility of the peace-inducing beauty of the natural world. The poem—rather than incuding the spirit of dialogue or contentiousness in the poet and reader—encourages an inwardness of spirit.

Hazlitt was twenty years old in 1798, the year that saw to light much of this great new poetry. Over two decades later, in "My First Acquataince with Poets," he recalled the excitement of meeting Wordsworth and Coleridge in 1798 and of experiencing what amounted to a coalescence of identity around the uplifting power released by the beauty of the Romantic poem. In Coleridge he found a man in whom art and religion joined forces to organize the possibility for individual integrity and sympathy in an age perceived as battered by international and domestic disappointment. At the time this effect of beauty upon sympathy must have fit with Hazlitt's independently developing concern with "disinterestedness" as a natural principle of sympathy. Writing against the eighteenth-century philosophical view that sympathy was a specially cultivated state, Hazlitt argued that "the same faculty of imagination which enables the self to will or act 'must carry me out of myself into the feelings of others by one and the same process by which I am thrown forward into my future being.' " And "I could not love my self, if I were not capable of loving others" (Kinnaird, pp. 29-30).

What Hazlitt could not see in 1798 was that the beauty of Romantic poetry—apparently that which could represent and inspire a "natural disinterestedness of mind"—in fact served the private interests of the poet far more than the interests of "the other" and fostered an egotism that precluded disinterestedness. In short it manipulated an illusion of disinterestedness while in reality simply re-establishing a set of power relations and confirming a society partly operating through and by them. The great intellectual and emotional drama—never fully concluded—of Hazlitt's life emerges through the competition between his desire to find in beauty, as practiced by the Romantic poets, a principle of the liberation of the individual and his slow-dawning realization that the Romantic poets' use of beauty tends to mask the continued centrality of power in human relations and tends to establish the ideological preference of capitalism for an imagined "spirituality" as the epitome of human existence—a preference for a view of the human subject as at its best an ahistorical being.

Both Kinnaird and Bromwich recognize that Hazlitt's importance for modern readers lies first in his reading of what Jerome McGann calls the Romantic ideology and second in his conviction that Romanticism (at least in its early phase) most characteristically seeks to divorce history from its vision of itself. Kinnaird, moreover, calls attention to Hazlitt's elevation—both in the style of his essays and in his interpretation of aesthetic objects—of passion as a means of knowing the subject in his true psycholocical and historical context. Given these basic similarities in their perspective on Hazlitt, how do the two reassessments differ from each other and how are we to evaluate their respective contributions? The decision to consider these particular books together comes partly from their sheer size and pretension and also from the odd fact that reviews of Bromwich's book have not given any assessment relative to this other recent major study of Hazlitt. (This may be a function of Bromwich's own reticence about Kinnaird: while not denying the latter's relevance to his own work, Bromwich has, to my mind, over-minimized Kinnaird's work in his thinking.)

William Hazlitt: Critic of Power has to date not make the impact on Romantics studies that it deserves to make. Perhaps when it first appeared (1978), the trendy world of criticism was not ready to embrace a study of a major critic of the Romantic ideology in his role as such a critic. For it is really only in the last few years (with the appearance of such books as Jerome McGann's *The Romantic Ideology* and Marilyn Butler's *Romantics, Rebels, and Reactionaries,* as well as isolated articles and MLA talks) that in this country, criticism has begun to question the venerable tradition of an idealizing and consoling view of Romanticism. Indeed, it is only in the present re-reading of Kinnaird's book—over twenty years in the making—that I have myself felt or seen its power. A grateful student of Lionel Trilling, Kinnaird seems to have internalized both his mentor's first principle that literature is a social and historical phenomenon (and the corollary for critics that one does not consider literature without considering its *effect*: "one does not describe a quinquereme or a howitzer or a tank without estimating how much *damage* it can do") and Trilling's seemingly contradictory deep wish to find in the great works of the past a locus for an ahistorical consolation. Kinnaird, whether or not he was enmeshed in the same web of critical impulses, has given us a Hazlitt so enmeshed and thereby has sketched out perhaps the most compelling drama of the Romantic intellect, a drama which—in his frequent lonliness— no other figure of the age submitted to with such commitment.

Perhaps both the drama and Hazlitt's loneliness can be indicated by a remark from his friend and fellow-essayist, Charles Lamb, in an unpublished review of Hazlitt's essays: "We have nothing to do with Mr. Hazlitt as a controversial writer; and even as a critic; he is perhaps too much a partisan, he is too eager and exclusive in his panagyrics or invectives; but as an Essayist, his writings can hardly fail to be read with general satisfaction."[1] Hazlitt, whom Lamb admires above all other contemporary prose writers, still needs to have divided his role as cultural critic and his role as artist ("Essayist"). It is precisely Hazlitt's struggle with the near-utopian possibility of art as an instrument for critical consciousness and political commitment that Lamb denies him. Lamb, I think, is far more muddled about the political power of art—and his own role in producing such art—than is Hazlitt. For Lamb's essays (such as "Dissertation upon Roast Pig" or "The Convalescent") as well as some of his correspondence about his preference for urban over rural life and values reveal him to be critical of the Romantic ideology almost as much as is Hazlitt. Yet he apparently does not see Hazlitt's essays as an indirect attack or critique on the Romantic view that art should exalt an ahistorical spirituality, conclusively distinct from social life. The great strength of Kinnaird's book is that it follows the young Hazlitt's desire to associate Romantic poetic beauty with a belief in natural disinterestedness and love to the older Hazlitt's growing conviction that an accurate knowledge of society must admit to the fundamental egocentricity or "self-love" of individuals, an egocentricity masked by beauty in Romantic art. Put in terms of the function of art, the older Hazlitt seems to demand the dissolution of the divisions of art into its "aesthetic" and its "political" aspects, and surely his best criticism shows this inclination.

But it is Kinnaird who makes us appreciate the tremendous hold that the consoling imagination of the early Romantics had over the thinking population of the early 1800s. Hazlitt appears as one unwilling—even in the face of his own contrary reasoning and instinct—to let go of the utopian idealisms of the new poetry. This includes his admiration for the aristocratic and conservative traditions in literature and education. And a surprising organizing feature of Kinnaird's book is religion which, through his father, moulded Hazlitt's thinking in youth and to which he returned in his last years as a "skeptical mystic." Hazlitt seems fully commited to the central place of the individual; but with an equally strong commitment to democracy and with perhaps the most acute awareness in the Romanic period of those features of contemporary culture most and least supportive of democratizing aims, he—like de Tocqueville and Stendhal—anticipates the potentially eroding effects of democracy upon individuality. Thus toward the end of his life he can sum up his complex reaction to his age by saying: "It is essential to the triumph of reform that it should never succeed." Paradoxically the Romantic imagination and its literature need to be fought against but not defeated, just as democracy must be fought for but not be completely victorious. In his difficult relationships with Coleridge and Wordsworth, his enormous respect and apparent contempt, Hazlitt embodies the confusions of the emerging democratic experiment.

A word never associated with Hazlitt but central to the Romantic ideology is "harmony." This, I think, is not merely a matter of temperament but belongs to his critique of ideology. Conversely the "passion" of Hazlitt's writing as well as of the object of his criticism stands for him in a mutually exclusive relationship to harmony, the latter being a mask for what is really the repression of the former. Kinnaird refers to what Hazlitt calls the "*ferae naturae* principle," close to what Freud calls the id, as that which controls most of our actions. Hazlitt sees the Romantic ideology waging war against this *ferae naturae* principle: most of his criticism assesses its object in these terms: "Individuality means for Hazlitt . . . the organic *indivisibility* of the self and its passions" (p. 179). Hazlitt is not, however, primarily a psychologist, unless one expand the term to include one whose view of individuality is that it is essentially wed to its environment and its relationships. For Hazlitt, Kinnaird makes clear, passion is the "force generated by . . . the motives of individuals as they exist *only* in combination with one another" (p. 179). The irony here is that the touted principle of "harmony," which ideally refers not only to the mind in contentment but also to a communion among sympathetic spirits, turns out to be far more egocentric and self-serving than the principle of passion as Hazlitt defines it. Similarly passion, particularly in its erotic embodiment in the sentimental novels of the eighteenth century, shows—as Jean Hagstrum has recently argued—the direction towards the democratization of society. In Hazlitt's own writing the great autobiographical essay, "The Fight," and the autobiographical novel of passion-love, *Liber Amoris*, point to the tradition in eighteenth-century writing to associate passion and the dissolution of class boundaries.

The relative inconsequence accorded Hazlitt's definition of poetry over the past 150 years (in comparison, for example, to that accorded Coleridge's) results, says Kinnaird, from "how intolerant we are to the concept of 'passion' in poetic theory (p. 203). This simple observation is perhaps the cornerstone of Kinnaird's revaluation of Hazlitt, for it gets at the crucial distinction between Hazlitt and Coleridge in the function of the poetic imagination, a distinction which from the Romantic Age to our own has consistently favored Coleridge. Coleridge's view is that the imagination is primarily a transcendentalizing faculty, a spiritualizing, harmonizing, unifying one. In this light passion shatters unity and harmony as it is opposed—in the usual thinking—to spirit. Hazlitt, in this regard, stands far closer to Blake, who saw imagination as at once the expression of passional energy and as that which could through such energy envision a world of egos erotized unfearfully towards love. Hazlitt, incapable of such apocalyptic visions, still loved great literature for its foregrounding of great passion—Chaucer, Fielding, and above all Shakespeare are so praised. And his praise of Wordsworth ("He does not affect to shew his power over the reader's mind, but the power which his subject has over his own"), a regard for Wordsworth's receptivity to the world around him, nonetheless leaves room for the following essential criticism: there is in Wordsworth "a total disunion and divorce of the faculties of the mind from those of the body."

When one reads this sentence in light of Hazlitt's associations from passion and the erotic to the key terms in Kinnaird's study, "power" and "intersubjectivity," he can better appreciate the boldness of Hazlitt's vision and tradition's resistance to it. For passion, though at times (as in the sentimental and *Sturm und Drang* literature) shattering and disorganizing, is for Hazlitt the necessary condition and expression of the real community of individuals, motivated—as they are—by *power*. A society that programatically denies its citizens passion denies the healthy growth and the rights of its members. And an art that prefers a community of "souls," that "chastens" (in a favorite word of Wordsworth) the individual of its drives, that values and assumes the independence of aesthetic endeavor from social and psychological forces, also favors the continuance and rigidification of traditional "base-superstructure" hierarchies in society. In Hazlett's maturity he envisioned a more mature individual, one of necessity living in the midst of passions and power-drives but who out of these could possibly attain more realistic and more equitable relations among his fellows—more (in Kinnaird's leaden but accurate masterterm) "intersubjectivity." The pantisocratic vision fostered by the Coleridgean and Wordsworthian imagination seems, in contrast, to be nothing more or less than the longing to return to the imagined bliss of the mother-child dyad.

Hazlitt, personally embroiled in such imaginings, can still emerge to give, "from within" and lacking the Marxian and Freudian analyses to which he would have been largely but not wholly sympathetic, the essential contemporary critique of Romanticism. Kinnaird provides us convincingly with this news. What does David Bromwich's more recent study add to this? A nice characterization early in his book sets the tone: "Hazlitt remains a rare instance of the speculative thinker who is also a representative observer—who can give a report on what

Romanticism and Hazlitt

lies directly before him which has the effect of prophecy" (p. 13). That is, Hazlitt stands both inside and outside his moment, he is at once philosopher and journalist, and—implied with hindsight—as he was an avid player at fives and admirer of pugilists and Indian jugglers, he is a great "player" at the sport of society and culture. Bromwich reflects what we might call the undefensive Hazlitt, a writer and thinker taking upon himself with a simple mixture of pleasure and seriousness the fundamental issues of his time. One consequence of this for Bromwich is that his Hazlitt is an undramatic figure: he does not "develop" over time or struggle through changes in perspective. Bromwich says that he is telling a "story" of Hazlitt, but it is hard to feel his commitment to any narrative at all; Hazlitt is always the same Hazlitt, moving from one concern to the next in approximately the same way. This "freer," at times breezy, Hazlitt I find a valuable and suggestive corrective to Kinnaird's more burdened (Trillingesque?) version.

From a slightly different angle Bromwich's book reminds me of the Victorian "appreciation" expanded to book length. He is at pains to "present" Hazlitt to a readership that still finds him foreign or minor. In this regard the timing of the book's publication is perfect: Hazlitt is just now coming back into focus. The writing is by-and-large uncritical, and part of the style is to present large quotations from Hazlitt with or without comment. In this regard a highly successful feature is the juxtaposition of Hazlitt with various contemporaries and of passages from Hazlitt with competing or reflective passages from other Romantics. Bromwich plays the stops right for Hazlitt, for the latter always appears to us in context, a reactive figure, one whose words never cease testing and defining the spirit of the age. The book serves us best, I think, when we see passages from Hazlitt and Coleridge on the imagination and on Shakespeare or when Hazlitt's style and Leigh Hunt's are compared: "Lighter in his graces and better equipped than Hazlitt to sound the by-ways of common emotions, Hunt is also less bold" (p. 113). The most radical strategy is to reconstruct Hazlitt's critique of the *poetry* of Wordsworth, Byron, and— at greatest length—Keats as a point of comparison and influence, by a juxtaposition of Hazlitt's observations with Bromwich's own reading. He also, with considerable interest for the reader, shows us Hazlitt revising his own essays, usually from a first to a second publication. And rightly, he contextualizes the revisions in the politics of the occasion.

As with Kinnaird, Bromwich's primary concern is to contrast Hazlitt's grounding of the poetic imagination in history and passion to Coleridge's and Wordsworth's (and in a different way, Burke's) wish to purify art and the imagination from its immediate context. Thus his comments on Coleridge and the imagination have to do with transcendence, the symbol, the ahistorical emphasis. And he shows convincingly that Coleridge views Hamlet at the core as a character, or type, untouched by event and history, whereas for Hazlitt, Hamlet would not be Hamlet without event. On the other hand, he does not argue convincingly against Kinnaird that Hazlitt always stood in this relation to Coleridge.

Bromwich, too, devotes much energy to literary context, including a chapter called "The Politics of Allusion." Often this is valuable and interesting. The subject, or at least the *fact* of literary allusion, is central to Hazlitt's style. But in the too-lengthy chapter on allusion not much is revealed about its workings that is not fairly obvious: some writers are better than others at capturing the resonances of their allusions and sources and refocusing them for a new purpose with power. And sometimes Bromwich misses opportunities right under his nose. Take, for example, his comments on Hazlitt's major evaluation of Wordsworth's Immortality Ode. Wordsworth, says Hazlitt, organizes his vision of human development upon a blissful past that has been lost, whereas he ought to have focused upon the future that has not yet come into being: both visions show the hunger of the mind for a perfect state, but to model the future is more in keeping with what people do. Bromwich, however, does not observe that Hazlitt's reading of Wordsworth is in an essay on *Romeo and Juliet* where his subject is the passion of young lovers! Part of Hazlitt's critique of Wordsworth is that the poet has left passion out of his analysis of human life.

I would extrapolate from this instance the weakness of Bromwich's overlong book: though he often presents in right combinations good raw material from Hazlitt and other writers, he does not treat these combinations with the significance they deserve. As a result, I did not learn from this study nearly as much as I was led to believe I would. The most glaring example of the book's weakness is the final chapter on Hazlitt's influence on Keats's Odes. Bromwich has done readers the service of documenting most, if not all, of the references—explicit or otherwise—in Keats to Hazlitt. But having accomplished this, he applies Hazlitt to Keats's poetry in unconvincing ways. In his chapter on Hazlitt's familiar essays, he says: "The best analogy for Hazlitt's essays is with Keats's verse-epistles, and in select cases with his odes" (p. 351)—a suggestive statement but one never proved. Of "On a Sun-dial" he says: "The essay, like a conversation poem, has begun fixed on a single object, rambled outward from that to kindred imaginings, and returning from its circuit at last settled into a new and long-earned repose of consciousness" (p. 361). The problem lies in the assumption and definitions of verse-epistles and conversation poems: *what conversation poem conforms to this description?* When he gives detailed "Hazlittian" readings of Keats's Odes, these problems of genre become acute, and the discussion does not convince us of Hazlitt's influence, nor does it force us to revaluate the Odes. A discussion of Hazlitt's influence could, I think, encourage such a revaluation, but it does not help to learn that Hazlitt's essay "On Dreams" bears the stamp of the poet who wrote the "Ode to a Nightingale" "in a kind of trance-like state" (p. 384), particularly since there is no evidence that Keats wrote the Ode this way. (If anything, Keats's confession that he composed the "Ode to Psyche" more slowly and painstakingly than he did previous poems and also presumably wrote with the same conscious care the succeeding Odes, would imply that the "Nightengale" was written with untrancelike deliberateness.)

Nevertheless, all aside, Bromwith has presented to us in new detail the mind and writings of Hazlitt. When considering this book in tandem with Kinnaird's fine study, students of Romanticism—professional or amateur—can no longer pass over Hazlitt's critique as quirky or minor. What neither Kinnaird nor Bromwich approach *in the detail deserved*, however, is the place of Hazlitt's novel *Liber Amoris* and his familiar essays—

those seemingly casual and abstracted performances on "universal" themes—in the scheme of his career-long evaluation of modern culture. For it is in the familiar essays that Hazlitt tries to situate "beauty" in the context of and in the service of a living cultural criticism. As Bromwich says at the close of his book: "Many of Hazlitt's victories are still to be declared" (p. 409).

Note

1. Quoted by Robert Ready, *Hazlitt at Table* (East Brunswick, N.J.: Associated Univ. Presses, 1981) p. 113.

Advancing toward Chaos in New Stevens Criticism

Barbara M. Fisher

David M. La Guardia, *Advance on Chaos: The Sanctifying Imagination of Wallace Stevens.* Hanover, N.H.: University Press of New England, 1983. 192 pp.

Leonora Woodman, *Stanza My Stone: Wallace Stevens and the Hermetic Tradition.* West Lafayette, Ind.: Purdue University Press, 1983. 195 pp.

There is something about Wallace Stevens that invites wildly divergent critical approaches. In the past thirty years or so, interpretations of the poetry have ranged from R. P. Blackmur's "examples" of a sleekly gestured lexis to Harold Bloom's Freudian assessment of Stevens as an Emersonian revisionist— in a way, his central example of a filial decorum of literary influence, crisis, and rebellion. Other influential readings establish perspectives so varied that—but for the occasional overlapping of quotations from the poetry—one seems to be introduced to the work of several different poets.

These variations in approach suggest something more than the need of graduate students to find a new point of entry into the canon. Apart from Blackmur and Bloom, contemporary criticism has provided at least thirteen ways of looking at Wallace Stevens. He has been read as a Hedonist (Winters), a Meditative (Martz), a Comedic Dandy (Fuchs), a Philosophe (Doggett), a Symbolist (Benamou), an Ironic (Vendler), an Iconic (Kessler), a Pathbreaker (Litz, Riddel), a Romantic (Kermode), a Poet of Reality (Miller), an Architectonic (Baird), a Decreationist (Pearce), and most recently, a Destructionist (Bové). Margaret Peterson recently pointed out, in a succinct evaluation of the critical heritage, that Stevens' poetry "has been called metaphysical, symbolist, imagist, neo-romantic and romantic-symbolist" and the poet described as "a Platonist, an eighteenth-century figure, a relic of the mauve decade, and an eminently modern poet."[1] Stevens has been aligned with Wordsworth and Shelley, Whitman, Laforgue and Verlaine; his poetics traced to Plato, Plotinus, Kant, Schopenhauer, Nietzsche, Bergson, James, Santayana, Husserl and Heidegger.

In fact, almost any critical bird can fasten a coppery claw into some portion of the work. Support for inventive approaches can be marshalled from the copious correspondence, edited by Holly Stevens, or adduced from the pithy "Adagia" in *Opus Posthumous*, edited by Samuel French Morse.[2] Peterson believes that the prevalence of divergent approaches reflects "a certain critical malaise," which may well be true, but this broad critical range exists also in part because Stevens himself supplies the material that feeds opposed points of view. He can be understood as a pragmatist and a visionary, as sensual and ascetic, as a reverent skeptic, in parallel modes that do not interfere with or "cancel" each other out. Stevens took a genuine pleasure in this sort of variety. In August 1940 he wrote: "The various faculties of the mind co-exist and interact, and there is as much delight in this mere co-existence as a man and a woman find in each other's company . . . . Cross reflections, modifications, counter-balances, complements, giving and taking are illimitable. . . . There is an exquisite pleasure and harmony in these inter-relations, circuits."[3]

Perhaps the single most persistent feature of Stevens' work is this predilection for complementary counter-balances. It nurtures the paradoxical quality that lies at the heart of his poetry. Although it tends at times to lead to obscurity, it is not the path of confusion. Rather, it illustrates in the form of a poetics the principle that Niels Bohr called *complementarity* in physics (introduced into the pages of this journal by Thomas McFarland four years ago): the theory that "a physical phenomenon may evoke two equally valid but mutually contradictory explanations." The two studies under consideration here contain contradictory interpretations for a number of poems. The question is not whether the "explanations" are

New Stevens Criticism

in conflict, but whether taken singly they add to our understanding of, or pleasure in, the poetry.

David M. La Guardia's *Advance on Chaos: The Sanctifying Imagination of Wallace Stevens* is a study "in American grain." It traces the joint influence of Ralph Waldo Emerson and William James on Stevens' poetry, and on his way of looking at things, and it puts Stevens in the poetic line of Whitman. The book is modest in scope, focused and workmanlike; the exposition relevant and readable if somewhat repetitive in the thrust of its argument, and La Guardia is in command of the intellectual background that forms the substance of his discussions. This strength may also be the main weakness of the book as the "thought" tends to overbalance the poetry. La Guardia seems more confident when addressing Emerson's transcendental natural theology or James' radical empiricism than when he is dealing with Stevens' verse. His discussions of *Owl's Clover*, "Sunday Morning," "The Idea of Order at Key West," *Esthétique du Mal* and *Credences of Summer* owe something to established readings, notably Joseph Riddel's. On the whole, however, this is a lucid study, deserving of attention, especially for its coverage of the many aspects of Jamesian philosophy and the relevance of these ideas to the shaping of Stevens' poetics.

In contrast, Leonora Woodman's *Stanza My Stone: Wallace Stevens and the Hermetic Tradition* draws upon a European model of "spiritual alchemy." Woodman extends the notion of hermeticism well beyond the writings of the obscure Trismegistus (exposed by Isaac Casaubon, Frances Yates tells us, as a chronological interloper) to include medieval laboratory searches for the "philosopher's stone," and material from the Kabbala, Gnosticism, speculative theology, mysticism, and Carl Jung's theory of archetypes. While the focus wavers over this extensive but questionable terrain, making the argument difficult to follow, the discussion itself is limited and reductive. Woodman sees Stevens as a sort of poetic Paracelsus. Her study concentrates on elements in the poetry that can support an "alchemical" reading and ignores all else, including context and Stevens' own declaration that he loathed "anything mystical."[4] *Stanza My Stone* is structured to a considerable extent on the kind of imaginative linking that so irritated Dr. Johnson in the metaphysical poets: the discovery of "occult resemblances in things apparently unlike."

La Guardia derives the title of his book from Emerson's famous essay, "Self-Reliance," noting that William James marked the passage in which Emerson exhorts men to think of themselves "not as cowards fleeing before a revolution, but as guides, redeemers and benefactors, obeying the Almighty effort and advancing on Chaos and the Dark." Stevens readers, of course, are well aware of the poet's self-professed connoisseurship of the Chaotic. The study is divided into five chapters that deal with poems thematically, but also in a roughly chronological order. La Guardia conducts the discussion of the three Americans (all Harvard men, Peterson points out) by systematically developing philosophical attitudes he finds common to all three: existence as flux; mind as shaper of reality; man at the (perceptive) center of his world; and interpenetration of subject and object (James' percept/concept relation).

The idea that a sense of sanctity pervades the secular sphere binds the thought of the three men, according to La Guardia, and he points out that Emerson's "challenge" to his generation was inherited by a later age:

The affirmation of divinity in a world of perpetual flux embodied for Emerson a challenge to his age to participate in divinity by more actively confronting the festival of life that reflected it. In the godless twentieth century, Stevens challenges his contemporaries to confront precisely the same festival, substituting for the divine the spirit of the holy that they generate in themselves by individual acts of the imagination's perception. [p. 6]

La Guardia's reading of Stevens' wonderfully evocative *Credences of Summer* relies on James' assertion, in *The Varieties of Religious Experience*, that "personal religious experience has its root and centre in mystical states of consciousness." From this, La Guardia concludes, too easily: "Since Stevens' visions subscribe to James's definition of a religious experience, they may be referred to as mystical states." He accordingly interprets *Credences* as a first-hand record of visionary experience rather than examining it as a rhetorically refined poetic statement. Stevens might have remarked that this was skating figure-eights on pretty thin ice. For example, La Guardia states that the first section of *Credences* is "the most important of the poem," and quotes the opening lines:

> Now in midsummer come and all fools slaughtered,
> And spring's infuriations over and a long way
> To the first autumnal inhalations, young broods
> Are in the grass, the roses are heavy with a weight
> Of fragrance and the mind lays by its trouble.

La Guardia notes Stevens' "intense concentration on the visionary moment," and reads the opening lines to mean: "In summer's ripeness, in the lull between spring's ascendence and autumn's decline, the imagination 'lays by its trouble' and basks in contemplative passivity." This valid reading underscores the "visionary" quality of the stanza. At the same time it is a partial reading, insensitive to ambiguities in the lexis. How is the reader to understand the accumulation of such terms as "slaughtered," "infuriations," "broods," "heavy with a weight," and "trouble"? Does the phrase "the mind lays by its trouble" mean that trouble has been put away, or that trouble is adjacent and present? Perhaps Stevens wishes us to sense a dark underside to the bright vision. Particularly if one is exploring Stevens' sanctifying imagination, one must remain open to the *double entendre* in a poet whose "Seigneur" is the "gaiety of language."

Other difficulties in *Advancing Toward Chaos* result from limitations of approach and from occasional fuzziness in definition. In "Amputation From the Trunk," the longest (50 pages) and least rewarding chapter, La Guardia investigates "decreation" in the poetry. To my knowledge, the one time Stevens used the term importantly was during a lecture on "The Relations Between Poetry and Painting," delivered in 1951 at the Museum of Modern Art.[5] He referred to Simone Weil's distinction between decreation and destruction: "She says," noted Stevens, "that decreation is making pass from the created to the uncreated, but that destruction is making pass from the created to nothingness." Having remarked the difference between thoughtful dismantling and arbitrary demolition he continues: "Modern reality is a reality of decreation, in which our revelations are not the revelations of belief, but the precious portents of our own powers."

Stevens goes beyond the noting of a boundary line between abolition and demolition here, and the idea of the "precious portents of our powers" is reflected in *The Sail of Ulysses*, written in the same period. Stevens predicts a time when,

> We shall have gone behind the symbols
> To that which they symbolize . . .
>
> Like glitter ascended into fire.

This is the note of hope in a dark time, more particularly the keynote of Bergsonian creative evolution and the idea of an élan vital energizing the human spirit. Possibly because of his approach, La Guardia ignores the influence of Santayana and Bergson in the poetry, as well as Stevens' approving reference to Bergson's notion of the Life Force in "A Collect of Philosophy."[6] The philosophy of creative evolution presumes an organic and spiritual development for the human race; it has little to do with a critical approach via William James and "perpetual flux." And it conflicts with one of La Guardia's major themes, the attribution to Stevens of a belief in a "nonteleological universe." For this critic, Stevens is deeply involved in process, but (as Donne might have said) "O to no end."

The second, less disturbing, problem involves the notion of "decreation." La Guardia does not clearly define the term and uses it throughout the lengthy "Amputation" chapter to signify both "abolition" and "demolition." It becomes a return to "primitive simplicity" (p. 41), "stark violence" (p. 58), a "tendency to 'unsettle all things' " (p. 65), "necessary violence" (p. 68), and the need to "remove all of the old scaffolding that prevents [the poet] from perceiving the world at first hand" (p. 70). Finally, La Guardia fuses the senses of "decreation" and "destruction" in a discussion of the poet's "heroic" aspect: "The role of the poet and the role of the hero fuse for Stevens" so that "by acts of decreative violence the poet experiences temporary apotheosis and replaces the deity at the creative center of existence" (p. 73).

La Guardia does bring into focus a number of Stevens' key images, among them the "man of glass" and the notion of "transparency." La Guardia traces these, rightly I think, to Emerson's remarkable figure of the soul as pure perception (*Nature*, I): "I become a transparent eyeball; I am nothing; I see all." Harold Bloom, of course, cited the relevant passage in *Poems of Our Climate* (Cornell Univ. Press, 1977, p. 61), but Bloom's insight has been substantially carried forward by La Guardia. His discussion of Stevens' metaphors of "center and edge" is lively and provocative, and it reveals an affinity between Stevens and James that manifests itself in imagery as well as in thought. La Guardia suggests that the "tentativeness of the central position" in Stevens' verse reflects the problem of the psychologist "who, in a pluralistic universe, seeks a center that, as quickly as it can be achieved, dissolves." He refers to a telling passage from James which I reproduce here:

I feel that there is a centre in truth's forest where I have never been: to track it out and get there is the secret spring of all my poor life's philosophic efforts; at moments I almost strike into the final valley, there is a gleam at the end, a sense of certainty, but always there comes still another ridge, so my blazes merely circle towards the true direction. . . . I cannot take you to the wondrous hidden spot today. Tomorrow it must be, or tomorrow, or tomorrow, and pretty surely death will overtake me ere the promise is fulfilled. [p. 27]

One is reminded of the poetic consciousness in Stevens' early "Valley Candle" in which "beams of the huge night" converge on the tiny flame with impersonal inevitability. La Guardia believes that James' statement "contains in miniature a characterization of the whole of Stevens' poetry," and rightly observes: "If James's figures of the flickering center are not a source for Stevens' figures of center and edge . . . they portray at least a brilliant example of the psychic affinity between the two writers." Although La Guardia relies a good deal upon previous readings of the poems (often turning, for instance, to

Joseph Riddel's *The Clairvoyant Eye*), when he is engaged in triangulating the thought of Emerson and James with Stevens' poetry the discussion is generally tightly-knit, well documented, and useful. Limitations of approach do not prevent him from developing a number of insights that help to illuminate Stevens' poetic vision of the world.

Leonora Woodman's title is intriguing, taken from the penultimate line of one of Stevens' best known and most unnerving poems. "The Man on the Dump" locates the poetic consciousness square on the trash of romantic ideals, heroic traditions, the remnants of *courtesie* and lyric flights of fancy. All the "images" of the moon are "in the dump": "You see the moon rise in an empty sky. / One sits and beats an old tin can, lard pail." It is a poem in which the tone alternates between cynical disgust, bitter despair, Chaplinesque whimsy, and a dogged determination to see "things as they are." The final stanza poses a series of stinging questions:

> Is it a philosopher's honeymoon, one finds
> On the dump? Is it to sit among mattresses of the dead,
> Bottles, pots, shoes and grass and murmer *aptest eve*:
> Is it to hear the blatter of grackles and say
> *Invisible priest*; is it to eject, to pull
> The day to pieces and cry *stanza my stone*?
> Where was it one first heard of the truth? The the.

Woodman's *Stanza My Stone: Wallace Stevens and the Hermetic Tradition* does not address itself to questions of time and place and a changing world. Instead, it endeavors to establish a linkage between Stevens' poetry and various schools of mysticism and alchemy. Her introduction maintains that Stevens was a "deeply religious poet" who " held a vision of spiritual regeneration which he repeatedly outlined in many poems. His subject is not 'natural' man but transcendental man . . . and it belongs to the venerable and well defined Hermetic tradition."

Two arguments are brought to support this thesis: Stevens' use of emblems such as the "giant red man," the "man of glass," the "rock" and "Ananke"; and the fact that the young Stevens visited a summer resort in Ephrata, Pennsylvania, where a community of Theosophists was undergoing its final decline. Not until the last of nine chapters does Woodman reveal the source of Stevens' supposed involvement in "spiritual alchemy." This chapter, entitled "Crispin and the Hermits of the Wissahickon," is in the nature of an appendix that provides the rationale for Woodman's study and is, unfortunately, the most readable section of the book

In this section, called "The Rosicrucians of Pennsylvania," Woodman recounts the history of the "forty eremites" who sailed from Germany to establish, in 1694, a " 'true Theosophical' . . . community grounded in the esoteric philosophy of the Kabbalah, the speculative theosophy of Jacob Boehme, and the teachings and art of hermeticism." These religious dissidents set up in eastern Pennsylvania, moved to Ephrata not long after, and continued there into Stevens' lifetime. Woodman quotes from Stevens' reference to the community in "Rubbings of Reality," an appreciation of William Carlos Williams.[7] According to Stevens, just as Williams' experiments in poetry, like Picasso's in painting, approximate "the grinding of glass, the polishing of a lens by means of which he hopes to be able to see clearly," so "the German pietists of the early 1700s who came to Pennsylvania to live in the caves of the Wissahickon and to dwell in solitude and meditation were proceeding in their way, from the chromatic to the clear."

Woodman, unhappily, proceeds in the reverse direction from the pietists of the Wissahickon. She begins by establishing an alchemical model which assumes increasingly complex or "chromatic" dimensions. The laboratory procedure that alchemists hoped would transmute a base metal into gold, "expressed in the adage *solve et coagula*" (dissolve and resolididy), goes hand in hand, we are told, with a search for the "life-germ or vital seed commonly known as the philosopher's stone." This stone represents on the one hand the "triune principle of godhead immanent in nature and man." and the *"prima materia"* or "centre" or "the point originated by God" which, on the other hand, is "often pictured as a two-headed hermaphrodite" (pp. 52-53). The reader is then introduced to "Mercurius Monogene," who chromatically "assumes various disguises" such as "Sol (the sun)," the "red man," the "Giant of two-fold substance," and the "Philosophic gold, described as crystalline and associated with glass and salt, symbols of the 'subtle' body of the divine androgyne, 'transparent as crystal, fragile as glass.' " He corresponds, we find, to "the bisexual Adam Kadmon" of the Kabbala, who is later connected with the "Persian Gayomart," a masculine earth symbol. The analogue of "spiritual alchemy" involves, among other elements, putrification, a purifying dissolution, a redemptive return to "nothingness," or "the center," and a spiritual "sacred marriage." These initial mystifications become for Woodman the descriptive *materia alchemica* of Stevens' poetry.

Both La Guardia and Woodman address themselves to the figure of the "subman" in *Owl's Clover*, and to the idea of the "hero." It is instructive to see how the approaches color the interpretations. The "subman" is Stevens' "man below the man, below the man, / Steeped in night's opium, evading day." Both critics sidestep a "Freudian" reading. La Guardia perceives the subman to be "Stevens' drab image for the bare self who sees the flux as it is and can animate it. He is Emerson's scholar, but living in a dungeon, Poe's spirit of beauty trapped in a rationalist's world" (pp. 63-64). For Woodman, the same "subman" is a Protean creature whose nature changes as one turns the page. Having rather suddenly advised the reader that "Stevens' poems are primarily concerned with Ananke" (p. 20), Woodman introduces the subman as "an Ananke surrogate." He survives for a while as "Ananke-subman" until he experiences a final transformation into the "Ananke-subman-portent: the dark-skinned Ananke-serpent" who "presides over Stevens' restored paradise" (p. 26).

For the Americanist, MacCullough—the "hero" figure in *Notes Toward a Supreme Fiction*—is "like Emerson's central man. He is a real man, not an apotheosis" even though he can be understood as a "parable of the Christ-fiction" (pp. 81-82). For Woodman, the "hero" is simply another avatar of Ananke:

Stevens' hero, whom I have urged as a variation of his Ananke-subman, is at once a psychic force [imagination] and a telluric spirit of nature [reality]; that though shrouded in darkness, he is a creature of light, often equated with the sun . . . . This figure, elsewhere labelled an 'impossible, possible philosopher's man' . . . is not at all a prototype of ordinary humanity but . . . the *homo maximus* or divine 'Son of the Philosophers,' more popularly known as the 'philosopher's stone.' [pp. 43-44]

La Guardia is least impressive in readings of the poetry where he tends to overlook the complexity and depth of Stevens' best work. He is firm and clear, however, in his presentation of the background material and his book contains valuable insights. Woodman has chosen an approach that would have been more appropriate to a study of Yeats. Instead of clear argument and reasoned discussion, Woodman deals in equivalences and correspondences; things turn alchemically into other things and continue their existence as part of a chain of hyphenated elements. As a result, the exposition in *Stanza My Stone* is a model of opacity. It is difficult to see, in the welter of mystical terminology, alchemical symbology, and comparative mythology, just where the connection to Wallace Stevens might be, except perhaps in "the blatter of grackles."

Notes

1. Margaret Peterson, *Wallace Stevens and the Idealist Tradition* (Ann Arbor: UMI Research Press, 1983), p. 1.

2. See *Letters of Wallace Stevens*, ed. Holly Stevens (New York: Knopf, 1966); and *Opus Posthumous*, ed. Samuel French Morse (New York: Knopf, 1957).

3. *Letters*, p. 368.

4. *Letters*, p. 428.

5. This lecture was published by the Museum of Modern Art as a pamphlet and is included in the collection of Stevens' essays that appeared in the same year: *The Necessary Angel: Essays on Reality and the Imagination* (New York: Vintage-Knopf, 1951), pp. 159-76. The reference to Simone Weil's *La Pesanteur et La Grace* is on p. 174.

6. *Opus Posthumous*, p. 187.

7. *Opus Posthumous*, pp. 257-59.

Five Versions of Milton at Horton

Richard S. Ide

A. N. Wilson. *The Life of John Milton.* Oxford and New York: Oxford Univ. Press, 1983. 278 pp.

Maryann Cale McGuire. *Milton's Puritan Masque.* Athens, Ga.: Univ. of Georgia Press, 1983. 208 pp.

Richard Helgerson. *Self-Crowned Laureates: Spenser, Jonson, Milton, and the Literary System.* Berkeley, Los Angeles, and London: Univ. of California Press, 1983. ix, 292 pp.

John Guillory. *Poetic Authority: Spenser, Milton, and Literary History.* New York: Columbia Univ. Press, 1983. xiii, 201 pp.

William Kerrigan. *The Sacred Complex: On the Psychogenesis of* Paradise Lost. Cambridge, Mass.: Harvard Univ. Press, 1983. x, 344 pp.

At a time in Milton criticism when increasingly interpretive theses about Milton's poetry are predicated upon assumptions about Milton the man, and when momentarily the skirmishes between supporters of a radically Protestant, prophetic Milton and those of a Christian humanist Milton will proliferate into the grand combat of the 1980s, it is disconcerting to realize how utterly confused we are about Milton's beliefs, aspirations, and sense of vocation during the formative years at his father's houses after Cambridge and before the trip to Italy. The Milton of the Horton period who emerges from the five works under review is alternatively Anglican or Puritan, gay-blade or kill-joy, self-assured or anxiety-ridden. He is a prelate or poet or prophet or pamphleteer who cannot get started with whatever it is he wants to do because 1) he does not know what it is, or 2) he is having too much fun not doing it, or 3) he must prepare further before doing it, or 4) even though he knows he wants to be a poet, he has nothing to write about, or 5) he has no mode in which to write it, or 6) he is waiting to be discovered by an aristocratic patron, or 7) he is incapacitated by developmental arrest, oedipal in nature. And this is only to scratch the surface of the incongruities.

It would be unfair to ask of A. N. Wilson's new biography of Milton that it bring order to this chaos, for the confusion survives the best efforts of giants (Masson, Tillyard, Hanford, Bush, and Parker, among others) and at any rate the prolific novelist and literary editor of *Spectator* has written his chronological review of Milton's life and works for a popular audience. Admirably readable, *The Life of John Milton* lacks authority as a scholarly document.

The strengths and weaknesses of Wilson's life of Milton derive from a thoroughgoing effort to transform the facts of biography into a fictional life. The first extended fictional passage, for example, which attempts to recreate the sights and sounds of Bread Street in the Jacobean era, finds William Johnson (landlord of the Mermaid Tavern) strolling down to the river before retiring for the night:

Most of the houses in Bread Street would be plunged into darkness, for men rose in those days at dawn. But, night after night, as he ambled down that fetid, narrow little street, the innkeeper who had served ale (in his day) to Shakespeare and Donne and Ben Jonson, would have seen a light burning in an upstairs window above the sign of the Spread Eagle. Every evening, defiant amid the surrounding blackness of London, the candles flickered at that window until midnight struck. It was not some learned divine, preparing a lecture for the morning; nor an advocate working late on a case; nor an alchemist dabbling in forbidden knowledge, though any passer-by might have guessed it to be one of these things. [p. 4]

It is the boy Milton, of course, and notwithstanding the melodramatic touch about the black alchemist, one is struck by the deftness with which biographical details of Milton's studious childhood are incorporated into Wilson's fictional scene-setting. Indeed, Wilson is at his best when describing the London streets, the insides of churches, or battles during the

Milton at Horton

civil war, and when speculating about Milton's relations with his wives and about his blindness. These latter matters, about which we have few facts, invite responsible speculation, and Wilson—penetrating and sensitive—responds as well or better than any biographer before him. But Wilson's fiction can also distort fact, as when—to return to the portrait of the young student—he elaborates on Aubrey's detail that John Milton, Sr. "ordered the maid to sit up for [young John]" when he studied late.[1] According to Wilson, "Already, he led a studiously eccentric life. The maids who sat up late with him complained that it would do no good to his eyes" (p. 4). There are now at least two maids, and they are not simply waiting up for him but sitting with him (to wipe his brow? to bring him sweets?) and fussing about him. Little John and his fluttering hens.

Mixed in with the fiction-making that sometimes distorts are some regrettable oversights and a good deal of humorous, cheeky editorializing. Nearly wholly dependent on Parker's biography, Wilson seems unaware, for example, that nearly everyone else believes that Milton had begun his education at St. Paul's School before Thomas Young was hired as a tutor, or that Grierson, Tillyard, Hanford, Shawcross, and Sirluck date "Ad Patrem" in 1637-38 rather than earlier. Indeed, reading Wilson's chapter on St. Paul's School, in which Gil's spelling, whipping, Spenser, and du Bartas are emphasized and the "safe" assumption made that Milton's schooling had little influence on him (p. 14), one must conclude that Wilson simply has not read D. L. Clark's *Milton at St. Paul's* or any other books on Elizabethan education and so is ignorant of the formative influence of rhetorical training on English Renaissance poetry. As for the editorializing, academics and private schools are the objects of some generally good-natured fun; less appreciated and less fun are the jabs at the Scots and homosexuals. [One is less than grateful for being instructed that the psychopathic Earl of Castlehaven was like most homosexuals in that he had the "classic homosexual delight in having love-affairs with men of the lowest class on whom he then bestowed great favors"—p. 43.] When Wilson places his substantial fiction-making talent in the service of an editorial stance, however, the reader has cause for feeling betrayed. One example of this editorial intrusion involves a subtle yet discernible anti-Cromwell bias that eventually burgeons into a direct attack on Christopher Hill (pp. 159-60). A more important example for us involves the extensive coloration of the portrait of Milton in the early 1630s.

The fictions that *maids* attended Milton when he studied late at night and that the privileged student began his education at the foot of a private tutor, together with Wilson's reading of Milton's schoolboy portrait ["This is not the face of a boy who is going to have to earn his living" (p. 9], are later supplemented by a description of a spoiled undergraduate who loved women and fun but was pent up in dingy Cambridge. Upon matriculation, this Milton, we are told, was a "social climber" who "deliberately chose, even though he had the support of his father and the means to live without the support of aristocrats to seek out the patronage of the Countess of Derby" (p. 36). Why? Because by predilection he preferred to be "with people of the world, with whom he was always more happy than with a narrow academic or literary circle" (p. 50). And who were the people of Milton's ideal world?

> When God addresses himself, as his manner is, to his Englishmen, one can be sure that the type of Englishmen Milton had in mind owned a few hundred acres and were merciful towards the poor of the parish, harsh to poachers, and handy with rod and line. [p. 178]

Neither radically Protestant nor zealously republican, Wilson's Milton at Horton is not even much of a Christian humanist. Indeed one intuits that this Milton, who at one point is termed a "passionate capitalist" (p. 55), would have made a perfect Tory gentleman of the eighteenth century.

Wilson's version of Milton at Horton, as one might well imagine, has interesting implications for the biographer's readings of *Comus* and "Lycidas." On the whole, one must remark, Wilson's readings of the major poems of the 1660s are pedestrian: not unexpectedly, *Samson Agonistes* is read as a biographical document, and the familiar links to Mary Powell, Salamasius, and John Milton, Sr. are made; the positions of honor afforded Lewis and Empson in the discussion of *Paradise Lost* indicate that Wilson will provide no new revelations about

Milton's great epic; and *Paradise Regained* seems to have generated in Wilson little interest and less enthusiasm. But *Comus* is singled out as "the lightest and the most joyous of all Milton's poems" (p. 48). It is written by a courtier in the cavalier tradition, and its "most striking feature [is] that without any offensiveness, Milton has enabled Comus to retain the amusing, gay, and almost innocent debauchery that he has in Jonson's masque" (p. 50). In "Lycidas," in turn, Milton speaks from a "very Anglican" perspective against Catholic infiltrators (" 'The grim wolf with privy paw'' is a clear reference to the Jesuits"—p. 68). Not until the trip to Italy did Milton turn toward religious and political radicalism. Wilson's biography of Milton during the 1630s, from *Arcades* through the radicalizing trip to Italy, is easily the most interesting and surely the most controversial segment in this new life of Milton.

Years ago, James Holly Hanford cautioned that even though Milton was temperamentally "poles apart" from the aristocratic circle for whom he wrote *Arcades* and *Comus*, some future biographer might be tempted to misread the evidence: "No writer of historical fiction, to my knowledge, has undertaken to show us a Milton interrupting his studies to present himself at Harefield and exchange courtesies with the awe-inspiring dowager, the socially experienced Lord Brackley, and the soon to be marriageable Lady Alice, but the opportunity to do so obviously exists."[2] Wilson has seized the forelock with both hands. Maryann Cale McGuire, on the other hand, in *Milton's Puritan Masque*, refuses even to acknowledge that such an opportunity exists, for reasons that will soon become clear.

McGuire's Milton was a committed Puritan early in the 1630s. Milton undertook his studies at Horton to prepare himself for the sectarian pamphleteering of the 1640s, and *Comus*, far from reflecting simply a "nascent Miltonic libertarianism," as Angus Fletcher would have it,[3] is in fact "a crucial turning point" for Milton, a shift from the largely "apolitical or even conformist attitudes of his early writing [to] the Puritan partisanship evident in 'Lycidas' and his prose works" (p. 6). McGuire's specific thesis is that *Comus*'s violation of conventional masque formulae constitutes a Puritan rejection of the traditional royalist attitudes associated with those formulae.

McGuire derives her thesis from "a contextual reading of the masque—one that takes into account its general historical milieu and the individual mind that produced the work" (p. 2); unfortunately, neither the ideological contexts she constructs for *Comus* nor the Puritan mind-set she adduces for Milton are convincing. There is no question, of course, that Milton's beliefs and temperament fostered adaptations of traditional masque formulae; *Comus* is distinctly Milton's masque—moralistic, didactic, dramatic, misshapen, idiosyncratic. But the reader is by no means convinced that it is Milton's *Puritan* masque. In fact, if Milton were so committed to the radical Puritan program regarding an essentially royalist form of entertainment, could such a Puritan fail to recognize the obvious: that however well intentioned his efforts to reform the genre and to register his antipathy toward royalist attitudes, the mere fact of his accepting a commission to write a masque defending the reputation of an aristocratic family would tend to confirm his complicity with the "enemy." There is good reason for McGuire not to want to consider Milton's "exchang[ing] courtesies with the awe-inspiring dowager": the implications of such an exchange war against her thesis.

The first of McGuire's four central chapters is fundamental to her argument. In it she contends that Milton sided with the Puritans against the Anglicans in what is termed the "recreation debate." Even if one were to grant that such a debate existed—one distinguishable from the more narrow controversy concerning recreation on the Sabbath—McGuire not only fails to make her case that the debate "had a massive and complex impact on Milton's writing of his masque" (p. 39) but unwittingly leads the reader to precisely the opposite conclusion: that Milton was closer to the Anglicans than the Puritans in his attitude toward recreation. For example, because McGuire's attempt to link Milton with the hysterical Prynne (*Histriomastix*) carries so little conviction, one's immediate reaction is to embrace Annabel Patterson's notion that Milton's masque constitutes a rejoinder to Prynne rather than an endorsement of him.[4] Indeed, to associate Milton with the Puritans on this issue requires an intolerable distortion of evidence on McGuire's part, one effect of which is to transform *The Declaration of*

Milton at Horton

Sports (reissued in 1633) into a libertine document. But the Anglicans never asserted that pleasurable recreation on the Sabbath was tantamount to an abrogation of moral responsibility (McGuire's simplificaiton); in fact, by stating that only those who have attended church may engage in lawful recreation, official policy *subordinated* Sabbath recreation to religious obligation. Moreover, to read *Comus* as a Puritan document in this regard necessitates a desperate interpretation of the masque's ending: specifically, that the final rustic dance before the presentation of the children to their parents is somehow a threat to the moral life of Ludlow (pp. 162-63).

McGuire is on safer ground in the second and third chapters where she demonstrates how Milton adapted to his own purposes masque conventions relating to character, plot, and rhetoric. She is quite right in attributing the dramatic emphasis in *Comus* to Milton's "intensely dramatic moral vision" (p. 64) and in distinguishing his conception of spiritual journey (as Christian quest, warfare, race) from the merely processional journeys of conventional masques. (Spenser is not mentioned as an influence in this regard, presumably because that might suggest a literary heritage for the masque rather than a strictly doctrinal, Puritan heritage.) And McGuire's interpretation of the children's journey as a dynamic, educational experience is legitimately conceived and fairly presented. In the third chapter devoted to the rhetoric of *Comus*, a lengthy review of the dispute between Ben Jonson and Inigo Jones over the relative importance of verbal and visual "rhetoric" in masquing leads to a justifiable differentiation between the Anglican and royalist preoccupation with the "eye" (ritual, beauty, appearance, image), which is promoted by Comus in Milton's masque, and the Puritan priority on the "ear" (sermons, the Word), which is generally associated with the Attendant Spirit and the Lady. But again, however, the *Puritan* thrust of McGuire's argument is somewhat vitiated by at least two factors. First, the absence of spectacular scenery may have been dictated merely by physical necessity (the performance was at Ludlow, not at court), not by conscious Puritan predilection, or, alternatively, there may have been more scenery and devices in *Comus* than we have heretofore thought.[5] Second, and more important, arguably the distinction most insistent in *Comus* is not an intramural one between eye and ear (as the chapter proceeds, in fact, McGuire concedes that the senses must be used to check each other), but a hierarchical one between sense and spirit. There are sensual songs and heavenly songs, outer lights and inner light, brute forms and intellectual ideas: the body may be frozen, but the mind is free. That is to say, the substantive distinction in *Comus* is not Puritan at all, but neo-Platonic.

In the final chapter McGuire launches her most provocative interpretive sortie, one for which her book will probably gain its place in omnibus footnotes and future variorum commentaries. What is the meaning of chastity in *Comus*? That McGuire's response can be simply put, "chastity is Milton's version of charity" (p. 138), reflects neither clarity nor depth of insight in this instance, but a single-minded ingenuity that overleaps text, doctrine, and logic in attaining—one must assume—the point at which it began. Reformed theologians, we are told, understood charity principally as love for God, and often used "betrothed" as a metaphor expressing that love. To follow God's will faithfully was to live a "chaste" life, avoiding the "fornication" of sin. Charity was thus spoken of metaphorically as chastity. This is well and good (never mind for the moment that the Castlehaven scandal is essential to the masque's context, and Milton's text repeatedly associates chastity with virginity), but the points McGuire must make in order to support her thesis are first, that chastity was spoken of metaphorically as charity, and second, that the metaphor in fact bespeaks a fundamental doctrinal identity between the virtues. This McGuire fails to do, yet she presses forward, assuming the interchangeability of the terms. By the time we are told that "Nature is thus ruled by the same principle of chastity, the outward and active conformity to divine will, that ought to guide human life" (p. 158), and chastity has been elevated to something like Dante's *"La gloria di colui che tutto move,"*[6] this reader has long since abandoned ship.

Milton's Puritan Masque is an earnest book which is worth reading for its suggestions as to how Milton adapted the conventions of the Caroline masque for *Comus*. But the reader should be cautioned that its central thesis about the Puritan program of *Comus* and its most provocative interpretive point about chastity are dubious at best.

Richard Helgerson, for one, would certainly not be convinced by McGuire's thesis. His version of Milton at Horton in *Self-Crowned Laureates: Spenser, Jonson, Milton, and the Literary System* is that of a poet too much caught up in the impoverished literary milieu which McGuire thinks he set out to reform. For Helgerson, *Comus* is a quintessentially Caroline poem which—in spite of Milton's effort to distance himself from the cavalier poets figured by Comus (pp. 268-69)—fails to assert the author's full poetic autonomy.

> By its genre and structure, by its themes and style, by its social, political, and professional affiliations, *Comus* declares itself a work of its time . . . . [It is] an Orphic poem, a mannerist poem, an occasional poem, a poem dependent on the systems of patronage and artistic collaboration. [pp. 258, 271]

Comus is not the work of a laureate poet, and certainly not that of a Puritan poet.

Self-Crowned Laureates is a major achievement. Its conception is dazzlingly strong and simple, its argument deployed with economy and force, its style lucid, its tone unpretentious. The ways Spenser, Jonson, and Milton present themselves as "laureate poets" occupy the foreground of the study, but the broad canvas of literary generations Helgerson creates as backdrop for the poets' self-presentation is for me the more impressive critical achievement. Helgerson displays a sure command of English literary history from Spenser to Milton, and in giving definitive shape to the generational conflicts that dominate that history—between Elizabethan amateurs and the satirists of the 1590s, between the satirists and the cavalier poets—he articulates more clearly than in any work I know how genres become generational markers, as if so many traits by which an individual poet and his coevals identify themselves. But this eclectic critic is much more than a sophisticated student of genre theory. He is also influenced by the "new historicism," especially evident in his insistence upon evaluating history as ever-changing, in this case as a generational succession of synchronies; by contemporary semiotics, evident in his application of semiotic analysis to each literary generation, determining principally through generic signs that generation's identity; and by the new "socio-criticism," evident in his recognition (with Greenblatt, Montrose, Whigham, and others) that the poet's struggle to achieve a position of individual authority and preeminence, to fashion a public sense of self, must be carried out under certain inescapable "social and cultural constraints" (p. 15). Although Helgerson would distinguish himself from some socio-critics (Jonathan Dollimore, for recent example)[7] whose Althusserian materialistic bias leads to the notion that the gestures of selfhood are virtually programmed by society (as if by cultural imprint), and would preserve the integrity of the "irreducible and active self" (p. 19) of these three writers, the critical emphasis of *Self-Crowned Laureates* is on reading literature in terms of its symbolic codes and interpreting the poets' self-presentation in terms of socially symbolic roles, of recognizing—that is—that the "differences by which the self declares its identity must necessarily be located in a synchronic system, in a communally established sense of social reality, a sense renewed and revised with each successive generation" (p. 282).

Helgerson begins by establishing some constants in the laureate poet's self-presentation: that the laureate self is "a virtuous, centered, serious self, characterized by its knowledge of and fidelity to itself and the governing ethos of the age" (p. 102), and that this self identifies with the literary system of its generation but, through calculated opposition, distinguishes itself from that system. Helgerson then turns to his important chapter on Spenser, balancing the poet's self-presentation in *The Shepheardes Calender*—marked by uncertainty as Spenser tries to free himself of the amateur identity he shared with his coevals to assume the work of poetic responsibility—with that of the late works where, especially in Book VI of *The Faerie Queene*, the fusion of love poet and vatic poet achieved in the 1590 edition of the epic disintegrates.

The chapter on Jonson is the most powerful in the book. Locating Jonson in a generation when the "golden poetry of Sidney and Spenser was played out" (p. 108) and the new genres of elegy, satire, and epigram were in vogue, Helgerson turns to *Poetaster* to evaluate Jonson's Horatian identity in light of Ovid (who represents Jonson's amateur coevals) and Virgil (who represents Jonson's daunting predecessors, Sidney and Spenser). From this time forward, Jonson's laureate presentation focused on "exercise, imitation, study, art, and, above all, moral goodness" (p. 122). The next sections on the laureate satirist and the laureate dramatist, detailing how Jonson attempted to elevate an antiromantic, antiheroic genre and to transform an unsavory profession into vehicles for his laureate ambition are for me the highpoints of the book, the treatment of Jonson's antitheatrical prejudice being especially fine: "So long as the pressure to define himself remained strong, so long, that is, as the accurate construal of his status remained in doubt, he could be a laureate poet in the theater only by opposing the theater, by unmasking the moral emptiness of its mimicry, its metamorphoses, and its plotting" (p. 161).

Milton had the misfortune of being born into an era of literary belatedness, one characterized by homage to predecessors, by a mannerist style, and by close association with court and society. The Caroline poets' generation lacked a literary idiom, and Milton by political and religious inclination was not disposed to present his laureate self as servant of Charles and Anglicanism. Later, however, Milton's too close association with the Commonwealth became fatal to his laureate ambition: "Church-outed by prelates, Milton was laureate-outed by a political, religious, and literary situation that first gave him nothing to do and then gave him too much" (p. 242).

The factors that release Milton from this paralytic situation are chiefly two (and these are Helgerson's two most important points in the chapter). First, the cavalier interest in heroic poetry in the 1650s—Davenant's Preface to *Gondibert*, Benlowes's *Theophila*, Fanshawe's translation of *The Lusiads*, and Cowley's *Davideis*—created precisely the generational idiom which reignited Milton's laureate ambition and enabled its fulfillment. Second, Milton "found in blindness and defeat [of the Old Cause] a new autonomy for poetry and poet" (p. 251): "Neither the King's laureate nor the laureate of the English people, Milton was freed by defeat to assume the prophet's posture of divinely inspired alienation, a role adumbrated but never fully realized in his earlier work" (p. 250). Milton became God's poet.

There can be no question but that the lack of a literary idiom early in Milton's career and the lack of poetic autonomy later in his career are plausible contributory factors in the great "delay" between the announcement of Milton's laureate ambition and its fulfillment. That they are at most *contributory* factors, however, indicates the relative limitation of Helgerson's thesis when applied to Milton. Far more than Spenser and Jonson, Milton appears answerable to systems other than the literary system. The man given over to an expansive study of history and the church fathers at Horton—while writing virtually nothing—seems deliberately to be hedging his bet: would he be a prelate, after all? a religious pamphleteer and activist? a poet? a scholar-teacher? (philosopher? theologian? historian? logician?). Helgerson says "poet," and so only one of several possible informing systems, the literary system, and only one dominant branch of it at that, cavalier non-dramatic poetry, are brought to bear on this formative period of Milton's career. But questions remain. Why could not the publication of Donne's and Herbert's work provide an acceptable idiom for Milton? Why could Milton not set out to reform cavalier genres, such as the masque (as McGuire says he did), or more obviously (given his love for classical tragedy and plans for a biblical tragedy) the decadent cavalier drama? And what if religious or educational or psychological "systems" were in conflict with the literary system in Milton's conscious or unconscious mind, counselling that fame through poetry was wrong, that religious or civic service was the proper use of Christian talent, that inaugurating a poetic career would launch the "boy" into unwelcome manhood? And what if Milton's chief affiliation were with a diachronous system of literary history after all (the world of Homer, Virgil, Ariosto, Spenser, and others), not the synchronous system of cavaliers? Such questions do not refute Helgerson's thesis, but merely point to limitations which make it relatively less successful when applied to Milton. It is certain, however, that even if one were disposed to account for Milton's "delay" in terms other than the incapacitating dynamics of his interaction with the cavalier literary system,

Helgerson's book ensures that never again will the great poet be thought of as standing in splendid isolation above and apart from his literary generation.

It is John Guillory's misfortune that the announced concerns of his *Poetic Authority: Spenser, Milton, and Literary History* make its pairing with Helgerson's book irresistible. Ideally, I suppose, the books ought to be complementary: Helgerson's new historicist, socio-critical approach to Spenser and Milton being balanced by Guillory's emphasis on intertextuality, deconstruction, and the psychodynamics of literary influence. Unfortunately for Guillory, however, sharp differences in execution tend to place the books in a contrastive, not complementary, relationship. *Poetic Authority* lacks *Self-Crowned Laureates'* clarity of conception, learning, and quality of argumentation. And where Helgerson's style is lucid, Guillory's is opaque; where Helgerson is authoritative, Guillory is given to discipleship. Guillory places formidable obstacles in the reader's path, and this is too bad; for the author of *Poetic Authority* has a keen intelligence, and the patient readers who surmount the book's maddening excesses will discover a provocative central thesis to compensate them for their effort.

Guillory's thesis is that modern, secular poetry, with its emphasis on creative imagination, comes into prominence with the demise of a vatic mode of poetry which subordinates imagination to inspiration. At the time of this revolution in poetics, Spenser and Milton were waging an unsuccessful rearguard action against secular poetry; their efforts were pointed against the imagination, which can produce its poetry only at the great moral risk of prizing its own creation *ex nihilo* over God's creation. The reason Spenser's attacks against the authority of the imagination may be said to fail is that his efforts to associate his own poetry with a sacred, authoritative source and to use allegory as a means of expressing sacred truth contain their own severe critique [this predicated, of course, on Guillory's success in deconstructing key passages from *The Faerie Queene* (Chap. 2) and *The Mutabilitie Cantos* (Chap. 3)].

The thesis as it relates to Milton is more interesting, and Chapters 4 and 5 are the most important in the book. Guillory posits that "the relationship between poets can range from an identification, by means of which an origin is found, to a usurpation, by which an authority is displaced" (p. 21). In *Comus* especially, Milton identifies with Spenser and displaces Shakespeare. If the identification with Spenser—carefully qualified—recommends Guillory as a sensitive student of literary family dynamics, the putative displacement of Shakespeare—largely unqualified—cannot be passed over without the rejoinder that Guillory seems deliberately to set out to provoke.

Guillory's Milton-Shakespeare antithesis is shaped by a fierce critical reductionism, according to which "Shakespeare" in Milton's mind stands for a mode of imaginative, irrational, secular poetry created *ex nihilo* in opposition to sacred poetry's revelation of God's creation. One discerns this Miltonic attitude, Guillory claims, as early as in "On Shakespeare," Milton's ostensible tribute to Shakespeare placed at the head of the Second Folio:

> For whilst to th'shame of slow-endeavoring Art,
> Thy easy numbers flow, and that each heart
> Hath from the leaves of thy unvalu'd Book
> Those Delphic lines with deep impression took,
> Then thou our fancy of itself bereaving,
> Doth make us Marble with too much conceiving;
> And so Sepulcher'd in such pomp dost lie,
> That Kings for such a Tomb would wish to die.
>
> [9-16][8]

Here, we are told, the older poet first becomes suspect in Milton's poetry: "The condition of arrest or paralysis is everywhere morally suspect in Milton's poetry. This Shakespeare possesses the paralyzing magic of the enchanter, Comus" (p. 19). But not quite everywhere, and not with this particular figure. What Guillory fails to point out is that the closest analogue to this passage, in "Il Penseroso," which describes Contemplation's moment of Platonic ecstasy as forgetting herself "to Marble" (see 37-43), has no such negative implication. But more important is what Guillory does to the significant pre-texts of *Comus*, which are *A Midsummer Night's Dream* and to "a slightly lesser extent" *The Tempest* (p. 75). The problem lies not in that we are supposed to discern a direct allusion to *A Midsummer Night's Dream* every time Milton uses the words "faery" or "aery," but in what these allusions are said to signify. According to Guillory, Milton derives Shakespeare's "antithetic poetic" from Theseus's famous speech in Act 5 of *A Midsummer Night's Dream*:

The poet's eye, in a fine frenzy rolling,
Doth glance from heaven to earth, from earth to heaven;
And as imagination bodies forth
The forms of things unknown, the poet's pen
Turns them to shapes, and gives to aery nothing
A local habitation and a name.
[5.1.12-17][9]

Although Guillory earlier acknowledges that this poetic is "very mediated indeed in the mouth of the unimaginative Theseus" (p. 18), he subsequently forgets his own caveat when placing great pressure on the word "nothing" and interpreting it (as Milton supposedly did) as Shakespeare's own endorsement of imagination's creation *ex nihilo*. But we know, of course, that at no other moment and with no other word is Theseus more skeptical and revealed to be more wrong. In comic contrast to Theseus's materialistic skepticism [i.e., what is not experienced by the senses and not rationally accounted for does not exist ("nothing")], the existence of the faeries, not just in the wood but right there in Theseus' house, symbolizes the existence of natural principles—no less real for being imperceptible ("nothing")—governing the lovers' behavior. In short, this poetic is "very mediated indeed in the mouth of . . . Theseus"; one may say, in fact, that it stands as a foil to the Shakespearean poetic in *A Midsummer Night's Dream*. And yet Guillory identifies Theseus' poetic with Shakespeare's, and so Shakespeare with Comus, and later with Satan—all creators *ex nihilo*. [Presumably Guillory would have us (and Milton) fail to recall that nowhere is the moral risk of indulging the imagination's creation *ex nihilo* depicted more pointedly and with such admonitory force as in the genesis of Macbeth's evil design (see I.iii.134-42) or Leontes' evil suspicion (see esp.

I.ii.138-42).] An even more perverse reading of the *Dream* occurs or Leontes' evil suspicion (see esp. I.ii.138-42).] An even more perverse reading of the *Dream* occurs later in the chapter when the play is adduced as "the most proper intertexual locus" (p. 88) for Comus's seduction of the Lady—not the obvious subgenre of the seduction poem, mind you, the *carpe diem* themes and witty seducer of which Milton replicates in *Comus* and the typically dull seducee Milton pointedly transforms, but *A Midsummer Night's Dream*, that well-known libertine manifesto!

And what of *The Tempest*? First, we are to understand Comus himself as a critique of Prospero, as opposed to a black magician like Archimago or Sycorax. But this is not easily done, of course, for it means that specifically we are to associate the theme of debased nature, which is everywhere insisted on in *Comus*, not with Caliban, but somehow with the supposed *base* designs of Prospero's *natural* magic. Further, we are to disremember that Prospero makes a stern speech enjoining Ferdinand and Miranda to pre-marital chastity and often insists on the civilizing mission of art, for these emphases would smack of the Spenserian mode more than the naturalistic Shakespearean mode. Moreover, we are not to recall that Prospero, a far more likely surrogate for Shakespeare than Theseus, is fully aware of the imaginative vision's "baseless fabric." And when attention is fixed on Comus's magic rod, we are to remember Prospero's staff but simultaneously to forget that the Attendant Spirit and two brothers attacking Comus must then necessarily be related to Caliban, Stephano, and Trinculo. In sum, while one could argue that *Comus* is in its way an upside-down version of *The Tempest*, it is not at all clear that Milton's attitude toward this particular pre-text for *Comus* is wholly negative. And, in general, while there is no question in my mind that Milton's incorporation of Shakespeare into his work to some extent involves a critique of the older poet, the topic is as complex as it is important, and is not served well in this case by Guillory's reductionism.

The fifth chapter is more successful and should be read by serious Miltonists. The conflict Guillory locates between Milton the poet and Milton the prophet, the association of Satan with the imagination and with its secular poetry, and—as mentioned above—the discussion of Milton's identification with Spenser are important points responsibly formulated. This is Guillory at his best, and Guillory at his best is very good indeed. The final chapter on "History and the Language of Accommodation" is less cogent. Not only is the fundamental link between the two titular subjects of the chapter tenuous, but the theses that topical history saturates *Paradise Lost* and that the reality of history subverts Milton's vision of history are not strongly supported, and so are proffered as interesting ideas rather than evidential arguments.

Unquestionably the finest recent achievement in Milton criticism is William Kerrigan's, *The Sacred Complex: On the Psychogenesis of Paradise Lost*. Intelligent, learned, clearly conceived and beautifully written, *The Sacred Complex* is a masterpiece of interdisciplinary criticism. Here, as in no other work I know, the principles of psychoanalysis are brought into a fruitful, harmonious, mutually illuminating relationship with those of literary criticism. Although Kerrigan insists that "The survival of literature as anything more than artifact depends on our ability to extend its original reference into a genuinely revelatory description . . . of the world we inhabit now" (p. 2), his ideal psychoanalytic critic is fundamentally a literary historian: "Although he broadens the usual notion of intentional meaning to include the unconscious, the psychoanalytic critic cannot find this extended intentionality without first having found the customary one: the intended meaning, the minimal possession of all literary study, is the meaning he interprets" (p. 3). When "brought to literature with respect for the cultural life of symbols, psychoanalytic principles can disclose new configurations in the structure of a work or a career" (p. 3). Conversely, a literary study of Milton's works can also bring much to psychoanalysis, particularly as it suggests how some people, "not all of whom have written books, undergo through religion an authentic reshaping of the self that psychoanalysis has yet to recognize adequately" (p. 73). Freud's views on religion notwithstanding, religious affirmation associated with the sacred complex (as distinguished from the oedipal complex) refashions the superego:

The superego may make us ill, may make us ordinary, or may fade into an ego ready for solitary self-regulation: but there is another and uniquely religious vicissitude of the superego. Traced to the turmoil of the oedipus complex, God appears to be illusion. Such an illusion, due in part to the process of excavation by which it has come into our ken, seems at first overwhelmingly conservative—a strategy for preservation. Yet it may have a future. The dynamics of the sacred complex turn against the oedipal settlement they also preserve, liberating the ego to some degree from its secular submission. Through religious symbols Milton was able to empower himself in a manner directly opposed to the dissolution of superego into ego. The way beyond the complex began inside the complex. [p. 8]

After establishing the centrality of temptation in Milton's work—that moment of existential revelation when the interior communities of law and desire claim allegiance—and after suggesting how "Milton created through poetry effigies of his self-determination" (p. 19), Kerrigan charts in one breathtaking sweep Milton's psychic history as revealed in *Comus* (Chap. 2) and *Paradise Regained* (Chap. 3). Central to Kerrigan's reading of *Comus* as "the masque of the superego" is Milton's "feminine identification in the oedipal context" (p. 49), an identification enabling us to see him working through his own oedipal problems in the figure of the Lady. If the Lady's virginity is a "root-bound virtue, caught in a reaction formation to oedipal temptation" or "in bondage to the desire denied" (p. 55), Milton's virginity, which was for him a sign of his separateness as God's poet and prophet, is also a desire root-bound because of "his reluctance to begin and his fear of exposure" (pp. 53-54). The epilogue to *Comus*, which "releases the erotic and aggressive wishes whose denial bound virtue to its root, . . . gestures toward a new negotiation of the oedipal settlement" (pp. 59, 61) in Milton himself. Not long afterward, the death of Milton's mother, the assumption of paternal roles as surrogate father and teacher of his nephews, the decision to marry, and the early pamphlets through which he "was reforming from within the structure of his superego" (p. 65) reveal Milton successfully exorcising the "static obedience memorialized in the Lady of *Comus*" (p. 66).

Turning to *Paradise Regained*, Kerrigan follows Freud in insisting on the superego as a vehicle of culture and boldly departs from Freud in his assertion of a "sacred complex" by which "religious devotion may permit a creative 'immaturing' of the fallen superego":

> By reenacting the oedipus complex in the sphere of religion, Milton composed the terrors and ecstasies bound to his ambition while simultaneously he gave life to the symbols of his faith. . . . If the first complex thrusts us from nature into culture, the second transforms the profane into the sacred culture [pp. 77, 80]

This large claim is buttressed by a brilliant reading of *Paradise Regained* "as a Freudian psychomachia," at the climax of which "the ego as rival to the father falls into repression [i.e. Satan], while the ego-ideal, obediently correlated with the ways of the father [i.e. Christ], ascends to its sovereign position in the structure of conscience" (p. 81). Highpoints during the course of the argument are discussions of the Oedipus simile at the poem's climax (pp. 83-85), of Christ as the founder of a new culture (pp. 86-87), of symbolism, metaphor, and Milton's use of the symbolic mode (pp. 103-05), of phallic symbolism in the poem (pp. 110-11), and of the Athens temptation (pp. 111-14). Principally, however, the thrust of the argument is that the Son, encouraged by his mother, transforms his desire into the will of the father, seeking identification, not conflict, with his "matchless Sire."

In Chapter 4 Kerrigan turns directly to the psychogenesis of *Paradise Lost*. The argument is focused on the invocation to light (III, 1-55) and a time in Milton's life when, owing to his blindness, his full psychic history—elaborated in the discussions of *Comus* and *Paradise Regained*—is recapitulated *in parvo*. If the pace and intensity of the argument slacken while Kerrigan reexamines the ontology and symbolism of light in *Paradise Lost*, we are off and running soon enough with an examination of Milton's blindness, specifically with how seeing is associated with guilt and blindness with guiltlessness, and consequently how blindness enables Milton to recover the lost innocence of the primal scene. The pivotal identification of

Milton's muse with the preoedipal mother then clinches Kerrigan's thesis on the poem's psychogenesis: that *Paradise Lost* is enabled by the sacred complex's restructuring of Milton's superego.

It is as if the structure of the superego, when stretched out in the cosmic dilations of religious symbolism, loosens to reveal its full contents. A muse was hidden in the strict taskmaster. The mother, too, inhabits this psychic agency, and she is more than another voice to obey. . . . She is not the dominant pole of the first superego. But through obedience to the paternal law, the boy supplies himself with the possibility of reencountering, in a future of lessened severity reached through this obedience, maternal intuition. It is in this sense no merely symbolic truth that only the Father can dispense the presence of the Muse. Finding this sense, Milton ended the antagonism between oedipal father and the narcissistic ego whose symbol was once the paralysis of *Comus*. [p. 181]

Kerrigan then completes this central chapter with another stunning observation, detailing how *Paradise Lost* is printed on the blank book of Milton's blindness. Milton, like a maternal vessel waiting for God's seed ("There plant eyes"), is linked with the Son, whose role is also that of mother, of materializer:

It is the Son, the feminine Son, the first *lumen* to receive the divine *lux*, who stands as the prototype of strength that comes from weakness, exemplifying the movement from self-emptying obedience to self-fulfilling exaltation Milton would imitate in the blank book that becomes *Paradise Lost* and the ever-during dark of blindness that becomes a womb full of futurity. [p. 186]

In the next and longest chapter dealing with Milton as the "Christian Lucretius," Kerrigan leads the reader through a fascinating revaluation of the scientific elements in the epic, his purpose being to suggest how these elements stand as symbols of Milton's personal crisis over his blindness. If the scholarly discussions of medicine, digestion, spirit, monist ontology, and the like are authoritative and intriguing, the real excitement resides in the psychoanalytic reverberations of Milton's association of blindness with the failure of digestion (pp. 204-

05), of the angel body with an ego ideal (pp. 222-23), and of knowledge as both nourishment and poison, as a wish to be both indulged and resisted. The concluding section on the pathology of the Fall and the cures of Michael, more specifically on the pathogenic fruit and the exogenous cure of inspiration, tie the strands of the chapter together by suggesting how the poisoned Adam whom Michael enables to see reflects on the blind poet's private theodicy:

As blindness is equivalent to the curse of the fall, so the writing of the poem, which the guilt of this blindness paid for, must be unconsciously equivalent to the guilty aspiration of the fall. . . . [But] *As blindness is punishment, so seeing is forgiveness, and the visionary composition of the epic renders the poet symbolically guiltless.* [pp. 258, 259]

The "enfolded sublime" of the epic's final lines, where Milton offers us "the nonsectarian wisdom he had harvested from the long work of mastering the sacred complex" (p. 271), centers Kerrigan's concluding discussion. The final challenge facing the poet who proclaims the *felix culpa* is to define what it is in our present historical state of homelessness that is "more wonderful" than the paradise now lost; in psychoanalytic terms, "In what way does Milton's presentation of the *felix culpa* pass beyond. . . the pleasure principle?" (p. 281). The answer—and Kerrigan's reader has now been trained partially to anticipate it—resides in the uncanny appropriateness of the oedipal solution which the reader of *Paradise Lost* achieves in the final identification with our first mother and father, Eve and Adam: "Milton's catharsis is a *pax christiana* for illnesses residual from the first conflicts of life" (p. 296).

This final psychoanalytic thrust, like the others in *The Sacred Complex*, is perceived by the student of Milton to be wholly appropriate; it articulates in a new but complementary vocabulary what we feel on our pulse to be true and have tried otherwise to articulate. It is finally this "strange sympathy" of Kerrigan's psychoanalytic criticism with our traditional Miltonic criticism that will ensure that Kerrigan's work not only be taken seriously but accepted and assimilated into the vast body of received knowledge on Milton's poetry. (Indeed, one easily predicts that psychoanalysts will have more trouble accepting Kerrigan's theories about religion and the sacred complex, the primal scene, and the pleasure principle than will literary critics his psychoanalytic reading of Milton.)

But this perhaps is to understate the extraordinary achievement of *The Sacred Complex*, which may do much more than teach us about Milton and *Paradise Lost*. This book has the potential—I believe—of fully legitimatizing psychoanalytic criticism in a community of Renaissance scholars still dominated by a conservative historicism, and in particular, of weaning Miltonists away from our habitual concerns with the formal and thematic properties of Milton's texts to a consideration of the fascinating pre-text of those texts, the poet's psyche. *The Sacred Complex* will be difficult but obligatory and rewarding reading for the scholarly community of Miltonists.

Having justly praised this extraordinary book, one remains obliged to remark that Kerrigan, too, leaves much to be said about Milton at Horton.[10] In concert with the other four books under review, *The Sacred Complex* intimates that no period in Milton's life is more shadowy, no time in his psychic history more problematical, than that of the early 1630s. Each work has given us at best a partial glimpse of Milton at his father's houses after Cambridge, partial by virtue both of their limited perspectives and of the limited truths those perspectives reveal. We have yet to achieve a fully integrated sense of the great poet during these formative years, and if we are soon to measure the relative strengths of his radical Protestantism and Christian humanism, it is time that we try harder to do so.

Notes

1. Quoted from *The Early Lives of John Milton*, ed. Helen Darbishire (London: Constable, 1932), p. 10.

2. James Holly Hanford, *John Milton, Englishman* (New York: Crown Publishers, 1949), p. 61.

3. Angus Fletcher, *The Transcendental Masque: An Essay on Milton's Comus* (Ithaca, N.Y. and London: Cornell Univ. Press, 1971), p. 18.

4. Annabel Patterson, "*Paradise Regained*: A Last Chance at True Romance," in *Composite Orders: The Genres of Milton's Last Poems*, ed. Richard S. Ide and Joseph Wittreich, *Milton Studies*, 17 (1983), 194.

5. See William B. Hunter, Jr., *Milton's Comus: A Family Piece* (Troy, N.Y.: Whitson Publishing Co., 1983), esp. p. 55.

6. *Paradiso* I.1, quoted from *The Divine Comedy: The Paradiso*, trans. with commentary Charles S. Singleton, 2 vols. (Princeton: Princeton Univ. Press, 1975).

7. Jonathan Dollimore, *Radical Tragedy: Religion, Ideology and Power in the Drama of Shakespeare and His Contemporaries* (Chicago: Univ. of Chicago Press, 1984).

8. Citations are to *John Milton: The Complete Poetry and Major Prose*, ed. Merritt Y. Hughes (New York: Odyssey Press, 1957).

9. Citations are to *The Riverside Shakespeare*, ed. G. Blakemore Evans, et al. (Boston: Houghton Mifflin, 1974).

10. Kerrigan's assumption—accepted without qualification from his earlier *The Prophetic Milton*—that Milton had no doubts about his poetic vocation, that from the beginning (i.e., 1629) he thought that his sacred poetry was wholly acceptable in God's eyes, seems unworthy of a psychoanalytic critic. James Thorpe, *John Milton: The Inner Life* (San Marino, Ca.: Huntington Library Press, 1983), has pointed out how Milton's early fantasies of fame and immortality as a poet convey "nothing about those hopes for heaven expressed in the resolution reached in the passage in 'Lycidas' " (p. 43). Are we really to assume that the guilt Milton attaches to the writing of *Paradise Lost* (Kerrigan, p. 258) was not at all present earlier during the period of delay when the anti-poetic sentiment of John Milton, Sr., may have been reinforced by the heavenly father's strictures against fame? One would like to hear more from Kerrigan about Milton and his father, and the text that begs for attention in this regard is *Samson Agonistes*, where the notion of a "divided father" seems so central.

Aesthetic Sensibility and the Idea of the Imagination in America

Robert F. Lucid

Louis J. Budd. *Our Mark Twain: The Making of His Public Personality.* Philadelphia: University of Pennsylvania Press, 1983. 266 pp.

John Raeburn. *Fame Became of Him: Hemingway as Public Writer.* Bloomington: Indiana University Press, 1984. 231 pp.

Louis J. Budd's *Our Mark Twain* is subtitled *The Making of His Public Personality.* The concept of a public personality—like the somewhat related concept of a cultural imagination, and the idea of an individual-at-large in the culture—is familiar enough, but Budd's may be the first full-length literary study to address it formally. His book was released only shortly before John Raeburn's *Fame Became of Him*, which is subtitled *Hemingway as Public Writer.* This may be the second full-length formal contemplation of the phenomenon. The two books are very ambitious compendia of research materials and would be, for this reason alone, extremely valuable. Neither gives more than perfunctory attention, however, to the immense amount of material to have accumulated since the death of these two subjects, so that from a compendia point of view both books should be followed by volumes devoted to the posthumous years. No doubt they will be.

As analyses of the material their research has uncovered, the two books are also immensely informative. Both suffer, however, from a kind of intellectual isolationism that, for example, prevents Budd from mentioning Hemingway (or anyone else) as following in the Twain tradition, and leads Raeburn, in his few references to Twain, always to insist upon (but never to explain) the great differences between his and Hemingway's public identities. Indeed, in their different ways both books tend to claim that their subjects are *sui generis*. The two works also reveal two very different ways of coming at the study of the public writer. Professor Budd worries repeatedly over the lack of an established scholarly method for conducting a study such as his, and justifies the work finally because of his personal belief in the greatness of Twain's accomplishment as a public figure. The book is deeply, almost apologetically committed to methodological caution, and, given its also very deep populist sentiments, it presents us with an unusual interplay between conservative and liberal scholarly impulses. Professor Raeburn, quite liberally unselfconscious about his methodology, presses strongly his personal belief that, at least as Hemingway lived it, the public literary life is a pointless and miserable waste. In the process he presents us with an interplay, also unusual, between a liberal openness of method (and of style), and an almost startlingly conservative espousal of high-cultural critical severity. By playing to the crowd, in this view, Hemingway had betrayed his art, and so grievous a sin could only call down upon him the most grievous consequences.

Whether the public Twain is actually established as a permanent hero in our cultural pantheon, as Budd maintains, and whether the public Hemingway is in the process of being permanently forgotten, as Raeburn more than implies, are questions difficult to discuss convincingly in a narrow context. And the contexts of both of these books are narrow, in that they focus only upon a single figure and, even then, propose no coherent, overarching idea of the public figure in America, in the light of which their particular figure can be examined. Thus the books, while extremely valuable in their ways, are perhaps most forceful in their catalytic capacity: they require us to reflect for ourselves upon the broad topic of the presence of the public artist figure in the culture, and to relate that presence to the culture's more general understanding of the idea of the imagination.

Ever since Plato banished the poets from his Republic, there has been an argument going on in Western intellectual history concerning the societal efficacy of art, the artist, and the artistic community. At issue was the question whether the cultivation of the aesthetic sensibility was a way of strengthening the cultural imagination or, on the contrary, was actually a fatal means of debilitating it. In America, however, the argument seemed to end, for we began our culture on the assumption that the jury had found for the prosecution: we not so much banished the poets as we rehabilitated them, openly articulating the proposition that telling stories, fashioning poems, or in any other way attempting to create aesthetic experience was not fit work for a grown man's hand.

The legacy which succeeding generations have received from this ancestral source is complex and far-reaching, but its most obvious and immediate effect is to be found in the way we have finally brought into existence the figure of the American artist, the structure of the American artistic community, and the full canon of American art. All are marked indelibly by their inherited sense that they perhaps should not exist at all, just as they are also marked by an almost messianic sense that they have been brought into existence for some intensely important purpose. One way of identifying this purpose is to remark our artists' sense that they are the keepers of the culture's imaginative flame; that as artists they relate to the imagination for its own sake, rather than for the purpose of accomplishing some utilitarian task; and that in their lives and artistic concerns they offer living examples of what close, long-term cultivation of the aesthetic sensibility can produce.

Of course the idea of the imagination in America can be approached without this special reference to our artists. For something like the first two-hundred years of its existence, after all, the culture assigned few if any of its major imaginers to the production of art, and if we now identify an artist's imagination at work in the careers of William Bradford, Cotton Mather, Jonathan Edwards, Benjamin Franklin, and Thomas Jefferson, we should do so while understanding that none of them would have taken such identification as a compliment. That the imagination is not the exclusive possession of the artist, but is rather the exclusive possession of *homo sapiens*, would presumably have been Plato's position. So approached, an attempt to engage the idea of the imagination in America would address the understanding and employment of the imagination not by the artist but by the individual at large in the culture. A way to do that, in turn, might be to set up an investigation of those figures in the culture upon whom the imagination of the individual at large has unquestionably been fixed: icons in the many pantheons the culture has created are, after all, fashioned by people in the culture to serve their imaginative needs. Our political and economic and military heroes, our scientist and educator icons, even our figures of legendary athletic prowess not only speak to, but to a significant degree emerge from, our imagination. To analyze their identities and infer from them the internal condition of the individual at large in the culture is, at least theoretically, an achievable goal, and what might be called the imaginative state of the culture might thereby be ascertained.

But the more direct avenue into the subject does, indeed, appear to be through American art, the artist, and the artistic community. For one thing the avenue has clear borders, in contrast to the immensity of the general subject of cultural heroes and hero-worship; and for another thing the area of art offers us an attractive kind of self-reflection with respect to the subject. The artist, after all, is by definition the figure of the imaginer, and when we address the way the audience undertakes to envision such a figure, we encounter (if one may say it) the imaginer imagined. An intensity of dynamic is possible in such a dialectic that would be most difficult to discover with any other figure, and this, combined with the fact that the history of the work, world, and life of the artist in our culture has charted such an unusual course, leads us almost inevitably to contemplate this aesthetic arena.

To contemplate the aesthetic in America is, immediately, to encounter the Platonic societal question: Is aesthetic experience a source of strength or of weakness for the individual engaged in the larger cultural struggle? Indeed, insofar as the artist does anything besides produce works of art, is aesthetic experience a source of strength or of weakness to the artist himself? The career of every American artist speaks in some way to this question, and the careers of what Professors Budd and Raeburn call our "public" artists speak to it directly. The public artist is properly identified as an exemplum, and what is being exemplified is the way close, prolonged association with aesthetic experience affects the figure's ability to deal with life outside the aesthetic sphere. What of the relationship with nature, with society and institutions and communities other than the artistic? What of the figure's relationship with the family, the other, the loved one or the nemesis or, finally, the self? These are the relationships required of all men and women, and they constitute what often is called reality. Imagination, as the idea is traditionally and centrally conceived, is the peculiar human quality that responds to reality, and is thought, historically, to be at once our most powerful weapon and our greatest weakness. An excess of imagination is said to make us unrealistic with regard to the experience life requires of us: we imagine things to be other than they are, and we must suffer the consequences. At the same time, an insufficiency of imagination strips us of our power to cope, to reply to reality with imaginative strategies and tactics, and in our helpless literal-mindedness we must suffer the consequences. How best, then, to condition and employ the imagination is a question of such seminal importance that it might be said to be definitive in any culture, anywhere.

In our culture the question, long regarded as settled according to the Platonic prescription, now sets us at war with ourselves. The possibility that cultivation of the aesthetic sensibility might actually prove redemptive to the cultural imagination conflicts publicly with its opposite: the possibility that the inadequacies of our imagination are the direct result of too great a cultivation of the aesthetic sensibility. In the face of such a conflict we turn to our artists themselves, and most specifically our public artists, to resolve the conflict. What does the life of Mark Twain say to the question? What does the life of Hemingway say? The lives of both artists constitute arguments for the defense. Their relationships with nature, with society, and with institutions and communities other than the artistic are made, by them and by us, very large and important parts of their life stories. As adventurers in nature, pressing always close to the vanguard of some kind of frontier, they are offering a proof, just as they are when they simultaneously attack the institutions of society and yet amass fortunes and honors there unachieved by the most dedicated servants of "reality." They are not, as Raeburn would have it, abandoning the life of the artist; they are celebrating that life for an audience in search of instruction. It is *because* they are artists that they are able to command an audience while acting out, in these other spheres, these other roles. The connection between the prior artist identity and the subsequent non-artist role is vital and unbreakable. The same may be said of their roles as heads of families, and formidable friends and foes, as loner adventurers in search, at last, of themselves. We cannot determine whether or not they are successful until we understand what they are trying to do. They are trying to exemplify how the cultivation of the aesthetic sensibility adds force to the imagination as it engages the world of non-aesthetic experience. They are rebutting a prior cultural argument. And they are doing so because an eager audience in the culture—of which they are themselves no doubt a part—wants them to do so.

Twain and Hemingway are of course only examples, if very good ones, of the phenomenon. Each was a member of an artistic community that contained many other important figures who shared the artistic stage, and those communities themselves served, as the artistic community serves now, as examples to individuals in the larger communities outside. Further, both the individual public artists and their communities form into a chronology of tradition that is itself subject to analysis in the terms that have been suggested here. It is certainly proper to select out a single figure from a single community and concentrate upon that figure, but the danger is that the figure, in such isolated focus, can come to seem *sui generis*. Twain and Hemingway, considered as public figures, are anything but *sui generis*. They are representative spokesmen for a cultural point of view, and should be considered in that context.

Ruth apRoberts, Matthew Arnold, and God

David J. DeLaura

Ruth apRoberts. *Arnold and God.* Berkeley: University of California Press, 1983. xi, 299 pp.

One of the several virtues of Ruth apRoberts's insouciantly titled book is her nearly entire sympathy, her "inwardness," with Matthew Arnold's lifelong preoccupation with religion. Her ambitious and wide-ranging study of Arnold's "vocation" proves not only that "the religious perspective reveals a hundred hitherto unperceived concords in his work" (p. vii), but that the issues engaged by Arnold—notably the possibility of a "religious" view of life amidst the general collapse of metaphysics in the modern world—remain the permanent issues of modern theology. This is a thoughtful, well-informed, and daring book; and no student of Arnold, the Victorians, or literature-and-religion will fail to profit from reading it. She is far too self-deprecatory when she refers to her work as merely provisional, no more than "an essay, perfectly expendable" (p. ix).

Some will object to a certain diffuseness of statement and I will point to a lack of rigor in some of her central arguments. And she may give too free a rein to effusiveness: "simply grand"; Super's "beautiful edition of Arnold's prose"; Arnold's "splendidly British-empirical loose ends," his "grand inconsistencies," etc. But the book maintains a general high-spiritedness, unusual in such material; the lively turns of phrase are entirely appropriate when dealing with Arnold, himself the master of a dangerous "vivacity" of style. The book is also spiced with a wealth of modern allusions; though a surprising number are journalistic or ephemeral, many are worth following up, and some actually "correct" what (as I will argue) are her distorting emphases.

apRoberts's enviable command of German has enabled her to make the most complete case yet attempted for the "German" influences on Arnold's career (which others, including myself, have tended to treat rather briefly and unsystematically). She has translated numerous passages in Arnold's *Note-Books*, which the mostly Germanless students of Arnold have passed over. (On the other hand, her habit of giving scores of longish passages in both the original and English—instead of focusing on the key or telling phrase—is for the most part cumbersome and unilluminating.) One other bonus of her angle of approach is the fresh treatment of neglected areas of Arnold's thought: for example, his Isaiah project (Chapter II), his relations with Tolstoy (pp. 275-80), and his long-continued fascination with Judaism (pp. 163-75)—though these two latter sections may be too long for their explanatory role in the book.

But there is also a surprising number of matters of method and substance that deprive the book of its full impact. I found myself repeatedly stirred to a mood both admiring and "objecting." (She refers to my own work favorably throughout; and that only makes my task more difficult.) I have detected only a few outright errors: for example, Carlyle did not "bring out" his translation of *Wilhelm Meister's Travels* in 1839 (p. 59n.), but rather in 1827; and apRoberts repeats R. H. Super's error of finding a source for "sciolist" (in "the Grande Chartreuse") in the running summaries for *Sartor Resartus*, which so far as I can determine were not added until about 1857. But there is a disconcerting incidence of loose and sometimes I fear uncandid use of evidence. Too often we hear, without proof or analysis, generalized claims like this one: "Arnold's studies in anthropomorphism *must owe something* to Berkeley's understanding of God as wisdom, order, law, virtue" (p. 33; my emphasis). Similarly, she calls Connop Thirlwall's remarkable study "On the Irony of Sophocles" (1833), "an essay Arnold would have known" (p. 82). But the essay appeared in a short-lived journal and was not collected again until 1877, and apRoberts does not pause to offer either verbal or argumentative links. Her sense of the transmission of ideas is even wobblier when she mentions Thirlwall's translation of Schleiermacher's *Essay on St. Luke* (1825), and

Arnold and God

then summarizes the main points of Schleiermacher's religious thought: a basis in experience, religion as self-consciousness, and "God" as a relationship of dependence—all these, she says, "concepts clearly contributory to those of Matthew Arnold" (p. 69). But the St. Luke essay does not mention these ideas *at all*, and she makes no effort to show any real influence on Arnold, who mentions Schleiermacher I believe only twice, both times in 1867, and only in passing.

Again, she cites a passage in Herder, that Arnold read and marked in the late 1860s, on the difficulty of a man attaining "the pure image of man that lies in him," and she calls this idea "a model of the quest in 'The Scholar-Gipsy' and 'Thyrsis' " (pp. 43-44). But *model* surely implies precedence and both poems were written well before Arnold read the passage, and the implied correspondences, which are not even argued, remain entirely nebulous. In her fresh and interesting pages on Arnold's relations with modern Judaism, she says, "Arnold writes. . . that 'the conception of Christianity and its Founder, is probably destined to become the conception which Christians themselves will entertain' " (p. 167). A footnote indicates that this is Arnold's paraphrase of a statement by Charles Réville, but "Arnold writes" and the context ("an effect on his religious thought") suggest concurrence. In fact a check of Arnold's original text shows that Arnold does *not* in fact endorse the opinion.[1]

apRoberts's difficulties in handling the dating of inconvenient evidence are particularly clear in her use of Arnold's *Note-Books* (1952). She cites Arnold's reference to Lessing in *Culture and Anarchy* as one of the great men of culture, and then she gives Arnold's transcriptions from Lessing's *Erziehung*. But though she twice mentions Richard Tobias's important article on the dating, she is totally silent about his careful judgment that these pages in General Note-Book No. 2 mirror "Arnold's thought between 1876 and 1888," long after the time of "Sweetness and Light."[2] Similarly, when she judges that Arnold's citation from Quinet cannot be "earlier than 1863" (the date of the original: pp. 159-60), she again implies an influence in the crucial 60s and ignores Tobias's argument. (Confusing the reader even further, she is franker about dating such a late item in a note on page 230.)

But this is a book about sources and evidence in a much broader sense. apRoberts treats the major themes of Arnold's career, from the earliest poetry to the final essays on literature and religion: "poetic vocation, the function of myth and of metaphor, education or the transmission of metaphor, the nature of religion and of language itself" (p. viii). She covers the widest range of sources ever assembled—especially "the Germans," Spinoza, the English Broad Church tradition—and in doing so extends her net much further than earlier source studies by Basil Willey, William Robbins, R. H. Super, and others, including myself. Indeed, the book becomes one well-read student's version of modern intellectual history as a whole, with a strong German emphasis. Arnold's interest in myth, metaphor, symbol puts him, for apRoberts, centrally in "the Historicist line [that] developed the doctrine of *Bildung*, the dialectical method of Hegel, the provisionalism of Nietzsche, and . . . the philosophy of fictions" (p. viii). Never has Arnold, the British empiricist, been viewed as so "German"!

A not untypical summary: "Out of Herder's work, and Humboldt's and Goethe's, emerges the great concept of *Bildung*, that process of moving toward the fulfillment of the capacities of *Humanität*, both in individual civilizations and in individual human beings, the process which Arnold denominates 'Culture' and makes his subject." And even "Darwinism" (in a broad sense of the term) "can I think be best viewed as one aspect of the larger concept, Historicism, Herder's philosophy of history with its *Entwicklung*, or 'development,' its relativism and its humanism. Darwin's *Descent of Man* is really understood [by whom? one asks] as an *ascent*, into ever higher forms" (p. 54). *Out of emerges and ascends . . .* : these are like biblical "begats," and every evolutionary, progressive, and processive thinker of the modern world seems instantly enrolled in a sort of universal marching chorus—and there is no membership test in this happy modern parade moving forward. "Darwinism" (even in the very broad sense she uses here, borrowed from Michael Timko) is particularly puzzling in this jumble of the most incongruous elements, extreme naturalisms and the most highly abstract spiritualisms—though I would grant that, somewhere off the horizon, monisms of this sort do "meet."

Arnold and God

apRoberts's cheerfully uncritical syncretism does not allow her to pause to consider that Darwinism, in *any* historically valid sense of the term, simply cannot be accommodated within even the loose, sub-philosophical framework of Arnold's "humanism," a point well explained by A. Dwight Culler.[3]

Arnold is thus in constant danger of being viewed as a great intellectual sponge, absorbing the most heterogenous "influences" in an undiscriminating way. Things *in the air* suddenly become specific "influences" and "lines"; with more patience this running stream of hints, obiter dicta, plausible hunches, and striking insights could have been built into a solid and more permanent structure. A good test case for the weighing of evidence is that of Vico, who in a general way, she acknowledges, lies somewhere behind her central figure, Herder. "It is quite likely," she asserts, "that Arnold by his early privileged exposure to Vico [that is, in his father's historical writings] acquired this expressionist perspective, which by resting weight on symbol, myth, and fable rests on metaphor (sub-suming all three) as the distinctively human response to the world" (p. 221). But this "acquisition" is simply never established; on p. 63n., she pooh-poohs Vico as a direct source for Thomas and Matthew Arnold, in favor of Herder, both directly and indirectly; and Arnold refers to Vico on only two occasions and in passing (1:145; 10:86,88), and he did not put Vico on his crucial reading lists of the late 1840s. apRoberts speaks elsewhere of "that Viconian-Herderian historicism that he [Thomas Arnold] and Carlyle both arrived at by their somewhat different routes" (p. 56). But though she notes that the "radical religious implications" of Carlyle's early work "would have escaped Thomas Arnold," it would have been more to the point to note candidly that the historians associated with Thomas Arnold, however "liberal," were orthodox Christians, and far more cautious about the deterministic forces of history than were Vico, Herder, or even Carlyle.[4] Attention to the careful groundwork laid by Fisch and Bergin,[5] giving dates and English sources (notably Coleridge), would have made possible a reasoned assessment of the lines of transmission.

The Coleridge-Matthew Arnold connection, which still has not found its proper historian and interpreter, is handled in a similarly breezy way. apRoberts cites Arnold's late (1885) endorsement of the "great Coleridgean position" that Christianity is based on "necessary and eternal facts of nature or truths of reason," and she adds: "The Coleridge influence was early, and by way of Thomas Arnold, and it simply became integrated with his line of thought" (pp. 57-58). But was it? Though Coleridge was no doubt a "presence," Arnold was suspicious of and distant from Coleridge at all periods—and on grounds similar to Carlyle's, and there is very little evidence of influence.[6] Her treatment of the Carlyle influence is even more curious. She makes very broad claims: the "radical religious implications of *Sartor Resartus* . . . are the ground of Arnold's religious thought" (p. 56); the early Arnold "saw how the [new German] Historicism needed a retailored, nonsupernatural Christianity, and for him Carlyle's religious thought became a phase on his own way toward restabilization" (p. 67)—but she makes no real attempt to assess the quality and extent of this "ground." (It is a little awkward to note that she makes no reference to my own attempt to detail Arnold's continuing religious debts to Carlyle—no mere "phase.")[7]

This book seems to me especially weak in dealing with Goethe as a source of the *Bildung* notion, one of the central issues in Arnold studies. Though apRoberts refers to Goethe admiringly again and again, she regularly glosses over Goethe's shortcomings in social, moral, and "educational" vision, by her own and Arnold's standards. The passage she cites from Goethe (p. 97), on "perpetual *Bildung*," as a parallel to Arnold's notion of culture, is strikingly deficient in its characteristic *lack* of such a social focus. Indeed, this whole book would have been strengthened if apRoberts had directly confronted the cogent analysis by W. H. Bruford, in two books she uses for other purposes, of the ways in which the Germans of the Weimar period were divorced from social realities.[8] This evasion of difficulties is particularly evident in apRoberts's presentation of excerpts from Arnold's extensive, previously unpublished notebook citations from an 1863-64 series of articles on Wilhelm von Humboldt (pp. 93-96). They came at a vital moment for Arnold, since Humboldt's benign and moralized ideal comes closer than virtually any other of these "development" models—

Arnold and God

closer, in my view, than Herder's—to the "public" ideal Arnold endorsed from the late 1860s on. But her summary statement—"Humboldt embodies the Arnoldian paradigm: retirement, withdrawal into oneself or the region of ideas, and return to man, to society with something of value"—finds no echo I can detect in these citations, none of which stresses the strongly public and even pragmatic character of Arnold's emerging idea. Indeed, the very French critic Arnold is citing (Challemel-Lacour) explicitly notes that the effect on "general civilization" was a secondary consideration for Humboldt.

But the issues of attribution and of the legitimate use of evidence in the history of ideas come to a head in apRoberts's great central claim regarding Herder as the chief source of "the Historicist line of thought": for example, "whole tracts of Herder's thought are incorporated into the base of [Carlyle's] fabric and in spite of Arnold's frequent ostensible rejection of Carlyle, these same tracts undergo a further incorporation by Arnold" (p. 39). The new and important fact brought forward is that Arnold, in 1867-69, read and marked the first ten books of Herder's *Ideen zur Philosophie der Geschichte des Menschheit*—that is, volume I up to page 282 (on "the cosmic, comparatist, and anthropological philosophy of history": 42), rather than the ensuing history of mankind. More specifically, she claims that Arnold finds in Herder "the font and text of the *Humanität-Entwicklung-Bildung* line of thought. He grasps the vision of the coextensiveness of language, literature, and religion under the rubric of *Bildung*-Culture, and this becomes the controlling idea of *Culture and Anarchy*" (pp. 142-43). Two points are beyond contest in all this. First, there did arise in the late eighteenth century a "large German comparativistic, anthropological vision" (p. 39), in some ways anti-Enlightenment in tone, with momentous and long-continuing effects on European culture—and in this "line" Herder is perhaps the chief *Ur*-source. Moreover, Arnold's reading of the *Ideen* came simultaneously with the writing of *Culture and Anarchy*, where we observe Arnold's intensest struggle with the notion of "culture." A small host of other problems arise, however, regarding Herder's role in Carlyle's and, especially,

Arnold's thought, that I think apRoberts does not manage convincingly.

Above all, Arnold's own development-doctrine had been evolving for a decade, at least from the time of the inaugural lecture at Oxford in 1857, and it was clearly strengthened by Arnold's reading in Humboldt in the mid-60s, among others. There is no reference to Herder in Arnold's writings before the farewell lecture at Oxford in June 1867, and the passages Arnold marked in the *Ideen* seem to be much more nebulously related to the specifics of *Culture and Anarchy* than the views of Humboldt and others. The conclusion one feels forced to draw is that Arnold's reading of Herder in 1867-1869 was an important confirmation of an already well-established drift in Arnold's thought toward a more evolutionary, optimistic, and comparatist point of view, but that Herder cannot be viewed as a truly *primary* source.

If it is argued, as apRoberts tends to do, that, well, Herder was the "father" of such evolutionary thinking anyway—and there is some degree of truth in the claim—a question remains as to what extent Arnold *specifically* perceived Herder as the "font" of such a widely diffused point of view. She acknowledges this diffusion problem at one point, but only backhandedly, in a note: "No one in Arnold studies seems to have recognized that what appears to be Vico is often in fact Herder, in Thomas Arnold's case by way of Niebuhr and Carlyle, as well as directly from Herder's *Ideen*" (p. 63 n.) Six major names here, in a veritable cat's-cradle of criss-crossing "influences" and "flowings."[9] But since no one, including apRoberts, has showed Herder to be a central influence in *Thomas* Arnold's work either, the problem surfaces again, in two stages: if Thomas and Matthew Arnold are both virtually unconscious of Herder's influence, how legitimately can the "historicist" point of view in their work be referred to regularly, and tendentiously, as "Herderian"—all the more, after a century of being "in the air"?

And that leaves Carlyle as a possible source or conduit of Herderian ideas; apRoberts claims that "in all probability [Matthew Arnold] knew much of Herder early, through Carlyle" (pp 37-38). But Carlyle's *doubts* about *Humanität* and Herder's

Arnold and God

ideas on the Bible and religion, as expressed in a key passage of 1826 in his notebooks, led Harrold virtually to deny any central influence;[10] the first nine volumes of the *Letters* (up to 1837) contain scarcely a handful of references to Herder, and though friendly, they are totally lacking in substance; and the few references in Carlyle's published writings lack any reference to Herder's characteristic intellectual positions. Hill Shine made the broadest claims for Herder's influence on Carlyle, and I do not doubt that Herder contributed to Carlyle's rapidly evolving views in the late 1820s; but the parallels Shine draws, mostly about history, are disconcertingly vague.[11] More to the point, whatever (controverted) role Herder played in Carlyle's career, little about positive influence and little of any substance could be detected by any later reader of Carlyle's printed works. This fact, and Arnold's nearly entire silence about Herder even after reading part of the *Ideen* in the late 60s, leads one ineluctably to conclude, again, that Herder's influence on Arnold was largely "collateral," supporting a drift in his thought that can claim a number of other converging stimuli and sources.[12]

Herder, in short, threatens to become apRoberts's King Charles's head. The aggrandizing term "Herderian" runs like wildfire throughout the book, and is applied to every "developmental" theory of the century. To take one example, she cites a passage from Joubert in Arnold's 1863 essay, on the uniqueness of man's moral and intellectual development, and comments: "How stunningly this accords with Herderian ideas of *Humanität* . . . !" (p. 119). Well, the reader can only respond, the citation comes years before we know Arnold read Herder, and this is obviously a set of widely current ideas. And yet, though this book verges at times on becoming a gigantic example of special pleading, it is not uncommon of course for even quite "general" studies to have a bias, or even a slightly off-center originating insight or germ. One is tempted to suggest, only half facetiously, that the reader should systematically deduct or correct for the torque in apRoberts's exuberant missionary work on Herder's behalf; for the essential question, even after the deductions, is, how authentic and convincing is the intellectual portrait of Arnold that remains?

In her largely chronological series of summaries with commentary, apRoberts has come closer than anyone else so far to defining Arnold's "vocation" as a "religious mission" that binds all aspects of his career (p. 20). And she sees the doubleness in the young Arnold, a central seriousness and concern for religion, along with a worldly and "dandy" manner. On the other hand, she seems to me to lack an adequate sense of changes, pressures, and vital decisions in Arnold's career, especially before the mid-1860s. The figure that emerges is less daring and much less "divided" than the Arnold of previous studies. This blander Arnold, strangely "alike" at all periods, is involved in a lifelong "great humanistic cause": building "the rationale for the value of the classics, the tradition, the Celtic element in literature, the 'Oriental' poetry of the Hebrews" (p. 13). What is lost here, put simply, is the sophisticated tension and the lively dialectical interplay of elements in Arnold's treatment of history and human nature *in all periods*: Hebraism *and* Hellenism, Celtic *and* Germanic, the *two* kinds of poetry in "Maurice de Guérin," etc., etc. In her treatment of "Maurice de Guérin" (pp. 111-13), in fact, apRoberts simply ignores Arnold's clearly expressed doubts and hesitations about the Keats-Guérin ideal of the "hovering" poet, a precarious balance that he corrected even further in the Celtic lectures.[13]

As a result of this "homogenized" reading of his career, apRoberts tends to read Arnold's poems as if they came out of a single, invariable matrix or set of attitudes. Though she has something interesting though overstated to say about "Empedocles on Etna" (pp. 39-40 n.), her approach to the poem (pp. 18-19) makes Arnold into an untroubled "humanistic" figure, instead of a romantic rebel, reacting *against* the severely moralistic, Apollonian vision of Callicles.[14] Similarly, she makes the strongest claims yet advanced for Glanvill—a sort of Broad Churchman before his time, with a "strong sense of the limitations of reason"—as a substantive influence on Arnold's two Oxford elegies, as if the two poems were saying pretty much identical things (pp. 11-12). For her, "The gipsies' lore . . . symbolizes that great humanistic cause" (p. 13) Arnold was increasingly to stand for—in a word, "Culture." But this straight-line reading requires her to conflate the Scholar-Gipsy's

Arnold and God

totally intuitive "spark from heaven," in one of Arnold's most "regressive" poems (and, as a large critical debate has showed, an *anti*-Oxford poem), with the far more public and rational character of the culture-ideal of the late 60s.

Confusion is confounded when this theory of "the religion-poetry continuum" is applied to the paean to Oxford ("queen of romance," etc.) in the Preface to the *Essays in Criticism* (1865), and Arnold's complicated ironies and hesitations regarding Oxford (and Newman) are entirely left out of sight. This tendency to collapse all phases of Arnold's career is also evident in her reading of the second Obermann poem (composed 1865-1867), which she calls "of all of Arnold's poems the most explicit on his religious views and purpose" (p. 155). This seems true, but only to the extent that the poem is a sort of prospectus, laying out the broad basis of *any* religious resettlement. But when she goes further, and says the poem urges man to "turn to the imitation of Christ," one can only protest: the poem totally lacks the more fully Christian note of *Literature and Dogma*; and though it acknowledges the power of Jesus in the *early* Christian centuries and commits Arnold to seek *"One common wave of thought and joy"* anew, it does *not* urge the imitation of Christ. The simple fact is that, in the mid-60s, Arnold was not yet prepared to answer those questions and admitted needs in explicitly Christian and biblical terms.

apRoberts attempts to give definition to "the great shaping idea of Historicism—development, that is; the ideal of *Bildung* with its inwardness and never-ending process toward perfection," especially to the extent that, in Arnold's case, "all this is rationally reconciled with Christianity—rationally, nonsupernaturally, experientially" (p. 214). The spread of a "developmental" view of history and of ideas is unquestionably central to almost all varieties of thought in the past two centuries, and notions of development pervade the entire spectrum of thought from the left-wing Vico, Herder, and Hegel to the orthodox John Henry Newman. But in a not untypical, show-stopping formula like the following—"It seems to me . . . that Organic Filaments binding all together is a vision of Herder's holism, that *Sartor* is the very text and flower [sic] of Herder's *Entwicklungsphilosophie*, and that the *Entwicklung* is Carlyle's

'Eternal Growth' and Arnold's 'Becoming' (as well as Browning's 'Development')" (p. 38)—all the individual contours and shadings of at least four important careers are simply lost, especially when "Darwinian evolution" (p. vii) is more than once dropped into the mix.

Even after carefully making one's way through this book, the actual shape that this view of "perpetual becoming, the ever shifting relativism of history" (p. 45), takes in Arnold's work, remains frustratingly problematic. apRoberts's implicit model seems to be that all of historicist thinking flows into Arnold, who refocuses it and enriches it, and it then flows out again in many new channels. The effect is to claim a much more central position for Arnold in modern intellectual history than has ever been claimed before. Apart from Vico and Carlyle, however, mentioned above, and some reference to figures like Spinoza and Renan, her emphasis, legitimately, is on the Germans. But her "Germans" tend to move along in one direction, like a cheerful holiday party, as on page 142, where the "pagan" Goethe, the moral Schiller, the Promethean Beethoven—and Matthew Arnold!—join hands in a sort of quadrille; whereas other readers will be inclined to see them instead as a jostling and rather motley crowd. Her other most original claim is that Arnold's "realm where poetry and religion are undifferentiated" has a "native" basis in Coleridge and an expanded version of the Broad Church traditions (p. 7).

But Matthew Arnold, though in a real sense "papa's continuator," is *not* a British Broad Churchman like Coleridge and his liberal Anglican followers, including Thomas Arnold— all of whom were Trinitarian Christian theists, however suspect their theology was to the severely orthodox. apRoberts can, infrequently, make such distinctions, as when she remarks that Thomas Arnold distrusted current German biblical scholarship "as tending to disbelief" (p. 63), or that "Schleiermacher, though considered 'liberal,' was still among the faithful, but D. F. Strauss ultimately left the fold" (p. 51). But she even more regularly elides the cautious liberal Anglicans with "the new German philosophy of religion" (pp. 158-59), including figures like Feuerbach who lie outside the confines of even a scrupulous agnosticism. Even by the end of the book, in fact, it remains

Arnold and God

unclear whether such distinctions—important enough to those involved—are crucial in any way to *her* inclusive historical scheme. And when she expands her very-broad-church tradition to include figures like Bunsen and Max Müller, she becomes deaf to the rather cool and even patronizing praise Arnold extends to such "nebulous" and "splay-footed" Teutonic sages. She conveniently overlooks Arnold's wounding treatment of the "abyss of platitude" in "the German nature," a theme insistently stressed in the Celtic lectures, written in the mid-60s. Matthew Arnold had much less of his father's earnest reverence for German thought and thinkers than this study would imply. To put the matter schematically, Arnold carefully positioned himself, after the mid-60s: on the one side, he moves toward Christianity and thus "beyond" the Weimar Germans, as well as Spinoza and the classical Stoics, asserting now the need for a religion of warmth, joy, and cheerful self-sacrifice; on the other side, he carefully distances himself from his apparent allies, the "broad" Christians, judging them provincial, since they had failed to make his own decisive break from the world of ecclesiasticism and metaphysical theology.

It *is* illuminating to locate Arnold directly in this German historicist line of thought, the line of natural supernaturalism—or, as the less accepting put it, supernatural naturalism. But crucial questions immediately arise that remain unasked in this study. Most obviously, apRoberts's various summaries of Herder's thought are attractive (e.g., p. 141), and the passages in Herder that Arnold marked are suggestive. These include the notions that *Humanität* is the attainment of "the pure image of man," a goal high, extensive, and infinite; that "it is in culture [*Bildung*] that the solidarity of mankind is to be sought"; and, above all, that in the "rubble" of history, individuals pass away, but through the "chain of development" (*Die Kette der Bildung*), "the human spirit lives, immortal and prevailing" (pp. 43-45). But, rather disconcertingly, apRoberts never (so far as I can see) holds up these high-flown statements for careful comparison with specific passages in *Culture and Anarchy*. Perhaps the most "Herderian" notions there would be that the individual seeking perfection must do "all he can to enlarge and increase the volume of the human stream sweeping thitherward," and that the idea of total human perfection, "adding to itself the religious idea of a devout energy," is destined to "transform and govern" religion itself—the first, an attempt to "moralize" culture, the latter a notion that troubled Arnold's first critics, of all parties (5: 94, 100).

She seems to me on even shakier ground when she treats Arnold's notion of "development" and "transformation" in the specifically religious writings as having a "solid Herderian base" (pp. 125, 186), and offers no corroborating texts. Herder is indeed one of the "great men of *culture*," but the single reference to Herder I find in all of the religious writings, though favorable, does not concern development or even religion, but the right method of "literary" interpretation (5: 113; 7: 333). It seems evident that Herder was simply not Christian or even "religious" enough (not to say, "English" enough) for Arnold's purposes during this phase of his career. But, as I have suggested, the ubiquitous if shadowy Herder is not, finally, the problem: it is apRoberts's continual plucking of the single note of "Historicism and developmentalism" (p. 221), her two key terms, and "Arnold's relativism, the sea of more-or-less [sic] and of constant change, that German historicism cast him into" (p. 232). I do not doubt that this is indeed the sea on which Arnold sails (if sometimes against the tides), the most fruitful locus of "modern" thought, as Arnold avoids the Scylla of a supernaturalist literalism on the one side, and the Charybdis of a "blank" or aggressive rationalism on the other. But this is also a far more fluid, unstable, and (to use Coleridge's expressive term) "streamy" Arnold than anyone has before detected—or, I think, than the totality of the evidence warrants. *Do* we recognize the authentic Arnold when apRoberts asserts: "With Arnold, everything is in process; our myths are provisional and of their time, not absolute or final" (p. 218)?

What apRoberts does not do, with any system, is even to follow the thread of "change" and "evolution" in Arnold's own career; her point is largely assumed and reasserted as she bears down on a comparative handful of "evolutionary" passages. Even more predictably, this unrelenting emphasis virtually ignores Arnold's real resistance to change and fear of the flux of history, as well as central counterbalancing elements of his thought (acknowledged if not approved by virtually all other students of Arnold): his search for what is lasting, enduring, even absolute—and in that one-sided emphasis she misses, I judge, much of the feeling-tone of Arnold's work. (She has been emboldened in this single-minded pursuit by a brilliant but unbalanced article by Epifanio San Juan, which argues, on the model of I. A. Richards, for a totally subjectivist and psychologistic Arnold.)[15] By arbitrarily ignoring the "transcendentalizing" side of Arnold's work and personality, apRoberts not only misses the essential tensions of Arnold's career, but evades the philosophical issues of "relativity" itself, which is relational and demands a living sense of the enduring, both in personality and in culture. Hers is a "modern" world of Heraclitean flux, with no Parmenidean counter-moment. William Madden, in his important book, seized this relativistic line and made Arnold seem almost as "aesthetic" as Pater;[16] apRoberts presents a more religious and moral version of a similarly simplified figure. There are as a result few if any *costs* in apRoberts's benign developmental modern scheme; she seems to me to miss the pathos (well known to Arnold in all periods), not to speak of the comedy and tragedy, of the "modern" experience, conceived by Arnold and most other serious modern thinkers as a series of painful, if necessary, losses and substitutions.

A careful tracing of the two intertwined themes would reveal the earlier, "alienated" Arnold as more resistant to the zeitgeist, understood as meaningless change standing in opposition to eternal values, and the more optimistic Arnold of the 60s, willing to find this "cosmic spiritual power" at work in historic time.[17] But even in this later period, Arnold gave "change" a fairly arm's-length welcome. apRoberts is so fixed on an Arnold devoted to "change, . . . the relative, . . . [and] the non-absolute" (pp. 11-12), that she fails to note that even Arnold's notion of a "flexible" critical spirit seeks "the infinite" (pp. 128-28), and that even the Hellenistic component of the culture-ideal has a surprising affinity for the permanent and unchanging. Her parti pris also leads her to overlook the plain implication of the evidence she herself adduces. She reads the poem "Progress" (1852?) as representing "the developmental view of religions"

(p. 43 n) instead of (as Kenneth Allott clearly sees) Arnold's irony and "impatience . . . with liberal ideas in religion."[18] Similarly, she cites Arnold approvingly citing Senancour on the "passion for order and harmony," but seems unaware that exactly such a passion on Arnold's part strongly qualifies her own insistence on "change, development, progress" (p. 153).

As for culture itself, it does include in the first place an ideal of the "expansion" of the human powers that implies ethical and intellectual development, a matter deserving more direct attention than it receives in this book. As for the *content* of culture, however—conceived by Arnold as a program and (by the early 1880s) a sort of first version of the modern liberal arts curriculum—it remains resolutely backward-looking, a museum of texts and an amalgam of carefully selected traditional values, that were to be salvaged and somehow "applied" to the chaotic present and the fearsome future: the world of current "change," and certainly contemporary literature, are rarely if ever seen as *sources* of value. The religious writings, which more fully develop the earlier notion of the ethics of Hebraism (read: historic Christianity) as "an eternal possession" (5: 255), are even less "developmental," as what she herself considers Arnold's "best definition of God"—"What subsists," or "*I am*," or the "Eternal" (p. 155)—should have clearly signaled. As with culture, that is, the feeling states, the spiritual truths, and the moral contents of Arnold's "reconstituted" Christianity are entirely traditional, and not at all subject to "change." What is scientific or "progressive" in the religious writings is Arnold's uncommonly daring willingness to apply modern critical scholarship to the texts, in order to disengage precisely the *enduring* spiritual kernel from the husks of metaphysical and historical error (see the opening of "The Study of Poetry"). apRoberts's thesis prevents her from seeing that Arnold is regularly contemptuous of "progressive" thought in precisely the central areas evoked by the terms culture and religion.

apRoberts, as will be evident by now, makes the least qualified assertion ever offered for the equivalence or identity of religion and culture in Arnold's thought. She rejects T. S. Eliot's notion that Arnold "substituted" culture for religion, which she calls "a simple idea of exchange" (p. 271), in favor of the view that

"Arnold's idea of Culture, . . . embracing *Bildung*, subsumes all humane activities: science, politics, art, literature, and religion" (p. 281). This may indeed be the tendency of the key "Greek" (and "Herderian") passages in *Culture and Anarchy*, noted above; I can only briefly summarize my own reading of the evidence, which I have developed elsewhere. Briefly: "culture by no means simply swamps or engorges religion—even Arnold's residual and spiritualized religion of morality touched by emotion"; and partly in response to his first critics, *after* 1869 "culture becomes a highly refined mode of knowing and discrimination, . . . and conduct and religion emerge and remain [as] a distinct and generally *superior* area of experience."[19] This retreat from the high but momentary holism of *Culture and Anarchy* came from a deepening perception of the contemporary religious crisis, and is reflected in the interplay of two kinds of touchstones, secular and religious, in Arnold's writings. apRoberts continually refers to the "continuum" of poetry and religion—"the element," "poetry-religion"—as if it were totally unproblematic, whereas there is in fact a large, confused, and contentious body of early- and mid-Victorian discussion of poetry-and-religion that throws essential light on these issues.[20]

Likewise, the notion of a Goethean *Bildung* or self-development, far from being a positive and uncontroversial ideal as presented by apRoberts, divided and disturbed the English intellectual and literary community for forty years before it was taken up and in effect domesticated by Matthew Arnold in the 1860s—"Herderized," if one likes.[21] I have little appetite for thus citing my own work: my point is that, by failing to face candidly the context and the problematics of her material (recognized in the very first "culture" reviews Arnold received in 1867), or to fit her strong assertions into either the complexity of the primary evidence or the state of current opinion, apRoberts does not achieve for her thesis anything like the "public" character it might well have assumed nor in the process securely advance our understanding of these issues of continuing significance. Most importantly, perhaps, apRoberts's rush to collapse categories prevents her from measuring how far Arnold went "beyond culture," almost in Lionel Trilling's sense of that phrase—and thus from capturing the depth and authenticity (and distinctness) of his religious ideal. Again, to speak too categorically, apRoberts's favorite Germans are the major sources of Arnold's culture, but not (as she incautiously claims: e.g., pp. 90-91, 206-207) of his religiousness. A closer look, I suggest, would reveal that the "inwardness" of Arnold's religious ideal lies at a distinct remove from the naively imperious personal assertion and intellectualism of so much in her German tradition, even the benign but post-Christian Herder.

With more space, I could do more justice to apRoberts's achievement, and—no doubt—reluctantly "quarrel" with her even further. Chapter 2 is an excellent introduction to the Higher Criticism; and Chapter 10, "Metaphor," is particularly informative in developing her view of "the symbolic method" common to poetry and religion, in a series of overlapping terms: metaphor, symbol, simile, synechdoche, and metonomy. This is the "grand consistency" in all of Arnold's writings, which, drawing on earlier work of her own, she ties to the notion of the *provisional* and "our modern critical concept of *fictions*" (pp. viii, 217). But even in claiming, a bit dizzyingly, that "The main line of scholarly biblical criticism today appears to be Arnoldian," all deriving ultimately of course from "Herder and the whole expressionist school" (p. 235), apRoberts so far detaches Arnold from any definite "meaning" that she makes him sound like an advanced deconstructionist. Most revealingly, even citations from her key modern witness, Rudolf Bultmann— that myth expresses "man's conviction that the origin and purpose of the world . . . are to be sought not within it but beyond it" and that man "is not lord of his own being" (p. 234)—fit very questionably with her own extremely "immanentist" reading of Arnold's not-ourselves.

No informed reader today would deny that attributing "personality" to the divinity is fraught with difficulties; the category-problems that beset the study of Arnold's religion are common in the history of modernist theology. Therefore it is not surprising that the least substantial part of this book is apRoberts's scattered attempts to pin down her announced topic, Arnold and God. She is not untrue to Arnold's spirit in stressing in effect his "negatives," a tradition of refusal to "denominate" that Arnold derived from Goethe and Carlyle ("Who dares name

Arnold and God

Him?"): in seeking to define "the common nonsectarian ground of religion," Arnold refuses to view God as "a literal personage," and he witheld belief from "any miracles, resurrection, afterlife—or any form of the supernatural" (pp. 106-107). The Kingdom of God is simply a metaphor for the moral "movement toward perfection"; and the conception of the not-ourselves-that-makes-for-righteousness she boldly turns back inward, considering it a myth expressive of a "psychological need," "an invention, a noble fiction, a personification—God" (p. 233). "God," if not more palpable, becomes a bit more self-subsistent when defined as a metaphor for "reason, . . . something like Milton's 'Right Reason' or German 'Vernunft' " (p. 143).

Still, as noted above, the power, if not "personal," is not quite so "figurative" as construed by apRoberts, who brushes aside without examining the persistent "transcendental" torque in Arnold's thought detected (if deplored) by Robbins (pp. 162-63 n., 228; and see p. 91 on the "absolute and eternal"). Certainly the power making for righteousness is *functionally* more powerful than her radically "provisional" and "as if" theory of fictions allows; indeed (as T. S. Eliot, for all *his* opposite disapproval, saw) a doctrine of *grace* runs all through Arnold's religious writings. She would have gained a solider historical setting if she had examined R. H. Hutton's assertion that Arnold's "prejudices" about divinity were fixed in the 1840s, the era of natural supernaturalism, by Spinoza as well as by Goethe, Carlyle, and Emerson, who mediated German thought in specific configurations.[22] Arnold eventually developed a rich theology which continually strained against the metaphysical boundaries erected by his own intellectual honesty. The tensions can become quite extreme: Arnold's submission to the order or "tendency" of righteousness could kindle to the point of happiness and even joy, though the word "love" is conspicuous by its absence. The anomalies deserve frank probing. For example, experience has quite generally been viewed as a testing-ground for morality but can only questionably serve as its *source*. Even more pointedly, how can we, the "subjects" of the order to which we submit in a devout spirit, be more conscious of righteousness than the order / power / source / tendency itself? The God-problems flood back, irresistibly.

And so it is not wrong, in these circumstances, for apRoberts to concentrate on the epistemological *limitations* Arnold felt obliged to observe in the search for God-definitions. But the epithet "rationalist," which she repeatedly applies to Arnold, gives a misleading cast to her argument, even on her own terms. She seems at times to mean by the term what Arnold (and she) approve as Goethe's "profound, imperturable naturalism" (p. 110). The term *is* applicable to the extent that Arnold sought an independent "Goethean" point of view, apart from dogma and metaphysics, and insisted that the religious impulse must, like everything else, be brought before the bar of rational inquiry. But the term causes difficulties when insistently applied to "Arnold's thoroughly rationalist turn of mind" (p. 106). For Arnold carefully distances himself from the tone and many of the arguments associated with European rationalism from the eighteenth century on. Despite his radical rejection of the entire apparatus of dogma, miracle, and philosophical theology, Arnold almost never indulges in the hostility toward historic Christianity of the outspoken London freethinkers of his day— Huxley, Harrison, Stephen, or Morley.

More substantively, though reason was a norm of inquiry and it set certain limits to his thought, it is harder to see (as the term rationalism certainly implies) that Arnold gave to abstract reason the highest priority among the central human faculties and humanizing activities. As the *Encyclopedia of Philosophy* (which apRoberts uses for other purposes) makes clear, *rationalism* is usually contrasted with *empiricism*— and it is with this latter tradition that she more often and more convincingly aligns Arnold.[23] She speaks of Arnold's "nonsupernaturalism, or *empiricism*" and of "the Arnoldian scale of values: the limits of intellection, and the supremacy of 'behavior'—of 'Imitation [of Christ]' " (pp. 114, 129). But the categories collide jarringly when she speaks of Arnold's "Spinozist experiential gauge of ethics" and "that Spinozist-Arnoldian-William Jamesian line that takes experience as paramount" (pp. 5, 51)—for Spinoza (see *Encyclopedia of Philosophy*) is one of the most abstractly rationalistic and *in*experiential of thinkers. Pragmatism, yes, and an important variety of "agnosticism" (a term which, puzzlingly, she avoids), one unusually open to the experience of the joyous surrender to the moral order—whatever *its* status! Also helpful might be terms like "skepticism," or an extreme nominalism with regard to all philosophical categories.

Inevitably, even in this substantial volume, some important issues receive sketchy treatment. There is, for example, a strong "mystical" side to Arnold's religiousness, early and again late in his career, that is neglected (except for a brief note on page 273) in apRoberts's resolutely non-supernaturalist reading of Arnold's thought. (Her dismissal of John Henry Newman as a "mystic" [p. 199] is both revealingly prejudiced and uninformed, since Newman's phenomenology of the act of assent is at least as "experientially" that of a British empiricist as Arnold's own approach.) And, despite her constant emphasis on change and Historicism, she is silent on the notable "visionary" element in Arnold's view of history, detected by John Holloway and others; Arnold has a developed reading of historical periodicity as well as a final apocalyptic note that throw light on the central issues of this book.

Even more interesting would be a consideration of the influence of Arnold's *kind* of religious thinking over the past century. Although apRoberts makes sweeping claims for Arnold's centrality and refers to a scattering of important and less important twentieth-century figures, she simply overlooks Arnold's vital and provable role in the Modernist movement, both the Protestant and especially the Roman Catholic varieties.[24] But the modern that apRoberts's view of Arnold kept reminding me of most regularly is the once-influential Paul Tillich and the philosophy of "ultimate concern": a detailed comparison would be revealing. apRoberts boldly asserts: "Matthew Arnold remains satisfactory to us now" (p. 217); the finally most interesting question is how well such thinking has in fact survived, and whether men and women do still find satisfactory an Arnoldian "provisional" and "as if" position (as apRoberts defines it). I do not deny that, at least until recently, many "humanistic" and literary people could be described as "devout agnostics" who implicitly subscribed to a kind of Arnoldian amalgam of religious and literary values—although 1) this inchoate canon was probably neither so consciously "religious" nor (paradoxically) so resolutely nonsupernaturalist as apRoberts suggests, and 2) the public ideological consensus involved (in effect, the spiritual basis of the liberal arts curriculum that rose and fell over the last century) has steadily disintegrated in recent decades.

Perhaps the most instructive question to pursue is that of the limits of transformability in religion, even of the extreme non-supernaturalist sort. apRoberts takes Arnold's statement, that Christianity is "the greatest and happiest stroke ever yet made for human perfection" (6: 232-33), as proof of two quite different kinds of assertion regarding Arnold's "developmental theory of religion": "Christianity is capable of improvement. Prediction and miracles *were* useful fictions, and now no longer are" (p. 203). Adopting a hyper-Kuhnian view of a wholly "relative" and "provisional" physical science, perpetually abandoning its propositions for new and more "adequate" ones, she directly applies this dubious model to Arnold's religious paradigm: "A hypothesis must not be a creed but a policy, which we adopt temporarily as the best basis for the next stage of investigations" (p. 281). One can only wonder how indefinite the number of "stages" between the religious and the non-religious attitude are either theoretically or practically possible; and the whole question of authority and continuity in religious matters is cheerfully ignored in this view of religion in kaleidoscopic forward motion. A fundamental distinction is needed, one that calls all of this benign flux into doubt. Arnold seeks to cast out prediction and miracles—the world of dogma, creed, and false tradition (9: 161)—to create a post-metaphysical basis for Christianity, and that is no doubt a "progressive" process requiring the critical intellect; but the positive *content* of Arnold's moralized residual Christianity (the true "idea" behind the alleged "fact") is derived wholly from the ethical, emotional, and imaginative materials of the *past*, a quite *un*improvable "deposit."[25]

For me, apRoberts allows her own inevitable prejudices and predilections to misshape her presentation of Arnold as well as her more implicit account of the fate of "religiousness" in modern culture. Everywhere, an extreme and stupid dogmatism and religious literalism are conceived as the only alternatives to her culture-religion; and nowhere does she even take up the widely discussed role of scientism, technologism, secularism, and sheer spiritual indifference as the more obvious enemies of a religious attitude. She seems not to see that there has existed a kind of "parasitic" relationship between syncretic "Christian" spiritualisms of the sort she in effect champions and the maintenance of a traditional belief-basis in the community—and if that is so, as I believe, the two will predictably (and observably) decline in tandem, as the cultural deposit "runs out." The broad synthesis she seeks to define—that of a Herderian *Kette der Bildung*—does form a loose, benign, post-ideological, "educational" tradition, in which people of varied philosophical and pragmatic allegiances can participate and cooperate. But in effect, it is with a narrower if attractive tradition, that of Broad-Church Anglicanism, running from Hooker and the Cambridge Platonists to the liberals of Thomas Arnold's generation, that apRoberts repeatedly seeks to align Matthew Arnold—and I think herself. The simplest unanswered question (a naive one, apRoberts might judge) is this: what, exactly, are the common elements, if any, between the broadest Christian theism (or even an "open" agnosticism) and Matthew Arnold's resolute non-supernaturalism (as apRoberts conceives it)—and what, then, is the propriety of positioning Arnold within the Broad Church party?'

The tone adopted at points by apRoberts will make some readers uncomfortable. She seems to me startlingly complacent about Arnold's own assumptions, and about the endurance of a very "English" culture. There is a disquieting consciousness of superior taste and cultivation as she dismisses the irrationalism of the "masses" that threatens "our [sic] bulwarks of Hellenism" (p. 3). She approves the traditional "gentleman's education" in the classics, and totally misses Newman's deep reservations regarding that ideal (p. 135). This is, finally, a traditional "Arnoldian" literary intellectual's sort of religion, in effect the self-congratulatory enclosed garden of Eng. Lit. And that will not, for most readers, religious or non-religious, be good enough.

Arnold and God, in opening the large issues of Arnold's relations to "Germanism" and the role of developmental historiography in nineteenth-century England, raises issues of enduring significance, as the troubled humanities seek to redefine themselves. More particularly, apRoberts has persuaded me to speak more cautiously regarding the content of Arnold's God-talk, and to see him as perhaps more thoroughgoing in his naturalism than I have in the past acknowledged. We now have some fairly distinct versions of Arnold's career to choose among—ranging from the "totalizing" views of apRoberts and Madden, across a spectrum, toward the more disjunctive and dialectical Arnold I have been arguing for. The disappointment detectable in the present review derives from apRoberts's unwillingness (despite the apparatus of notes and references) to advance our understanding of the issues by bringing her assertions into the arena of public debate and clearly positioning them with reference to competing views. This review is meant to be one beginning of that process of sifting and winnowing. What, then, *does* Matthew Arnold "mean"? The question, rather amazingly, is more open than ever.

Notes

1. *The Complete Prose Works of Matthew Arnold,* ed. R. H. Super, 11 vols. (Ann Arbor: Univ. of Michigan Press, 1960-77) 5:251; hereafter cited by volume and page alone in text.

2. Richard Tobias, "On Dating Matthew Arnold's 'General Note-Books,'" *Philological Quarterly* 39 (1960), 426-34.

3. A. Dwight Culler, "The Darwinian Revolution and Literary Form," *The Art of Victorian Prose,* ed. George Levine and William Madden (New York: Oxford Univ. Press, 1968), pp. 224-46.

4. Duncan Forbes, *The Liberal Anglican Idea of History* (Cambridge: Cambridge Univ. Press, 1962), leaves the decisiveness of Vico's influence on Thomas Arnold up in the air; but in general he tends to downplay the influence: e.g., p. 17.

5. *The Autobiography of Giambattista Vico,* ed. Max Harold Fisch and Thomas Goddard Bergin (Ithaca: Cornell Univ. Press, 1944).

6. See, e.g., my "Coleridge, Hamlet, and Arnold's Empedocles," *Papers on Language and Literature,* 8 Supplement (1972), 17-25.

7. See "Arnold and Carlyle: The Religious Issue," in *Carlyle Past and Present,* ed. K. J. Fielding and R. L. Tarr (London: Vision Press, 1976) pp.

Arnold and God

127-54. Also overlooked is "The Future of Poetry: A Context for Arnold and Carlyle," *Carlyle and His Contemporaries*, ed. John Clubbe (Durham: Duke Univ. Press, 1976), pp. 148-80, in which I provided a broad early- and mid-Victorian context for the increasing "confusion" of religion and poetry—the "continuum" which is at the center of the present work.

    8. See W. H. Bruford, *Culture and Society in Classical Weimar* (Cambridge: Cambridge Univ. Press, 1962), and W. H. Bruford, *The German Tradition of Self-Cultivation: "Bildung" from Humboldt to Thomas Mann* (Cambridge: Cambridge Univ. Press, 1975).

    9. There are further ways of tracing this pentagram of influences. The long and important essay on Vico by John Kenrick, in Hare and Thirlwall's *Philological Museum* (2 [1833], 626-44), refers to Niebuhr but minimizes the parallel between the two men's work; and there is no reference to any other German figure. This is the very issue in which Thirlwall's notable essay on Sophoclean irony appears, referred to by apRoberts, and noted above. And Duncan Forbes, in *The Liberal Anglican Idea of History*, prints a most revealing letter of 1812, in which the supposedly "liberal" Niebuhr writes, "Herder was no longer the same man when he ceased to be religious." My own point: Herder was simply not *Christian* enough to serve as a central figure for apRoberts's own Broad Churchmen.

    10. Charles Frederick Harrold, *Carlyle and German Thought: 1819-1834* (1934; Hamden Ct.: Archon Books, 1963) p. 157. And one would wish that a study like this would also be willing to quote Carlyle's dismissive remark about the "*Blarney* about history" emanating from the Germany of Herder, Wieland, and Goethe. See *Two Note Books of Thomas Carlyle*, ed. Charles Eliot Norton (New York: Grolier Club, 1898) p. 36.

    11. Hill Shine, "Carlyle's Early Writings and Herder's *Ideen*," *Booker Memorial Studies*, ed. Hill Shine (Chapel Hill: Univ. of North Carolina Press, 1950), pp. 3-33.

    12. There *are* ways in which the running claims for "the influence of Herder," especially on Arnold, might have been tested. For example, volume 5 of *The Reception of Classical German Literature in England, 1760-1800*, ed. John Boening (New York: Garland, 1977), shows that only eight reviews of Herder appeared in England during the fifty-five years between 1805 and 1860, many of them short; so knowledge of Herder was far from widespread. On the other hand, two of these, written in the 40s, were important introductions to his thought; the elements emphasized there would be those especially "available" to Arnold in that crucial period.

    13. From Arnold's essay of 1863, apRoberts cites Guérin's *Le Centaure*—not, of course, a "poem," as she calls it—and comments: "I think this sense of ocean . . . contributes to the awesome mystery of the 'luminous home of waters' in the end of 'Sohrab and Rustum' " (p. 113)—the latter a poem

written in 1853. And she had earlier claimed that *Le Centaure* "helped to shape Callicles' songs" in "Empedocles on Etna," which Arnold was writing in 1849 (p. 81). But there is simply no evidence for what she calls "the intimacy of the de Guérin influence" (p. 113) before 1863.

14. This is the persuasive argument of Linda Lee Ray in her "Callicles on Etna," *Victorian Poetry*, 7 (1969), 309-20.

15. Epifanio San Juan, Jr., "Matthew Arnold and the Poetics of Belief: Some Implications of *Literature and Dogma*," *Harvard Theological Review*, 37 (1964), 97-118.

16. William A. Madden, *Matthew Arnold: A Study of the Aesthetic Temperament in Victorian England* (Bloomington: Indiana Univ. Press, 1967).

17. These are important points first solidly established by Fraser Neiman in "The Zeitgeist of Matthew Arnold," *PMLA*, 72 (1957), 977-96, and in *Matthew Arnold* (New York: Twayne, 1968); apRoberts pauses only long enough to brush him aside (p. 187 n.)

18. *The Poems of Matthew Arnold*, ed. Kenneth and Miriam Allott, 2nd ed. (London: Longman, 1979), p. 275.

19. David DeLaura, "Arnold and Literary Criticism: Critical Ideas," *Matthew Arnold, Writers and Their Background*, ed. Kenneth Allott (London: G. Bell, 1975), pp. 118-48). This collection of essays, a standard work in contemporary Arnold studies, is nowhere referred to by apRoberts, though it also contains Basil Willey's last statement on Arnold's religion.

20. See David DeLaura, "The Future of Poetry."

21. The immediate background is well explained in Sidney Coulling, *Matthew Arnold and His Critics: A Study of Arnold's Controversies* (Athens: Ohio Univ. Press, 1974).

22. Richard Holt Hutton, *Essays on Some of the Modern Guides to English Thought in Matters of Faith* (London: Macmillan, 1888), p. 133.

23. *The Encyclopedia of Philosophy*, ed. Paul Edwards, 8 vols. (New York: Macmillan and Free Press, 1967).

24. We now have Nicholas Sagovsky, *Between Two Worlds: George Tyrrell's Relationship to the Thought of Matthew Arnold* (New York: Cambridge Univ. Press, 1983). Sagovsky is ably reviewed by James C. Livingston in *The Arnoldian*, 11, 2 (1984), 70-74.

25. The continuing liveliness of the issues of "change" in religion is evident in the widespread discussion provoked by Thomas Sheehan's article, "Revolution in the Church," *New York Review of Books* (14 July 1984), pp. 135-39.

Emily Dickinson:
The Poet as Experienced Virgin

Jerome Loving

    William H. Shurr. *The Marriage of Emily Dickinson: A Study of the Fascicles.* Lexington: University of Kentucky Press, 1983. x, 230 pp.

    Vivian R. Pollak. *Emily Dickinson: The Anxiety of Gender.* Ithaca: Cornell University Press, 1984. 272 pp.

If *The Scarlet Letter* had been written by Emily Dickinson instead of Nathaniel Hawthorne, Arthur and Hester would have never made it out of the dark wood in which Pearl was presumably conceived. This most famous of Puritan couples would always be waiting for the ecstasy for which, as the poet tells us in J. 125, "We must an anguish pay." Hawthorne, of course, solved the problem of presenting the unpresentable by beginning his story *in medias res.* His characters are forever looking over their shoulders into a past that makes them feel guilty about the present. Dickinson's supposed persons, on the other hand, usually hope to remain back before the Fall of Man. Always on the edge of experience and seldom in its aftermath, *her* Arthur and Hester are always anticipating that final moment before they are stripped of their innocence and—as the American Adam and Eve driven out of the New Eden—realize their nakedness. They are forever attempting to return to the moment when, as Dickinson wrote in J. 322,

        The Sun, as common, went abroad,
        The Flowers, accustomed, blew,
        As if no soul the solstice passed
        That maketh all things new—

This is the instant of ecstasy when we remember to forget—as Emerson so cautiously laments in "Experience"—"the discovery we have made that we exist."[1] Dickinson locates this moment in many of her poems, but the most famous example is found in her most famous poem, "Because I Could Not Stop for Death" (J. 712). It comes just before the narrator realizes that her "hansom" man is also the undertaker and that every desire for Love is a wish for Death. At such "extatic" moments it is even possible to pass "the Setting Sun" instead of being hopelessly controlled by the "harmony" of nature ("Or rather—He passed us"). It is—as the imagery in "There Came a Day at Summer's Fall" (J. 322) suggests—the June 22nd of our lives. Ever afterwards we know that the sun sets upon our existence, insisting that nature must kill in order to "maketh all things new." Dickinson's Arthur and Hester make love in a "House" that becomes "A Swelling of the Ground."

It is precisely Dickinson's ability to talk about this crucial aspect of experience that draws out the literary detective in us. Her poems make us importunate. We want to know more about the life experience that allowed her to see so acutely the ratio between success and failure. We want to know how she could have seen so much and also have led a life which, as she told Thomas Wentworth Higginson, had "been too simple to embarrass any."[2] Virtually every possibility has been whipped into a thesis for a book-length study: that she was disappointed in love, that she was a lesbian, that she was a closet feminist, an agoraphobic. Indeed, the post-mortem analysis of her life and work resembles that for Poe in that she has been accused of everything *but* necrophilia. In other words, the poet had to be in some manner abnormal in order to write what still have to be called "abnormal" or wildly unconventional poems. With the publication of Richard B. Sewall's definitive biography in 1974, the various and divergent theories began to consolidate into one of two schools of thought. The first sees Dickinson as conventionally religious (believing in a domestic heaven) and sexually normal (meaning heterosexual). The other finds her (at one extreme) agnostic and (at the other) vaguely homosexual. One might say that sex is sentimentalized by the first school and sanitized by the second: Dickinson wrote from either a broken heart or a heart that was really a head in the sense that gender was a reason for writing instead of mating. The two studies under consideration here appear to present these opposing viewpoints most comprehensively: William H. Shurr's *The Marriage of Emily Dickinson: A Study of the Fascicles* and Vivian R. Pollak's *Emily Dickinson: The Anxiety of Gender.*

In reviewing R. W. Franklin's *The Manuscript Books of Emily Dickinson* for this journal in 1983, I suggested that the facsimile of her holographs takes us back full circle to the problems faced by the poet's first editors, Higginson and Mabel Loomis Todd; that is to say, we are now faced with unfinished productions—poems with alternate endings and, thus, multiple versions. What I never quite imagined, however, was that the edition might also take some critics back full circle to the 1890s and the Victorian myth about the poet's writing from some "secret sorrow." The phrase is not Shurr's, but the argument is. The poems in the fascicles and sets presented in *The Manuscript Books*, Shurr believes, "suggest meditations on events as they happened, meditations shared with a specific addressee" (p. 4). The poems address a particular lover, most likely the Philadelphia clergyman Charles Wadsworth, and it is highly probable that their "marriage" was consummated and may even have resulted in pregnancy. Undaunted by the danger of inferring biographical facts from the artist's work, Shurr at least stops short of finding evidence of a fetus buried in the garden.

Doubtless there are readers who will find this closely argued theory intriguing if not convincing, but this reader feels it is imposed upon Dickinson's work much in the same way the wedding veil is superimposed on the photograph of Dickinson that illustrates Shurr's dustjacket. And even if these parallels between the life and work do literally exist, their discovery tends to focus our attention not on the poetry (which makes Dickinson worthy of attention in the first place) but on the private life that went out of existence almost a century ago. Furthermore, seeing the poems as an emotional chronicle instead of an artistic structure (as Shurr does), we are left not with a personal reaction that opens out, as great poetry does, into the universal but with simply a sentimental—at times, rather lugubrious—poet. For example, at one point in the study the final lines of Whittier's

"Maud Muller" are quoted to illustrate the depth of the poet's "aloneness":

> For of all sad words of tongue and pen,
> The saddest are these, "It might have been."

Surely, Dickinson would not have agreed with Whittier in such matters but rather with her contemporary in realism Bret Harte, who, in "the only genuine sequel" to "Maud Muller," suggested that love and "marriage" were hardly ever the same thing. In his parody, the western wit concludes:

> If, of all words of tongue and pen,
> The saddest are, 'It might have been.'
>
> Sadder are these, we daily see,
> 'It is, but hadn't ought to be.'[3]

Perhaps the only "marriage" Dickinson ever allowed herself was that between her mind and the matter it so eloquently contemplated.

To assert, as Shurr does, that the fascicles "were written not as public works of art but as private communications to a specific lover" (p. 10) is to reduce to a single dimension the work of one of our most complex and mystifying poets. If indeed her poems were initiated by a personal crisis or romance, surely they were not sustained by one. Her indentity-theme, it seems clear, was not the loss of a lover but the loss of love itself. Relentlessly, the target of her "Loaded Gun" is the union of Love and Death, not the love of a married clergyman from another city who, incidentally, did not even know how to spell the poet's last name.[4] If we owe Shurr a debt, it is not for his admittedly clever reading of the poems but for his attempt to find a structure—any structure—to these puzzling clusters of poems and for the meticulous care he takes in trying to make the pieces fit his story "of the marriage made in heaven, prevented on earth, but to be celebrated eternally in heaven" (p. 125).

Professor Pollak's argument is not nearly so tidy as Shurr's; however, it does give us a more credible portrait of the poet.

Emily Dickinson

The fundamental question asked in half of Dickinson's poems is why the "nearest Dream" recedes "unrealized." In the rest of her poems, however, "happiness is not an issue" (p. 9) because life is a quest for sexual identity. Which is to say that the "Laureate of the dispossessed," however, is also the "laureate of sexual despair" (p. 9). It is not always clear to the reader (and perhaps not to Pollak) whether the object of her identity quest is heterosexual or homosexual. But the early chapter (indeed, the first three are models of criticism in their use of biography) on the poet's relationship with her future sister-in-law is excellent in showing the complexity of Dickinson's sexual fears. By the early 1850s Susan Gilbert, we learn, "had become the vehicle for a set of rich and intensely gratifying fantasies" (p. 59). The possibility that Emily participated vicariously in many of Sue's romances seems to answer a good many questions about her later life and poetry which celebrated sex in the subjunctive.[5]

The depth of Pollak's critical inquiry is generally impressive. Although she sides with Shurr on the identity of "Master" as Wadsworth instead of a psychological "other," she also emphasizes that it is the inaccessibility of Dickinson's lover that appeals to the poet's artistic sense. And whereas Shurr cites J. 322 as a celebration of Dickinson's "marriage day," Pollak treats the same poem as a "marriage fiction." The distinction is crucial to an appreciation of the poet's theme of sex—and indeed life—in the subjunctive. For Shurr the lovers "will meet beyond the grave," but for Pollak the emphasis is usually on the life that must be lived in the present. The marriage fiction is, accordingly, "more successful in conveying the urgency of [Dickinson's] quest for psychic integration than in persuading the reader that the union . . . has ever been fully accomplished" (p. 169).

The idea that Dickinson "rejects her world in order to endorse it" is explored in a number of ways. If Pollak's thesis here falters, it is in her insistence that the world the poet rejected was a male one. It is not exactly the ghost of Shurr's Emily come back to haunt us, but what emerges in the discussion is its sentimental twin, the castrated female. The argument, however, is never successfully integrated into the one that Dickinson rejects the imperative to live (more fully) in the subjunctive. Obviously, the poet did experience a sense of alienation when it came to the male gender, but the greater alienation in the poems surely came from experience itself. This Pollak correctly observes when she notes that Dickinson was fascinated by the human desire to have it both ways: to fall in love and at the same time preserve one's psychological freedom.

Pollak's thoughtful study might well have been concluded with her sixth chapter on the poems to and about male figures. To quote from it would be illustrative but also redundant. Suffice to say that this critic has shown, probably more clearly than others, how the poet's sense (really fear) of male sexuality was the catalyst that transformed potentially morose and sentimental poems into profound psychic insights. The final two chapters reinforce this idea, but their feminist argument adds little to the already established and penetrating psychological reading of the poet and her work. We are given interesting examples of how the important men in her life were also menacing. Higginson, for example, is chastised for his chauvinist imagery in "Letter to a Young Contributor," but we must not forget his important role in her career and, in fact, her statement to him in the 1860s that he had saved her (literary?) life.[6] Generally, the feminist "slant" (surely a neutral word in Dickinson's case) scatters the force of an otherwise important book.

The two studies suggest a good deal of unhappiness on Main Street in Amherst, but the deprivation Dickinson experienced may not have been viewed as dramatically in the nineteenth century as we want to view it in the twentieth. Any poet who could reach her literary zenith not only when her country was engulfed in civil war but also when her side was losing must have been fairly secure about herself and her literary vision. She once told Higginson: "I find ecstasy in living—the mere sense of living is joy enough."[7] Perhaps we ought to pay more attention to Dickinson the philosopher—more to the disembodied voice of her poems and less to the unmarried lady. Though her art doubtless reflected the problems of personal love and female oppression, her central concern was for that dazzling ratio between life and death. Dickinson did indeed reject life in order to savor it.

Notes

1. *Selections from Ralph Waldo Emerson*, ed. Stephen E. Whicher (Boston: Houghton Mifflin, 1957), p. 269.

2. *Letters of Emily Dickinson*, ed. Thomas H. Johnson (Cambridge: Harvard Univ. Press, 1958), II, 330.

3. *Writings of Bret Harte* (Boston: Houghton Mifflin, 1870), XII, 290.

4. In a letter written around 1860, Wadsworth addressed the poet as "My Dear Miss Dickenson"; *Letters*, II, 392.

5. For a short discussion of this idea, see Albert Gelpi, *The Tenth Muse: The Psyche of the American Poet* (Cambridge: Harvard Univ. Press, 1975), p. 242.

6. *Letters*, II, 460.

7. *Letters*, II, 474.

On Measuring Shakespeare's Theatre

William H. Allison

John Orrell. *The Quest for Shakespeare's Globe*. Cambridge: Cambridge University Press, 1983. xv, 184 pp.

Occasionally a work of scholarship thrills the intellect by opening prospects for understanding of mysteries which have seemed permanently unassailable, forever obscured by the lack of evidence for further study. John Orrell's book *The Quest for Shakespeare's Globe* is in that good tradition. Like Champollion seeking an understanding of the ancient Egyptian language through the enigmatic evidence of the Rosetta stone or like Hawkins applying computer technology to reveal meaning in the relationships at Stonehenge, Orrell has approached the Globe Theatre's evidence with fresh insight and has found means for comprehending what has been there all along for us to see.

Contemporary evidence from the Globe Theatres is extremely meager; we know that the second Globe was built on the same site and foundation as the first and that it had a tiled roof. The external appearance of the second Globe was depicted in a contemporary sketch by Wenceslaus Hollar. It cost £1400 to erect, a high figure for that time, and was praised as "the glory of the bank." There is very little evidence to work from, and that little has already been examined assiduously by countless scholars, a most daunting prospect for any researcher. Orrell states at the outset his intentional use of the singular 'Globe,' signaling his contention that both theatres of that name were closely similar, enough to be considered interchangeably for most of what his research treats on. Professor Orrell has made careful study of the best work of his predecessors and fellow scholars, as his statements of credit for their contributions amply indicate. Principal among those helpful sources were the 1924 site study by W. W. Braines; John Cranford Adams's impressive marshalling of the evidence in 1942; C. W. Hodges's excellent books on the subject, first in 1953 then in 1973; and the fine research and closely correlated recent conclusions of Richard Hosely, which have been published over the past decade in various books and articles.

The key points about Professor Orrell's book are that he presents discerning and persuasive interpretations of old evidence in order to reach some new conclusions and to reinforce a few of the old ones. He reconciles his observations and his reasoning in a manner which brings assurance and fresh clarity of understanding to Globe Theatre scholarship. He believes that the sketch of "The West Part of Southwarke Toward Westminister," by Wenceslaus Hollar, with its contemporary (ca. 1640) view of the second Globe Theatre, was done using a mechanical sighting and sketching device, probably the topographical glass.[1] That sketch had, in Orrell's judgment, the "authority of a photograph" (p. 75)—a reliability in detail which was previously not guessed at. From that confidence in the drawing he develops a statement of the theatre's width (101.37 ft. to 103.32 ft., p 2%) and of the Globe's similarity in size to the Hope Theatre, thus making a case for playhouses of that period having a standard plan, by which the Theatre, the first Globe, second Globe, the Hope and Swan Theatres were all nearly identical in major dimensions. Furthermore, he presents startling evidence (the more so since the source of his information is not new, but is only newly appreciated for its true meaning and value) of the seating and audience passage dimensions and conditions typical for dramatic presentations in early seventeenth-century England.[2] He describes the method of calculation used for laying out theatres and stages as being the "ad quadratum" and "ad triangularum" methods commonly used by surveyors of Shakespeare's time. Guided by the geometric practice of those methods, and working with the standard measuring tools of the period, Orrell has discovered that certain configurations, relationships, and measurements were predictable and were evident in the drawings and contract information which exist from the Elizabethan theatres. Orrell describes misleading conditions of the Hollar drawing, particularly the distortion which results from the viewing plane of the topographical glass not being at right angles to the direct line of sight to the Globe Theatre. He also comments on the anamorphosis effect by which any cylindrical shape is distorted when recorded on a viewing plane as described above, and with the cylinder (the Globe Theatre, in this case) being at some distance from the central line of view to that plane. Those distortions have misled other scholars to fairly serious misjudgments; Orrell corrects and explains.

The iteration of trigonometric calculations and of the many cartographic projections which establish the surprising accuracy of Hollar's drawings, while slow-moving, are necessary for establishing credibility. Once assimilated by the reader, those passages set a high level of confidence in the author's method and the thoroughness and reliability of his procedure, supporting all that follows.

The language of John Orrell's presentation is clear, direct, and eloquently communicative; it serves his purpose admirably for the arrayal of his facts and reasoning, enlisting the reader's interest and commanding respect with the breadth of knowledge, proofs, and arguments which he brings to bear on his subject. He soon builds confidence by proceeding from basic evidence to well-documented conditions of proof. His reliance on the earlier work of other scholars is fairly stated. When he has taken his argument to the limits of his proof, he clearly states what he projects in theory beyond the assurance of supporting evidence.

The final chapter, in which the author speculates about the origins of the Globe Theatre form, seems inappropriately placed. His first appendix begins with the statement "Thus far in this book I have tried to offer the reader as little speculation and as much established fact as possible" (p. 158). His chapter "The Globe and the Sun" should most appropriately have followed that statement, since it deals mostly with speculations. That is not to gainsay the value and the fascination of Professor Orrell's final chapter. He makes interesting comparisons with other building forms and weighs their merits thoughtfully and instructively. And he presents one last demonstration of his mathematical and cartographical brilliance, by which he proves that the axis through stage center of the Globe points directly at the rising sun when it is at summer solstice. That remarkable observation, coupled with the coincidence of near identity between the diameter at post centers for both the Globe and the sarsen circle at Stonehenge, seems to imply more than can reasonably be claimed for any purposeful relationship between those two great structures. Even adding the further coincidence of exciting recent advances in research, illuminating both structures with the startling clarity of new understanding, the argument goes nowhere, as Orrell quickly avows.

John Orrell's exposition is logically developed. He begins with the statement and proof of his major thesis—that the accuracy of Wenceslaus Hollar's work, both in the drawing "The West Part of Southwarke Toward Westminster" and in his etching the "Long View of London," is reliable to a degree previously unrecognized. When the rules which governed Hollar's work are properly understood, that work reveals nearly exact information on major aspects of the Globe Theatre's design and measurement. Orrell's confidence in the Hollar sketch is without reservation: "This drawing signals to the inquirer across more than three centuries with all of the precision of an optical instrument. We have long sought a measured survey of Shakespeare's Globe, and here it is" (p. 83).

A nice touch in the course of the many proofs of Hollar's accuracy is Orrell's disquisition on the now vanquished sketch by which Hollar recorded his pacings and observations of Thames Street—not for direct application to the drawing, but for a better understanding of relationships than could be obtained from a distance, with a jumble of buildings intervening. No direct information about the Globe is involved in that, but it gives great assurance for Hollar's carefully analytic study of the theatre when he did turn his eye and glass in that direction.

The Hope Theatre depiction by Hollar has fostered the belief that the Hope was smaller than the Globe; being close to the latter in the drawing, it appears to be much the smaller of the two. Orrell's research, compensating for distance, perspective, anamorphosis, and the distortions of registration on a slanted plane, reveals the two to have been almost identical in dimension. And since the building contract survives for the Hope, certain

Measuring Shakespeare's Theatre

revelations of that document can now be read into the Globe's condition—the building's height being a particularly useful reinforcing detail of information. It was from that height specification that Richard Hosely was able to give a deceptively simple proof of the Globe's width, deriving a width of 100 ft. from the Hollar sketch, based on the 3:1 relation of width to height shown there.[3] His conclusion very neatly corroborates the width calculated by Orrell.

Described elsewhere by other scholars, the conditions of the dismantling and moving of the Theatre from its original site in Shoreditch to become the new Globe Theatre in Southwarke on Bankside adds importantly to the verisimilitude as well as to the narrative interest of Orrell's writing. In Orrell's words, "The Globe was the Theatre transpontine, but not transformed" (p. 120). Helpful to the reader in this section is the description of Peter Street, the carpenter, contractor, and surveyor who probably built the Fortune Theatre, imagined in the discharging of his responsibility to dismantle the Theatre and to lay out and assemble the Globe.

The careful statement of the laws and the rigors of their enforcement at the time of the building of the second Globe gives us persuasive evidence that the two Globe Theatres were of the same size, the second having been built exactly on the foundation of the first. And also by law of that time the jettying of the galleries was prohibited; upper levels rose directly above those beneath.

A matter frequently commented on by scholars of Shakespeare's theatre (often with reservations concerning its accuracy) is the Spanish ambassador's statement in 1624 that the second Globe held more than three thousand spectators; it is here reviewed for proof by reference to contemporary records of seating provisions in other theatres of the period. Orrell presents us with a remarkable "discovery" in this case—a detailed technical account of the stage and seating installation at Christ Church, Oxford, for a performance in 1605, a document previously commented on by other scholars who did not understand its relevance to early seventeenth-century English theatre scholarship. Professor Orrell dispels the misunderstanding which has prevented the acceptance of this document as a guide. A seating width of 18 inches was common throughout; and leg room varied from 18 inches to 30 inches. Thus, for a theatre with a diameter of approximately 100 feet as many as 3,350 audience members could be accommodated. Seeking further afield to extend the basis of his proof, Orrell comments, "In Italy the Teatro Olimpico still stands to remind us that the English were not alone in their astonishing compressibility" (p. 129).

Over forty years ago John Cranford Adams, beginning the account of his ambitious study of the first Globe Theatre, dismissed the Hollar views of the Globe, preferring the Visscher panorama (which showed it as an octagon) for its "contemporary representation of the famous theatre."[4] He commented on the Hollar depiction of a cylindrical second Globe as being probable evidence of a brick exterior wall. The differences of scholarly interpretation which have been developed in the interim are instructive.

Orrell, in his "Speculations" appendix, argues persuasively for a polygonal structure, giving the following reasons for believing that the second Globe was a many-sided polygon, simplified in drawing by representation as a cylinder:

The Hope Theatre was polygonal, as described in the extant contract; and the drawing shows the same appearance for both theatres.

The roof ridges of the two theatres were surely built of wood and therefore were polygonal, but they were represented by curved lines.

A curved wall is most improbable for a timber building. And there is no existing indication that the second Globe may have been clad in brick.

Furthermore, Orrell agrees with Richard Hosely in preferring to believe in a 24-sided building configuration, stating these reasons:

Only a many-sided polygon would have seemed appropriately presentable as a cylinder.

Measuring Shakespeare's Theatre

By comparison of the characteristics of a range of polygons and considering the building problems for placement of the superstructure, the 24-sided figure works best, particularly for the 77.5° angle of alignment calculated by Orrell from study of the Hollar sketch.

A 24-sided polygon is readily constructed by geometrical layout. And from the carpenter-surveyor's point of view, it is one of the most readily verifiable of forms.

That form works best in accordance with the window configuration on the Globe Theatre wall, as shown in the Hollar sketch.

The bays would be easily spanned by timber—9.14 ft. inside and 12.92 ft. outside.

A 24-sided polygon would influence design so that the superstructure would not quite reach the center of the theatre—a condition shown on the Hollar sketch of the "West Part of Southwarke Toward Westminister."

Thus it is that Orrell builds his case for a fresh understanding of Shakespeare's theatre—developing one line of reasoning until he has established it as persuasively as possible, then dropping back for a new beginning through which to develop another chain of proof by different means. A fascinating exercise and in all a most impressive statement of new conditions for our understanding of that theatre. Surely no one now intending to build a replica of the Globe should do so without thinking their plans through fundamentally with Orrell's new proofs and strong arguments clearly in mind.

The many scholars who have worked so diligently to derive a fully believable Globe theatre from the few and easily misleading scraps of surviving evidence have well deserved the respect of the scholarly community. But one's genuine admiration is aroused by John Orrell who, after so many already have derived so much from so little, had the fortitude and the special qualities of mind with which to look yet again and to discover new uses for evidence, extending and changing the conditions by which his successors will view their arcane subject hereafter.

Notes

1. John Orrell, observing that Wenceslaus Hollar's accuracy in drawing was on a level beyond what could be expected from unaided human skills, makes a case for Hollar's probable use of the topographical glass, based on the several publications describing that device, all of which were available in London early in the seventeenth century.

I have sought more direct corroboration of Hollar's use of a mechanical drawing device with but partial success, finding these excerpts from the diary of Sir William Dugdale (an associate of Wenceslaus Hollar for many years) in Richard Pennington's *A Descriptive Catalogue of the Etched Works of Wenceslaus Hollar 1607-1677* (Cambridge: Cambridge Univ. Press, 1982), p. xxxix: Dugdale wrote on 6 September 1649, " 'I took the prospect of Kenilworth Castle' and on the next day 'I took the prospect of Warwick.' " A phrase published later in the diary, from James Fish's letter, dated 27 May 1682, to Dugdale, refers to "that instrument you were pleased to shew me with which you tooke the prospects of Warwick, Coventry, etc." All that one can make of this statement is that some mechanical or optical sketching device was used by (or perhaps for) a man who worked closely with Hollar in his later years and with whom he may have been acquainted prior to the sketching of "The West Part of Southwarke Toward Westminster." Several conditions tied them together closely enough in that time that their acquaintance seems distinctly possible, but it was only a matter of record in later years. And we know that Dugdale is nowhere else credited with being an artist.

Richard Pennington's speculations are interesting: "Was this perhaps the screen with its crossing wires that artists are sometimes shown making use of when drawing a portrait?" He continues, "In a footnote Hamper (the printer of Dugdale's Diary) suggests that the contrivance was possibly a camera obscura" and "the use of a camera obscura was known in Dugdale's day and even before, and the description of a portable apparatus is to be found in a popular art manual, *Graphic or the most excellent art of painting* (1658)."

The dates, people, and places do not quite come together satisfactorily in the notes above, but these isolated bits of information do tie the use of a sketching device to the general time and place of Hollar's sketching of the Globe Theatre, and from that we can derive a guarded additional assurance supporting John Orrell's contention that Hollar's sketch (ca. 1640) of the Globe benefitted in accuracy from his use of a mechanical or optical sketching device.

2. John Orrell, "The Theatre at Christ Church, Oxford, in 1605," *Shakespeare Survey*, ed. Stanley Wells (Cambridge: Cambridge Univ. Press, 1982), pp. 129-140. The article states that "British Library Additional MS 15505 fol. 21 is cautiously cataloged as 'The plan of some theatre, probably in Germany,' and that it is . . . the work of a designer, not a mere observer. Indeed there is reason to believe that this sheet of paper carries the earliest English theatre design yet to come to light, the design of the arrangements

made in the hall at Christ Church, Oxford for the visit of James I in August 1605" (p. 129).

3. Richard Hosely, "The Shape and Size of the Second Globe," *The Third Globe*, eds. C. Walter Hodges, S. Schoenbaum, and Leonard Leone (Detroit: Wayne State Univ. Press, 1981), pp. 82-107.

4. John Cranford Adams, *The Globe Playhouse: Its Design and Equipment* (Cambridge: Harvard Univ. Press, 1942).

W. B. Yeats: A Commentary on the *New Commentary*

Richard J. Finneran

A. Norman Jeffares. *A New Commentary on* The Poems of W. B. Yeats. London: Macmillan; Stanford: Stanford University Press, 1984. xxxix, 543 pp.

In 1968 A. Norman Jeffares published *A Commentary on* The Collected Poems *of W. B. Yeats*. In many ways the volume was a very useful companion to the poetry, its major virtue perhaps being the citation of relevant passages from Yeats's other works, both published and unpublished. Though the work became a standard reference source for Yeats studies, it was not without flaws. First, it was inconsistent as to what kind of information was provided on a particular lyric: sometimes, for example, a summary of critical opinion was provided, often not. The entries were as brief as a single line ("To an Isle in the Water") or as long as sixteen pages ("Parnell's Funeral"). Secondly, Jeffares often provided lengthy quotations from Yeats's own notes on his poems without annotating them; given the allusiveness of Yeats's prose, this process was as frustrating as it was helpful. Thirdly, the *Commentary* engaged in a kind of one-for-one biographical annotation which reduced many lyrics to a level precariously near the bathetic—Yeats as an Ur-writer of soap opera. Finally, although no work of this scope can hope to be free of error, the number of what appeared to be simply careless mistakes was alarming.[1] As we shall see, these problems have not disappeared in the revised volume.

The main purpose of issuing the *New Commentary* was to make it compatible with *The Poems: A New Edition*.[2] Apparently, Jeffares was given a copy of the typescript of the new edition while it was in press. He then seems to have added about ninety-five percent of the new or revised information in *The Poems*, along with some material he had gathered on his own, and produced the *New Commentary*. This is of course a normal process. All annotators build on their predecessors: Jeffares borrowed from George Brandon Saul, I borrowed from Jeffares, Jeffares has now borrowed from me, and when *The Poems* is revised I shall again borrow from Jeffares.³ However, it is arguable that common scholarly courtesy would have called for the editor of *The Poems* to be informed of the disposition of his typescript, in which case I could have made certain that Jeffares received any last-minute corrections or additions submitted while the work was in the press. As it is, the *New Commentary* is several times simply wrong about what is said in *The Poems*. On the matter of "Herodias' daughters" (Nineteen Hundred and Nineteen"), for example, *The Poems* does not cite Reginald Scot's *The Discoverie of Witchcraft* (1584) but instead offers what is almost certainly Yeats's source, Jacob Grimm's *Teutonic Mythology* (1883-88).⁴ Likewise, *The Poems* does not cite Zigismond Perenyi in connection with "How Ferencz Renyi Kept Silent" but instead notes where Yeats found the legend (NC 456; PA11); and readers of the new edition will be puzzled by Jeffares's remark of "source not yet known" for the "Archangel Axel" in "[Come ride and ride to the garden]" (NC 471; PA52.11).

Another sign of the haste with which the *New Commentary* must have been produced is Jeffares's handling of quotations from Yeats's prose. Any prose quoted in *The Poems* was annotated; when the same passages are quoted in the *New Commentary*, the annotations are carried over (though occasionally one or two in a long quotation are omitted, for no apparent reason). Jeffares's usual method is to place the annotation in brackets, but that produces some typographical nightmares. For instance, Yeats is quoted as explaining that he "wrote Leda and the Swan because the editor [George Russell, AE, see note on Dedication to *Crossways*] of a political review [*The Irish Statesman*] asked me for a poem. I thought 'After the individualist, demagogic movement, founded by Hobbes [Thomas Hobbes (1588-1679) English utilitarian philosopher] and popularized by the Encyclopaedists [the authors of *L'Encyclopedie* (1751-72) who included Voltaire, Rousseau, Buffon and Turgot; they were edited by Diderot and D'Alembert, and influenced the course of the French Revolution (1789-99)] and the French Revolution . . ." (NC 246). However, on two occasions (NC 332-38, 350-51), Jeffares decided to place the annotations after the passage, citing them by line numbers. There are two problems with this method. First, no marginal line numbers are provided for the passages being annotated. Worse, the line numbers of the annotations do not correspond to anything in the *New Commentary*. They are, in fact, the correct line numbers for the passages only as they were printed in the 1968 *Commentary*! So prolific an author as Jeffares might have realized that the typographical layout of prose can change between different printings. Given such confusion, one may prefer the non-annotation of prose of the earlier *Commentary*.[5]

Yet another sign of the carelessness characteristic of the *New Commentary* is the treatment of Denis Donoghue's edition of Yeats's *Memoirs* (London: Macmillan, 1972; New York: Macmillan, 1973). Jeffares is aware of that volume, which is included in the list of abbreviations and even cited on one occasion (NC 465). But throughout the *New Commentary* Jeffares continues to cite the contents of *Memoirs* as either an "unpublished Autobiography" or an "unpublished MS.," on the one hand; or, on the other hand, as "the Diary begun in 1908," "Yeats's 1908 Diary," "Yeats's 1909 Diary," his "1909-1910 Diary," "Yeats's 1910 Diary," or simply "Yeats's Diary." Given the number of different unpublished manuscripts and diaries which survive in the Yeats Papers, this multiple citation form is bad enough; but there is even less justification for Jeffares' not revising his work to draw on *Memoirs* in light of the numerous errors in transcription and dating. Here are the same four sentences as presented by Jeffares and by Donoghue:

There is a small island entirely covered and still [indecipherable] empty castle. The last man who lived there had been Dr. Hyde's father who when a young man had lived there a few weeks. All round it were the wooded and hilly shores - a place of great beauty. I believed that this castle could be hired for little money and I had long dreamed of a king, an Irish Eleusis or Samothrace. [NC 23]

There is this small island entirely covered by what was a still habitable but empty castle. The last man who had lived there had been Dr. Hyde's father who, when a young man, lived there for a few weeks. All round were the wooded and hilly shores, a place of great beauty. I believed that the castle could be hired for little money, and had long been dreaming of making it an Irish Eleusis or Samothrace.[6]

It would not be difficult to continue citing errors of this sort in the *New Commentary*, but I will leave such of them as are worthy of note for the addenda provided at the end of this review. It is now time to take up two problems with the volume which are not the result of carelessness but of conscious choice.

The first of these might be called "multiple choice annotation." At times, rather than admitting that the first *Commentary* has been corrected by later scholarship, Jeffares will offer two or more glosses, occasionally attempting to defend his original annotation. This problem begins with the opening lyric of *The Poems*, "The Song of the Happy Shepherd," in which Yeats refers to "the cracked tune that Chronos sings" (P1.9). In the first *Commentary*, Jeffares annotated this as "Kronos or Cronos, one of the Titans" (C 4). *The Poems*, however, offers this annotation: "Chronos is the Greek word for 'time'; personified by Pindar as 'the father of all.' The similarity of Chronos with Kronos, one of the Titans, led to the latter's identification with Time in cosmogonic speculation." In the *New Commentary*, however, Jeffares simply reprints his 1968 notes and adds "The Greek word Χρόνος means time; but Kronos was only later interpreted as Χρόνος" (NC 4). Although no one should be denied the opportunity to display his Greek, that statement quite misses the point—which is precisely that Cronos was originally a deity distinct from Kronos. In *History, Time and Deity*, S. G. F. Brandon has offered examples of Cronos from as early as the sixth century B.C. (Pherecydes of Syros and Anaximander) as well as from Pindar.[7] Indeed, given the fact that Yeats studied Greek in the High School (Dublin), Pindar is a likely source.[8] Yeats might well have been interested in Pindar's second Olympian Ode—which explicitly distinguishes between Kronos (l. 11) and Cronos (l. 15)—not only because it is, in the view of Lewis Richard Farnell, "in some respects the greatest of Pindar's works," but also because of its Orphic doctrine.[9] Jeffares's gloss denies the difference between Cronos and Kronos, and also denies that the difference was known to either Yeats, the editor of the *Dublin University Review* (where the poem was first published), or the several later editors of the poem. Moreover, in the context of "The Song of the Happy Shepherd," the figure of Time is clearly more relevant than that of one of the Titans (the "cracked tune" neatly foreshadows "this voice that ninety years have cracked" of Ribh in "Ribh at the Tomb of Baile and Aillinn" [P309.5]). One should perhaps invoke here Occam's razor: if Cronos is appropriate, why believe Yeats intended Kronos?

Another example of this problem concerns the identity of the "Old Dublin merchant 'free of the ten and four' " (P112.3) in the opening poem of *Responsibilities*. In his 1949 study of Yeats, Jeffares correctly glossed this as Yeats's great-great-grandfather, Benjamin Yeats (1750-1795); he noted that Yeats's source of information was almost certainly two copies bought by Lily Yeats of what is called "Watson's *Gentleman's and Citizen's Almanack*" (in fact, Wilson's *Dublin Directory*), in which Benjamin is listed as one of the merchants "free of the six and ten percent tax at the Custom-house, Dublin."[10] However, in the 1968 *Commentary*, the ancestor is inexplicably glossed as Jervis Yeats (d. 1712), Benjamin's grandfather, thus repeating an error in Joseph Hone's biography.[11] *The Poems* reasserts the correct identification and offers evidence about the tax exemption from the second edition (1767) of Richard Eaton's *A book of rates inwards and outwards with the neat-duties and drawbacks payable on importation and exportation of all sorts of merchandise.*[12] Jeffares's solution in the *New Commentary* to the discrepancy is to state that "the merchant may be Jervis Yeats . . . or his son and inheritor Benjamin or Benjamin's son, also christened Benjamin (1750-1795) . . . a linen merchant like his father and grandfather" (NC 100). He offers as support only his 1949 study and *The Poems*, neither of which suggests anyone other than the second Benjamin.

The truth is that the identification of Jervis Yeats is quite impossible in this context. When Jeffares refers the reader to Eaton's work cited in *The Poems*, he overlooks the fact that the quotation was from the second edition. That was done not because of an inability to locate the first edition (1765; a copy is in the New York Public Library), but because the information on the six percent and ten percent exemptions is found only in the second edition. It is therefore obvious that the law must have been changed sometime in 1765-1767, or more than fifty years after the death of Jervis Yeats. As for the first Benjamin, his dates have not been cited in the scholarship, but it is probable that he was granted the tax exemption when the system was changed, later passing it on to his son Benjamin.[13] But in any case, it seems clear that as far as Yeats knew, it was the second Benjamin who enjoyed the tax exemption.

One final example of "multiple choice annotation" (more can be found in the addenda). In the original *Commentary*, Jeffares glossed the source of what he calls "The fabulous darkness' (actually "A fabulous, formless darkness") in "Two Songs from a Play" as "from a description of Christianity by Proclus, a fourth-century Neo-platonic philosopher (whom Yeats read in Thomas Taylor's translation of 1816)" (C 291). He cited not his probable source, Ellmann's *The Identity of Yeats*, but a scarcely relevant page in F. A. C. Wilson's *W. B. Yeats and Tradition*.[14] He also offered a misquotation of Yeats's reference in the 1925 *A Vision* to "a philosopher of the fourth century" who described Christianity as "that fabulous formless darkness."[15] By putting together Ellmann and Yeats, Jeffares presumably came up with "Proclus, a fourth-century . . . philosopher."

There are, however, three problems with such a gloss. First, Proclus was born, lived, and died in the fifth century. Secondly, despite an extensive search some years ago by the editors of *A Vision*, no such passage has been discovered in Proclus (Ellmann's misinformation probably came from Mrs. Yeats). Thirdly, as those same editors explained, E. R. Dodds noted in his *Missing Persons: An Autobiography* (Oxford: Clarendon, 1977) that Yeats found the passage in his 1923 *Select Passages illustrating Neoplatonism*.[16] *The Poems* draws on that research and offers a 1922 translation of the relevant passage from the Greek sophist Eunapius—who *was* born in the fourth century. In the *New Commentary*, Jeffares simply repeats his original note on the matter and follows it by citing the annotation in *The Poems*. Apparently readers are supposed either to make their own selection of the proper gloss or else believe that Yeats drew on both philosophers.

We now come to the final major question about the *New Commentary*: biographical annotation. The material is based on two implicit assumptions: 1) that virtually all of Yeats's poetry is a direct transcription of what happened in the life of William Butler Yeats (1865-1939) of Sligo, London, Dublin, and elsewhere—"Man and Poet," if you will; and 2) that the poems are best read in the light of such knowledge, whatever its sources (which range from the statements of Mrs. Yeats to the intuitions of critics). Now no one would deny the connection between Yeats's life and his work: indeed, what would have been the very first sentence facing a reader of the projected Scribner Edition of 1937-1938 begins, "A poet writes always of his personal life, in his finest work out of its tragedy, whatever it be, remorse, lost love, or mere loneliness . . . ." But what Jeffares and many other critics slight is the second half of that sentence: "he never speaks directly as to someone at the breakfast table, there is always a phantasmagoria."[17] I would argue that the purpose of the "phantasmagoria" is precisely to make the kind of biographical annotation offered in the *New Commentary* fundamentally irrelevant.

Doubtless not many readers find helpful all of Jeffares's biographical glosses, such as "Marriage can seem a very enfettering prospect to a bachelor of fifty-one" (NC 140, on "The Collar-Bone of a Hare"); "the refrain is a composite picture of Mrs. Yeats and Dorothy Wellesley, both gardeners" (NC 397, on "The Spirit Medium"); or "Yeats was suffering from heart trouble at the time of his visit" (NC 400, on "The Municipal Gallery Re-visited"). And when the reference to "Fit audience" in "Remorse for Intemperate Speech" is explained as "probably the friends Yeats made after he was thirty, Lady Gregory in Ireland, and many others in England" (NC 306), one can only wonder if the poor man had but a single friend in the country of his birth and none at all in America (John Quinn, for instance?). But what of the many comments on the order of this one: "The poem was written to Maud Gonne" (NC 51.

on "The Fish")? Jeffares seldom offers any documentation for such assertions, and he seems unaware of the problems of evaluating the disparate kinds of evidence for his claims.[18] For example, after an extensive study of the manuscripts, Curtis Bradford decided that "The Lover asks Forgiveness because of his Many Moods" was addressed to Olivia Shakespear, but Jeffares is silent on any biographical background to that lyric.[19]

As the *New Commentary* is so full of biographical annotation, I cite but a single example. Here is the first stanza of "The Results of Thought":

> Acquaintance; companion;
> One dear brilliant woman;
> The best-endowed, the elect,
> All by their youth undone,
> All, all by that inhuman
> Bitter glory wrecked. [P264]

Jeffares glosses this as *"Acquaintance*: not identified"; *"companion*: Mrs. Shakespear"; *"One dear brilliant woman*: Lady Gregory" (NC 305). The first question is, of course, how does Jeffares know? Yeats obviously had many "companions" in his life, and the reference does not necessarily mean a woman (cf. the reference in "The Two Kings" to "Companions of the Cheshire Cheese" [P113.2], an all-male group). And is "companion" the proper term for the woman with whom Yeats had his first liaison? Yeats might well describe Lady Gregory as a "dear brilliant woman," but would he describe her as "undone" by her youth or, shortly before her death, as "wrecked"? Why not, for instance, Florence Farr, whose declining last years Yeats had described in "All Souls' Night" (P239)?

Secondly, one might invoke an old-fashioned question and wonder if Yeats wanted the poem to be read in this fashion. Here the evidence does not always support the procedure of the *New Commentary*. For instance, in an unpublished letter to Macmillan (London) on 1 June 1934, Yeats's agent quoted what Yeats had written him about permission rights for J. H. Pollock's *William Butler Yeats*: "One thing however must be understood that we do not give any permission to quote from me . . . unless he cuts out all speculations as to the person or persons my love poems were addressed to."[20] Likewise, Yeats told Maurice Wollmann on 23 September 1935, "If an author interprets a poem of his own he limits its suggestibility."[21]

Yeats's belief in "suggestibility" leads to the final question about the biographical annotation in the *New Commentary*: is it helpful? Should we interpret and recall the opening of "The Results of Thought" as Yeats's remembrance of the decline of a few friends and look forward to the day when the identity of the mysterious "Acquaintance" will be disclosed? Or should we view the stanza as a statement about how the unfulfilled dreams of youth can lead to despair, about how man's own vision of "glory" can finally become "inhuman" and "bitter"?

There is indeed no simple answer to those questions, and many readers will continue to emphasize the biographical background to Yeats's work. But they need to be provided with the materials for such an approach in a more accurate and carefully annotated form than is found in the *New Commentary*. Jeffares and Knowland will doubtless revise *A Commentary on The Collected Plays of W. B. Yeats* in the light of David R. Clark's forthcoming edition of *The Plays of W. B. Yeats*. Let us hope that they do so in a scholarly and responsible manner.[22]

Selected Addenda

This list, which does not claim to be complete, deliberately excludes errors discussed above, obvious typographical mistakes which any reader will notice and be able to correct, misquotations from Yeats's *Memoirs,* or misquotations from other writers. I have also not cited the errors or misstatements in Jeffares's argument (pp. vii-x) that Yeats preferred the quasi-chronological arrangement of his poems planned for a projected edition in 1931-1932 instead of the two-part format used in the *Collected Poems* (1933), as I have written elsewhere on the matter.[23]

ix   Yeats died on 28 January 1939, not 25 January.

xiii	No publication date is offered for *Representative Irish Tales* (1891).
xiii	References to Wade's *Bibliography* should be to the 3rd ed., rev. Russell K. Alspach (London: Rupert Hart-Davis, 1968).
xiv	References to Ellmann's *Yeats: The Man and the Masks* should be to the new edition (New York: W. W. Norton, 1979).
xvii	*Fairy and Folk Tales of the Irish Peasantry* was published in 1888, not 1889. The meeting with Maud Gonne is listed last under 1889, yet it occurred on 20 January 1889. "Diana Vernon" is not identified as Olivia Shakespear; the *New Commentary* is inconsistent on this point throughout.
xxi	This discussion overlooks the new heading "[Parnell's Funeral and Other Poems]".
5 (P1.39)	The note is unclear: "rewarding" is not an "uncorrected misprint" in P. See my *Editing Yeats's Poems*, (London: Macmillan; New York: St. Martin's, 1983), 37-38.
5 (P3)	*The Island of Statues* is also in P (A1).
6 (P4.66-68)	For "Hermakuta" read "Hemakuta". Given the context of the poem and its other references to *Sakuntala*, Kasyapa and his various wives seems clearly the proper gloss for "the parents of the gods" rather than Richard Ellmann's hypothesis of Madame Blavatsky's masters.
7 (P5)	No dates are offered for Mohini Chatterjee (1858-1936). For "A E", read either "AE" or "A. E." (cf. NC 3, where "AE" is used). "Kanva on Himself" is included in P (A19).
10-11 (P9.3)	The quotation of "They were ... become Faeries" makes no sense. The "Gaelic writer" in Yeats's 1895 note is not identified but is in fact the one cited

Yeats and the *New Commentary* 173

	by Whitley Stokes in the essay mentioned in the gloss on l. 11.
11 (P9.55)	A tympan is not a kettle-drum (correctly tympanum or, in the more familiar plural, tympani), an instrument which Goll could scarcely find "Deserted on a doorway seat" and "carry to the woods with me", the end result being that "Our married voices wildly trolled". Rather, as Eugene O'Curry explained in Yeats's probable source, *On the Manners and Customs of the Ancient Irish* (London: Williams and Norgate; New York: Scribner, Welford, 1873), 3: 362-63, a tympan was "a stringed instrument . . . played on with . . . a fiddle-bow" (cf. 1: dxxvii-dxxix). In fact, the OED entry on tympan cites both O'Curry and Yeats's *The Countess Cathleen*.
11 (P10)	Yeats's note was not published until 1888.
19 (P16.7)	The horse was not named "Brown Dermot" but simply "Dermot": "My Dermot dear and brown" (l. 6). "Brown" is capitalized in "Brown Dermot" (l. 17) because it occurs at the beginning of a line.
24 (P17.3)	Yeats's reference to "Curtin" is not glossed: the American folklorist Jeremiah Curtin (1838-1906).
25-26 (P19)	Since Yeats's 1892 note (ignored here but mentioned in connection with 17.3) insists on Curtin as the major source, "Emer" must be an error for "Aoife." (The pronunciation of the two names is similar.) Jeffares is aware of this problem but still proceeds to gloss the poem as if Emer were correct. The only authority for Emer as instigator of the battle would be the "oral tradition" Jeffares cites.
27 (P20.5)	In the quotation from Yeats's note: for "symbolised in such poems" read "symbolized [in such poems]" for "in that it is imagined as suffering, with man" read "in that I have imagined it as suffering with man".

31 (P25)	Jeffares does not seem to realize that the epigraph comes from the Gaelic song cited in the note on l. 11.
32 (P28)	For "Quand Vous Serez Bien Vieille" read "Quand vous serez bien vieille".
32 (P29)	For *"Tier-nan-Oge"* read *"Tier-nan-oge"*.
34 (P33.1)	The spelling "Dromahair" was first used in *Poems* (1949).
35 (P33.13)	For "P 1896" read *"The Savoy* 1896."
42	The *Collected Works* was published in 1908, not 1906.
49 (P44)	Jeffares overlooks the fact that Yeats's translation of "A very old Arann charm" is included in P (A39).
65 (P67)	O'Curry's *Lectures* was not published in 1879; presumably Jeffares means to cite the 2nd ed. of 1878. O'Grady's *History* was published 1878-1880, not 1879-1880.
66 (P67)	The correct page numbers for O'Curry's commentary are 231-33. In this same paragraph, delete the [before "But", add a quotation mark after "book", and delete the elbow brackets around the final sentence.
80 (P84.11)	To gloss Clooth-na-Bare as a lake ignores the context of the poem. How can a "yellow pool' have "overflowed high up on" a lake? John Kelleher's suggestion that Yeats is misusing Clooth-na-Bare as the name of a mountain remains cogent.
81 (P86.2-3)	The source offered in P is clearly more to the point than the one provided by G. B. Saul.
86 (P92)	*Memoirs* establishes the date of composition as 18 April [1910], not 5-15 April.

Yeats and the *New Commentary*

86 (P93)	A review cited in section 9 of *Memoirs* establishes the date of the prose draft as quite definitely 22 January [1909].
88 (P95)	The draft of the poem is included not in section 7 but section 72 of *Memoirs*; that section is not "dated 26 February 1909" but can be dated [26 or 27 February 1909].
89 (P97)	For "Colville" read "Coleville".
91 (P100)	The poem is undated in *Memoirs*. The nearest dated entries are 8 August [1910] and 25 May 1911
92 (P105)	The draft in *Memoirs* is dated 7 August [1909], not 1910.
93 (P105.8)	The passage from *Memoirs* was written not in "September 1910" but on 16 September [1909].
95 (P107)	Jeffares dates the composition of the poem "May 1910", but the nearest dated entries to the draft in *Memoirs* are 8 August [1910] and 25 May 1911. The printing of the Cuala *The Green Helmet*, where the poem first appeared, was completed on 30 September 1910.
98 (epigraph)	For "Khoung-fout-seu" read "Khoung-fou-tseu".
101 (P112.11)	The Battle of the Boyne was fought on 12 July 1690, not 1 July.
114 (P115.19)	For "Mourn, and then Onward" read "Mourn— And Then Onward!" The poem is included in P (A27).
115 (P120)	The date of the poem in *Memoirs* is 5 April [1910], not 1909. Yeats wrote the prose subject on [3 March 1909]. The correct date for the passage from *Memoirs* quoted in the gloss on l. 2 is 18 May 1910, not 18 May 1912.

116 (P121.5)	Jeffares ignores the note in P that Dinneen is the only lexicographer to offer *libín leamhan*.
127 (P142)	There is no need for "probably:" Yeats travelled on the *Lusitania* on his way to America.
130	*The Wild Swans at Coole* was not dedicated to Edmund Dulac (or anyone else).
138 (P145.5)	"Reprisals" was not "written for *The Nation*". Yeats submitted it there only after it had been rejected by *The Times*.
139 (P146.1)	For "arms!" read "arms."
146 (P155.5)	Jeffares overlooks the apparent source of the name "Tom O'Roughley".
148 (P156.62)	The sentence beginning "It was published" in the note on l. 80 belongs at the end of the note on l. 62, and the correct publication date of the novel is [1977].
151 (P158.4)	For "*Memoir of Armagh Cathedral* (1882)" read "*Memoir of the Armagh Cathedral* [1882]". The passage cited is found on pp. 6-7.
152 (P159.30)	Jeffares does not explain the symbolic associations of "the Pestle of the Moon".
157 (P165.9)	Deslys was a dancer as well as an actress.
157 (P165.10)	The birth date of Ruth St. Denis has been elsewhere cited variously as 1878 or 1879. but 1887 is not an alternative.
158 (P166.6)	For "*Athene*" read "*Athena*".
161 (P173.1)	Pollexfen died in 1892, not 1890.

163 (P174)		It is possible to be more precise than "early forties" for the age of Mabel Beardsley when she died: she was either 44 or 45 (1871-1916).
165 (P179.9)		Not even Babar was capable of founding an empire at the age of three. The start of the Mogul Empire dates from his capture of Delhi in 1526.
166 (P181.1)		Yeats's comment on *Per Amica* should be cited from the Wade *Letters* (627), not from Hone's biography, where it is misquoted.
175 (P183.28)		The apparent death of Robartes at the end of "Rosa Alchemica" is alluded to not in "The Tables of the Law" but in "The Adoration of the Magi".
176 (P183.46)		For "Friederick" read "Friedrich".
181 (P186.1)		For *"specked"* read *"speckled"*; for "Yates" read "Yeats".
184 (P189)		Ellmann's dating of the composition of the poem in *The Identity of Yeats* as 1918 rather than 1919 is confirmed by Mrs. Yeats's annotation in a copy of the *Collected Poems*.
185 (P189.26)		Veronese was born in 1528, not 1525.
187 (P191.42)		The revised *Encyclopedia of Islam* has corrected the dates for Kusta ben Luka from (820-92) to (d. ca. 912-13).
190 (P193)		An unpublished letter from Yeats to Clement Shorter in the British Library (Ashley A2284) makes it clear that the private printing of "Easter 1916" dates from 1917 (prob. April), not 1916.
193 (P193.72)		No source is provided for the quotation from Pearse.
194 (P194)		For "Glashevin" read "Glasnevin"
197 (P197.6)		No source is offered for Yeats's statement that "we must be baptized of the gutter".

198 (P198.23)	Jeffares is free to invoke Mrs. Yeats an an authority for Yeats's sources, but the stag which he cites in Malory is less "of Arthur" (it is hunted and killed by Sir Gawain) than the one in *The Mabinogion*, which Yeats is known to have owned and read. What is called *"Le Morte d'Arthur*, III, 5" refers to Chapter 5 of Book III ("Torre and Pellinor") of "The Tale of King Arthur" in the standard edition of *The Works of Sir Thomas Malory* by Eugene Vinaver.
199 (P199.13)	Wentworth was Lord Deputy of Ireland until 1640, when he became Lord Lieutenant, not 1638.
207 (P201.57)	The correct date of the entry in *Memoirs* is not "1910" but 20 March [1909], and that text also makes it clear that "F" in *The Death of Synge* refers to Maud Gonne.
209 (P202.1)	No source is offered for the quotation from Aquinas by Villiers de l'Isle-Adam.
210 (P203.6)	Mrs. Yeats was born in 1892, not 1894.
210 (P210.6)	Jeffares's "Poet's Tower" is far more accessible in his *The Circus Animals* (Stanford: Stanford University Press, 1970), 29-46.
213 (P204.1)	A revised version of Bradford's important essay on the Byzantium poems has been available since 1963 in *Yeats: A Collection of Critical Essays*, ed. John Unterecker (Englewood Cliffs: Prentice-Hall).
214 (P204.14)	No particular passage is cited from *Journey to the Western Islands of Scotland*.
215 (P204.27)	Jeffares's "Yeats's Byzantine Poems and the Critics" was quickly superseded by James Lovic Allen, "Charts for the Voyage to Byzantium: An Annotated Bibliography of Scholarship and Criticism on the Byzantium Poems," *BNYPL*, 77 (1973): 28-52.

221 (P205.57)	The correct date for *The Secret Rose* is 1897, not 1907.
221 (P205.65)	The alternate meaning for "bawn" is not a "cattle ford" but a cattle-fold. Jeffares's citation of *"Notes and Queries,* I, ii, 60" is in fact to vol. 2, no. 34, of the First Series of *N&O* (22 June 1850), where "bawn" is described as "applied in the south of Ireland to the spot of ground used as a place for milking the cows" (60).
221 (P205.79)	As "the dog will have its day" is a common expression, the citation of York Powell's translation of Paul Fort is misleading without a reference to Yeats's essay on "Modern Poetry," where Fort is quoted (*Essays and Introductions,* 498).
221 (P205.85)	The note on "the Great Memory" has been misplaced below the note to l. 95.
224 (P206.9)	The note on Homer which belongs here will be found at 207.9.
250 (P221.7)	The phrase "mummy wheat" does not occur in "All Souls' Night".
252 (P222.34)	The citation of Porphyry's *"On the Cave of the Nymphs* (1917) 22" is clearly incomplete.
255 (P223)	Yeats based his version of *Oedipus Rex* on Jebb's translation as well as Masqueray's, and he did not begin work on it until January 1912.
256 (P256.9)	Of the apparent three choices offered for "the gymnasts' garden", the Academy is the correct one, as can be seen by the note and map in Jebb's edition. The Lyceum was neither a garden nor a place for gymnastics.
261 (P232.5)	The note on Hector is misplaced below the note to l. 15.

262 (P237.6)	The "God-hated children" are not identified.
265 (P239.46)	As in the note to ll. 52-53, "Sir Ponnabalam Ramanathan," not "Sri".
266 (P239.63)	Yeats's "Postscript" (not "Postcript") was written in the same year as the essay, 1901, not six years later. Jeffares fails to note that the texts of those two exceedingly rare items can be found in George Mills Harper's *Yeats's Golden Dawn* (London: Macmillan, 1974).
268	Jeffares does not indicate that he has only quoted part of the Dedication to Dulac.
271 (P242.25)	For "Osafume" (twice) read "Osafune," a small village in Bizen renowned for its swordsmiths.
276 (P244.3)	For *The Life of St Teresa* read *The Life of Saint Teresa*.
285 (P253.9)	Douglas Hyde was not the "author" of *Love Songs of Connacht* but rather their editor and translator.
288 (P254)	The correct title, as given on p. 131, is "Coole and Ballylee, 1931." The superseded title is also found at pp. 170 and 292 and in the Index to Titles (p. 523).
291 (P255)	For "Lady Gregory's grandchild" read "one of Lady Gregory's grandchildren".
291 (P256)	Jeffares is correct in stating that " 'World-besotted' is Yeats's importation", but so is the first line of his poem.
292 (P278.11)	For *"Memories . . . of Sir Isaac Newton"* read *"Memoirs"*.
292-93 (P259)	Mohini Chatterjee is identified as a "Bengali Brahmin" twice within seven lines; his dates are not offered until the second time.

Yeats and the *New Commentary*

297 (P260.16)	Denis Donoghue did not write "An honoured guest on 'The Winding Stair.' " He did write a chapter entitled "On 'The Winding Stair' " in *An Honoured Guest: New Essays on W. B. Yeats*, ed. Donoghue and J. R. Mulryne (London: Edward Arnold, 1965).
298 (P260.33)	For *"Apotheosis and the After Life"* read *"Apotheosis and After Life"*. Jeffares offers citations to pp. 153, 195, and 266; he then proceeds to misquote from p. 216 and to attribute to p. 219 a passage found on p. 215.
300 (P262)	In attempting to date a letter, Jeffares writes "postmark, 23 November; letter dated 'Last Sunday', but there was another that month". The letter is in fact dated "November. Last Sunday". Since 23 November 1931 was a Monday. it would seem that Yeats added "Last Sunday" before posting the letter, thus dating its composition [22] November [1931].
302 (P262.29)	Yeats wrote "fortieth winter", not "fortieth year". Considered in biographical terms, the reference would be to the winter of 1904-1905.
302 (P262.35)	Jeffares is correct in stating that "Yeats was fifty in 1915-1916", but his "fiftieth year" refers to the period when he was forty-nine years old (13 June 1914—12 June 1915). At the age of say, one, a person has *completed* his first year of life. Cf. Dylan Thomas's "Poem in October", written when he was twenty-nine years old and describing his "thirtieth year to heaven".
304 (P262)	For *The Mystical Element of Religion* read *The Mystical Element in Religion*.
308 (P268.9)	*The Pot of Broth* was published in 1903, not 1902.
309 (P270.3-4)	The standard reading of this famous aphorism is "the tragedy of sexual intercourse is the perpetual virginity of the soul", not "souls". Jeffares's source here is William Rothenstein's *Since Fifty*, but Rothenstein is recalling what John Sparrow said

	to him. In his own *W. B. Yeats: Man and Poet*, 2d ed. (London: Routledge & Kegan Paul, 1962), 267, Jeffares quotes from Sparrow's notes made after the conversation with Yeats and gives "soul". Dorothy Wellesley also uses the singular when she quotes the remark made to Sparrow in *Letters on Poetry from W. B. Yeats to Dorothy Wellesley* (London: Oxford Univ. Press, 1964), 174. Jeffares cites the remark correctly on p. 330 (301.12).
312 (P274.18)	"Thraneen" is not an Irish word but an anglicized spelling of Irish *tráithnín*; and Yeats would have heard the word long before Synge used it in *Playboy*.
312 (P275.11)	No particular source in Blake is offered.
317 (P284.8)	For "Donald R. Clark" read "David R. Clark".
319 (P287.1)	For "J. E. Wells" read "John E. Wells"; for *Manual of Middle English Writing* read *A Manual of The Writings in Middle English 1050-1400*; for 492 read 493. Jeffares misquotes a passage from St John D. Seymour's *Anglo-Irish Literature 1200-1582* but seems unaware that Seymour provides the text of the poem which was Yeats's source (in a modern English version).
320 (P288)	Although the speaker of the poem may invoke the words of St. Cellach, that does not mean he *is* St. Cellach, who was not known for his abilities as a dancer.
321 (P289.7)	The poem is also found in P (A97). Yeats's source, wrongly given both here and in P, was "Donald and his Neighbours", which he included in *Fairy and Folk Tales of the Irish Peasantry* (1888).
325 (P294.1)	For "Grace Jackson" read "Grace Jameson". Jeffares does not make it clear that the work is an unpublished dissertation.
328 (P298.3)	F. P. Sturm was born in 1897.

Yeats and the *New Commentary*

343 (P304.15)	Yeats's note refers to a Cretan coin, not a Sicilian coin.
344 (P304.27)	No source for the account by O Súillebháin (not "O'Suillebhan") is offered.
345 (P304.II)	Jeffares does not follow the line numbering of P for part II of the poem.
346 (P304.II.2)	Yeats's first poem on Parnell is included in P (A27).
347 (P305)	No note is provided on *The King of the Great Clock Tower*.
351 (P320)	Jeffares offers no information on the Indian mountains referred to in Yeats's note.
351 (P320)	For "quotation from *Il*" read "quotation *Il*"; for "(1820), a" read "(1820), in a".
359	Jeffares ignores the new evidence about the order of the poems offered in *Editing Yeats's Poems*, 65.
363 (P322)	For "1739-03" read "1739-95".
367 (P325)	For "Bourdeille" read "Bourdeilles"; for "(c. 1540-1614)" read "(c. 1527-1614)".
381 (P334.7)	Lady Gregory was not "about seventy" when the incident occurred but was in fact seventy.
381 (P334.12)	No gloss on "Olympians" is offered.
381 (P335.14)	Ruddock did not write "O sea-starved" but simply "Sea-starved".
382 (P336.10)	Yeats's final text reads "great dane", not "Great Dane".
389 (P341)	For "Come Gather Round Me, Parnellites" read "Come Gather Round Me Parnellites".
393 (P348.16)	For "Manini" read "Mannini".
395 (P350)	Jeffares fails to cite Masefield's "A Prayer for the King's Reign".

399 (P354.2)	No birth date for Seán Keating is provided (1889).
399 (P354.8)	For "blessed;" read "blessed."
400 (P354.13)	Jeffares's title of "Hazel Lavery at her Easel" is not attested to in any of the standard sources.
402 (P354.48)	No source for the Synge quotation is suggested ("Prelude").
409 (P357.III.11)	Seán Connolly's first name is not given.
418 (P363.15)	The end of the last sentence of this note makes no sense. And "Innocents" may well be an appropriate description of the Immortals, purged of their sins during the journey to Elysium.
419 (P365.13)	For "[Human]Immortality and Pre-existence" read "Human Immortality and Pre-Existence". Again, Jeffares is free to invoke Mrs. Yeats as an authority on Yeats's sources, but the passage from *Human Immortality* simply has nothing to do with the reference in the poem to "may be substance can be composite, / Profound McTaggart thought so". *The Nature of Existence* is obviously Yeats's source.
426 (P373.27)	The Abbey Theatre was not founded until 1904, though Yeats had been involved with other theatrical groups since 1899.
429 (P375)	Jeffares questions the identification in *The Poems* of Josef Tulka as the probable author of the epigraph. He offers instead Charles Augustus Tulk and cites three of his books. Presumably, if the epigraph was found in one of them, Jeffares would have said so. Since he is silent on the point, either the quotation has not been traced or Jeffares has not read the books. The citation of *Aphorisms* (1843) is tempting, the full title less so: *Aphorisms On the Laws of Creation as Displayed in the Correspondences that Subsist Between Mind and Matter*. The epigraph is not found there. One could

Yeats and the *New Commentary*

	again invoke Occam's razor and suggest that if an appropriate Tulka is available, some substantial evidence is needed to prefer a Tulk.
431 (P375.I.63)	Jeffares has badly garbled the quotation from Yeats's note. The text in P is correct.
433 (P375.II.84)	For "trees in" read "trees, in".
435 (P375.III.179)	For "Creeverow" read "Creeveroe".
435 (P375.III.222)	Jeffares offers no gloss on "the chain of small stones", whereas *The Poems* suggests a rosary. Has that annotation been rejected or simply overlooked?
436 (P376.69)	Jeffares gives a cross-reference to his note on l. 41, but there is none.
439 (P377.76)	For "Felimid" read "Fedlimid".
442 (P380.162)	No gloss on "Druids" is provided.
445 (P382)	Harun Al-Rashid was born in 766, not 716.
446 (P382.2)	No annotation of "Abd Al-Rabban" is given.
446 (P382.6)	Yeats's note on "the banners of the Abbasid Caliphs" is not quoted.
446 (P382.184)	The line number is missing from the note to "All, all those gyres".
453 (PA7)	There is no epigraph to *Mosada* in P.
455 (PA11)	There is no significant doubt that Renyi was a fictitious character. The article on "A Hungarian Hero of '48" was first published in the *Pall Mall Gazette* (17 Sept. 1886); Jeffares does not offer the precise date of its reprinting in the *Pall Mall Budget* (23 Sept. 1886), nor does he give the date of Molnar's article on Renyi (1975).

457 (PA14)	Jeffares is quoting from the second edition of *Irish Popular Songs*. No information is offered on Eamon an Cnuic.
461 (PA28.12)	For "(pp. 855-1919)" read "(1850-1919)". A 1917 text should not be cited when suggesting a source for a poem published in 1892.
463 (PA34.1)	The line number for the note is missing; for "May" read "may".
467 (PA44.3)	The line number is incorrectly given as 15. Jeffares's gloss on "white-scarfed riders", carried over from the *Commentary* on the plays, is far less likely than that offered by McGarry: an alb is not a scarf.
468 (PA47.8)	For "(c. 1530-c. 1500)" read "(c. 1530-c. 1600)".
489 (PA84.1)	For "Attrecta" read "Attracta".
501 (PA101.II.24)	For "(b. c. 1540)" read "(1550-1616)". Since Jeffares considers Owen Roe O'Neill only a "remote possibility . . . as one of the two O'Neills", it is difficult to understand why the body of his gloss states "possibily Shane O'Neill . . . but probably Hugh O'Neill". Who, then, is the other O'Neill of "both O'Neills"?
508 (PA111.15)	For "Athene" read "Athena".
514 (PA122.7)	There is no comma after "dream" in the text in P.
518 (PA125.20)	This note is incorrectly assigned to l. 21.
523	Add brackets around "Crazy Jane on the Mountain".
532	Add brackets around "Why should not Old Men by Mad?"

Yeats and the *New Commentary*

Notes

1. The two Commentaries will hereafter be cited parenthetically as C and NC by page number. In what may be the best-kept secret in Yeats studies, Jeffares explains that the first *Commentary* "was revised in four subsequent printings in the light of fresh information" (NC vi-vii). So far as I can tell, the errors in the text of the 1968 *Commentary* not corrected in *The Poems* remain unchanged. The Chronology has been partly corrected, no doubt in response to a list of errata provided by George Mills Harper in his review of Jeffares and A. S. Knowland, *A Commentary on* The Collected Plays *of W. B. Yeats* (London: Macmillan, 1975), in *The CEA Critic*, 38.3 (March 1976): 34-37.

2. W. B. Yeats, *The Poems: a New Edition*, ed. Richard J. Finneran (New York: Macmillan, 1983; London: Macmillan, 1984), hereafter cited parenthetically as P by poem and (when appropriate) line number. The English editions of *The Poems* and the *New Commentary* were published simultaneously.

3. Most importantly, I had forgotten that Sheila O'Sullivan had provided glosses on the "Wood-of-Wonders" and the "Wood-woman" ("Under the Moon"; cf. NC 81-82 and P86.9) in her "W. B. Yeats's Use of Irish Oral and Literary Tradition," *Hereditas*, ed. Bo Almqvist, et al. (Dublin: The Folklore of Ireland Society, 1975), 266-79. However, if Jeffares had looked at the source offered by O'Sullivan, Douglas Hyde's edition and translation of *Giolla an Fhiugha or, The Lad of the Ferule; Eachtra Cloinne Righ na h-Ioruaidhe or, Adventures of the Children of the King of Norway*, Irish Texts Society, 1 (London: by David Nutt, 1899), he would have discovered that it provides the correct annotation, contrary to that offered in *The Poems* and reproduced in the *New Commentary*, for "golden-armed Iollan" in *The Shadowy Waters* (P380.406; NC 442-43). "Golden-armed Iollan" (p. 127) is an important figure in the "Adventures of the Children of the King of Norway."

4. See *New Commentary* 42 and 234-35 vs. *The Poems* 213.118.

5. Many of the passages in the *New Commentary* are indeed not glossed, leaving readers in the dark on such matters as "Aretino" (NC 177), "Bardaisan" (NC 179), "Firmicus Maternus" (NC 342), "the Hymn of the Kouretes" (NC 341), "Lunacharsky" (NC 240), "Petra" (NC 170), "Simeon Solomon" (NC 168), and "Sherogues" (for "Sheogues"; NC 71), among many others. Jeffares claims that "passages of prose have been annotated where this has seemed likely to be useful" (NC vi), but with rare exceptions only those passages annotated in *The Poems* are annotated in the *New Commentary*. See, for example, the long note quoted in NC 42-44: the last two allusions, to O'Grady and to P. W. Joyce, are not included in the version quoted in *The Poems* and are not glossed in the *New Commentary*.

6. *Memoirs*, 123. Since in *Memoirs* "errors of spelling and punctuation have been silently corrected" (15), some of the minor variants between Jeffares

and Donoghue should be disregarded. Although Yeats's handwriting is difficult to read, Donoghue had access to a full transciption by Curtis Bradford, and my spot-check of the microfilm has not disclosed any instance where the *New Commentary* is correct and *Memoirs* incorrect.

7. Brandon, *History, Time and Deity: A Historical and Comparative Study of the Conception of Time in Religious Thought and Practice* (Manchester: Manchester Univ. Press; New York: Barnes & Noble, 1965), 49. See also his entries on Cronos and Kronos in *Dictionary of Comparative Religion*, ed. Brandon (New York: Scribners, 1970), 195, 400.

8. Opinions vary about the extent of Yeats's knowledge of Greek. In a 1939 essay, John Eglinton notes that "the patience and docility required in the early stages of the study of Greek and Latin were not his characteristics, and he had his crib spread out inside his textbook when called upon to translate." But an anonymous classmate writing in *T. P.'s Weekly* in 1912 claims that "in classics he held his own fairly well." See *W. B. Yeats: Interviews and Recollections*, ed. E. H. Mikhail (London: Macmillan, 1977), 1: 4, 2.

9. Farnell, *The Works of Pindar: Translated, with Literary and Critical Commentaries* (London: Macmillan, 1930), 14. Farnell notes that "Pindar is here expounding a doctrine taught in Orphic circles: the doctrine of a posthumous moral judgment of all souls, of Purgatory whereby the impure stains contracted by the soul while in the flesh might be removed, and of the cycle of a triple incarnation" (15), topics which interested Yeats for his entire life.

10. Jeffares, *W. B. Yeats: Man and Poet*, 2d ed. (London: Routledge & Kegan Paul, 1962), 2; 299, n.14. The *Almanack* and *Dublin Directory* are often bound together.

11. Hone, *W. B. Yeats, 1865-1939*, 2d ed. (London: Macmillan, 1962), 1.

12. I am grateful to the late F. S. L. Lyons for calling my attention to that source.

13. Little is known of the first Benjamin. He is not listed in the surviving British Library copies of the *Dublin Directory* for 1752, 1760, and 1765-1772, and his existence is apparently overlooked by William M. Murphy in *Prodigal Father: The Life of John Butler Yeats (1839-1922)* (Ithaca: Cornell Univ. Press, 1978), 20. Murphy makes Jervis Yeats the father of the second Benjamin. The later Benjamin Yeats first appears in the *Dublin Directory* for 1773 (*W. B. Yeats: Man and Poet*, 2; the British Library does not have an issue for that year). The system of indicating which merchants had the tax exemption did not start until the issue for 1783. Benjamin Yeats is so listed from 1783-1794, but not in 1795, the year of his death.

14. Ellmann, *The Identity of Yeats*, 2d ed. (London: Faber, 1964), 262; Wilson, *W. B. Yeats and Tradition* (New York: Macmillan, 1958). Jeffares

Yeats and the *New Commentary* 189

cites p. 59 in Wilson, which discusses Yeats's reading of some other works by Taylor but not his translation of Proclus; there are four references to Proclus elsewhere in Wilson's study, but none in connection with "Two Songs from a Play."

15. *A Critical Edition of Yeats's* A Vision *(1925)*, ed. George Mills Harper and Walter K. Hood (London: Macmillan, 1978), 190. Jeffares's citation is "185 ff."

16. Harper and Hood, notes, pp. 52-53.

17. Yeats, *Essays and Introductions* (New York: Macmillan, 1961), 509.

18. See especially Carolyn Holdsworth, *"The Books of my Numberless Dreams": A Manuscript Study of Yeats's* The Wind Among the Reeds, diss., Tulane University, 1983, 40-49.

19. Bradford, *Yeats at Work* (Cardondale and Edwardsville: Southern Illinois University Press, 1965), 18.

20. British Library, Additional Manuscripts 54902, f. 110. Yeats was, of course, interested in protecting the identity of living persons, but his motivation may have been poetic as well. In *William Butler Yeats* (London: Gerald Duckworth; Dublin: Talbot Press, 1935), Pollock did as he was told. I am grateful to Dr. John S. Kelly and the Oxford University Press for permission to quote from Yeats's letter.

21. *Letters of W. B. Yeats*, ed. Allan Wade (London: Rupert Hart-Davis, 1954), 840. See also *The Poems*, p. 612.

22. The notices of the *New Commentary* that have so far appeared serve as a sad commentary on the present state of scholarly reviewing. In "The editor takes possession," *TLS*, 29 June 1984: 731-33, Warwick Gould noted but a single error—which later turned out to be no error at all, as demonstrated by Mary FitzGerald (Letter, *TLS*, 20 July 1984: 811). In "What to make of W. B. Yeats," *The Guardian*, 14 June 1984: 21, John Montague described the *New Commentary* as "the fruit of a lifetime's thinking about Yeats, and probably the best book on the poet so far." One might protest that Gould is not a widely published scholar and Montague is a poet, but one despairs to find Denis Donoghue, not only a major critic of modern literature but also the editor of the ignored *Memoirs*, stating in "Textual Choices," *The Times Higher Education Supplement*, 8 June 1984: 20, that "Professor Jeffares's commentary is quite splendid" and "the commentary as it stands is superb."

23. "The Order of Yeats's Poems," *Irish University Review*, 14.2 (Autumn 1984): 165-176.

H. L. Mencken and the Harlem Renaissance

Fred Hobson

Charles Scruggs. *The Sage in Harlem: H. L. Mencken and the Black Writers of the 1920s.* Baltimore: Johns Hopkins University Press, 1984. viii, 213 pp.

Henry Louis Mencken is a strange case—a conservative who, in the 1920s, attracted mainly liberals as his followers; a vicious satirist who blasted the "hellawful South" and called it a cultural desert, yet drew scores of Southerners to his side; a man who wrote of "kikes" and said most Jews were "inherently incapable of civilization," yet numbered not only some Jews but *mostly* Jews among his best friends; and, as Charles Scruggs demonstrates in this book, wrote of "coons" and "darkies" and "niggeros," yet played a central role in the Harlem Renaissance of the 1920s.

What manner of man is this? Mainly one who, at some point in his fifty years of writing, attacked nearly every American group in the abstract—and also one who, bold-spirited and vigorous, loved the color and vitality of colloquial American speech. Why use "Negro" when "blackamoor" was more colorful? Not logic for the sensitive, but Mencken threw bricks and was never very concerned about breaking windows.

Thus it probably isn't as surprising as Scruggs contends that Mencken both issued racial slurs and championed black writers. It is really very easy to see why he was attracted to them, and they to him. They saw in him a kindred spirit, a writer who saw the mediocrity and hypocrisy beneath high American ideals, and one who blasted and ridiculed life in these United States, which meant life in the *white* United States, particularly below the Potomac. And he saw in them a critical detachment which matched his own, a spirit which, in literature, was naturally predisposed to the realistic or naturalistic vision he preferred. Most black American writers, he reasoned, had *lived* realism and naturalism; they could not write any other way.

But to contend that Scruggs's thesis isn't striking or altogether original is not to say that his study is not valuable. It is a first-rate book, well-researched, well-written, and sound in its judgments and conclusions. If most Mencken-watchers already knew that Mencken helped some black writers, Scruggs spells it out chapter, page, and verse. Drawing on the rich body of Mencken correspondence in the New York Public Library and on collections of the papers of black writers at Howard University, Fisk University, and other university libraries, he describes Mencken's friendship with James Weldon Johnson, Walter F. White, and George Schuyler (sometimes called the "black Mencken") and his influence on these writers and numerous others, including W. E. B. DuBois, Alain Locke, and Richard Wright. If he occasionally overestimates Mencken's influence on the Harlem writers—I would doubt, for example, that very little drama came out of the Harlem Renaissance just because Mencken wanted it that way—in general he convinces me that Mencken did indeed play a greater role in the Harlem movement than any other white American, and certainly a much greater role than Carl Van Vechten, who is often seen as the white link to the Harlem Renaissance. And Scruggs does this while accomplishing something else that many writers on Mencken have not: he sees the Sage dispassionately, astutely assessing his virtues and his shortcomings.

Scruggs begins by describing Mencken's taste in literature and his attitudes toward the Negro. Although he prefers to believe that Mencken was not a racist, Mencken certainly was in the sense that he believed Negroes tended to have certain traits different from those of Caucasians. But even well-meaning racial liberals of his day believed that, and besides it is pretty certain that Mencken preferred black Americans, different or not, to white puritans, philistines, prohibitionists, prudes, poetasters, and poor whites-no-longer-poor.

After outlining Mencken's expectations for black writers—and giving us that famous episode from Richard Wright's *Black Boy* in which Wright, as a young man in Memphis, discovers

Mencken's work and is liberated by it—Scruggs traces the growth of Mencken's interest in black literature beginning with the period just after World War I. Mencken had already been acquainted with certain black writers, notably James Weldon Johnson, before war's end. But in 1919, as Scruggs maintains, Mencken—the outspoken German-American who had been alienated from his country during the war—probably felt a certain bond with alienated black intellectuals. He took a new interest in black writers, and in his columns in the *Smart Set* and the Baltimore *Evening Sun* he urged them to write critically and realistically. In letters to several aspiring black novelists he said the same thing. He opened to them the pages of the *American Mercury*, which he began in 1923, and he approached publishers on their behalf. In certain cases, his enthusiasm for the new Negro literature compromised his critical standards. Scruggs tells us how Walter F. White manipulated Mencken to gain his assistance in publishing *The Fire in the Flint* (1924), a novel, chronicling Southern savagery, which drew its inspiration from Mencken's essay "The Sahara of the Bozart" (1920). *The Fire in the Flint* was hardly an artistic success— White had written it in twelve days—but White insisted that it had been rejected by the first publisher to whom he sent it because he had been too rough on the South. Mencken responded as White had hoped, approached his own publisher, Alfred Knopf, who then published the book.

Mencken's influence upon black writers came in part because he was the dominant influence on *all* rebellious American writers, black or white, in the 1920s; but it also came because he was not condescending as other white critics tended to be toward Negro writers. He was usually tough-minded and honest in discussing their work. But his bluntness alienated many black writers when he wrote two essays in 1927—a time when the Harlem Renaissance was in full swing—in which he announced that Negro writers had not, after all, lived up to the potential he had seen for them in 1920. Except for James Weldon Johnson (who actually preceded the Harlem Renaissance) and the social critic George Schuyler, the Negro renaissance, he maintained, had produced no first-rate writers. Since Jean Toomer, Claude McKay, Langston Hughes and other writers had become widely celebrated by 1927, it appeared Mencken was ignoring them. Whether he truly meant what he said (he probably did), or whether he felt that Negro writers had become smug and complacent and needed to be taken down a peg or two, his essays had an effect. The black literary establishment began to attack Mencken, while the rebellious younger black writers, the "Young Wits," echoed his criticism.

Mencken's influence upon black American writers was never the same after that. As the 1920s waned he lost a vital interest in literature in general, and, in any case, with the 1930s his distaste for the New Deal and liberal politics hardly endeared him to black intellectuals—except for Schuyler of the *Pittsburgh Courier* who remained a companion in spirit. But Mencken had served the black writer in the 1920s in precisely the role in which he was needed most. "The most powerful personal influence on this whole generation of educated people" (as Walter Lippman called him), "the most powerful private citizen in America" (according to the *New York Times*), he had given the new black literature legitimacy and respectability. But most of all he had given its writers self-confidence.

The role he played in the Harlem Renaissance of the 1920s, in fact, is remarkably similar to the role he played in the Southern literary renascence of the same decade (although Scruggs does not mention this similarity). Both white Southerners and black Americans had produced little truly significant literature before 1920. In that year Mencken issued his challenge to both—and, indeed, one might contend that his serious interest in black American writing grew out of his serious interest in the literary deficiencies of the white South: nothing would insult white Southerners more than to say that black Americans could write better.

After his challenges of 1920, both black Americans and white Southerners flocked to Mencken, writing him, praising "The Sahara of the Bozart," and asking his advice. He began a lengthy correspondence with both white Southerners and blacks, and the tone of his letters to George Schuyler and James Weldon Johnson and Walter F. White is remarkably similar to that of his letters to Howard W. Odum and Gerald W. Johnson and W. J. Cash. In nearly all cases, he advised realism, and the more critical, the more graphic, the better. Both the white Southern culture and the black American culture were subcultures which Mencken, in his passion for getting at the truth about America, believed had to be explored. To demythologize, to get beneath and beyond stereotypes to *reality*: this was his aim—although, in each case, in his insistence on scientifically determining the truth, he ignored the power of myth-making and missed the value of any literary art which went beyond satire and critical realism. He urged black writers, as he urged white Southerners, to get rid of the influence of religion, although in doing so he dismissed much of the richness of black—and Southern white—folk culture. (If black Americans had taken Mencken's advice to root out the influence of black preachers, they might never have listened to Martin Luther King.) And as far as matters strictly literary, in both the Harlem Renaissance and the Southern Renascence Mencken bet on the wrong horse. In Harlem he championed Walter White—and virtually ignored the greatest of the Harlem writers, Jean Toomer. In the late Confederacy he championed Odum and Julia Peterkin and Frances Newman—and missed William Faulkner.

Finally, even the charges and the cadences of his public utterances about the literature of Dixie and that of Harlem were similar. The indictment of "The Sahara of the Bozart" is familiar:

Once you have counted James Branch Cabell . . . you will not find a single southern prose writer who can actually write. And once you have—but when you come to critics, musical composers, painters, sculptors, architects and the like, you will have to give it up, for there is not even a bad one between the Potomac mud-flats and the Gulf. Nor an historian. Nor a sociologist. Nor a philosopher. Nor a theologian. Nor a scientist.

The charges in "Hiring a Hall," one of Mencken's essays on black literature, are nearly the same:

No Negro novelist has ever written a novel even remotely comparable to such things as *Babbit* and *Jurgen*. No Negro writing short stories rises above the level of the white hacks . . . . Even the Negro publicists make a sorry showing considering their opportunities. . . . Even on the subject of their race's wrongs they do not write as well, taking one with another, as the white scriveners who tackle the same subject. All the really first-rate books written by American Negroes since the Civil War could be ranged on a shelf a foot long.

The difference in "The Sahara of the Bozart" and Mencken's indictment of black literature is that "The Sahara" appeared in 1920, at the *beginning* of the (white) Southern Renascence; the charges against black writers came in 1927, near the *end* of the Harlem Renaissance which Mencken had helped to bring about. The difference is significant. In the case of white Southern literature, Mencken began as its most severe critic and wound up in the mid and late 1920s as its greatest booster. In the case of Harlem, Mencken began in 1920 as its most influential booster, predicting that a great Negro literature would emerge, but in the late 1920s he announced that it had not.

What does this say about Mencken? That he was a true southron after all (as he sometimes said he was), and that he was flying his true colors at the end? Of course not. If anything it shows (as Scruggs points out) that Mencken in 1927 felt the Harlem writers needed challenging—just as white Southern writers had in 1920. It shows again that tough-mindedness Harlem had admired in him from the beginning, a state of mind which refused to see the Harlem writers as exotics, as primitives, as special cases, but rather saw them, as he had earlier seen Catholic immigrant writers, Jewish writers, and Southern and Midwestern provincials, as contributors to an increasingly broad and representative American literature.

Failed Splendor: Edward Brunner's Remaking of *The Bridge*

L. S. Dembo

Edward Brunner. *Splendid Failure: Hart Crane and the Making of* The Bridge. Urbana and Chicago: University of Illinois Press, 1984.

This book will no doubt give every Crane scholar something to think about for a long time. Having grown accustomed to interpretations that are little more than changes in terminology for familiar themes and patterns, we've come to expect no real departures from a methodology and perspective established by the first wave of revisionists in the late fifties and early sixties. That Brunner could inspire an old pro like Brom Weber ("a radically illuminating and persuasively written evaluation of the poet," "a dramatic and intellectually gripping book") suggests that something new has indeed come upon the scene.

Up to a point, I share Mr. Weber's enthusiasm—or at least his wonder. To call Brunner's ideas original would be sheer understatement. And it's not just a matter of a few new insights. He seems to add an entirely new dimension to what critics usually see in Crane. Unfortunately, he adds it also to what Crane is generally thought to have seen in himself.

Brunner is a reconstructionist who finds in Crane the materials from which to rationalize a poetry seemingly fuller and more complex than Crane was ever thought to have written. That's one reason Brunner's insights appear to be so convincing: the image of Hart Crane that emerges is far more "perfected" as an artist. I'm afraid, however, that we are stuck with the original, for the more we read of Brunner the more we come to realize the utter unreality of the Hart Crane that he has portrayed and the more we come to see his book as the brilliant fantasy it is.

I begin with a cloudy bibliographical matter—a crucial one in that it touches upon the very design of Brunner's book. We are told by the publisher that Brunner "convincingly argues that the 1926 version is both superior to the final 1930 version and much closer to Crane's original intentions." But we cannot be sure there even was a 1926 *version* of *The Bridge* in the first place, if by that we mean a separate document substantially distinct in text as well as in sequence of poems. When Brunner quotes he cites no special text and no "1926 version" appears in an appendix to differentiate itself. So far as I can tell, Brunner's quotations could just as easily come from the standard version (1930).

Then we find Brunner saying, "Not only is the 1926 version an impressive poem in its own right, it is free of the confusion created by Crane's own assemblage of the poem." Own assemblage? Does this mean there is a different sequence from the one Crane made? We need, I should think, a great deal more information as to how and when the sequence developed and why Crane ultimately rejected it for the sequence in which the final version appears. And another complication: Brunner asserts that in the 1926 order, the poems emerge spontaneously and freely from each other. How, we wonder, can this opinion be reconciled with the fact of Crane's working on several sections at the same time?

In any case, on the Caribbean Isle of Pines in July of 1926, Hart Crane went into a frenzy of creativity and completed a large part of *The Bridge*. Brunner argues that, bogged down in his work on the poem—and defeated by his own social and cultural theories—Crane had a sudden illumination that allowed him to transcend "the strain and falsity of his effort . . . to be affirmative at all costs." Crane's biographers cite a number of reasons for this resurgence, among them Crane's reading of, and "triumph over," Spengler, but nowhere do they even hint at the kind of illumination that Brunner proposes, a total reorientation of certain fundamental attitudes. Crane, we learn, has come to a new understanding of motion and stasis and the involvement in these states of the "multitudes," whom he now sees not as "listless shells, content with their torpid routine, lying as corpses in a graveyard awaiting a poet to resurrect them

Brunner's Remaking of *The Bridge*

with his potent act of naming," but as just the opposite: they are "restless and driven with outbursts of undirected energy; and no one pauses for a moment to ponder their situations, to consider why they are so fervently on the move. Everyone simply desires to escape from the difficulties that constrict them; they long to blur themselves into some dynamic activity that postpones all conflict." Crane, Brunner argues, knew from experience the consequences of this urge to be in motion:

> To be on the go is to wish to avoid any complicated involvement, any lasting relationship with another individual. With everyone on the move . . . the modern city seems composed of isolated selves, each one intent on maintaining its own momentum. Just as a younger Crane had entranced himself with talismanic words, using language to stir events in motion, so the multitudes abuse the new mobility that is theirs in order to stream ahead in endless movement. Just as Crane matured, recognizing the emptiness that lay behind his own ingenious use of language, so the multitudes could be made to realize the hollowness behind their own infatuation with flight.

Still, in upholding "the notion of involvement as a countering effect to the lure of endless movement, surging momentum, soaring flight . . . he is involved with his own restless earlier self even as he turns to address the multitudes." Brunner goes on to say, "At one and the same time, [Crane] discovers that he has an audience for his poetry, that he himself is both intimately connected with that audience yet also in touch with an answer to its problems. The new sequence of poems rises directly out of his new ability to turn and view himself as he was in the past [i.e., restless, infatuated with motion], as he would not be in the future—and to see the action necessary in the present in order to link his past and his future." Believing that this illumination freed Crane from "all his ponderous plans and ambitious outlines," Brunner concludes that in the ten poems written in the summer of 1926, Crane "composes a long sequence virtually flawless in its execution . . . a personal epic that does not enunciate cultural synthesis of values in terms of our America (as Crane had once promised) but reveals . . . how it is possible for an individual to take bearings within a culture that offers no immediate support for such a task."

This, I believe, is the essence of Brunner's argument and it determines the perspective from which he views each of the sections, as well as the whole, of *The Bridge*. As I've implied, it is a perspective that distorts as much as it illuminates. Brunner transforms Crane's personae (Columbus, Maquokeeta, Van Winkel, Pocahontas, et al.)—and Crane himself—into complexities that are *"not here / nor there."*

Brunner's Columbus, for example, is a three-dimensional tragic hero; he has a complicated psychology that comes not from Crane's thought but from Brunner's alone.

> [Columbus] moves through a disorder whose origin he recognizes in himself: out of his new insight into himself, he redirects his own thinking, mentally changing course, and with his return to Europe vouchsafed, he is granted a vision of the universe as a jewel beyond value. The virtue he demonstrates is the ability to rise above disorder by recognizing the part he played in contributing to disorder.

And this notion leads to this interpretation of the opening stanza of "Ave Maria": "[Columbus is] crowing like a braggart, congratulating himself on his own superiority. Though he is in the midst of a pounding storm, his concentration is turned toward the accolades he expects at his triumphant return."

First of all, Columbus is not in the midst of a pounding storm. That's the whole point: the storm is over and he has once more survived. Relieved that his ship is still afloat but, at the same time, fearful that it will be lost in another storm and with it news of the existence of "Cathay," he calls out to his two loyal friends:

> Be with me, Luis de Angel, now—
> Witness before the tides can wrest away
> The word I bring, O you who reined my suit
> Into the Queen's great heart that doubtful day....
> To you, too, Juan Perez, whose counsel fear
> And greed adjourned,—I bring you back Cathay!!

These lines are straightforward; they reveal all of Columbus' "character" that Crane intended to reveal. When Columbus says "I bring you back Cathay!" he's speaking of the "word," not literally. But for Brunner, this statement epitomizes Columbus's "sin:" "His vindictive boasting and his determination to clutch Cathay is a form of greed that should be more alarming to him than any death by water."

Surely this is nonsense. "Ave Maria" is concerned not with the sin and redemption of a tragic hero possessed of a complex inner life but with the question of faith in a divine order in a world of violence and destruction. There are, it is true, many images of Columbus that Crane might have chosen. The one he did choose (mainly from Prescott) was that of a man driven by the belief that the mission to discover Cathay (or the Indies or whatever land lay beyond the setting sun on this "turning rondure whole") was divinely appointed.

Arguing that "in the multitudes of the new world are flaws that Crane's Columbus displays himself, precisely in order to counteract them and move beyond them," Brunner totally ignores the crisis of faith that I take to be the central issue. Our interpretations not only differ from each other, they are irreconcilable on every level of analysis. Brunner has little or nothing to say on the very lines and images that I believe unify the poem, as, for example, these on Columbus' longing for a sign from God:

> Into thy steep savannahs, burning blue,
> Utter to loneliness the sail is true.

Or:

> And Teneriffe's garnet—flamed it in a cloud
> Urging through night our passage to the Chan

Columbus took this eruption of an island volcano as a sign given to him on the outward voyage when

> faith, not fear
> Nigh surged me witless

Finally, in the brilliant night after the storm, God reveals himself in the constellations, just as the stars, as aids to navigation, blaze forth the means of safe passage:

> This disposition that thy night relates
> From Moon to Saturn in one sapphire wheel

> The orbic wake of thy once whirling feet,
> Elohim, still I hear thy sounding heel!

Sign, prophecy, and deity merge in a final vision:

> round thy brows unhooded now
> —The kindled Crown: acceded of the poles
> And biassed by full sails, meridians reel
> Thy purpose.

Brunner, however, sees in these lines an expression of the "total sense of the dynamic harmony of the universe" felt by Columbus not because God, who "grindest oar, and . . . Subscribest holocaust of ships," has again revealed himself and reaffirmed his Purpose, but because Columbus has transcended his moral weaknesses and now enjoys a self-awareness that makes it possible for him to see cosmic harmony.

I don't say that Brunner's reading is without appeal, especially to a reader inclined toward idealism; the vision of Elohim is not given to Columbus, it appears as a reflection of his "new magnanimity." Brunner then extends this pattern to Crane himself, who "like his Columbus had been boastful and possessive, insistent on the rightness of his vision; he had learned to modulate his ambition, and in the process had begun to find answers that had eluded him for years."

This may be fascinating but we accept it at a price. The poem cannot be an account of Columbus's moral regeneration and of his crisis of faith at the same time. Faith is tested by absence and violence, and God reveals himself at his own will; that is, gratuitously, not through the moral triumphs of the hero. Aside from shifting interest away from the theme of faith, which I can only once again assert to be virtually self-evident in its centrality, Brunner's thesis demands a sinful Columbus, and this in turn leads him to the kind of reading he gives to the opening stanzas. As for his application of the thesis to Crane's life, whether it is a valid description or a matter of circular reasoning, I leave it to Crane's biographers to decide.

Burnner's portrayal of Columbus is not an isolated case in his book: a similar argument underlies his reading of every poem in *The Bridge* (including those written after 1926) as well as *White Buildings* and *Key West*; roughly, the hero or persona is morally discredited and then redeemed. What is criticized as inferior poetry is considered deliberate, Crane's attempt to express the fallen world. I confess that I found the variations on this theme neither tedious nor without intellectual appeal—it's just that they are *wrong*. Here, for example, is Brunner on "The Dance," generally agreed to be the climactic poem in the "Powhatan's Daughter" sequence and an expression of the poet's ecstatic initiation into the mythic world of the Indian: "Crane depends . . . on his skill in evoking an Indian's view of a landscape tinged with excess, a landscape too masculine or too feminine. This requires no small amount of confidence in one's prowess, and it is understandable why Crane should have been pleased with the result." This argument calls for a dialectical interpretation of Crane's treatment of the landscape, an interpretation that until this time no commentator on Crane had even the remotest thought of making. The trouble comes immediately:

> The swift red flesh, a winter king—
> Who squired the glacier woman down the sky?
> She ran the neighing canyons all the spring;
> She spouted arms; she rose with maize to die.

Guided by Crane's marginal gloss, and no less by common sense, we assume that this is the poet's initial vision of Pocahontas, an earth goddess once fulfilled, yet now unfulfilled. For Brunner, however, Crane is simply giving an example of the Indian's habit of personifying nature, a habit from which Crane, for the moment, "withholds any appreciation." "There is even the suggestion," Brunner adds, "in the lines 'a winter king— / Who squired the glacier woman down the sky' of something old fashioned and outmoded in such gallantry."

If it comes as a surprise that these lines are meant to depict outmoded gallantry among Indian gods, Brunner's further application of his thesis brings nothing less than shock: "As Crane, the feminized Indian, floats downstream, he . . . hopes to create in the reader a distaste for the dissolution he displays. There must be sensuality described, but it must be a sensuality that is slightly overripe, fulsome, as in the luxuriant sound 'Feet nozzled the wat'ry webs of upper flows with its unctious zzz' sound and the lip-smacking 'wat'ry webs.' " This is really too subjective to argue with, but even "the Bawds of Euphony" must cry out when Brunner quotes only the first three lines of this quatrain:

> What laughing chains the water wove and threw!
> I learned to catch the trout's moon whisper; I
> Drifted how many hours I never knew . . .

and asserts, "The dainty languor of the 'I,' poised prettily over the line break, seems to mark indulgence, calling attention to its prominence." This would have been more convincing if the last line hadn't been "But, watching, saw that fleet young crescent *die*." It's obvious that there was only one reason for the "I" to be poised prettily over the line break and it was wholly prosodic.

Unable to accept, on the face of it, Crane's explanation of "The Dance," Brunner insists on calling these passages "deliberately overdone, arch and mannered." He brings the same bias to Crane's portrayal of Maquokeeta, arguing that "if the streams and valleys are haunted by the shade of genteel ladies' verse, the Indian council of war conveys a fantastic world of business men unleashed, a Rotarian club meeting gone wild." The rhetoric of this section, he claims, is pure bombast to reflect the bluster of the world being described. Brunner is telling us, in effect, that lines like "Now snaps the flint in every tooth; red fangs / And splay tongues thinly busy the blue air," if not bad poetry themselves, at least are meant to describe a bad situation. Now, all the lines quoted by Brunner as being something other than what they are strike me as being typical of Crane and his wide-ranging style. They are meant to be neither parodies nor expressions of any situation other than the one that they appear to be expressing; and to manipulate them as Brunner has done is to reveal a fundamental contempt for much of Crane's writing. It is a contempt that in Brunner's case is cloaked in admiration, though an admiration not of Crane as he is but as Brunner has created him.

Thus, in Brunner's conception of "The Dance," the most important motif is the opposition of a "feminine" landscape— "luxuriantly passive, alternating with spasms of wild hysteria"—and a "masculine"—"active," "but with activity [that] verges on pure frenzy, on displays of dazzling might." This opposition supposedly finds a synthesis in the last several stanzas: "The transformation now come over the landscape conveys the knowledge Crane values in the Indian: the perfect union of man and woman, a union that guides passivity and calms violence." This opposition and resolution has its roots, Brunner conjectures, in Crane's concern about the relations of his mother and father.

I cannot deny that there is a certain plausibility to all this. The trouble is that, once again, we find Brunner challenging Crane's own view of what he was describing in this case, "the conflict between the two races in this dance." "This note is puzzling," says Brunner disingenuously, "because such a conflict between races is barely evident at all; Crane may have had in mind not the effort to heal the conflict between the two races but rather . . . between the two sexes."

I shall not burden the reader with another interpretation of "The Dance"; I wish to say only that I am persuaded that conflict between the races is not only more than "barely evident" but is in fact the central motif of the poem and perhaps the entire work. "Greeting they sped us, on the arrow's oath: Now lie incorrigibly what years between." It has been the poet's mission to redeem the white man by recovering the Indian past of the continent or, in mythic terms, by uniting with Pocahontas, just as time, cleaved from space by the white man's iron, will be reunited by the Bridge. Only when the poet becomes Maquokeeta, assuming both ecstasy and suffering, at once burning at the stake and merging with the goddess, can the incorrigible years be redeemed.

Splendid Failure is probably the most important book on Hart Crane in the last ten years. But it is important not so much for what it persuades us as for what it does not. Brunner's Crane is a subtle poet, indeed a kind of poetic genius; he is, however, only the Platonic idea of the actual Crane. As to Brunner himself, his mind is obviously a keen instrument, "strung to a vast precision," but it is not one that yields "by inference and discard . . . true appointment from the hidden shoal."

Nightmare to Daydream to Art

Arnold B. Fox

Andrew Wright. *Anthony Trollope: Dream and Art.* Chicago: Unviersity of Chicago Press, 1983. 173 pp.

In his *Autobiography* Anthony Trollope speaks of the "burden of many pages" which novelists faced at a time when only the three-decker could hope to achieve popularity. Although many modern critics eagerly accept this burden and produce voluminous studies, Andrew Wright displays admirable restraint, and his criticism has been characterized by a welcome brevity. This new volume on Trollope consists principally of short discussions of three groups of novels. The opening and closing chapters present what appears to be the thesis of the book, a proposed explanation for the drive which led to such phenomenal productivity.

Trollope's readers were hardly prepared for the revelations of his *Autobiography*, revelations which explain his refusal to publish that book during his lifetime. The story of his boyhood misery is extremely moving, even if we allow for some self-indulgence on the part of the adult looking back. He considered his boyhood as unhappy as it could have been. He suffered horribly, felt himself a pariah, believed himself an object of scorn to those he most admired. Until the Post Office transferred him to Ireland as a surveyor's clerk, he experienced years of wretchedness, enough to make him wish he had never been born. It is true that he says his unhappiness disappeared the day he set foot on Ireland. However, the memory of his early years left him with a fear that was frequently an alloy to his happiness.

Wright's contention is simply that Trollope's difficulties led him to daydreaming as an escape, and that from these daydreams he turned to writing fiction as a means of making his life bearable. The need to write novels became an obsession. It started as a form of play—imagining a tale and working on it for months. The tale became a means of taking control of the nightmare of his existence and converting it into tolerable form. This outlet proved so important that he was never more happy than when working on a novel. Indeed, when he finished one, he was sometimes ready to start the next on the following day. His ability to create versions of life which ended well gave him increased confidence in the pleasures that he experienced and helped allay the fears of what the next day might bring. In his early years he was the hero of his daydreams. Later he was able to separate himself from his protagonist. In Wright's view the novels became Trollope's device for capturing and domesticating the nightmares of his early years, making of them comic structures which ended happily.

Where Wright holds close to the account in the *Autobiography*, there is little reason to argue with him. If Trollope maintains that he never included the impossible or the violently improbable in his daydreams, we can find here an indication that his powerful impulse towards realism goes far back in life. His ability to separate himself from his characters in later life can offer a possible explanation for the introduction of darker and more powerful strains into some of his later novels. But finally we are left with a sense of disappointment as we realize both too much and too little is made of this thesis.

Trollope's sufferings and dissatisfactions may indeed have led him to fiction. But the misery that he describes in the *Autobiography* seems to have diminished so markedly in later life that it is difficult to be convinced it continued to motivate him throughout his long career. The example of his mother is a far more likely explanation for his decision to make literature his second career. His own explanation is that he chose writing because it was the only career available to him, and the novel was the only form of which he considered himself capable. If he wanted a second career as a means of improving his status and his finances, surely that is not sufficiently unusual to require a complex explanation.

It is disappointing that Wright's book does not use this thesis fruitfully. Indeed, it appears only in the opening and closing sections, and the book remains a series of largely disconnected comments which the thesis fails to hold together. It never appears in the discussions of individual novels because it seems to contain no insights relevant to the discussions. I assume Wright believes that his approach explains Trollope's decision to limit himself to comedy, but this view is nowhere developed. His comment that "in the shoes of Phineas Finn he could walk with the natural grace denied him in actuality; and in the devoted statesmanship of Plantagenet Palliser he could project much of his wishful life" (p. 23) is unconvincing since Trollope could easily have chosen more impressive characters with whom to identify. The dull Palliser and the opportunistic Finn could hardly be the characters through whom Trollope would most likely compensate for the dissatisfactions of his own life.

A critic of Trollope can hardly avoid dealing with the question of authorial intrusion, and Wright returns to it again and again. Perhaps he would have done better had he dealt with it thoroughly at one point; his scattered discussions are too diffuse and leave the impression of indecisiveness. At times he treats the question with clarity and effectiveness. At other times he strives for a subtlety which proves self-defeating. And it does not strengthen his case that he seems always to defend Trollope. There is room for more uncertainty than he allows. Rejecting James's criticism that authorial intrusion destroys the illusion, he reminds us that fiction and actuality should not be confused and that art matters by virtue of being art. Unfortunately that does not prove a justification for Trollope's particular method. It may be true that Trollope's intrusions promoted fuller and more precise delineation. However, that is not the best line of defense, for there have been novelists who achieved such results without Trollope's constant reminders to the reader that he is only creating a fiction and can do with his story whatever he wishes.

It is probably true, as Wright suggests, that the primary effect of Trollope's intrusions is to reassure the reader of the comic quality of the story. But it is not certain that this constitutes an artistic defense. We might ask why such reassurance should be necessary. Perhaps the question is not the presence of intrusions so much as it is the quality of the intrusions. Do the narrator's comments increase our confidence in him by revealing qualities we admire and trust, or do they merely reveal a garrulous individual of limited intelligence? In *Barchester Towers* the narrator makes a direct plea for the confidence of the reader, and Wright interprets the plea as requesting "respect for the integrity of the relationship between the story and imaginative capability, what may be called the verisimilitude of the fanciful" (p. 41). In the course of constructing pleas of this kind, we should perhaps keep in mind the possibility that more successful techniques might have made them unnecessary.

When we refer to Trollope as a comic writer, we are communicating only on a highly generalized level. We may be understood to mean that his subject matter will include more or less gentle criticism of human weakness and that the outcome will be favorable, whatever catastrophe may be threatened. When the outcome is not favorable, the nemesis will be mild and will strike only those who deserve it. But comedy is a complex concept, and when a writer means something less than the obvious in using this term, or when he applies it to an ambiguous instance, it is a kindness to the reader to clarify his meaning. I occasionally had difficulty with Wright's use of the term. When he says that *Dr. Thorne* obeys "the laws of comedy" (p. 46), we can only wonder what laws are referred to. And as we come to Trollope's later and grimmer novels, in which the comic element struggles with an increasing awareness of the darker aspects of human behavior, it seems more evasive than illuminating to be assured that these novels too are "comic."

If Trollope persists in writing comedy, it is nevertheless true that he keeps pushing against the limits of this form, though certainly never as hard as he might. Wright's suggestion that *The Small House at Allington* should be seen as parody of the sentimental tradition is excellent. Such an approach seems the best way to contend with Lily Dale. But it is less helpful to be told that *Can You Forgive Her?* is "overpoweringly comic" and that it reveals "the ironies and shadows which comedy exists to compose" (p. 85). Perhaps we need more attention to the counterplay to comedy which exerts so powerful a force in this work and in so many others. When the comic impulse exists in almost constant conflict with opposing perceptions, it is not enough to impose the label of comedy on a work, for too much is brushed aside. The same difficulty arises in the discussion of *He Knew He Was Right*. It stresses all the parallels with *Othello* and sketches the sad disintegration of a young man whose story began so promisingly. But it ends with an insistence that we are still dealing with comedy, for after all, prudence gives way to romance and we encounter a large number of marriages. If this is the author's view, he might have concerned himself with the manner in which Trollope integrates his bourgeois tragedy with his comedy and the effects he sought to achieve through this integration. Does this novel reveal faintness of heart in an author who did not dare look at the tale he was writing? Does it show a sardonic streak that led him ironically to combine this squalid story of a failed marriage with a series of other marriages beginning with equal hope? Or was the book written for an audience that could tolerate only limited amounts of reality and needed to have that sweetened with an allotment of romance?

When Wright concludes that *Mr. Scarborough's Family* "is a grim comedy, but it is a comedy" (p. 148), we must certainly agree with him, but the comic impact of that novel probably needs clarification. Mr. Gray, who at first appears to be a highly sympathetic character, proves to be a comic figure, for not only is he easily taken in but he is a man who apparently has spent a lifetime deluding himself. We finally become aware of the fact that he is less committed to justice and morality than to legality. To many readers Scarborough is an appealing rogue, and we delight in his victory over the money lenders. In the end, however, he is only another comic figure, for we see that all his efforts are misdirected and vain as Mountjoy proves incapable of saving himself. And Henry Annesley is as sadly comic a figure as is Squire Prosper, for the guarantee of an inheritance turns this potentially useful young man into another otiose member of the gentry. In no other book does Trollope deal so sharply with the comic ironies of the pursuit of money.

Wright presents welcome clarification of Trollope's views. Trollope was certainly not an apologist for his age, despite his conservative stance. His treatment of the Thornes of Ullathorne is assurance enough that he was not committed to the past.

He was aware of social changes and traced the emergence of new groups with appreciation for their virtues but without sentimentality. He never failed to see the deficiencies of the aristocracy, and the society he presents often seems hopelessly dull despite its polish. The church almost never reveals religiosity, politicians are either time servers or entrenched incompetents, and money proves a corrupting goal. No careful reader will find a sense of complacency in Trollope's work.

The bulk of Wright's study is given over to brief discussions of seventeen of the novels. One of the more interesting passages analyzes Lizzie Eustace, but it is unfortunate that Wright follows Trollope in comparing Lizzie with Becky Sharp. Lizzie certainly doesn't have Becky's intelligence, and she never wins our admiration as Becky does. As we watch her efforts to keep the Eustace diamonds, we don't find it easy to sympathize with her. She most resembles Becky in the ironic disposition which the author arranges for her at the end. Perhaps it was from Thackeray that Trollope learned to choose so many unheroic protagonists. Trollope's leading men are often in the process of growing, of discovering more about themselves and the world, and thus they display error, weakness, and misjudgment. We see an example of this in Frank Greystock, whose behavior Wright describes as a challenge to the reader's generosity.

Wright's reading of *Phineas Finn* is perceptive. He reminds us that while Trollope describes Phineas as promising and impressive, we don't really see the basis for this evaluation. We never know what he stands for, and his earlier conduct hardly prepares us for his vigorous assertion of principle at the end. We never hear his eloquence; we merely hear of it. But Wright is correct in defending Phineas against the charge of being morally footloose. However he may be devoted to advancement, he is a serious and reasonably moral young man who attaches himself to the one highly principled member of Parliament whom he finds. And we must certainly share Wright's distaste for Harry Clavering in *The Claverings*. If he is an earlier version of Phineas Finn, we can clearly see how the two differ. Where one grows, the other seems only to regress. Phineas can attribute his success at least partly to his ability and his diligence. Harry owes his prosperity only to a trick of fate.

Wright's comparison of Louis Trevelyan and Josiah Crawley seems to me misguided, although I realize that other critics have also found a parallel here. Whereas Trevelyan becomes psychotic, Crawley is never really in danger, and this is the key. Crawley has an innate confidence in his rectitude, while Trevelyan can fall back only on a conventional insistence on his right to dominate. Trevelyan cannot discuss his problem intelligently with anyone because he refuses to allow any possibility that he is wrong in claiming power over his wife. It is this refusal to look at his own actions or to consider his wife's views that makes him so thoroughly unreasonable. In contrast, Josiah Crawley is constantly in doubt about what he may or may not have done and yet is never in doubt about his own moral rectitude. He is prepared to pay for any crime he may have committed, yet he is certain that he has never knowingly committed any. If he seems on the verge of insanity, that is because the world is proving unmanageable, irrational, and unjust. He is saved by the fact that he is committed not to his own ego but to a set of values. He doubts the facts, but not himself. Trevelyan has many doubts, but he keeps suppressing them. As a result, they force him into outrageous actions.

The principal shortcoming of Wright's book becomes apparent as soon as we try to arrive at a summary judgment. This study is constantly weakened by its desultory approach. While it promises a unifying thesis, that thesis soon disappears, and we are left with a series of random comments which do not add up to a point of view. The impression the work leaves is one of aimlessness. The absence of a controlling purpose appears to leave the author uncertain about the direction to take in his comments on individual novels. The chapter on *Orley Farm* opens with a comparison with *Great Expectations* and a suggestion that the novel is a study of the criminal conscience, but then it proceeds in a different direction. The discussion of *The Claverings* begins in a promising way and disintegrates into little more than summary. In brief, while the book has many enlightening passages, the serious student of Trollope is likely to find it disappointing.

Approaches to Biography: Two Studies of H.D.

Fred D. Crawford

 Barbara Guest. *Herself Defined: The Poet H. D. and Her World.* Garden City, N.Y.: Doubleday & Company, 1984. xv, 360 pp.

 Janice S. Robinson. *H. D.: The Life and Work of an American Poet.* Boston: Houghton Mifflin Company, 1982. xxii, 490 pp.

A reader expects much from a literary biography or from a biographical literary study. Leon Edel sums up the process in three words: "understanding, sympathy, illumination."[1] Understanding requires considerable objectivity on the biographer's part, not only concerning discrepancies between the subject's account and the biographer's discoveries, but also discrepancies between the subject's view and the perspectives of those who knew the subject and provided conflicting accounts of specific events. Sympathy requires similar objectivity when the biographer discovers evidence that reflects little credit on the subject, for the biographer must explain (without necessarily justifying) the subject's action or point of view rather than conceal it. Illumination requires new information based on solid research. This research requires flexibility when a discovery flattens a hypothesis, originality when the biographer draws unexpected conclusions from "new" material, and scrupulous documentation when the biographer identifies the sources on which original conclusions ultimately rest.

 The life of H. D. poses especially serious problems. H. D.'s circle included Ezra Pound, William Carlos Williams, Richard Aldington, D. H. Lawrence, Amy Lowell, John Cournos, Robert McAlmon, Kenneth Macpherson, Lord Hugh Dowding, Havelock Ellis, Sigmund Freud, Brigit Patmore, May Sinclair,

Dorothy "Arabella" Yorke, Ford Madox Ford, Bryher (Winifred Ellerman), and many others. These people are themselves the subjects of numerous biographies and literary studies which provide brief glimpses of H.D. from varying perspectives. They also wrote poetry, fiction, autobiography, criticism, and letters in which H. D. figures prominently. As if the sheer bulk of material, published and unpublished, were not enough to discourage a biographer from trying to research H. D.'s life thoroughly, much of the written record is contradictory, ranging from the extremely self-flattering portrait in H. D.'s *Bid Me To Live* (written and rewritten during the 1920s, 1930s, and 1940s, and ultimately published in 1960) to the highly unsympathetic portrayal by John Cournos (who admitted he hated H. D.) in *Miranda Masters* in 1926.[2]

Barbara Guest has managed to overcome the problems imposed by the welter of existing material. After reading her balanced portrayal, one cannot help sympathizing with H. D.'s personal and literary struggle to define herself. Guest's biography is noteworthy for the wealth of otherwise unavailable material it contains and for her efforts to be fair and even sympathetic to those with whom H. D. clashed. She strives for that objectivity required by understanding, sympathy, and illumination, and on the whole she is successful. She indicates in her preface that her focus is on H. D.'s life rather than on her work. Except for referring to H. D.'s perspective at the time of composing—e.g., " 'Asphodel' was written during a bitter and sometimes distraught period of her life" (p. 34)—she rarely discusses the art beyond drawing brief parallels with the life. This general neglect of the art suggests that the life of H. D.'s creative mind is less important than her actions, but Guest compensates by drawing extensively from H. D.'s correspondence to trace her artistic and intellectual concerns. Still, one might reasonably regret what Leon Edel has called "an absolute divorce between biography and criticism."[3]

The most intriguing events of H. D.'s life occurred in London from 1911 to 1919, when she became part of the Imagist movement and developed several lifelong relationships. Although she lived for another four decades, her post-war associations with other figures (excepting Freud) have been less interesting to scholars of literary history. Here more attention to H. D.'s art would have added to the value of Guest's book. Her post-war activities tended to involve either the constant writing and rewriting of her poetry, fiction, and autobiography, or the personal relationships chiefly of interest to herself. As Guest acknowledges, after the entrance of Bryher in July 1918, her biography becomes Bryher's story as well as (and perhaps even more than) H. D.'s, for the two lives were inextricably entangled. Bryher formally adopted H. D.'s daughter Perdita in 1927, supported H. D. for many years (even after H. D. had become wealthy in her own right), traveled with her, helped her to become briefly involved in film (notably *Borderline* in 1929), convinced her to become both analysand and student of Freud in 1933 and 1934, and saved her life or preserved her health on several occasions, from an influenza epidemic of 1919 through a subsequent series of psychological and physical breakdowns.

From Hilda Doolittle's birth on 10 September 1886 in Bethlehem, Pennsylvania, to her death on 28 September 1961 in Switzerland, Guest presents the major (and minor) events of her life in great detail. In the first thirty pages, she describes the events of H. D.'s early life—her Moravian upbringing, her efforts to please an undemonstrative and unsympathetic father, her engagement to Ezra Pound (while he was simultaneously engaged to at least one other woman), her leaving Bryn Mawr in 1906 after failing (of all subjects) English literature, her "equivocal" renewal of the engagement to Pound, and her departure for Europe with Frances and Mrs. Gregg in 1911.

Guest conveys understanding of H. D.'s responses to these experiences and influences by evaluating her subject's preferred interpretation of them. Thus, Guest describes H. D.'s departure from Bryn Mawr:

The reason Hilda gave for dropping out of Bryn Mawr was that she had become ill. She hinted at a nervous breakdown. This was untrue. Inexplicably, she failed English. "I loved *Beowulf!*" she wept. She also did badly in her other classes. She left Bryn Mawr because she had one failing mark, and the others were low passing. This was enough to discourage her in her mid-sophomore year, and possibly the administration as well. The truth was that she was facing dual worlds: an authoritarian institute of learning, and an equally authoritarian poet. It was either Ezra Pound or Bryn Mawr. "Remember," wrote Hilda about her abrupt departure, "I was an outcast." Pound, an outcast himself, was responsible for this. [p. 5]

Guest continues with H.D.'s settling in London, her involvement at the center of the Imagist movement, her marriage to Richard Aldington on 18 October 1913, her miscarriage in 1915, the various extra-marital entanglements of both Aldington and H.D. that led ultimately to the collapse of their marriage, the birth of H.D.'s daughter Perdita on 31 March 1919 (Cecil Gray was the father), and the friendship with Winifred Bryher that began in 1918 and continued until H.D.'s death in 1961.

Most admirers of H. D. who have written about her marriage have excoriated Aldington, but Guest scrupulously points out that both H. D. and Aldington suffered in the relationship and that fault lay on both sides. Guest does explore the relationships Aldington developed with Flo Fallas, Arabella Yorke, and Brigit Patmore during the war, but she also presents a balanced view, as when she describes the early phases of H. D. and Aldington's relationship:

She showed him her poetry; he formed an opinion, which was to remain with him, of this early, very early work that she was one of the finest poets of their era. He acknowledged her superiority over the other Imagists, and mostly over himself. Further, he was entirely sympathetic with the relationship she had had with Frances. Aldington encouraged freedom among lovers, and no doubt he was surprised to be challenged and chastised when his own path diverged. He could behave like a cad when it suited him; there was indeed a dubious quality in him that [Virginia] Woolf had sensed, and so had the young Hilda [who was almost 27; Aldington was 21]. But he was capable of deep love and abiding loyalty and affection. [p. 35]

Guest is explicit about H. D.'s refusal to have sexual intercourse with Aldington after her miscarriage in 1915 (due to her very real fear that she might die in childbirth), about her agreement with Aldington to have a "modern" marriage, and about her enjoyment of the siren's role.

Guest presents the opportunistic side of H. D.'s romantic "crushes"—after her engagement to Pound, she turned to Frances, then to Walter Rummel, then to Aldington, and later to Bryher. When Aldington was in the trenches (he enlisted following the Conscription Act of 1916), she flirted with John Cournos, tried to go beyond flirtation with D. H. Lawrence, and, after Lawrence rejected her, went to Cornwall with Cecil Gray, by whom H. D. became pregnant. The complicated relationships were the subjects of several novels, including H. D.'s *Bid Me To Live*, Cournos's *Miranda Masters*, and Lawrence's *Aaron's Rod*.

When Aldington learned that H. D. was pregnant, he took the matter calmly at first, partly because of his involvement with Arabella Yorke:

He knew that [H. D.] had a passionate sexual side; he had proof of it. He believed, however, that he had a moral obligation to Arabella, who if betrayed might become a "fallen woman." There is much conscientious dissecting of love and sex in [H. D.'s] letters. H. D. must have made him feel very guilty for his quite natural passions. And he generously wrote her that "damn it, Dooley, I believe in women having all the lovers they want if they're in love with them." Boy or girl, he had added. Aldington understood better than anyone what Frances had meant to H. D. He would never taunt her with her lesbian loves. [p. 99]

However, his attitude soon changed:

Between August and December of 1918 Aldington begins to make his exit; he starts to equivocate. Having had such an intense and intimate correspondence with Aldington all the time she had been at Bosigran [with Gray], H. D. had believed she understood his various moods. His first letter after the new year of 1919 surprised and unnerved her. He disavowed any plan to help her. He told her she must take care of herself and the child without relying upon him at all. He saw himself as helpless and poor. Worse, although he was being demobilized, he announced that he would not be able to visit her before she went to the hospital. She must plan her own life without depending on him. [p. 101]

Part of his change, as Guest indicates at the end of her chapter, resulted from H. D.'s new relationship with the wealthy Bryher and Aldington's knowledge that Bryher would care for H. D. He also knew that Professor Doolittle still sent H. D. an allowance of £200 annually (about $10,000 in today's buying power), hardly enough to make her wealthy but certainly enough to leave her better off than Aldington, whose prolonged absence from London during the war made him justifiably nervous about his prospective literary income.

Guest feels that H. D. was more fortunate in her marriage to Aldington than Frances was in her marriage to Louis Wilkinson: "Frances had made a mistake about Aldington. He may have thrown a stone or two at H. D.'s pedestal, but she remained where he had once placed her. In contrast, Wilkinson displaced Frances" (p. 38). Guest also acknowledges the important role Aldington played in the development of H. D.'s writing:

Aldington was not only useful to her writing, he was necessary. Throughout H. D.'s manuscripts and letters the reader does battle with her spelling and punctuation. Aldington adjured her *never* to submit her manuscript until he had been over it. He reminded her that she made careless errors in both spelling and syntax. With a blessing he adds: "H. D. cannot afford to be anything less than perfection." [p. 101]

H. D. was not always appreciative of such help. As Susan Stanford Friedman notes, H. D. "wrote angrily to Bryher about Aldington's 'psychotic' attitude toward her spelling."[4]

Reading Guest's biography, one assimilates a picture of H. D. that combines extremely attractive features with less admirable traits. By including both sides of H. D.'s character and evaluating H. D.'s motives, Guest helps her reader to view her in a sympathetic light. H. D.'s relationship with Frances Gregg is particularly well handled: "Beginning with Frances Gregg, her first and strongest love, the Fayne Rabb of *HERmione*, she was cherished and even adulated by the women of her circle, her lovers and friends. A lonely woman, H. D. was surrounded by a court, if at times provincial and limited"

(p. xi). After Frances married Louis Wilkinson, H. D. and her future husband Aldington met the newlyweds at the Victoria Station Hotel in 1912. H. D. "quickly credited Frances with taste, and it must be admitted, because it seeps through her account, she was jealous. Frances had triumphed over her" (p. 37). When Wilkinson invited H. D. to accompany the pair on their honeymoon, H. D. decided to drop everything to do so, but fortunately Ezra Pound "stopped this impulsive and ill-judged step" (p. 37).

When H. D. met Frances again in 1925, their situations had altered. Wilkinson had left Frances, who lived in London with her mother: "The two Gregg ladies now shared a single room. H. D. had spotted Frances in the neighborhood, but, to her discredit, had been so shocked at the circumstances in which she had found Frances that she tried to avoid her. She even wrote to Bryher, in reference to Frances, how much she hated poverty. She wondered how two women could live in one room; it was so uncivilized!" (p. 178). Instead of leaving matters here, however, Guest accounts plausibly for what superficially appears to be callous disloyalty:

H. D. had other reasons for wishing to avoid Frances, and they were complicated ones. Frances represented an episode of her youth, a love from which she had never detached herself. Further, Frances, who was the closest observer of the original H. D., would not be a likely person to permit the present H. D. to escape her stern and critical eye. H. D. could neither vamp, nor pretend, nor cast any more spells with one of the former conspirators of her theatrics. Frances had wounded H. D. by helping Wilkinson write *The Buffoon* (1916) with its brutal distortions of her friend. More than anyone else, Frances was seen by H. D. as a shadow goddess of herself. [p. 178]

Frances had earlier distracted the attention of Pound from H. D. during their engagement. Ironically Frances later fell in love with Kenneth Macpherson, who himself fell in love with H. D. and then eventually became Bryher's second husband. Frances, her mother, and her daughter were killed in 1941 by the German bomb that hit their Plymouth home. By tracing such relationships in all their complexity, Guest provides an objective treatment that is cautiously sympathetic to H. D.

In addition to meeting criteria of understanding and sympathy, Guest's book is illuminating, not only in the exhaustive tracing of H. D.'s actions and relationships, but also in less obvious ways. Of special note is Guest's account of the true state of H. D.'s financial circumstances. Despite the prevailing view that H. D. was poor until Bryher made lavish settlements on her, Guest reveals that H. D. had other assets.

In 1940 after she had returned to London from Switzerland, Bryher settled £70,000 on H. D. (today about $2 million) with an income for life of £2,450 yearly. H. D. already had inherited money from her family. Her businessman brother Harold had invested wisely for her. Indeed, she was well-off. And yet H. D. always considered herself impoverished—not exactly poor, but she feared to spend any money. [p. 264]

When Bryher saw Harold Doolittle in the United States during the early 1950s, she "learned to her surprise that H. D. was a wealthy woman in her own right. Now she chose to speak out to H. D. about money. She had always paid all bills willingly, but the idea of money idling away in a bank was too much for her" (pp. 295-96).

Bryher wrote to H. D., "I think you don't realize it but you have over £50,000 tucked away with [Harold] in good American dollars and he is worried *because you never spend any of it,* and if anything should happen to you, due to death duties, the American government would take about half of it. . . . Why you've got almost as much as I have" (p. 296; italics Bryher's, ellipsis mine).

Guest comments that "Together with Bryher's 1940 settlement on her, H. D. in today's terms would have been worth several million dollars" (p. 296), but she does not leave matters here. To explain H. D.'s attitude, Guest points to H. D.'s lack of money during her early years in London and to the financial difficulties of most of H. D.'s literary friends.

In reality there was this other side to the story. H. D. was in fact extremely well-off. Her brother managed her affairs superbly, and after the sale of family property in New Jersey she was a rich woman. There is the ring of the miser when H. D. writes Aldington that as she cannot get funds through to Switzerland and is only living on an income, which she infers [sic] is small, that she will be able only to send him one hundred dollars a year. After much hesitation, she continued to do so. Ezra Pound always thought H. D. lived off Bryher and that was the main reason for her remaining with Bryher. In fact, Bryher was constantly sending checks to H. D., which were usually hoarded. At the same time H. D. was very thoughtful about pointing out to Bryher writers who deserved financial aid. [pp. 296-97]

Such objective handling of these and similar details adds credibility to Guest's interpretation.

It comes as a disappointment that Guest, very careful to be fair to Aldington as well as to H. D. when marriage is the issue, would be so unfair to him in other areas. She says, for example, that his poetry "is a hair's breadth from the Georgians', self-indulgent and sentimental, especially in the celebrated 'A Dream in the Luxembourg Gardens' [sic]" (p. 82). She also objects to "a typical Aldington emphasis" on "price and sales" (p. 288), as if somehow income should be beneath the concern of someone supporting himself solely by his pen since 1912. Most unfair is her belief that Aldington's "army career . . . had not been all that disagreeable," based on her comparison of Aldington's novel *Death of a Hero* and Robert Graves's *Goodbye to All That* (pp. 85-86). Another lapse occurs in Guest's claim that during World War II, "Aldington . . . was living in Hollywood at the Garden of Allah, escaping the war and basking in the sun" (p. 273). "Escaping" does not fairly describe Aldington during these years. Born in 1892, he was over military age, and he had left England in 1928, long before the discomforts and dangers of war-time London. Nor does "basking" seem appropriate for Aldington during these years, when he wrote screen-plays and numerous articles, researched an authoritative biography of the Duke of Wellington, and compiled a monumental anthology of English literature.

These erroneous impressions may have been gleaned from Guest's sources, but the reader has no way of knowing, since Guest does not document those sources. In the preface, Guest apologizes for any "mistakes made by a writer unaccustomed to the strict overtures of research" (p. xii), but her problem does not seem to involve the actual research. She has interviewed scores of people, reviewed reams of correspondence at many locations, and visited the places H. D. knew. She has provided an impressive, if not quite up-to-date, selected bibliography of published sources—omitting, surprisingly, Susan Stanford Friedman's *Psyche Reborn* and many articles on H. D., although Guest acknowledges Friedman's "research and kindness" (p. xiii). Guest has also summarized the manuscript holdings of nine major repositories. Nevertheless, further documentation is necessary to make her sources useful to scholars. She quotes Aldington, for example, describing his mother as "a country wench. She copped the old fellow down hunting" (p. 34). If Aldington published this statement, where does it appear in print? If it is from a letter, which seems more likely, who was the recipient, where is the document, and when did Aldington write it? Without knowing the date or, for that matter, the recipient, one has no context for Aldington's statement. H. D., among others, often tailored descriptions to accommodate the biases of her correspondents and revised her perspective as time passed, placing key statements into contexts which qualified their meaning. A reader must be able to see features of context to understand the mere wording. The omission of notes in this book was unfortunate.

Despite the lack of documentation and the infrequent lapses from objectivity (usually, it must be admitted, in matters only peripheral to H. D.), Guest has made a valuable contribution to our understanding and knowledge of the poet. One might wish that Guest had paid more attention to the relationship between H. D.'s experience and the development of her art, but the reader must ultimately appreciate the thoroughness with which Guest has uncovered and presented the details of the poet's life. In terms of Edel's criteria, Guest's biography will remain an invaluable source for those interested in the development of modern British literature and, particularly, H. D.'s role in that development.

The subtitle of Janice S. Robinson's *H. D.: The Life and Work of an American Poet* suggests an approach different from Guest's. At first the reader feels that the book will attempt to integrate the life with the art, and the early sections of the book seem to keep this promise. In her early discussions of H. D.'s

Moravian heritage, for example, Robinson lays the foundation for useful application of this information to H. D.'s later poetry and prose, and she states early that H. D.'s work with Freud will provide the context for her critical approach. Overall, however, Robinson's biography fails to provide understanding, sympathy, and illumination because she did not really set out to investigate the life of H. D. Instead, she has preferred to embark on a search for biographical clues which support an extremely narrow reading of H. D.'s work.

Any biography or biographical / critical study must ultimately depend on valid research and the kind of mental flexibility which Guest demonstrates when she concedes that she has "willingly exchanged fantasy for fact" (p. xii). Instead of responding to the complexity and subtlety of H. D.'s poetry, Robinson reduces H. D.'s poetic genius to the mere encryption of her experience into verse, and H. D.'s character becomes mere caricature.

Robinson's thesis is that H. D. and D. H. Lawrence became lovers after the Lawrences stayed in H. D.'s sitting-room flat at 44 Mecklenburgh Square in 1917 and that the subsequent writing of H. D. and D. H. Lawrence consists solely of coded retellings of their "affair." According to Robinson, Ezra Pound, Richard Aldington, and D. H. Lawrence, in their several ways, dominated, victimized, and abused H. D. Pound, after awakening H. D.'s poetic gift and drawing her to Europe, sought to keep her under his control by burying her in the short-lived Imagist movement. Lawrence supposedly abandoned her after becoming potentially liable for a paternity suit. Aldington, however, is the real villain of Robinson's book. She alleges that Aldington ruined H. D.'s life, cold-bloodedly and spitefully, and then spent his subsequent career trying to minimize her literary achievement, to conceal her purported affair with Lawrence, and to establish himself as the foremost writer of their circle.

Robinson's dastardly Aldington—who bears little resemblance to the novelist, poet, biographer, and critic of the same name—was insidiously clever in his manipulation of literary history. Robinson gives Aldington full credit for almost pulling off the literary fraud of the century, foiled only by Robinson's superior cleverness. Here, according to Robinson, is how he did it:

[In January 1953] H. D. received from Aldington a bibliography of his writings on D. H. Lawrence. The list contained four book-length essays, including his recently completed *Portrait of a Genius, But* . . . , as well as eighteen other books of Lawrence's poems, essays, letters, or novels that he had edited and supplied with introductions. In several of his editions of Lawrence's work Aldington made silent editorial changes to the original text. Most of the volumes of Lawrence's work now in print have been altered by Aldington. The full extent of these adjustments will not be known until a scholarly edition of Lawrence's work is produced.

Until H. D. received the bibliography of Aldington's work on Lawrence, she was completely unaware of the extent of his involvement in creating the Lawrence legend that excluded her. Of course, she never became aware of the hundreds of letters Aldington wrote explaining and interpreting Lawrence's work and supplying character identifications and biographical information to a large number of correspondents. Much of this information was useful, but there was also a considerable amount of invention and misleading advice which has become enshrined as fact over the years. [pp. 349-50n]

According to Robinson, Aldington not only excluded H. D. almost entirely from his "recently completed" biography of Lawrence (actually the book had appeared in print in 1950), but he also "helped" Harry T. Moore and Edward Nehls in their biographies to be certain that none of the "truth" about H. D. and Lawrence would emerge.

As one finally learns after a well-spaced series of progressively damning innuendoes—Aldington's "testimony on this matter is not entirely reliable" (p. 29), "Aldington had taken advantage of the situation" (p. 59), Aldington had a "habit of fabricating stories that have no factual basis" (p. 66), "Richard Aldington was jealous of H. D.'s relationship with Lawrence" (p. 137)— there was a cover-up:

A good part of the cover-up was accomplished by Richard Aldington, whose motives could be interpreted as noble; perhaps he was trying to protect his wife from scandal. But since he in no way behaved in a protective role in other aspects of their relationship, it is more realistic to interpret his motives as related to his pride; he was attempting to protect *himself* from a scandal. [p. 142]

Now why would Aldington want to do this? According to Robinson, both H. D. and Lawrence spent their subsequent careers writing exclusively about their relationship. Thus, in *Lady Chatterley's Lover*, Mellors is Lawrence, Lady Chatterley is H. D., and Sir Clifford is Richard Aldington. Aldington, supposedly terrified that readers would recognize him as Clifford, cleverly pretended to support Lawrence as a great writer because he had an ulterior motive: he could thus impose his point of view on an unsuspecting public.

These accusations may hold some charm for those who are predisposed to demean Aldington (indeed, Robinson frequently uses the obligatory *bitter* to describe Aldington and his books), or to conspiracy theories in general. However, the charges are patently false. Indeed, they were demonstrably refuted before Robinson raised them. As one can document almost everywhere except in Robinson's book, Aldington consistently praised H. D. above the other Imagists (including himself), helped her to find publishers, and edited many of her manuscripts (chiefly for spelling—H. D.'s was worse than Yeats's). Aldington did not always approve Lawrence's work with the blind adulation of most of Lawrence's early defenders (for example, he disliked Lawrence's sneering depiction of H. D. in *Aaron's Rod* and felt that Lawrence's obscenity in *Lady Chatterley's Lover* would distract readers from the novel's purpose). Nevertheless, Aldington wrote approving reviews of Lawrence's work and provided Lawrence scholars with the first reliable biography. He also helped distribute copies of *Lady Chatterley's Lover* when such activity was illegal and remained on friendly terms with Lawrence as late as 1928, when Lawrence and Frieda visited him at Port-Cros. These are not the acts of a man who saw himself in Lawrence's protrayal of Sir Clifford.

Robinson matches Aldington with Sir Clifford in this way:

Like Aldington, Sir Clifford is a writer. Like Aldington he fought in World War I. It is a well-known fact, admitted by Aldington, that he broke down psychically after the war. But Clifford is of course more than a simple portrait; he is a class type, and his attributes resemble other characters from Lawrence's past. After her husband's death, Frieda identified Clifford with Lawrence. Yet to Richard

Aldington the psychic and situational resemblance to himself was all too recognizable. [p. 144]

There are problems here. Aldington was hardly in the same social class as Sir Clifford. If being in the war and being a writer are sufficient identifying marks, Sir Clifford could as easily have been Osbert or Sacheverell Sitwell, Edmund Blunden, or many many others. If shell-shock were sufficient to explain Sir Clifford's use of a wheelchair, thousands more would qualify, although not necessarily Aldington, whose resilience to his shell-shock suggests an unusual psychological strength. Besides, it is *not* a "well-known fact" that Aldington "broke down psychically after the war"—that is an extreme overstatement. It is true, and admitted by Aldington, that after-effects of the war troubled him for many years, but not to an extent that would justify the word "breakdown." Frieda Lawrence, to put it mildly, is scarcely a reliable source for any information, whether about herself or Lawrence. In short, the implication that Aldington recognized a resemblance between Sir Clifford and himself requires some sort of evidence. the absence of such support in Robinson's book suggests that there is none to be had.

When Paul Delany (whose book appeared long after Aldington might have been able to help him) treats parallels between the Chatterleys and the Asquiths, he has the advantage of being able to support them. Delany notes that Lawrence

used the Asquiths' marriage as a principal source for the Chatterleys in *Lady Chatterley's Lover*. In both cases they married when the bride was twenty-three, the groom twenty-nine; Connie, like Lady Cynthia, is of Scots ancestry; Clifford, like Herbert Asquith, has an older brother who is killed in 1916, is shattered by a war wound, and dabbles in literature. The novel is the culmination of Lawrence's perennial fantasies of carrying off an imagined English aristocrat rather than a real German one; having chosen the path of exogamy and exile, he nonetheless hankered after an ideal reconciliation with English womanhood and thus, indirectly, with England itself.[5]

Delany's parallels are more numerous and more convincing than Robinson's, particularly since Delany cites correspondence between Lawrence and Cynthia Asquith to support them.

Robinson's thesis requires that Aldington be the enemy of both H. D. and Lawrence, and to this requirement any pretense of objectivity toward Aldington must yield. She quotes Aldington's letter to H. D. of 17 January 1953 to establish his supposed lack of enthusiasm for her "Madrigal" (ultimately published as *Bid Me To Live*):

"I finished reading Madrigal with [a] temp of about 101°, which probably accounts for the fact that towards the end I found myself rather exhausted, by the intensity of all these self-absorbed emotionalists." Characteristically, he reacted with sarcasm, saying that "Madrigal" might be material for a three-act play. "It seems to me, thinking it over, that if you could hit the right structure and tone, you have the material for a good 3-act play. Of course, for the stage, it would have to have some violent ending—tragical or farcical." He told her that although the book was excellent he didn't know who would publish it, and asked if he might show it to a publisher. [pp. 348-49]

Guest provides an earlier portion of the letter which Robinson omits:

It is awfully good, Dooley, really good, authentic and concentrated, better than the equivalent chapters in *Aaron's Rod* where Lorenzo was in one of his fits and guying us all.
  You bring out splendidly L's mimicry and you were right to do so. It was something much more than monkey tricks, because he could also do it on paper, when it becomes genius. It was that plus his refusal to take people at their own valuation and his seeing through their self-deceptions which made him so hated . . . . [p. 288; ellipsis Aldington's]

Robinson's inclusion of a passage that seems to support her thesis and her exclusion of a passage that seems to refute it suggest careful selection on her part. Her notion that Aldington tried to suppress *Bid Me To Live* does not accord with Aldington's rejection of H. D.'s plan to use the pseudonym

"Delia Alton" rather than her familiar initials. Aldington, like Horace Gregory, Bryher, and Norman Holmes Pearson, felt that without the familiar H. D. signature, the public might not read *Bid*.

Another instance of Robinson's misuse of sources occurs in an insinuation that is unfair not only to H. D., but also to Ford Madox Ford, Aldington, and Harry T. Moore:

> H. D. implies that Aldington was in some way behind Lawrence's troubles in 1917 and 1918. They were also due, of course, to "war-hysteria." But why was Lawrence suspect in the first place? It has been suggested by David Garnett and reported by Harry T. Moore that Ford Madox Ford might have warned the government in 1915 that Lawrence was a pro-German, thus causing all of Lawrence's troubles during the war years. It should also be noted, however, that during the time that Ford is alleged to have taken this action Richard Aldington was serving as his private secretary. [p. 202]

Careful research and judicious interpretation are lacking here. Moore reported the idea of Ford's warning the government about Lawrence as something Garnett "believes," and then he quoted Aldington's comment (which Robinson omits, although it is on the very page she cites). In Aldington's letter to Moore of 5 May 1960, he wrote,

> I'd hate to think that fat Fordie'had been so goddam mean as to put in an unfavourable official report on the civisme of Lorenzo and Frieda. If he did, what a bastard. Of course, he needed to whitewash himself—he looked as much a Hun as Hindenburg—and, it is true, that pre-war he was friends with the Minister of Education, C. F. G. Masterman.[6]

In Robinson's version, Garnett's opinion (which Moore did not accept) has become Moore's, and Aldington's uncertainty about Ford's role has become Aldington's complicity simply because he worked with Ford briefly (he quit, in his words, after he became "fed-up" with Ford). The basis for H. D.'s supposed opinion that Aldington had something to do with Lawrence's troubles, as Robinson indicates in her notes, is a short story, "Pilate's Wife." In any event, Robinson's case is less plausible than another reason for the government's interest in Lawrence. His wife, Frieda, was related to Baron von Richthofen, so a report to the government about Lawrence's German connections was hardly necessary in the first place.

A major flaw in Robinson's research technique results from her principles of selection and the nature of the sources she draws from. Those writers involved in H. D.'s life during her associations with Lawrence include Aldington, Cournos, Arabella Yorke, Brigit Patmore, Cecil Gray, and Frieda Lawrence. These wrote many novels, poems, letters, and autobiographical accounts addressing events from vastly differing perspectives. What occurred among the Lawrences, Arabella, Brigit, Cecil Gray, Aldington, and H. D. remains confusing, for how does one reconcile the conflicting accounts of Cournos's *Miranda Masters,* Lawrence's *Aaron's Rod,* and H. D.'s *Bid Me To Live?* Two years before Robinson's book appeared, Peter E. Firchow (not cited by Robinson) concluded that on the basis of existing material, no single explanation would likely resolve all the contradictions.[7] Robinson fails to appreciate this complexity. She also fails to see that despite other contradictions, every account agrees that H. D. and Lawrence did not become lovers.

Faced with conflicting testimony, Robinson dispenses with secondary sources and resorts to H. D.'s art for clues to the "truth." As she says, "If we have the keys, we can read a poem as a message to a friend as well as an 'objective' statement" (p. xiv). This strategy works, in Robinson's view, because "each of H. D.'s Imagist poems is a palimpsest, and learning to read its images is like learning to read Egyptian hieroglyphs which have lost their meaning to all but the initiated" (p. 70). By deciphering the "hidden inner language," we are able to "read" from H. D.'s poetry "the inner biography of the poet's life" (p. 71). To minimize conflicting testimony further, Robinson proposes the following: "In our attempt to understand their work, we propose in this study to take the testimony of the artists—H. D. and D. H. Lawrence—more seriously than the testimony of their respective [sic] spouses, Frieda Lawrence and Richard Aldington" (p. 165). This injudicious strategy reduces

Aldington's credibility to the level of Frieda Lawrence's, and it also quietly ignores versions offered by other writers.

Aaron's Rod poses another problem. Lawrence's novel is uncomfortably distant from H. D.'s version of actual events, if that is what they are, in *Bid Me To Live*, and even embarrassingly close to Cournos's version in *Miranda Masters*. Thus, although Robinson gives ample space to *Lady Chatterley's Lover*, she refers to *Aaron's Rod* only peripherally. She says that Lawrence began the novel at 44 Mecklenburg Square (p. 159), that he later completed it, that *Aaron's Rod* and H. D.'s *The Flowering of the Rod* "come from the same source" (p. 222), and almost everything else except the nature of Lawrence's portrayal of H. D. as Julia Cunningham in the novel.

The view that poetry and fiction are no more than disguised versions of history eliminates the need for a careful examination of secondary sources. Thus Robinson feels free to charge that Aldington misled several scholars or attempted to censor their biographies without referring to their own testimony. Similarly, Robinson states that Aldington altered Lawrence's manuscripts, but she apparently did not visit the University of Texas Humanities Research Center where she might have sought evidence of Aldington's tampering by comparing Lawrence's manuscripts with the published texts.

Coupled with this dependence on poetic and fictional material is Robinson's selection of biased sources. Drawing almost exclusively from H. D.'s correspondence and manuscripts at the Beinecke (Yale), the Houghton (Harvard), and the Morris (Southern Illinois), Robinson limited herself to a one-sided view of H. D. She apparently has not read the extensive correspondence and manuscripts of Aldington and Lawrence which tend to contradict her theory. While she acknowledges H. D.'s letters held at Southern Illinois, she does not refer to the 716 letters from Aldington to H. D. or to the 2000 or so other letters by Aldington at SIU, or to the 149 Aldington letters at Harvard, or to approximately 1135 Aldington letters at Yale.[8]

In Robinson's view, virtually every one of H. D.'s works— *Helen in Egypt, Bid Me To Live*, "Asphodel," and the rest— retells a triangular story of Aldington, H. D., and D. H. Lawrence. This false assumption leads to insoluble difficulties.

In reference to the matching of fictional and poetic figures with their actual prototypes, Robinson asks, "How do we know who is who?" It is really quite simple; we need to know the biographical situation upon which the imaginative reconstruction is based. The novel is simply a more elaborate presentation of events than the Imagist poem" (p. 170). The matching of biographical situations with art is not always so certain, particularly when the artist changes. Robinson confidently reports that in *Helen in Egypt*, H. D. is Helen, Ezra Pound is Menelaus *and* Odysseus, Lawrence is Achilles, and Aldington is Paris. Guest, who has paid more attention to H. D.'s perspective at the time she wrote *Helen in Egypt*, identifies H. D. as Helen, Ezra Pound as Odysseus, Richard Aldington as Menelaus, and Eric Heydt as Paris. For Friedman, H. D. is Helen, Heydt is Paris, and Lord Dowding is Achilles. One problem here is that Robinson attempts to explain H. D.'s art as if no experiences after 1919 might have influenced her, whereas in truth H. D. wrote over a period of four decades after the Mecklenburgh Square entanglements.

H. D.'s perspective and memories suggest other problems which might explain why *Bid Me To Live* did not appear until 1960. Were *Bid* the straightforward autobiographical account that Robinson claims, surely H. D. would have had considerably less trouble finishing it. However, H. D.'s *Bid* is only partly autobiographical—after reading the renditions of Mecklenburgh Square by Aldington, Cournos, Lawrence, and others, H. D. was responding as well as recording. Only after her work with Freud in 1933 and 1934 did she begin to treat Lawrence as a major influence on her life or art. At one point she was incapable of remembering any of the events in her life from 1910 to 1920, and one wonders how reliable her restored recollections might be. As Robinson admits, "After World War I it was sometimes hard for H. D. to know whether something *really* happened or she imagined the occurrence so vividly it seemed real," and she also admits that "we may never know the real story, for all the Madrigal novels present a different perspective on it" (pp. 269-70).

I got out the vol. of letters of D. H. L. *The letters of D. H. Lawrence,* edited by A. Huxley . . . in it, are letters to Grey [sic] and letters from 44 Mecklenburgh Square, with dates and so on and the insinuating letters after Port Cros and the bust-up with R. A. [Aldington] and Bgt. [Brigit Patmore]. These letters . . . put a whole lot on the map for me, and it is as well anyhow, I think to have this printed record (though not explicit / no mention of my name or anything to give it away, of course) of my stay in Cornwall, the dates and so on. [p. 282; ellipsis and bracketed insertions Robinson's]

Apparently H. D. found research more helpful than did Robinson.

Because Robinson eschews secondary sources, she frequently makes errors of fact. She claims that H. D. left Bryn Mawr due to "poor health" (p. xvii), which she later calls "the physical breakdown that forced her withdrawal from Bryn Mawr" (p. 21), when in fact H. D. withdrew after failing English. Robinson describes St. Elizabeth's Hospital, where Pound was confined after World War II, in Pound's phrase, as a "hell-hole" (p. 21), although Pound was both privileged and comfortable there.[9] She calls Pound's selection of the "H. D., Imagiste" signature "traumatic" for H. D. (p. 34), whereas H. D. welcomed the alternative to "Doolittle," which she found embarrassing. As evidence of H. D.'s reluctance to surrender her poems to Pound, Robinson cites Pound's statement to Harriet Monroe that "it was only by persistence that I got to see [these poems] at all" (p. 36), overlooking the context in which Pound tried to interest an editor in the work of an unknown poet, whose "reluctance" would seem to Pound a rhetorically apt fabrication. Robinson says that H. D.'s miscarriage occurred "after some war news was broken to H. D. in a brutal fashion" (p. 103), which she further explains in a note:

The war news that so upset H. D. was Aldington's report of the sinking of the *Lusitania* by the Germans on May 7, 1915, with a loss of 1198 lives, including many Americans. Aldington greeted this news with excitement because he felt it would bring the Americans into the war. [p. 103n]

However, as Friedman had earlier pointed out, H. D. herself

denied this version in her comments on the *Magic Mirror* manuscript:

> Here and later in a repetition of this memory, H. D. added to the typed manuscript the pencilled words: "(But this never happened. Surely this was fantasy.)" This suggests that Aldington never actually burst in so angrily, but that her later fantasy connected him with psychological brutality and the death of their child.[10]

Guest suggests that this child was unwanted by H. D., which seems a more plausible reason for H. D.'s subsequent guilt after the child died.

Many other statements contradict verifiable facts. For example, Robinson says that "Aldington began to live with Dorothy Yorke" in 1917 (p. 151), two years too early. Robinson claims that H. D. "was very happy" at Perdita's birth, although H. D. had considered abortion (in 1928 she did abort when she became pregnant by Kenneth Macpherson). Robinson says that H. D. never named Perdita's father, yet H. D. made Gray's paternity a matter of public record, as Guest reveals in her narration of the divorce proceedings which H. D. and Aldington underwent in 1938.

In H. D.'s Petitioner's Statement at the High Court of Justice, Probate Divorce and Admiralty Division, she testifies that she was living with Gray in Cornwall for about six months, during which time "misconduct took place between us on several occasions. *About the end of July I found I was going to have a baby, whose father would be Cecil Gray.*" In her statement, H. D. quotes Gray as asking her to divorce Aldington and marry him. She, however, "decided to accede to my husband's request and return to him as soon as the baby was born." H. D.'s statement includes a description of Aldington's rage when he discovered that after the child's birth, and when she was living with him at the Hotel du Littoral, she had gone out and registered the child in his name. [p. 241; italics Guest's]

In a letter to Bryher, H. D. wrote, "My triangle is mother-brother-self.... I have HAD the baby with the brother, hence R. A., Cecil Gray, Kenneth" (Guest, p. 194), thus identifying the three men who had impregnated her. The evidence of public record and H. D.'s correspondence is more convincing than inferences drawn from H. D.'s poetry and fiction.

Throughout the book, one can find non-sequiturs such as this: "Because her perspective is feminine rather than masculine, she interprets events in terms of the timeless natural world rather than in terms of the historical process" (p. 56). Sometimes the connection between assertion and support is hard to discern: "In H. D.'s mind *Helen in Egypt* and 'Madrigal' were inexorably bound together. To Pearson she wrote: 'To me *Madrigal* and the *Helen in Egypt* are sacrosanct!' " (p. 354). To elevate H. D.'s importance, Robinson makes much of a supposed connection between a hut in Lawrence's *John Thomas and Lady Jane* and a hut in H. D.'s "Paint It Today," for Lawrence's hut "has the same primitive, outdoorsy, woodsy quality" (p. 148). Her implication is that without H. D.'s "Paint It Today," Lawrence would not have known what a hut was. Robinson then suggests that the lovers' use of blankets in *John Thomas and Lady Jane* and in *Lady Chatterley's Lover* also derives from "Paint It Today." What might Mellors and Lady Chatterley have used had "Paint It Today" had no blanket?

Some of Robinson's phrases are unfortunate—at one point she describes the Virgin Mary as having given birth "out of wedlock" (p. 326). Fearing her reader might be in need of instruction or incapable of consulting a dictionary, she defines commonplace words:

> It might be illuminating at this point to think about the meaning of the actual word *temple*. The most common meaning is, of course, "an edifice dedicated to the worship of a deity." Both H. D. and Lawrence use the word in this sense, although their meaning of *deity* might be considered by some to be heretical. *Temple* also means, significantly, *tempora*—the space on either side of the forehead. (pp. 209-10)

(She does not comment on what *tempora* meant to Cicero.) Sometimes her emphasis on words goes beyond plausibility, as in her strained explication of some early lines from Pound: " 'Even in my dreams you have denied yourself to me, / And sent me only your handmaids.' i.e., poems (handmades)" (p. 389).

Well into her book, Robinson asks, "But the question remains: To what extent did the realities described in these works occur somewhere, somehow, in historical time at a particular place or location, and to what extent was the H. D.—D. H. Lawrence vision conceived and born within the temple of twin minds?" (p. 226). The question does indeed remain, not only here but well after one has finished reading Robinson's book. Another question remains: why did the venerable and usually conservative Houghton Mifflin publish this book? Although the thesis is certainly sensational enough, the exclusion of secondary sources in favor of contradictory fictional and poetical ones should arouse any reader's suspicions, while the dependence on H. D. as the primary source for information ought to suggest an extraordinary bias on the part of the author in the selection of evidence. According to the dust cover, Robinson "is currently editing a volume of H. D.'s collected letters." One would prefer to see H. D.'s correspondence entrusted to other hands.[11]

Notes

1. Leon Edel, *Literary Biography* (Garden City: Doubleday 1959), p. 154.

2. See Alfred Satterthwaite, "John Cournos and 'H. D.,' " *Twentieth Century Literature*, 22 (December 1976), 394-410.

3. Edel, p. 62.

4. Susan Stanford Friedman, *Psyche Reborn: The Emergence of H. D.* (Bloomington: Indiana Univ. Press, 1981), p. xiii.

5. Paul Delany, *D. H. Lawrence's Nightmare: The Writer and His Circle in the Years of the Great War* (New York: Basic Books, 1978), pp. 170-71n.

6. Harry T. Moore, "Richard Aldington in His Last Years," in *Richard Aldington: An Intimate Portrait*, ed. Alister Kershaw and Frédéric-Jacques Temple (Carbondale: Southern Illinois Univ. Press, 1965), p. 91.

7. See Peter E. Firchow, "Rico and Julia: The Hilda Doolittle-D. H. Lawrence Affair Reconsidered," *Journal of Modern Literature*, 8 (February 1980), 51-76.

8. Norman T. Gates, *A Checklist of the Letters of Richard Aldington* (Carbondale: Southern Illinois Univ. Press, 1977), pp. 72-75, 148, 149, 155.

9. See E. Fuller Torrey, "The Protection of Ezra Pound," *Psychology Today*, 15 (November 1981), 57-62, 64-66.

10. Friedman, p. 301 n. 20.

11. A Summer Faculty Research Award (1984) from the University of Oregon supported research for this essay.

Truth and Fiction: Carlyle Edited and Re-edited

Rodger L. Tarr

Michael K. Goldberg and Jules P. Seigel, eds. *Carlyle's Latter-Day Pamphlets*. Ontario: Canadian Federation for the Humanities, 1983. 594 pp.

George Allan Cate, ed. *The Correspondence of Thomas Carlyle and John Ruskin*. Stanford: Stanford University Press, 1982. xiv, 251 pp.

Fred Kaplan. *Thomas Carlyle, a Biography*. Ithaca: Cornell University Press, 1983. 614 pp.

1981—the centenary of Carlyle's death—marked the beginning of a new era in Carlyle studies, the signs of which were manifest in the previous decade. In the ten years before the centenary, an edition of his letters was well underway, several critical books were written, two collections of essays were published, a secondary bibliography was compiled, and a plethora of shorter studies was composed. All these and more were given impetus by G. B. Tennyson's *"Sartor" Called "Resartus"* (1965), which serves as the benchmark for what has followed. By 1981, the tenor of expectation was high; Carlyle the Man and Carlyle the Writer were to be the subjects of serious re-evaluation. Numerous celebrations of the centenary were held. In Edinburgh, a year-long series of events took place; in London, the National Portrait Gallery provided a special room for an exhibition; in Germersheim at the Goethe Institute, a full week of scholarly exchange was highlighted by a strong European contribution; in New York, the Modern Language Association devoted two sessions toward re-examination; and in Spokane and Chicago, regional meetings were organized. What has transpired since builds upon this renaissance of interest. The Duke-Edinburgh Edition of the *Collected Letters* is shortly to go to press with volumes 10-11, covering the years from *The French Revolution* (1837) through *Heroes and Hero-Worship* (1841); a descriptive bibliography of Carlyle's writings is near completion; and the project to re-edit selected works of Carlyle has just been officially taken on by the University of California Press. A promising future for Carlyle studies seems assured, and nowhere is this future more predictably evident than in the volumes under review here.

The edition of the *Latter-Day Pamphlets* (1850) bears witness to the renewed interest in Carlylean text. The work of editors Michael Goldberg and Jules Seigel is as ambitious as it is challenging. For the first time we have an attempt to establish an authorized text, founded upon manuscripts and appropriate editions, of a major work. And (the irony is inescapable) it should be the most controversial of Carlyle's major works. For the most part misunderstood, and usually quoted out of context, Carlyle's eight-pamphlet salvo against democratic institutions became the focal point for mid-Victorian polemics. Mill was characteristically appalled; George Eliot was quietly apologetic; Dickens was generally in agreement. In the Deep South of America, the segregationists were elated; and in the North, the abolitionists filled the newspapers with anti-Carlyle invective. Over a century later, little has changed. *Latter-Day Pamphlets* is quite simply the most controversial document written in Victorian England, unless that designation should go to Carlyle's "Occasional Discourse on the Negro Question" (1849), which was written for *Fraser's Magazine,* and which was retitled, re-edited, and reissued in pamphlet form as the *Occasional Discourse on the Nigger Question* (1853). Carlyle was to refer to this work as a "precursor" to the *Latter-Day Pamphlets,* and five years later he had them brought together as one for the Uniform Edition of his works.

Goldberg and Seigel have published these two works together for the first time in this century and have done so in a manner that adds to their importance. This edition can be divided into two areas of research: text and context. The former is somewhat disappointing, the latter more than compensates. The central problem with the text is the format, which is probably not the fault of the editors, but which no doubt results from the fiscal constraints placed upon them. The method of presentation is to photo-reproduce the actual copy-text, which is referred to as an "unmodernized critical edition" (p. lxix). In the case of the *Latter-Day Pamphlets*, it is the first edition; and in that of the *Nigger Question*, the first pamphlet edition. The quality of both reproductions is, unfortunately, very poor. Sometimes faded, sometimes blurred, the texts are a burden to read. Further, superscript numbers are interpolated into the texts; and, because there is not appropriate space for them, the whole appears clumsy if not amateurish in design. The superscripts lead the reader to the rear of the volume where the explanatory notes on all contextual matters appear. In addition to the awkwardness created by these superscripts, the facsimile text is also intruded upon by angled brackets to indicate reportorial comments. The thirteen substantive changes found from the comparison of the copy-text to the Uniform Edition (1858) and to the People's Edition (1872) are placed at the foot of each respective page. The complaint here is not directed at the accuracy of the editors' work, but rather at the doubtful wisdom of presenting in such an obtrusive manner these numbers, symbols, and notes. To keep a clear text, would it not have been more desirable to abandon these intrusions and adopt a system of identification that would have placed all emendations and additions at the end, in the manner done for the volume's textual notes? However, as previously surmised, some if not all of these decisions were probably the result of the collision of the editorial ideal with the financial reality. Photo-offsetting the text, however annoying to the eye, is the cheapest method. One can only regret that it was not done here with more care and forethought.

Whatever complaints might be lodged about the presentation of text, they are muted when the context of this edition is considered. The work is headed by a lucid introduction that traces adroitly the histories of the *Latter-Day Pamphlets* and the *Nigger Question*. One learns everything of consequence without feeling the intrusion of scholarly pendantry. The reception, the textual nuances, the manuscript problems, and the editorial policies are all explained fully. The annotations of text and context do not disappoint. The textual variants, both substantive and accidental, are identified by page and line number. The editors are especially scrupulous here, even though the comparisons of texts are done by the somewhat outmoded sight method. Until subsequent machine readings of the texts are done, and most assuredly in the future they will be, the sight collation of the editors must be trusted. Regrettably, what we cannot learn from the variants list is which of the substantives and which of the accidentals are in fact Carlyle's. However, the editors do speculate freely in the introduction on the problems of making such identifications in the absence of conclusive evidence, such as corrected proof and/or manuscript copy. Indeed, the distance between Carlyle and his compositors may never be fully known, particularly since the printing records have long since been destroyed. Therefore, in the case of text it was the editors' choice to use the copy-text as authority for accidentals.

As for the contextual annotation, it is here that the skills of Goldberg and Seigel are most in evidence. Their notations are crisp, precise, and pointed in style. The editors' assumption that the reader must be led through the vast archive of Carlylean allusion is a safe one. It would take an especially well informed reader to see the many subtleties of Carlyle's point-counterpoint. We are always given the facts surrounding an allusion, but more important we are often given the direction intended by the allusion. For example, after being told that Smelfungus is a name given to Tobias Smollett by Laurence Sterne, we are then advised: "Through the use of this and other pseudonyms, Carlyle allows himself wide flexibility of style and statement. He is able to quote his own works, notes, journals, and create hypothetical conversations, all of which allow for additional rhetorical creativity" (p. 527). Such annotation is valuable, for it leads the reader beyond mere fact toward critical interpretation.

There are a few occasions, however, when the text is actually under-annotated. The very next note on Elizur Wright's reaction to Carlyle's calling Americans "eighteen millions of bores" could have been more fully developed, at least to include a statement on Wright's quaint and rare little pamphlet, *Perforations in the "Latter-Day Pamphlets,"* and its place in the canon of abusive response. This is a minor criticism however. The fact is that the notes to the *Latter-Day Pamphlets* are excellent, as are the notes accompanying the *Nigger Question*, although substantive comment on the change in title might have been in order. The alteration from "Negro" to "Nigger" seems curiously out of tone with the twenty-three-paragraph apologia, headed "Do I hate the Negro," that Carlyle added to the pamphlet edition. Such an addition seems an effort to abate the abolitionist critics by disclaiming any innate prejudice. On this point, Goldberg and Seigel argue to the contrary, asserting that this nearly 5500-word addition has "practically no effect whatever" on muting the tone of the original article (p. lxxxvii). If this is so, then why did Carlyle bother adding such an extensive commentary, unless we are to assume he did so to exacerbate the already explosive situation? His letters and journals of the period are conciliatory in tone, even reflecting a certain degree of embarrassment. Finally, most of the variants listed for the *Nigger Question* are not given here "for the first time" as claimed (p. 569). Eugene August's edition of the text and my subsequent work on it pre-date this edition. Both August and I are acknowledged later by the editors, to be sure.

The bibliographies of manuscripts, of texts, and of reviews provided at the end are useful, though one might not agree with the categories to which the various manuscript fragments have been assigned. The index is thorough and the illustrations pleasing for their iconographic effect. In spite of minor irritations caused by the photo-offset text, this edition, together with its compelling introduction, is a major contribution to Carlyle studies.

George Allan Cate's *The Correspondence of Thomas Carlyle and John Ruskin* is no less an achievement. This edition includes 154 letters (39 from Carlyle to Ruskin and 115 from Ruskin to Carlyle), of which 80 are published here for the first time. This immense canon, which rivals in significance Joseph Slater's *The Correspondence of Emerson and Carlyle* (1964), reveals a relationship between Carlyle and Ruskin that heretofore was impossible to appreciate fully. Indeed, the discipleship of Ruskin, which at times bordered on reverence, allows us to see sides of both men that would be hidden otherwise. Ruskin came to refer to Carlyle as "Papa," and Carlyle for the most part responded accordingly. Of course there were rifts, misunderstandings, hurt feelings (especially on Ruskin's part), and even silences, but the two finally remained inseparable, even during Ruskin's initial bouts with insanity. Chronicled here are nearly thirty years of friendship between Carlyle the Father and Ruskin the Son.

The text of Cate's edition is handsomely presented. In fact, if there is one noticeable difference between it and the Goldberg-Seigel *Latter-Day Pamphlets*, it is in the lavishness of composition afforded by the Stanford University Press. The notes to the text printed at the bottom of each respective page, the wide margins, the high quality paper, and the readable font are illustrative of the care taken in presentation. Cate's style of notation is effective: each note is headed by an identification and/or statement of provenance for each manuscript. If appropriate Cate also reveals where and under what circumstances the letter was previously published. This textual information is followed by contextual annotation, which in itself serves to enlarge the text. It is as if Cate were positioned between the reader and each letter. His carefully worded notes create context for the text; they amplify without intruding and sharpen the focus of allusion. Most readers will know generally what Carlyle and Ruskin mean in their exchanges, but few will know it with the particularity demonstrated by Cate.

For the sake of argument, however, one might question on occasion the extent of Cate's documentation. Does one need to be told, for example, that Gehenna is one of Carlyle's favorite words without being told why? Further, do we need to know that Gehenna is near Jerusalem and is thought, because of its perpetual flame of refuse, to be the signatory for the Old Testament Hell? In the first instance, one needs more information to make the comment meaningful; in the second, one hardly needs as much as is given. And then there are times when Cate teases by giving suggestive information and then stops short of full development. Take Ruskin's reference to a "little minature" (p. 103), which Cate surmises—based upon a notation to the text by Alexander Carlyle—is a reference to Jane Carlyle's lost play, *The Rival Brothers*. We want to know more! What is this "little tragedy," as Alexander refers to it? (Actually Carlyle called it that first.) A note directing the reader

Carlyle Edited and Re-edited

to the *Collected Letters,* II, 291n, where the "little miniature" is discussed, and to VII, 361-68, where the surviving fragment is printed, would have been useful. Further, since we infer from Ruskin's comment and Cate's commentary that Ruskin once saw the complete manuscript, it would have been helpful to know whether the Ruskin papers have been searched for this important document. There is also occasional imbalance in how Cate presents his documentation. Here the Jane Carlyle play is only alluded to, yet later a great deal of space is devoted to the tiresome controversy (was it really one at all?) between Carlyle and Ruskin over the alleged ill condition of the Chelsea streets. Cate devotes four pages of his introduction (pp. 27-30) and an elaborate footnote to this niggling disagreement, which even Carlyle felt was blown out of proportion. Cate's notes also contain a few bibliographic oddities. At one point he uses for his authority Isaac W. Dyer's *A Bibliography of Thomas Carlyle's Writings and Ana* (1928) to show that Carlyle's revision of his *Life of Schiller* appeared in 1867. Actually, Dyer's notation is "n.d. [1867?]"; and it is incorrect. The edition referred to is a reprint of the Uniform Edition of 1857, and was in fact published in 1864. The revision Cate is alluding to is the note Carlyle added in 1872 to the supplement to *Schiller* in the People's Edition (1873). In spite of such lapses, the notes as a whole are excellently rendered.

What brings true distinction to the volume is Cate's thoroughly researched fifty-eight page introduction. In it he presents the facts of this Victorian friendship in a form accessible both to the generalist and the specialist. Ruskin's early discipleship is described in glowing terms, and Cate shows the reader just how this devotion finally grew into reverence. It is a touching story that reveals as much about Carlyle as it does about Ruskin. The affection that each held for the other is striking. Ruskin, as Cate points out, changed both in heart and in mind as a result of the association, and one suspects that Carlyle did too. Cate does sometimes blunder into timeworn generalities about Carlyle, especially regarding his alleged impotence. On this subject there is absolutely no evidence for such an allegation, other than the highly questionable secret that Froude claims was communicated to him by the known hyperbolic Geraldine Jewsbury, who fancied herself a confidante of Jane Carlyle. But what is more surprising, Cate uses Waldo Dunn as his authority to confirm Froude. Dunn's *Froude and Carlyle* (1930) is admittedly devoted to proving Froude correct on all matters pertaining to this regrettable controversy. Cate again relies upon the pro-Froude Dunn for his examination of the equally regrettable controversy raised by Froude's edition of the *Reminiscences* (1881), and here Cate refers to Dunn's book as a "valuable work" (p. 43). Dunn's bias against Carlyle is never mentioned. We should expect Cate to be more perspicacious than he is here. At the very least, both sides should have been presented, with acknowledgment given to Alexander Carlyle's *The Nemesis of Froude* (1903) and to David A. Wilson's *The Truth About Carlyle* (1913), two notable anti-Froude documents. There are two more modern assessments of Froude's treatment of Carlyle to which Cate would have had access— namely, K. J. Fielding's "Froude and Carlyle" in *Carlyle Past and Present* (1976) and John Clubbe's introduction to his abridgement of Froude's *Life of Carlyle* (1979). The former strikes a balance; the latter is silently pro-Froude; each attempts to bring an air of objectivity to the controversy. As Cate carefully argues on another occasion, even Ruskin was bitter about the shabby treatment accorded Carlyle by the anti-Froude scholar Charles Eliot Norton, who appointed himself moral arbiter and re-edited the *Reminiscences* (1887). To a large extent Ruskin was correct in his condemnation of Norton's machinations, even though the shrillness of his language compromises his beliefs. Certainly, we must agree with Cate that the real loss in all this is that Ruskin, because of his increasing bouts with insanity, was not able to write his promised biography of Carlyle. One suspects that it would have had no rival.

If there are two things wanting in the introduction, they are sustained remarks on Ruskin's influence upon Carlyle, and extended commentary on Ruskin's fondness for Jane. These chapters in the story of the association are still unwritten. Cate's edition does provide a useful body of forty-five additional letters written by various correspondents (including the two principals) that shed light upon the significance of the primary correspondence. An index is then provided to the whole.

Where the editors of the *Latter-Day Pamphlets* and the Carlyle-Ruskin *Correspondence* seek to edit Carlyle, Fred Kaplan in his *Thomas Carlyle: A Biography* seems committed to re-editing Carlyle, and as a result both perpetuates and creates fictions. Kaplan's task was, of course, enormous, and one must admire his persistence. As a biographer, he accomplishes the near impossible: he compresses the legend and the legacy of Carlyle into one volume. Carlyle's official biographer, James A. Froude, took four volumes: *Thomas Carlyle: A History of the First Forty Years of His Life* (2 vols., 1882) and *Thomas Carlyle: A History of His Life in London* (2 vols., 1884). Indeed, it took David A. Wilson a lifetime of research and six volumes to complete his anecdotal *Carlyle* (1923-1934), volume VI being completed by D. Wilson MacArthur after the death of Wilson. Until Kaplan's work appeared, one was forced to consult the mammoth tomes of Froude and Wilson-MacArthur, or else rely on less popular biographies, most of which were written in the nineteenth century. Clearly what was needed was an authoritative re-telling, in manageable length, of Carlyle's eventful life. Most Carlyle scholars therefore eagerly anticipated the publication of Kaplan's work, and many of them have been disappointed that Kaplan has not provided us with the essential Carlyle.

Perhaps it would be impossible to present Carlyle's life effectively in a single volume. He was born in the same year as Keats (1795), and he died when the Victorian period was beginning its decline (1881). There are so many facts that attend Carlyle's rise from his rural Dumfriesshire heritage to his role as the lion of Victorianism that it may be in fact impossible in one volume to do, in his own words, justice justly. To sort through the mountain of letters, journals, memoirs, reminiscences, and anecdotes written by and about Carlyle is an epic task. Carlyle was, as George Eliot declared, "An oak among acorns." No one in her generation, Eliot continues, escaped his influence, whether in England or America. In *American Notes* (1842) Dickens reported in amazement that Carlyle was known as the "Father of Transcendentalism"; in *The Warden* (1854) Trollope saw him with affection as "Dr. Pessimist Anticant." To each country he was many things:

preacher, philosopher, historian, essayist, critic, biographer, even novelist. Thus we cannot fault Kaplan too severely when he passes briefly, or not at all, over the myriad facts that attend Carlyle's life and works. The issue to be examined here is not what *should* have appeared in Kaplan's biography but what *does*, and how, on more than one occasion, fact is edited into fiction.

Kaplan's effort belongs to that vaguely defined genre called "psychoanalytic biography." Repeatedly Kaplan retreats to the arena of psychoanalysis, and in consequence surrounds the Carlyles in an aura of post-Freudian, post-Jungian, post-modern perspective. *Thomas Carlyle: A Biography* is an impressionistic interpretation, written from the viewpoint of the doctor viewing his patient. Kaplan believes that he sees, in Carlyle's life and letters, what no one has seen before; but his alleged insights are often not supported by the authorities he cites. The most misleading quagmire is the subject of the Carlyle's sexual lives. In fact, the whole framework of the biography seems built upon doubtful assumptions about this rekindled controversy. At the very outset we are informed suggestively that "the subliminal voice of his parents' community told him, among other things, that physical instinct came from the devil, not from God" (p. 18). This shaky generalization about Calvinism is typical of Kaplan's method: generalize, then follow with specific conclusions that often contradict or ignore the given documentation. After observing Carlyle's advice to Thomas Murray, " 'Do not get in love—if you can help it,' " Kaplan concludes, "Aware of what it meant to be '*goatish*' and what it meant to be pure, Carlyle shrank from contamination, the strict standards of his parents forbidding masturbatory sex as well as fornication. He never seems to have deviated from his parents' law" (p. 35). Nowhere in the letter cited, written on 22 August 1815, is there the slightest hint of what Kaplan alleges. In fact, the sentence before the one quoted by Kaplan paints quite a different picture. "You have no doubt," writes Carlyle, "a large quantity of female beauty in the shire, and I hope and trust that among those provincial cynosures, you pass your time with much *gaieté de coeur*" (*Collected Letters*, I, 58). Even more misleading is Kaplan's comment that Carlyle knew what it was like to be "goatish." In the letter cited, written to Murray on 28 November 1815, Carlyle does not use that word as Kaplan implies he does. The word actually appears in a footnote supplied by the editors, and is from the pen of Murray, not Carlyle (*CL*, I, 63). In any event, there is no mention anywhere of masturbation, and the reference to someone else fornicating is clearly an instance of teenage gossip. How is it, then, that Carlyle "shrank from contamination"? On what authority is Kaplan basing his conclusion that Carlyle never "deviated" from his parents' wishes on masturbation and fornication? Indeed, what is the reason for raising this undocumented issue, other than the obvious intention to establish a scenario that Carlyle from youth was sexually maladjusted? By 1824, the plot has thickened. Now Kaplan is willing to assert that the source for many of Carlyles' aberrant anxieties was his mother. We are told that while in Paris, Carlyle attended a performance of Voltaire's *Oedipus*. According to Kaplan, it was "a play whose relevance to his own life probably eluded him" (p. 106). Here we have the fact of Carlyle's attending a production of *Oedipus* manipulated into the fiction of sexual psychoses. By the next year, 1825, Kaplan can safely conclude, "For Thomas, the return to the ministering arms of his mother fulfilled a long-held fantasy" (p. 111). The message is clear: Carlyle was molded by Oedipal instincts that sustained him throughout his life, but "particularly as long as his mother was alive" (p. 268). I trust that rebuttal is not necessary. These insinuations are entirely unfounded. The non sequitur is rooted in the language of the inference and in the method of documentation.

The error of Kaplan's methods is best demonstrated in his treatment of the love life of the Carlyles. Hinted at by Froude, proclaimed by Frank Harris, and alleged by Waldo Dunn, the declaration simply is that the Carlyles never consummated their marriage. First, what is the import of such a declaration, particularly when it is beyond proof? Second, what is the evidence for such a declaration, other than the alleged confidence of Geraldine Jewsbury (we will treat her later) to Froude that Jane confided in her about Carlyle's sexual problems? Third, why does Kaplan devote so much attention to this and attendant subjects, especially since a century of inquiry has been unable to unearth anything beyond common innuendo? Kaplan's story of the Carlyles' problems continues with the assertion that the then Jane Welsh "was frightened of marriage because, among other reasons, she was frightened of sex" (p. 72). This conclusion is founded upon Jane's idealized view of Rousseau's *Julie*, which Kaplan would have us believe caused her to set an "asexual standard" for her suitors (p. 73). Is it possible that Jane could have translated her reading to reality? Would her Byronic passions have been that misleading to her several suitors, among them Edward Irving? And how can one possibly conclude that she was "frightened of sex," unless one enjoys the privilege and position of the psychiatrist? As for Carlyle, Kaplan wonders openly why Carlyle did not worry as to "whether his state of mind would allow his 'unhealthy' body to perform effectively in a sexual relationship" (p. 110). The Carlyles, of course, are now doomed: Jane fears sex and Thomas cannot perform. Yet Kaplan seems to contradict his thesis when he tells us later that Jane did not want to marry Thomas because "she neither loved him in a romantic way nor felt toward him the sexual attraction that she always imagined she would feel toward the man who would become her husband" (p. 109). We are now asked to believe that she was capable of experiencing natural sexual instincts in the face of her apparent fear of sex and her resulting asexual standard. How is this possible—no evidence is provided—except in the general trepidation felt by all humans before their initial sexual encounters? But this natural sexual anxiety is not what Kaplan is referring to. Rather, his argument is that both Thomas and Jane suffered from deep-rooted sexual maladjustment, a fact which affected their whole lives. One must repeat, there is no strong evidence to support such an assumption; and certainly there is a great deal of evidence to suggest the opposite. The obvious devotion exhibited in the so-called *Love Letters* (2 vols., 1909), when considered in its entirety and not out of context, leaves an impression much different from that which Kaplan creates.

By the time of their marriage on 17 October 1826, the Carlyles, Kaplan concludes, had compromised their misgivings and inadequacies and had agreed to a union of mind over matter. It is important here to quote at length Kaplan's impression

Carlyle Edited and Re-edited

of their marriage night, for it reveals something of the biographer's commitment to proving Thomas deficient and Jane unresponsive:

> In his eyes it was a failure not of love but of a body that would not do love's bidding, the result of ill health and confusion. He had made his excuses in advance, and Jane had openly wondered whether she was in love with him as a wife should be with a husband. Clearly, Puritan inhibitions and Romantic idealizations were in the seven-foot wide bed with two sexual innocents. Fragile evidence suggests that though they were able to express affection with whispers and embraces, their sexual relationship did not provide physical satisfaction to either of them,[5] despite the efforts made during the first half-dozen or so years of the marriage. Whispers and embraces indicate that their affection did take physical form, but the account of the abysmal marriage night, the early retreat to separate beds and rooms, the vehement distaste for children, the constant pressure of ill health, and the general tone of physical repression provide convincing circumstantial support for the claim that sexual intercourse played little or no role in the routine of their relationship during almost forty years of marriage. [pp. 118-19]

The suggestive, leading inferences and conclusions in this passage speak loudly enough of Kaplan's thesis, a thesis based upon letters that do not remotely say what is said here. Indeed, it is Kaplan's abuse of his sources, here and elsewhere, that permits in turn the creation of such unfounded remarks. In the above passage, for example, it is important to note the position of the superscript "5," which is there presumably to justify the conclusion that the Carlyles' marriage night was a "failure." Kaplan goes further. He would have us believe that Carlyle made "excuses in advance" to Jane, and that "fragile evidence suggests" that there was no "sexual satisfaction" for either of them on the "abysmal marriage night" or for that matter during "almost forty years of marriage." What is Kaplan's evidence for such conclusions? Superscript 5 sends us to four letters, one written seven months before they were married, two written six months after, and one written twenty-six months after. Specifics are not quoted from these letters; we are simply directed to them without comment. Upon examining these letters, one can find nothing to support what Kaplan suggests.

The first letter, written on 7 March 1826, seems to concern a lover's quarrel, and in it Carlyle implores Jane to "forget the whole misunderstanding" (*CL*, IV, 53). We are not told exactly what the misunderstanding is, but certainly we cannot infer from the affectionate, passionate language that Carlyle is admitting "in advance" (p. 118) sexual inadequacy, particularly since he refers to the misunderstanding in the plural as "perplexities," and more particularly since we are still seven months from the marriage date. Carlyle does say that whatever the problems are, they are "not want of tenderness to you, but confidence in myself." In context, this comment cannot possibly allude to sexual problems, unless we are to presume that he and Jane already discussed sexual matters. It is unthinkable that they would have, even during the most intimate premarital discussions; and it is certainly unthinkable that Carlyle would have expressed any such discussion in a letter. The second letter Kaplan refers to is one written by Jane to Thomas on [16 april 1827], six months after the marriage. In it she expresses hope that Carlyle will be able to settle matters on their future home Craigenputtock, which has caused "perplexities and suspenses" (*CL* 4, 213). She then adds, "But health and spirits will come back when my dearest Husband comes back with good news; ... to be separated from you even for one week is *frightful*." Nowhere in this letter does Jane imply sexual unhappiness; quite the contrary: "Oh I think I shall never be satisfied with looking at you, and holding you in my arms and covering you with kisses after this." The third letter that Kaplan cites to confirm the Carlyles' unhappiness is written by Thomas to Grace Welsh, Jane's mother, with a note appended to Jane. In this letter, dated 19 April [1827], written just three days after the previous letter, Carlyle writes to Jane, "No, I do not love you in the least; only a little *sympathy* and *admiration*, and a certain *esteem*; nothing more!" (*CL* 4, 217). Can it be possible that Kaplan does not see this as a lover's jest? It is followed by the affectionate, "O my dear best woman! But I will not say a word of all this, till I whisper it in your ear with my arms around you." What we have here is a tease, followed by a declaration of love. Where is there any hint of dissatisfaction, sexual or otherwise? The fourth letter that Kaplan cites is one written

Carlyle Edited and Re-edited 253

on 30 December [1828], more than two years after the marriage. In this letter, from Jane to Thomas, there is expressed the filial concern that, in her absence, Carlyle is not "getting any vitual" (*CL*, IV, 438). To this domestic comment, Jane adds, "Oh if I were there I would put my arms so close about your neck and hush you into the softest sleep you have had since I went away." We must ask again, where in this letter is it indicated that Jane Carlyle is unhappy with Thomas, or vice versa? Yet it is from these four letters that Kaplan deduces his extravagant thesis that the Carlyles' marriage night was "abysmal."

The conclusions offered in the passage quoted above on the marriage night are set up in the previous paragraph, where Kaplan begins by citing Carlyle's letter to his mother, written on 19 October 1826, two days after the marriage. In this detailed letter, written as the editors of the *Collected Letters* carefully point out, to satisfy his mother's ever-present curiosity, Carlyle describes his marriage bed as being "about *seven feet wide*," and then adds, "Besides she [Jane] herself (the good soul!) has ordered another bed to be made for me in the adjoining room, to which I may retire whenever I shall see good" (*CL*, IV, 153). Kaplan hints openly that the second bed was there as a retreat for Carlyle during periods of sexual dysfunction, when in fact it was put there to accommodate his general ill-health. The truth is that Carlyle is responding to a projected question from his mother: "You will ask about sleep: fear not for that, my good Mother; I shall sleep better than ever." Kaplan sees all of this as a specific comment on the marriage night, a letter of "astounding frankness" in which "the son made clear to the mother that the experience had been a failure" (p. 118). Carlyle does say, "I am still dreadfully confused, still far from being at home in my new situation," but then he adds "inviting and hopeful as in all points it appears." Nowhere in this letter is there a hint of sexual "failure"; Carlyle admits only to being "confused." Indeed, if there had been any sexual problems, his mother would have been the last person Carlyle would have turned to, especially since the avowed purpose of the letter is to quiet "motherly anxieties." As for the innuendo about the two beds, that is refuted in a letter Carlyle wrote to his mother on 16 November 1826, one month later: "I sleep quite passably in our giant bed" (*CL*, IV, 157). This comment is neither quoted nor alluded to by Kaplan.

Instead of carefully measuring the language of hope and love that dominates the letters in question, Kaplan cites a letter by Carlyle to his medical doctor brother John, written on [24 October 1826], one week after the marriage. In it Carlyle writes, "I would give sixpence to see you here yourself at this very moment. I want to speak with you about many things, *ut cum fratre, ut cum medico*. When will you come? Jane will be delighted to see you; and for me your presence would be a lamp in a dark place" (*CL*, IV, 154). Carlyle goes on to explain that he must be quiet about "my matrimonial views; for I am yet in a maze, scarce knowing the right from the left in the path I have to walk." From this letter, and the previous one to his mother, Kaplan concludes that there was "some lack of physical responsiveness [in the marriage] so private it could not be detailed" (p. 118). It is true that this letter is suggestive. Carlyle is asking for personal as well as medical advice. The crucial question, however, is concerning *what*? Must we assume, as Kaplan does, that Carlyle's entreaty is evidence of sexual dysfunction? How do we not know that it was Jane who was unresponsive? How do we know that the problem was shared by both? And, even if we assume that there was a sexual problem, what is the point? What would be unusual about this in the first and early days of a virginal marriage? At the very least, not one of the comments in these two letters, or in the others considered here, proves the thesis that Kaplan wants us to accept—that the Carlyles were sexually inadequate and that this affected the whole of their domestic and literary lives. Kaplan simply does not provide the "convincing circumstantial evidence" (p. 119) that he claims. Finally, when he surmises that Carlyle vowed to give up tobacco as an "expression of penance for sexual failure" (p. 119), the whole of his unfortunate thesis is carried to the level of absurdity.

In the end we are left to accept the undocumented possibility that initial sexual failure led to life-long sexual frustration. Without evidence the reader is further assured that "Jane had quickly and quietly accepted the value of a marital life that did not depend on sexual satisfactions" (p. 122). Kaplan goes

Carlyle Edited and Re-edited

on to dismiss as "highly unlikely" (p. 179) the possibility of Jane's having been pregnant in the summer of 1831, but in his discussion of this controversial topic he fails to acknowledge the "family tradition" (*CL*, V, 433n) that she was and that she even gathered baby clothes in anticipation of the event. Whether or not the Carlyles had intercourse, whether or not Jane was pregnant, all and more seems of little consequence when Kaplan hints that a possible lesbian relationship existed between Geraldine Jewsbury and Jane. We are told that by the 1840s Jane was desperately unhappy, and that on one occasion at least she approached Carlyle's radical friend, Mazzini, and was rebuffed, with the warning to do her duty to her husband (p. 278). Apparently the time was right for Geraldine who, says Kaplan, was "at least partly conscious of her lesbian desires" for Jane (p. 300). In the meantime, Jane, who was obviously not fully aware of Geraldine's overtures, was jealous of what she saw as Geraldine's advances toward Carlyle. Carlyle all the while was interested in Lady Ashburton and so encouraged, unwittingly it would seem, the special friendship of Geraldine and Jane, "who had no hope for her own marriage" (p. 377). Here again, who was in bed with whom and why is of little consequence. What is crucial is that the seed has been planted in the reader's mind of a lesbian relationship, requited or unrequited, between Jane Carlyle and Geraldine Jewsbury. All this is evidenced, says Kaplan, by the "passionate personal letters" Geraldine wrote to Jane (p. 299). We ask in response, since no other evidence is provided, is it not possible that Geraldine's declarations are no more than the romantic delusions of a lonely, confused woman, not the advances of a lesbian? It seems incongruous that at one point Geraldine is purportedly to have approached Jane, at another point to have approached Carlyle's brother, Dr. John Carlyle, and still at another point to have approached Carlyle himself (p. 301). Are we to believe that she was bisexual? Or is it more likely that she was a sheer opportunist, willing to ingratiate herself to anyone, male or female, who would listen?

We are, of course, not arguing here that the Carlyles' marriage was not volatile, a natural occurrence of events when two emotional, sensitive, and intelligent individuals are married.

Where Kaplan errs is in taking this fact and transforming it into sexual neuroses. By dramatizing every traumatic situation, Kaplan turns, through inference, innuendo, and implication, the Carlyles' marriage into a tragic failure. Nothing, I submit, can be further from the truth. The depth of Kaplan's misperception is illustrated late in the biography in his analysis of Tate's painting of the Carlyles in 1857, a work called *A Chelsea Interior*:

Carlyle leans gracefully against the mantlepiece, his pipe in hand. He seems to have "world enough and time" in this extended moment of thought and relaxation. Jane sits comfortably on a chair in a corner, as if contentedly patient, approving of details of their life. The room, well decorated and comfortable, is uncluttered. Though there are no children, the husband and wife seem a family. Carlyle wears the dressing gown that his mother had made him. There are no lines of illness or anxiety on Jane's face. [p. 411]

The patronizing language of equivocation applied to Jane Carlyle needs no comment, nor does the inference contained in the comment, "Though there are no children." Kaplan simply does not see what is there. If anything Jane looks bored, impatient, *and* sick. Kaplan has missed what Tate has captured. The "Victorian image" is lost in Kaplan's icon of the Carlyle marriage.

To be fair to Kaplan, one must admit that his weaknesses are sometimes his strengths. He gives an engrossing account of Carlyle's rise to fame. He begins with a circular metaphor and weaves it throughout the biographical narrative, finding it also as a technique in Carlyle's own works, such as his essay on "Biography." Yet Kaplan's metaphors on occasion betray him. Referring to Carlyle during his formative years as "an intellectual fish who is out of his water" (p. 37) is an example. Nevertheless, Kaplan's experiments with language often lead him to elegiac moments. His description of Carlyle's rude parents, his perception of Carlyle's removal to London, and his understated account of Carlyle's death and burial are among the better passages in the biography. There are, however, specific subjects that Kaplan leaves mysteriously undeveloped. The quarrel with Antonio Panizzi, the Keeper of the Books at the

British Museum, and Carlyle's resulting stewardship in the founding of the London Library need more attention. Carlyle was one of the central figures in the movement to provide adequate lending libraries in London, and he was active in the vitalization of the National Portrait Gallery, facts which are not mentioned at all. We would have also liked more detail on Carlyle's championship of beleaguered individuals who, like George Eliot and George Lewes, turned to Carlyle in their darkest hours. Eliot referred to Carlyle's support of her right to live with Lewes out of wedlock as a "noble letter of sympathy," and in the next year Lewes dedicated his *Life of Goethe* (1855) to Carlyle. This episode and others, like the support of Chopin and the Rossettis, all contradict Kaplan's general thesis that Carlyle was unable to appreciate the realities of physical life and love.

We must also question some general facts given by Kaplan. Did Carlyle "hate" wandering and wanderers (p. 17)? There is good reason to argue otherwise: the conversion of *Sartor Resartus*, the apocalypse of *The French Revolution*, the impulse of *Past and Present*, the prophecy of the *Latter-Day Pamphlets*, all point toward the creative (and the paradoxical) advantage found in the journey. One might argue that Carlyle was a Romantic first, a Victorian second; yet in both, the journey without utilitarian end is a common motif. No matter. Kaplan seems to contradict his own premise when he points out later that Carlyle, through his vision of Richter, became the "uninvited pilgrim wandering in their [the critics'] wasteland" (p. 131). And what exactly does Kaplan mean when he says, in his discussion of the essay on Richter, "Carlyle, of course, was incapable of writing anything but disguised autobiography" (p. 130)? Are we being asked to believe that *all* of Carlyle's intellectual essays written during the 1820s are "self-projections"? Indeed, are we being told that *all* of Carlyle is autobiographical? Such a judgment is at best a gross simplification; at worst it is totally inaccurate, unless Kaplan's point is that all writers are incapable of Arnoldian disinterestedness and that all incorporate self-expression into critical perception. But even this generalization is open to dispute.

One cannot help but be greatly disappointed with *Thomas Carlyle: A Biography*. Perhaps in part it is because Carlyleans anticipated too much. Perhaps in part it is because Carlyle is finally too eclectic to be handled in one volume. Or perhaps it is because Kaplan's work is too often cast as an exposé rather than as a biography. The real disappointment, however, occurs when Kaplan's perceptions of the truth are considered. His unproved innuendos and his undocumented conclusions will be discounted by those knowledgable on the particulars of the Carlyles' lives. But what of those coming to Carlyle for the first time? Will this sometimes engrossing but too often misleading biography nurture a revival of the school of psychoanalytic studies? At the turn of the century, Carlyle's reputation was nearly destroyed by such work. One can only hope that such a thing will not happen again. As it stands now, *Thomas Carlyle: A Biography* is an inspired but, regrettably, a flawed work. It does not stand on the firm ground of scholarship, as do the editions of the *Latter-Day Pamphlets* and of the Carlyle-Ruskin *Correspondence*. In the end one perhaps should turn to Carlyle himself, who in his essay "Biography" (1832) reminds us: "It is good that every reader and every writer understand, with all intensity of conviction, what quite infinite worth lies in Truth."

The Story of a Lie:
A Sequel to *A Sequel*

William E. Fredeman

John Carter and Graham Pollard. *An Enquiry into the Nature of Certain Nineteenth Century Pamphlets*. Second Edition with an Epilogue, ed. Nicolas Barker and John Collins. London: Scolar Press, 1983. [10], xii, 400, [31] pp.

Nicolas Barker and John Collins. *A Sequel to* An Enquiry into the Nature of Certain Nineteenth Century Pamphlets. London: Scolar Press, 1983. 394 pp.

The world of books, which, as John Carter rightly observed in his generous obituary notice of Thomas J. Wise, is "a different place from the literary world," has long awaited the publication of a revised edition of *An Enquiry into the Nature of Certain Nineteenth Century Pamphlets* (1934), without challenge the most dramatic exposé in the history of bibliography.[1] Beside it, the earlier enquiries on which Carter and Pollard modelled their study pale by comparison.[2]

The scope of their investigation was appreciably broader, involving more than fifty fabricated nineteenth-century pamphlets purporting to be by established and avidly collected Victorian writers, and the genre they devised to reveal their discoveries melded the suspense of detective fiction with the rigorous demands of scientific scholarship in a style that, while elegantly allusive and scrupulously punctilious, managed at the same time, like the best dramatic monologues, to be obliquely but devastatingly accusatory. Masters of understatement and indirection, the Enquirers succeeded, by the sheer weight of negative evidence, in targeting (without ever naming him) the only possible source for the forgeries: the doyen of British collectors, Thomas J. Wise, whose Ashley Library was one of the finest collections in private hands and a treasure which it was hoped would one day come to the nation, and whose reputation as a bibliographer was universally acclaimed and seemingly unassailable.[3]

Nicolas Barker and John Collins have made no attempt in their *Sequel* to assume the mantle of the Enquirers, although Barker was hand-picked by the authors to complete the revision on which they had been engaged for over four decades. In electing to provide a "counterpart" rather than a revision of *An Enquiry*—a volume "complete in itself if unintelligible without the original" (p. 12)—the Sequelers were motivated by a desire to preserve the "classic" quality of Carter and Pollard's investigation. To this second edition of the *Enquiry*, the editors have added a preface, a section of corrections and notes keyed to the text, and an epilogue by the original authors on the publication of the book and its aftermath, which was to have been the introductory chapter to their own revision of the *Enquiry*. Barker and Collins' decision was surely the correct one, for it would have been impossible to integrate the new materials into the *Enquiry*, or even to add the authors' draft chapters, as first planned, without fracturing the delicate stylistic suspense that characterized their literary "whodunit." Fifty years on, the outcome is no mystery, but the brilliant allusiveness, subtlety, and innuendo that won Carter and Pollard a mock Nobel Prize for "written understatement," still commands the highest admiration.[4] The two books are simply too dissimilar to be merged: published together they not only provide a complementary reference set on the subject of the forgeries, but they also invite comparisons of methodology, style, and presentation, of which the Sequelers are all too aware: "How they [Carter and Pollard] would have reacted to the discoveries we made we could all too easily imagine" (p. 12).[5]

The *Sequel*, it should be said at the outset, makes no attempt to assimilate everything that has been written on the forgeries in the half-century since the publication of the *Enquiry*. The book is after all not a history.[6] The preface and prologue offer brief retrospective accounts intended to bring the story of the forgeries full-circle with the epilogue appended to the first volume; but the *Sequel* is a documentary account of the second stage of the investigation launched by Carter and Pollard in 1934 and extended by them and other scholars in the intervening years. Essentially it explores three main areas: first, the collaboration between T. J. Wise and H. Buxton Forman, buttressed by parallel chapters on the lives of the two men in Part I, a complete examination of the course of the crime in Part III, and their exchanged correspondence in Appendix 4; second, an elaborate typographical investigation of the 100 items in the List of Works now indicted (Appendix 7), with a detailed analysis in Part II and a thorough survey in Appendix 6 of all the type and ornamental stocks used in the fabricated editions; and third, full dossiers on 54 items: 8 reassessments of dossiers in the *Enquiry* and 46 completely new dossiers—10 titles by the six new authors added to the canon, and 36 by authors treated in the *Enquiry*—including works identified between 1936-1969, others that were dismissed by the Enquirers, either as genuine editions or for want of sufficient evidence to convict, and a final group, different in kind, mainly by Swinburne and Morris, the latter associated almost exclusively with Forman, whose role in the enterprise was unknown until a year after the publication of the *Enquiry*.[7]

The publication of the *Sequel* offers a unique opportunity to review the whole of the Wiseian saga in the context of the original *Enquiry*, to comment on the subsequent contributions made by the Enquirers and their collaborators to the exposure, and to examine the new evidence marshalled by Barker and Collins. The remainder of this essay will survey briefly the publication and aftermath of the *Enquiry* leading up to the *Sequel*; examine specific aspects of the *Sequel* itself, with special reference to the Forman-Wise collaboration and the prominence given Forman by Barker and Collins; provide new evidence to support the displacement of Swinburne's *Cleopatra* as the first of the jointly produced fabrications; and offer a brief summary evaluation of the contributions made by Barker and Collins in the *Sequel*. The article concludes with a Master List of Indicted Works designed to give the reader readier access to the statistical and factual information relating to the fabrications than is provided in the *Sequel* or elsewhere.

With a minor substantive alteration, the concluding sentence to W. B. Todd's brief Preface to *Centenary Studies* (1959) could serve as the epigraph to Barker and Collins' *Sequel* to Carter and Pollard's *Enquiry*: "The subject is inexhaustible, the villain[s] beyond all understanding." Weeks before the publication of *An Enquiry into the Nature of Certain Nineteenth Century Pamphlets* on 2 July 1934, the book had already become a *cause célèbre* among booksellers, bibliographers, librarians, scholars, and collectors. The most prominent of the last group was England's then greatest living collector, Thomas James Wise, who, by his prepublication letter to the *TLS* (24 May 1934) retracting his account of the discovery of the Reading *Sonnets* of Elizabeth Barrett Browning, the black orchid of all the forgeries, delivered into the hands of the Enquirers the weapon to administer his own *coup de grâce* in the "Stop Press" to their sensational exposure.

Their book—and indeed their investigations—had begun with the *Sonnets*, and to have the Master himself indite the perfect ending by indicting himself was a stroke of unexpected good fortune.[8] Any doubts they (or their readers) may have harboured about the identity of the culprit withered in the face of Wise's pathetically disingenuous admission that in his published record of this momentous event in bibliographical history he had misremembered the book he had acquired on that day "somewhere about 1885" when he took "high tea" consisting of "hot buttered toast and sausages" at the table of Dr. W. C. Bennett, who had invited him home to examine the *Sonnets*, of which he had several copies.[9] On reflection, he explained, what he had secured was *not*, after all, Elizabeth Barrett Browning's love poems written to her husband and privately printed for her at Reading in 1847 by her friend Miss Mitford— the most romantic book that could possibly be imagined in the entire annals of English Literature short of the undisinfected manuscript of Rossetti's poems buried with Elizabeth Siddal. Rather—at least by implication, if the second half of his earlier account was to be believed and made consistent with his later rendition—he had hurried back from Camberwell to inform his collector friends—Forman, Gosse, Slater, and others—of the "good news" that he had discovered a cache of Dr. Bennett's

My Sonnets, published at Greenwich in 1843, two copies of which he had "carried . . . home rejoicing" (E, p. 17).

Wise was clearly led into this piece of stupidity by panic, engendered—not unintentionally—by the conscious tactics employed by the Enquirers. It is no reflection on Carter and Pollard, particularly given the enormity of the crime they uncovered, to suggest that from the point in their researches when they decided to confront Wise personally, they were engaged for all practical purposes in a sting operation in which they hoped to entrap the collector. They doubtless embarked on their enterprise in all innocence, with little idea where their searches might lead them; but their investigations soon shifted from the area of literary to forensic evidence, as they moved into the examination of type faces and paper analysis. Their identification of Henry Clay & Sons as the printshop from which the pamphlets had derived, and particularly their discovery of Herbert Gorfin and his records—both of which led directly to the Ashley Librarian as the source, if not the perpetrator, of the forgeries—also brought them face to face, owing to the purely circumstantial nature of their evidence, with British libel laws and the legal implications of their discoveries.[10]

Published with an epigraph quoting Wise's *Bibliography of Swinburne* on the impossibility of fabricating reprints "in such a manner that detection cannot follow the result,"*An Enquiry* launched not only a world-wide controversy but also a whole new field of bibliographical exploration. On both sides of the Atlantic, pro- and anti-Wise forces squared off. Many collectors were simply unwilling or unable to concede that a man of Wise's prominence and esteem—former Honorary Secretary of the Browning and Shelley Societies, a member of the exclusive Roxburghe Club, Honorary M.A. (Oxon), Fellow of Worcester College, Oxford, Past President of the Bibliographical Society, author of dozens of authoritative author bibliographies, editor of the catalogue of the library of the distinguished American collector, Henry Wrenn, and compiler of the (then) ten-volume catalogue of his own magnificent Ashley Library, and all-round *bibliophile extraordinaire*—could in any way be involved in a plot so criminal in its intent, so pernicious in its effects, and so machiavellian in its execution.

Caught in a leg-hold trap, from which he could escape only by dismembering his reputation, Wise responded with animal instinct rather than reason, resorting to bluster, threats, name-calling, paranoic denial, counter-accusations, appeals to sympathy owing to ill health, and transfer of responsibility. In an interview with the *Daily Herald* two days before publication, he returned to a tactic he had unsuccessfully attempted to use on his bookseller Herbert Gorfin, identifying Buxton Forman as the source of the pamphlets and proclaiming himself to be only the "messenger lad who took the goods for delivery." "They [the pamphlets] were planted on Forman and not on me," he protested, while at the same time maintaining that "a large proportion of the books condemned are genuine." His two published defences in the *TLS*—one before, one after publication of the *Enquiry*—and his unpublished article written for Charles F. Heartman's *American Book Collector* were lame responses, unworthy of his talents and reputation.[11]

In the epilogue to the new edition, Carter and Pollard survey the "preliminary rumblings" and the aftermath generated by their exposure of Wise; Pollard's confrontation with Wise and his reaction; the evidence of Herbert Gorfin and the subsequent destruction of a number of his records by his family; the various attempts either to silence their investigation or to discredit the authors; the legal implications of their book (see above, n. 10); the defence committee formed at Oxford to protect Wise; the controversy in the press and the impact of the reviews; Wise's public stance; the reaction among collectors; and (at length) the ramifications of the discovery of the Pforzheimer proofs, condemning Forman as Wise's collaborator in crime and thereby confirming the previously unproved accusations of the University of Texas Rare Book Librarian, Fannie N. Ratchford, that the forgeries were the work of a "ring" or "factory" (see above, n. 7). It is difficult in retrospect to recreate just how sensational the Carter-Pollard disclosures were, or—to judge from the number of column inches devoted to the *Enquiry* in articles and reviews—how much the episode caught the popular and journalistic imaginations.

Once alerted to the fraudulency of so many nineteenth-century rarities, librarians, scholars, and collectors became increasingly skeptical of the authenticity of other pamphlets in their collections. Carter and Pollard made no claim that their list of forgeries was complete, and between 1936 and 1969 ten newly identified forgeries were added to the canon, together with eight items suspected but not proven in the *Enquiry*. Eleven of these discoveries were made by the Enquirers themselves, but scholars from as far afield as California, Texas, and Kansas in the United States and London and Manchester in England collaborated in compiling these later dossiers. In the enthusiasm of the chase, perhaps not unexpectedly, two pamphlets were incorrectly labelled as spurious. These were later exonerated—George Borrow's *The Death of Balder* (1889) and Tennyson's *To Her Royal Highness Princess Beatrice* (1885)—proving only that all that glitters isn't guilt.

At the same time, because the condemned pamphlets had taken on a new and different kind of scarcity and interest, libraries prepared inventories of their holdings of Wise forgeries and even took perverse pride in possessing a complete, or nearly complete, run. In 1934, only the University of Texas Library had all the forgeries; by 1946, when Texas mounted a full-scale exhibition of *Certain Nineteenth Century Pamphlets*, that library was no longer unique in owning all the blacklisted titles—Harvard and the Huntington by then having completed their sets—but Miss Ratchford could still boast that the Texas copies had a distinctiveness, "having come directly from Wise with a fictitious provenance to fit each book as he reported it to Wrenn." Prices rose well beyond their pre-exposure levels, until gradually the forgeries have become almost unprocurable at any price.

Over the years there have been no fewer than eleven exhibitions of Wiseian artefacts: the first in Ann Arbor in the year of the exposure; three at the University of Texas—the one cited above in 1946, a second appropriately opened on All Fools' Day in the Centenary Year (1959) by John Carter, and one devoted exclusively to Morris items (1973); one each at the Grolier Club (1935), the Turnbull Library in Wellington, New Zealand (1935), Colby College (1938), the British Museum (1961), the Peabody Institute in Baltimore (1962), Syracuse University (1967); and, the largest of all, *Wise After the Event*, an exhibition at the

Central Library, Manchester, on the occasion of the thirtieth anniversary of the publication of the *Enquiry* (1964). The Manchester exhibition, organized by G. E. Haslam, was drawn principally from the collection of Sir Maurice Pariser, a city alderman who had amassed the most representative assortment of Wiseiana in private hands. From correspondence between Forman and Wise in the Symington Collection at Rutgers, Pariser proved that Morris' *Two Sides of the River* was a forgery. At the Sotheby sale of Pariser's Wise collection in December 1967, where prices for the forgeries went from a high of £800 for Arnold's *Alaric at Rome*—the scarcest of all the fabrications, only three copies having been located, *Alaric* set the record among the 522 lots in the sale—to a low of £20 for Ruskin's *Leoni*, the great majority of the items were acquired by the House of El Dieff for the University of Texas, whose collection of Forman and Wiseiana is now unrivalled.

Texas's interest is consistent with the distinguished contributions to the Wise legend made by Fannie Ratchford and by William B. Todd, to whom the Sequelers award collaborator status with the Enquirers, and compatible with its rich collection of forgeries. But their interest is also based on possession of roughly half the located leaves stolen by Wise from seventeenth-century plays in the British Library to perfect his own Ashley copies and those he passed on to his customers, Wrenn (75) and George A. Aitken (6), which are now at Texas. As reported by David Foxon, who made the discovery in his second "enquiry" into this even more nefarious side of Wise's activities, *Thomas J. Wise and the Pre-Restoration Drama: A Study in Theft and Sophistication*, this new evidence added a dimension of villainy and a degree of scandal to the already blackened portrait of Wise that even a George Bernard Shaw could not have explained away as an elaborate practical joke "that hurt nobody, and gave keen pleasure to collectors."[12]

The practice of sophisticating copies of books is bibliographically controversial to begin with; but that Wise should have vandalized the early printings, many of them David Garrick's personal copies presented to the Museum, from the very institution destined to receive his Ashley Library, and, even worse, that in a number of instances he should have mutilated unique copies of perfect books, such as Ben Jonson's *The Case is Alter'd* (1609), is a heinous violation of the artefacts to which he devoted his life as bibliographer and collector. But with Wise there always seems more to uncover: in 1959, Foxon identified a total of 206 leaves "stolen from the Museum's quartos"; in 1982, Arthur Freeman reported another 102 loose leaves that Quaritch had inherited from Pickering and Chatto's purchases from the Hampstead sale of Wise's widow in 1939, eighty-two of which relate to the "known thefts from British Library quartos." Freeman called them "melancholy relics" of the "Wise workshop."[13] Freeman's discovery, cited in the "Stop-Press" to Barker and Collin's *Sequel*, is but the latest shock-wave emanating from the bomb dropped by Carter and Pollard in 1934.

The publication of the *Sequel* is a fitting capstone to fifty years of research into the life and art of Thomas J. Wise and (but to a far lesser degree) his collaborator, H. Buxton Forman. Behind it lie more than twenty separate publications and at least a hundred articles, not counting various reviews and numerous exhibition, sales, and booksellers' catalogues. Wise has been the subject of two full-scale biographies by Wilfred Partington; a collection of nearly 500 of his letters has been edited by Fannie Ratchford; his complete output as bibliographer, pirate, publisher, and forger has been charted by William B. Todd in his "Handlist" appended to *Centenary Studies*, which he also edited; and his accomplishments as a bibliographer have been dispassionately evaluated in the presidential address to the Bibliographical Society by Simon Nowell-Smith, who reviewed the original *Enquiry* anonymously in the *TLS* in 1934 and who also wrote the introduction to Dawson's reprint of the *Catalogue of the Ashley Library*.[14] That none of Wise's honest bibliographer-contemporaries has received such attention is an ironic comment on the perennial fascination of roguery.

At once the most important and controversial aspect of the *Sequel* is the prominence Barker and Collins assign to H. Buxton Forman as the instigator of the forgeries and the mastermind behind the whole operation: he is given star billing over Wise on the title page, and his biography, rather than Wise's, launches the first section of the book. In consciously allowing Forman to eclipse Wise in the *Sequel*, Barker and Collins may well have been prompted by the fact that most of what is new in their volume pertains more directly to him than to Wise, or they may have been influenced by the wealth of documentation on Forman that has come to light in the past two decades; but it is also probable that they share the second half of A. W. Pollard's reservations about Wise's role, expressed in a letter to Falconer Madan in 1935: "I think he is too honest to have done it, and I also greatly doubt that he is clever enough!"[15]

To judge from the later writings of Carter and Pollard, Forman seems never to have been a suspect in their conjectures over the identity of the forger during the course of their research on the *Enquiry*. While Sir Shane Leslie reported that the "cracker-barrel gossip" at the British Museum was "that Buxton Forman had manufactured the fakes, and that Wise, in spite of his almost godlike reputation as an authority, 'not being a scholar or a bibliographer,' had been taken in," it was Wise himself who first threw Forman's hat into the arena.[16] And Graham Pollard acknowledged in his introduction to Quaritch's 1973 catalogue of *Books and Pamphlets from the Library of Maurice Buxton Forman* that it was only towards the end of an unfruitful interview with Forman's son, following his *TLS* letter supporting Wise's allegations that Forman was the source of the pamphlets, "that it first occurred to us that the only explanation of Maurice Buxton Forman's attitude must be that he knew that his father was deeply involved with Wise in the forgeries." Until that point the Enquirers had assumed Wise was simply trying to make Forman "the scapegoat for his crimes."[17]

Meanwhile, in America, the Pforzheimer document surfaced and was shown to Carter in March 1935, with strict injunctions against publicizing or publishing its contents. Independently, with no specific knowledge of the secret document but drawing on Gabriel Wells' revelation about the authorship of the article on "The Building of the Idylls" in *Nineteenth Century Anecdotes* (see above, n. 7), Fannie Ratchford indicted Forman on an accumulation of circumstantial evidence—including his "satire" on Gosse's story of the Reading *Sonnets*, his sponsorship of the forgeries in various publications, and indications of his involvement in his correspondence, much of which is reproduced in the *Sequel*. By the early 1940s, Miss Ratchford too had been made privy to the Pforzheimer proofs, and in the expository section of her *Letters to Wrenn* (1944) she openly accused Carter and Pollard of suppressing evidence pointing to Forman's complicity. The controversy that followed—involving reviews and counter-reviews, accusations and counter-accusations, and a particularly unpleasant exchange over the publication of the Pforzheimer manuscript, culminating in Carter's commissioned "Postscript" to *Between the Lines* (1945), which was so devastatingly ironic and which so angered Pforzheimer that he refused to allow its publication—was invidious on both sides. Learning from Carter's *Atlantic Monthly* review of her *Letters to Wrenn* that he had known of the document and shared his knowledge with Pollard while Wise was still alive, she renewed her attack on the Enquirers in her *Review of Reviews* (1946), a long and defensive diatribe on the whole episode. Jealousy, proprietary claims, and no doubt even a little spite probably contributed to the controversy. Had the war not interrupted the investigations, removing the Enquirers temporarily from the scene and leaving the field clear for competitors, the sequence of events might have been quite different; but the fact remains that the matter of Forman did not bring out the best in either camp.[18]

None of the subsequent evidence against Forman has carried the weight of the direct confession in Wise's own hand contained in the Pforzheimer proofs.[19] The Symington letters published by Pariser exposed Forman's role in Morris's *Two Sides of the River* from his correspondence with Wise and established its forged status; and the sale in 1972 of M. B. Forman's library introduced a whole new range of materials for consideration, which Graham Pollard addressed in his introduction to Quaritch's catalogue (1973). While the younger Forman's library contained manuscript and printed materials associated with Meredith and other authors, the most important cache related to Morris and the production of his father's bibliography, *The Books of William Morris* (1897). In his "preliminary enquiry" in the *Book Collector* (1972), John Collins, who had prepared the Sotheby catalogue of the sale, identified eleven works to which some degree of suspicion attached as to production, description, imprint, or authorization.[20] These, together with two additional Morris dossiers, constitute more than a third of the 36 new works condemned in the *Sequel*.[21]

The general rumour for several years before the deaths of Carter and Pollard was that the long delay in publishing a second edition of the *Enquiry* was, in part at least, owing to a disagreement between the Enquirers involving both the importance of Forman and his precise role in the conspiracy. Whether true or not—and it may be significant that Carter published nothing on Forman subsequent to the 1972 Sotheby sale—it must be said that many of the new works added to the canon in the *Sequel*, particularly those by Morris, do not by and large share the same homogeneity that characterizes the originally indicted or suspected pamphlets. All of those, with the exception of the "Binary" copycats, were "creative" editions—"factoids" in Norman Mailer's usage—of books that never were but which either *might* have or *ought* to have been produced by their authors. All had traceable pedigrees and auction records, and all conformed to a similar though not identical format.

By contrast, many of the new works—principally those by Morris, which clearly derive from Forman—are unique, eccentric, or (in at least one instance) non-existent. Others, notably the five works by Carroll, Meredith, and Thomson, have so little to do with Wise and Forman that it is difficult to see why the Sequelers included them. And the Sequelers have had to devise a whole new rubric to describe the subspecies that their careful and detailed examination of typefonts has netted: chimaeras, changelings, ghosts, embryo piracies, blinds, counterfeits, and other deceptive productions, several of which are wrappers for Morris pamphlets that Forman clearly "invented" to sophisticate his own copies and to "dress up" the entries in his bibliography.

This distinction is in no way intended to minimize the contribution of the Sequelers. By widening the scope of the investigation, they have extended the known boundaries of the forgers' activities and perhaps laid the groundwork for new discoveries. "Like the story of Frankie and Johnny," they conclude their chapter on "The Process of Partnership," "this story has no moral, this story has no end. If we have taken it a little further, we end with the certainty that there is more still to be found out than we thought when we started. What it goes to show, beyond the obvious, only time will tell" (p. 182). In fact, this epilogue is too modest to define the major additions the Sequelers have made to the story, for, while the *Sequel* necessarily synthesizes an enormous amount of previously available detail, it also marshalls an amazing bounty of new information relating to the biographies of Wise and Forman; to the extensive range of types employed in the fabrications, which are so crucial in dating; to the auction histories of the pamphlets; and, of course, to the artefacts themselves.

The structure and organization of the *Sequel* are generally convenient; the three expository sections—on "The Lives of the Forgers," "The Typographical Enquiry" (the most recondite part of the book), and "The Course of the Crime"—are followed by the Dossiers and a series of seven Appendices, many of which have already been discussed.[22] Chapter 9, the summary of the typographical section, might profitably have been combined with the introduction to the following section since it is more apposite to the collaboration than to an examination of type, but that is the only major displacement in the volume. Some readers may cavil that the dossiers are not perfectly consistent or that the auction records stop at 1920, which admittedly does make comparisons with the figures cited in the *Enquiry* almost impossible; but these strictures are less serious than the authors' decision not to annotate the letters of Wise and Forman in Appendix 4.

Factually, the *Sequel* is unusually reliable, though inevitably there are errors, one or two of which are major.[23] Two of Wise's letters to Forman (pp. 272 and 275), for example, are both dated—the one 3 November 1886, the other 5 November 1888; from the contents, however, they would seem almost certainly to be contiguous and one or the other date wrongly transcribed. Similarly, the two reports on the valuation of Wise's library (pp. 58 and 123) do not agree; in the first instance Wise is quoted as stating that his books have cost him "barely £40,000" in the second, the same figure is cited as his valuation of his books when, in fact, he said "their value today is at least three times that sum" (p. 58).

Two important errors involve the Rossetti brothers, William Michael and Dante Gabriel. The first is of little other than chronological significance, but William's diary establishes that he did not meet Forman in 1876, as the Sequelers say (p.32), but on 8 March 1877. The second, however, may well be crucial to the dating of the first documentable forgery on which Forman and Wise actually collaborated. In this context, it will be useful to supplement the *Enquiry* dossier on Rossetti's *Verses*, 1881 (pp. 218-21). Carter and Pollard, reluctantly conceding that "there is no positive evidence from type or paper to prove the book a forgery," could only rank it a piracy, but they add: "There seems to be the strongest possible evidence, short of the conclusive, for assigning to it the higher degree of culpability" (*E*, p. 220). The pamphlet is condemned in the *Sequel* on grounds of type.

William Michael reported in his diary on 4 April 1881 that "from something which Sharp told him [Gabriel] has a suspicion that there may be a pirated edition of his poems on sale"; that piracy, if it existed—William doubted the likelihood and it is never again mentioned—could not have been *Verses*, owing to the use of anachronistic types not manufactured until 1883, a discovery that also gives the lie to Wise's statement to Wrenn in a letter of September 1900, that "D. G. R. himself caused the little tract to be printed and gave the copies away gratis."[24] Rossetti, of course, never saw this pamphlet, though the two poems it contains do have a curious history. The second poem, the sonnet, "After the French Liberation of Italy," was written in 1859 and set in type about the same time as *Poems (Privately Printed)*, 1869, though it was never included in any of the so-called trial books or in any edition of his poems until William Michael's illustrated edition of 1904. Copies of the fly-sheet, signed and dated "D. G. R. 1859," were fairly widely circulated and are not especially rare. The leaflet is No. 15 in William Michael's separately published *Bibliography* of his brother

(1905). The first poem, "At the Fall of the Leaf," was composed in September 1848, when Rossetti sent a fair copy of this "howling canticle," in five stanzas to his mother.

There is less agreement, however, about the date of publication. In the Contents to *Works* (1911), William gives the first date of publication as 1883, but he does not indicate that it appeared in the *Musical Review* for 6 January of that year; in the notes he says that the poem was set to music during Rossetti's lifetime by Edward Dannreuther, "and was published in that form—perhaps not otherwise" (p. 663). In his *Bibliography*, however, the poem appears as No. 41, under the date 1884, as having been published, along with five other previously published songs, with the title "Autumn Song," in *Love-Lily and other Songs, by Dante Gabriel Rossetti, set to music by Edward Dannreuther*, with a cross-reference to its earlier reprinting in *Verses* (1881), now included in the annotation to No. 15. Carter and Pollard also cite *Love-Lily* as the first publication of the poem. In fact, it was first printed— as "Autumn Song. (MS.)," with three stanzas—in the privately printed programme of a musicale held at "12, Orme Square, on Thursday, January 18th, 1877," entitled *Specimens from a Cycle of English Songs and Lyrics. / The Music by Edward Dannreuther*, containing in all 20 poems: 9 by Morris, 3 by Swinburne, two by Beaumont and Fletcher, one each by John Ford, Ben Jonson, and Tennyson, and, in addition to "Autumn Song," Rossetti's "Love-Lily." No music accompanies the text, but the names of the two male and two female singers are provided. The slight variations in punctuation and a single substantive alteration in the first line of the second stanza between the 1877 private printing and the forgery seem to indicate that *Verses* was set from either the 1883 or 1884 versions. The linking of the earlier title with the later text, although intentionally dissembling, may, however, suggest that the *Verses* version was set from a revised manuscript of the poem, antedating 1877, by which date the title had certainly been altered.

The first copy of *Verses* recorded at auction in the *Sequel* is in a Bang's sale for 10 February 1895, pushing back by nearly eighteen months the first recorded copy cited in the *Enquiry*

(Sotheby's, 31 July 1896) which, strangely, is not listed in Appendix 5. Like so many of the pamphlets, *Verses* was obviously produced several years before it was publicly marketed; how early may be central in establishing a priority among the forgeries. The earliest labelled forgery in the *Sequel* is R. H. Horne's *Galatea Secunda*, a work that exists in four recorded paper stocks. Putatively dated 1867, the B stock is watermarked "1873"—the tell-tale sign of a forgery. Forman's connection with the printing of Horne's work, the fact that a copy of *Galatea Secunda* appeared in Forman's first sale of 12 October 1884, and the further fact that the British Library copy (date stamped 14 October 1939) and more than 30 other copies bought by Elkin Mathews in 1945 derive from his son, Maurice, place firmly the responsibility for its manufacture on Forman. The Sequelers base their speculation on the probable dates of Forman's two Horne piracies and suggest that the pamphlet was "perhaps printed in 1881," which is at least five years before he met Thomas J. Wise and several years before the first joint forgery that can be dated with any confidence.

Establishing Forman as the father of this forgery poses a crucial pair of questions about which there can only be speculation: did Forman, recognizing a co-felon in Wise, recruit his junior by seventeen years to a scheme that he had already tentatively launched? Or had Wise already mapped out his own course by the time he met Forman, whom he found to be a compatible ally? With only two leaves, *Galatea Secunda* bears little resemblance to the forged pamphlets and is clearly a trial effort by Forman, analogous to the single 1884 issue of the *Hobby Horse*, which preceded the actual journal by two years. But it may not even be an intentional forgery: that so trivial a work is found in three states with four paper stocks, one with a later watermark—which could have been accidental, a possibility even more likely if it was produced as late as 1881—may indicate that it is no more than a deceptively dated piracy of the class of the much later *The Pilgrims of Hope*.[25] This is one of the two main recurring patterns associated with Forman, the other being the creation of fabricated wrappers, such as that done for the 1885 *Chants for Socialists* (of which only two out of a stated fifty are known), the second of the two works antedating

Forman's meeting with Wise. That two other contemporary piracies of Horne's work were produced at the same time lends credence to this theory.

If this hypothesis is correct, it suggests that the production of the more substantive pamphlets commenced only after their meeting; that the conception of the plan was closely linked to their access to printing facilities provided by the publication programme of the Shelley Society, the potential of which Wise, as Honorary Secretary, was quick to recognize and exploit; and that the earliest date for a joint production must be 1886. However, since both Wise and Forman by this date had produced independent piracies, the problem of influence remains up in the air.[26] Which of them actually initiated the scheme, how the proposal of a collaboration was ever broached between two men of such dissimilar temperaments, and how the practical logistics of the enterprise were managed will probably always remain enigmatic.

What is known is the rough sequence of publication of the early pamphlets. By consensus, the place of "honour" is given to Swinburne's *Cleopatra*. Barker and Collins, following Graham Pollard,[27] and on the evidence of Swinburne's letter to Wise of 27 April 1888, stating that he was "quite certain, quite positive, that I never set eyes on the booklet before, or heard of its existence," assert categorically that this is the "first attested date for any joint forgery" (p. 134). Several points are raised by their comment. First, though there is a wealth of negative evidence to convict this pamphlet—related type, provenance of a proof copy in the Wrenn Library, auction record, and imprint—Carter and Pollard had to conclude that "it is, in theory, possible that it is not a forgery" (*E*, p. 284); and no subsequent evidence of type or paper is provided in the *Sequel* to indict it. Second, no evidence is advanced to support the claim that it is a joint effort; the first forgery hinted at in their correspondence is George Eliot's *Agatha* in a letter from Forman to Wise dated 6 May 1889; the first directly mentioned is Rossetti's *Sister Helen* in the following year. *Cleopatra* was unquestionably in print by the date of Swinburne's letter, and Forman may have had a role in its production; but, lacking firm corroboration, it seems more likely that it originated with Wise, who certainly publicized and marketed the pamphlet. In any event, there is evidence, unexplored by the Sequelers, to suggest that the collaboration began several months before the date of Swinburne's letter—in the previous year.

The Troxell collection at Princeton contains Forman's annotated proof copy of Rossetti's *Poems*, 1870 (Lot 590 in the 1920 Anderson sale). The annotation consists of an initial note dated 10 June 1880, with a P.S. dated 15 November 1887. As both are evidential, they are quoted in full:

> These proof sheets of the first edition of Rossetti's Poems were sent to me by the publisher that I might be in a position to write an article about the book immediately on its issue. The interest I took in the matter was known from an article on Rossetti's scattered pieces which I had published in the series called "Criticisms on Contemporaries" in "Tinsley's Magazine"; and the article written from the proof-sheets appeared in the same magazine, under the title of "Dante Gabriel Rossetti, Poet," having been refused by Dr. Pope with many apologies as too preraphaelite (or something of the sort) for the "London Quarterly Review."
>
> Both articles were printed again in a revised form in "Our Living Poets."
>
> Rossetti did an enormous amount of redaction and cancelling before the book got to this state; and after that, even, he rearranged the contents, and added the four sonnets appended to these sheets in manuscript.
>
> The sonnet on the French Liberation of Italy was set in type; but it was agreed to withdraw it; and as far as I know it has never been published, tho' handed about in manuscript.
>
> There is not the slightest doubt of its authenticity. Apart from the internal evidence, I remember being consulted about it by Ellis; and certainly more than one copy, as set up in 1870, still exists. Ellis kept at least one himself: there is one in a set of sweepings up which W. B. Scott made at Penkill Castle, where Rossetti read the proofs when staying there with Miss Boyd; and I fancy E. W. Gosse has a similar set.
>   H.B.F.
> 10 June 1880
>
> P. S. Since the foregoing note was written some friends of Rossetti's have printed the Sonnet "After the French Liberation of Italy," together

with a poem of three stanzas, "At the Fall of the Leaf," in a very pretty pamphlet with the title "Verses / by / Dante Gabriel Rossetti" printed on vellum; but the whole issue must have been extremely small.

   H.B.F.
15 November 1887

 Barker and Collins are generally skeptical in the *Sequel* of Forman's endorsements in his personal copies of books and manuscripts, regarding them by and large as spurious and self-serving. But their notes 8 to Chapter 11 and 3 to Chapter 14 (pp. 142, 182), on Rossetti's *Verses*—the "earliest certain date" for which they say, with no tendered evidence, is January 1890—can only be regarded as either contradictory or self-cancelling. In the first, they assert that "no credence can be given to these dates" in the Princeton-Troxell copy; in the second, however, they allow at least for the possibility that Forman's endorsement may be literal: "the notes . . . may be genuinely dated; if so they are surprisingly early."

 That they are early is true, but even on the surface there is no reason to assume them to be dishonest. Forman, after all, knew Rossetti, though not intimately; he had corresponded with him about Keats and other subjects; and in 1870 he was one of the recipients to whom Rossetti instructed his publisher F.S. Ellis to send proof copies of his *Poems*, adding in a later letter (*c*. 10 March), "also please let me know if Forman seems frightened at *Jenny* or anything else." Forman's advance notice of Rossetti in *Tinsley's* in September 1869, the most extensive recognition he had received to that point, was influential in establishing Rossetti as a poet. In fact, it was directly owing to Forman's praise of "My Sister's Sleep" in his *Tinsley* article that Rossetti resuscitated that poem for inclusion in his volume, having to request Christina to make a transcription from *The Germ* as he had no copy with him at Penkill. Forman also defended Rossetti against Buchanan in 1871.[28]

 Forman's initial annotation is totally accurate, both about how he acquired the proofs and about the poems withdrawn from the published volume. The precise dating of both entries probably records no more than a collector's endorsement of his own property, a practice William Michael Rossetti engaged in all his life. The second date, 15 November 1887, may be accidentally or unintentionally honest, but there is no real reason to doubt its veracity. While the assertion that the pamphlet originated with "some friends" of Rossetti's is equally as disingenuous as Wise's bald lie to Wrenn that Rossetti himself had it printed and distributed it to his friends, this dated inscription appears to push forward the commencement of the collaboration between Wise and Forman and to establish *Verses* as their first created forgery. Admittedly, there is no direct evidence to establish that they collaborated on *Verses*; and applying the Sequelers stock-remainder yardstick, it might seem that Forman's letter of [18] November 1902 argues strongly for him as the more probable source. However, Wise's reference to the pamphlet in his review of Slater (1894) and the eagerness of both forgers in 1902 (see *S*, p. 288) to obtain William Rossetti's *nihil obstat* for the pamphlet in his *Bibliography* tend to confirm *Verses* as a more likely candidate for their first joint production than Swinburne's *Cleopatra*. In view of the propinquity of both forgers to William Michael Rossetti, whose friendship they courted and abused, it seems somehow ironically appropriate that they should have chosen a work by his brother to launch their infamous conspiracy.[29]

Whether Forman and Wise were friends as well as associates is not really evident in their exchanged letters printed in the *Sequel*, though obviously they shared a common bond as felons and collectors. Each brought to the conspiracy talents that complemented the intellectual and scholarly abilities as well as the personality and character traits of the other. But from the evidence of their letters to William Michael Rossetti—and their respective correspondence with Wrenn and Bucke reinforces the striking disimilarities between the two men—Wise clearly emerges as the more villainous, treacherous, and machiavellian of the pair.

Barker and Collins assume, and perhaps rightly, that Wise was neither the *primum mobile* nor the brains in the partnership, but they readily admit in their chapter on "The Process of Partnership" that the mass of new material that has surfaced in recent years complicates rather than clarifies the problems posed by the Wise-Forman collaboration. The Sequelers do not try to hide their dislike of Forman, owing to the "secretive, rather off-putting, nature of his personality," which contrasts with Wise's "genial," albeit "dishonest... affability." But the truth seems to be that Forman was a much more private and inherently discreet man than Wise: he sought fame and recognition through his published books and editions, but he did not publicize himself and his possessions as Wise did, nor did he revel in the limelight of public acclaim. A better bibliographer than his accomplice, Forman seems also to have had a genuine love of books as Wise did not. Wise may have taken a leaf from Forman's book in mimicking his pattern for creating books that never were, but, while Forman manufactured unique wrappers to case his privately printed treasures, it is hard to conceive of him ever mutilating a book—literally taking a leaf out of it—to sophisticate a copy to sell to someone else.

So, too, in his collecting, Forman was more attracted by the arcane and the unique—as so many items identified in the *Sequel* to be his work confirm—than to books as pecuniary objects. The avariciousness of a collector like Wise, who so often talks of his books in monetary terms, must, one senses instinctively, have been incompatible with Forman's more reserved and scholarly temperament. Forman left behind no Ashley Library to memorialize him. It may be true that in disposing of his books at an "institutional" price he envisioned having one day a rare book room in some university library named after him, but it is more likely that his primary concern was that his books should find a home where they would be housed intact.[30]

Taking their cue from Fairfax Murray, Barker and Collins conclude that "the partnership was an equal one" (p. 181) and it may have been—though the case is by no means proven—in terms of shared responsibility and joint profits; but it is significant that all the evidence amassed by the Enquirers in their original investigations pointed overwhelmingly, directly, and exclusively to Wise, not to Forman. And it was their refusal to allow Wise to exonerate himself by implicating Forman that forced Wise finally to stand mute. Would Forman, one wonders, in a parallel circumstance, have rested his defence on the grave of his dead partner? Even the Sequelers are forced to confess,

"It is by no means clear that Forman took the forgeries as seriously as he did Shelley and Keats" (p. 173).

No argument can be made to exonerate Forman, and none is advanced here: his complicity and guilt were established half a century ago when the Pforzheimer document came to light; but it is interesting to speculate with what certainty an indictment against Forman could be made to stick—in a court of law, say—even with the new evidence available in recent years, if that document did not exist.

Barker and Collins in their *Sequel* to *An Enquiry* have done John Carter and Graham Pollard proud in continuing the ongoing saga of the "Certain Nineteenth Century Pamphlets" that launched the original investigation so many years ago. If, like me, some readers remain skeptical about the emphasis given to Forman in the *Sequel*, the explanation lies not in the relative awkwardness of the appropriate adjectival form required to describe the origin of the forgeries—"Formanian" or "Formanesque" as opposed to "Wiseian"—but in something John Carter himself said in reviewing Fannie Ratchford's edition of the Wrenn letters, a decade after he became aware of the hard evidence to convict Forman: "Even if her readers now conclude, or further discoveries should suggest, that the forgeries were the work of a ring, I shall be much surprised if Thomas J. Wise has to be dethroned from his commanding position as the master mind."[31] To their credit, the Sequelers do not regard themselves as having "solved" the mystery: from their point of view, the case is altered, not closed.

Master List of Indicted Works

With the publication of the *Sequel*, the number of items identified as belonging to the Wise-Forman canon now numbers an even hundred. The dossiers for these items, however, are detailed and complex; not all of them are included in the *Enquiry* and *Sequel*, and there is nowhere available a summary of the condemned works that makes accessible the essential facts about each of the indicted items. This Master List is intended to fill that need. For each work, the following abbreviated information is provided:

Sequel to *A Sequel* 281

1) the *Sequel* and the Todd number;
2) the short title and putative date;
3) the location of the dossiers; commencing page numbers follow source abbreviations. An asterisk indicates the sources other than the *Enquiry* and *Sequel* in which a work was first condemned; abbreviations for sources other than *E* or *S* are indicated below;
4) the present status of the work, with the evidence, both abbreviated; status: forgery, binary forgery (F, BF); suspected, but not proven fabrication (S); piracy or chimaera (P, C); other deceptive work (DP); evidence: paper, type, collation, or imprint (P, T, C, I);
5) information about copies, including either the number or the location; the number handled by Herbert Gorfin—purchased from TJW (number only), on commission (C), or the number catalogued (*). The auction record includes the first appearance and the total accounted for in *E* or *S*, updated where a discrepancy exists between first sale recorded. Abbreviations in these columns are to the British Library, Bodley, and Cambridge (BL, B, C), and to the source of acquisition if TJW or his partner, Otto P. Rubeck (W, R); HBF in the auction column refers to his 1920 sale at the Anderson Galleries; MBF to the Sotheby, sale of 10 April 1972.
6) the probable date(s) of fabrication, where known;
7) evidence for responsibility or dating, and other notes.

As in the notes, the forgers are abbreviated TJW and HBF; MBF is HBF's son, Maurice; LA is *Literary Anecdotes* (1896); F numbers refer to HBF's Morris bibliography. Dates are abbreviated day, month, and year, as in 12.2.89.

Sources (with abbreviations)

(B) Roland Baughman. *Some Victorian Forged Rarities* (San Marino: Huntington Library, 1936); reprinted from *HLB*, no. 9 (1936), 91-117.

(R) Fannie Ratchford. "*Idylls of the Hearth*: Wise's Forgery of 'Enoch Arden'," *Southwest Review*, 26 (Spring 1941), 317-25.

(F) John Carter and Graham Pollard. *The Firm of Charles Ottley, Landon & Co.: Footnote to* An Enquiry. London: Hart-Davis, 1948.

(C) John Carter. "George Eliot's *Agatha* 1869—and After," *Book Collector*, 6 (Autumn 1957), 244-52.

(W) Graham Pollard. "The Case of *The Devil's Due*," in *Thomas J. Wise: Centenary Studies*, ed. W. B. Todd. Austin: University of Texas Press, 1959.

(G) K. I. Garrett. *"The Artist and the Author*: an Unidentified Edition of a Cruikshank Pamphlet," *Guildhall Miscellany*, 2 (October 1962), 170-72.

(P) Maurice Pariser. "H. Buxton Forman and T. J. Wise," letter to the Editor, *TLS*, 23 July 1964, p. 649.

(K) William D. Paden. "Tennyson's *The Lover's Tale*: R. H. Shepherd and T. J. Wise," *Studies in Bibliography*, 18 (1965), 111-45.

(WP) John Carter and Graham Pollard. *The Forgeries of Tennyson's Plays*. Working Paper No. 2. Oxford: Blackwell, 1967.

(D) James S. Dearden. "Wise and Ruskin II," *Book Collector*, 18 (Summer 1969), 170-88.

(T) William B. Todd. "Postscript on *The Story of a Lie*," in *Suppressed Commentaries on the Wiseian Forgeries*. Austin, Texas: HRC, 1969.

Sequel to *A Sequel*

MASTER LIST

Sequel/ Todd No.	Short Title & Putative Date	Dossiers	Status & Evidence	No./Location	Goffin	Auction Record	Fabrication Date	Evidence of Responsibility or Dating, and Other Notes
				MATTHEW ARNOLD (3)				
1 (1c)	Alaric at Rome (1840)	*B100/S193	BF (T)	3 (all U.S.)		[3.6.02]	Dec 1893	Date of TJW Facsimile
2 (4f)	Geist's Grave (1881)	E163	S (N)	C 1916-W		4.12.89 (21E+4S)	Dec 1889	Libbie Sale (Boston)
3 (3f)	Saint Brandon (1867)	E161	S (N)	BL 20.8.90-R	16	do (25E+5S)	do	do
				ELIZABETH BARRETT BROWNING (2)				
4 (69f)	The Runaway Slave (1849)	E169	F (P)	BL 16.8.88	107C	12.6.89 (28)	Aug 1888	BL
5 (68f)	Sonnets (1847)	E167	F (PT)	36? (E Census)	C	7.5.01 (19)	21.6.93	Letter Gosse:TJW (TJWOC, p. 275)
				ROBERT BROWNING (3)				
6 (84f)	Cleon (1855)	E177	F (PT)		14	10.6.03 (15)	1890	All three are listed in
7 (86f)	Gold Hair (1864)	E181	F (T)		19	30.1.95 (22E+2S)	1890	Anderson's Supplement to
8 (85f)	The Statue and the Bust (1855)	E179	F (PT)		18	7.5.01 (13E+1S)	1890	Sharp's biography
				LEWIS CARROLL (2)				
9	Some Popular Fallacies (1875)	S267	[F] (T)	12 (S)		Dec. 1923	1920+	Type; no HBF-TJW-MBF link
10	Love Among the Roses (1878)	S195	[implied F] (T)			1925	1921+	Date; MBF provenance (9 copies)
				GEORGE CRUIKSHANK (1)				
11	Artist and the Author [1872]	*G/S197	BF (PT)	9 located (G)	45	Hodgson's 1942	1900?	Wrenn copy: 5.12.1900; from "Hake"
				CHARLES DICKENS (1)				
12 (149f)	To be Read at Dusk (1852)	E185	F (PT)		50	7.6.93 (8E+15S)	15.5.91	Letter C. P. Johnson:Athenaeum
				GEORGE ELIOT (2)				
13 (156f)	Agatha ("2nd ed.")(1869)	E194/*C244	BF (PT)	50? (TJW)	19	[10.12.88]	6.5.89	Letter HBF:TJW (S275-6)
14 (157f)	Brother and Sister (1869)	E191/E2 p.15	F (PTC)	BL 23.10.88	24	17.11.91(30E+1S)	23.10.88	BL

283

284   REVIEW

-2-

Sequel/ Todd No.	Short Title & Putative Date	Dossiers	Status & Evidence	Information on Copies No./Location	Goffin	Auction Record	Fabrication Date	Evidence of Responsibility or Dating, and Other Notes
				RICHARD HENGIST HORNE (3)				
15	Galatea Secunda (1867)	S199	F (WaterM)	30+ (MBF)			1881?	Watermark:1873; HBF
16	Sir Featherbright [?1881]	S200	P			12.11.84	1881?	HBF; RHH inscriptions that
17	The Two Georges [?1881]	S201	P			12.11.84	1881?	neither published:Mitchell Library
				RUDYARD KIPLING (2)				
18 (171p)	White Horses (1897)	E201	P	BL 8.1.98	57	26.11.00 (22E+1S)	1897	First separate ed. of WH, but
19 (172p)	The White Man's Burden (1899)	E203	P	B 13.2.99	30	4.4.21 (15)	1899	neither pamphlet sanctioned by K
				GEORGE MEREDITH (2)				
20	Jump-to-Glory Jane (1889)	S202	P/F?	50 (certs. of		9.3.99 (10)	1889-92	Letter GM 15.11.92 (S202);
21	Twenty Poems (1909)	S203	P "orphan"	25 limitation)			1909	Both MBF?; Jane joint with HBF?
				WILLIAM MORRIS (15)				
22	Chants for Socialists (1885)	S204	C	Unique (50?HBF)		MBF	1885-97	Red wrapper only; F79
23	The God of the Poor [1884]	S204	F (T)			10.10.99 (6)	1893-97	F73
24	Gossip About Old House (1895)	S205	P	50 (HBF)-3+		27.6.12 (3)	1895-97	From sheets of The Quest; F162
25	Manifesto Socialist L. (1885)	S206	"Ghost"?			?	?	No copy known; F75
	do "New" [2nd ed. (1885)	S206	C				1885-97	Wrapper only; F76
26	The Pilgrims of Hope (1886)	S207	DP	BL 9.4.97-F		9.5.98 (15)	1886-97	Acknowledged piracy HBF; F93
27	The Reward of Labour (1892)	S208	C				1892?	Legitimate wrapper?; F137
28 (182f)	Sir Galahad (1858)	E207	F (PT)	Unique (Texas)	17	14.6.97 (16)	23.11.90	Inscribed copy WM:HBF
(183c)	do	S208	Counterfeit					F2; Temple-Scott, p. 1; Vallance F121
29	The Socialist Ideal (1891)	S209	DP (T)			27.3.03 (5)	1893-97	Unused wrappers (dated 1885, 1888,
30 [A]	The Socialist Platform (1888)	S209	C			MBF	1897	1890) for nonce edition; F102, 111
[B]	do (1890)	S210	F (T)			do	1897	Ambiguous title-page; A wrapper in
31 [A]	Socialists at Play (1885)		F (T)			21.10.01 (5)+	1897	red, B in brown; F77
[B]	do	E211/*P/S210	F	12.11.94	8	MBF (4)	17.2.90	Letter HBF:TJW (S276); F42
32 (184f)	Two Sides of the River (1876)	S212	C	Unique (50?HBF)		12.5.97 (23+HBF)	1891-97	Acknowledged HBF Wrapper only; F131
33	Under an Elm-Tree (1891)	S212	C	12 or less (HBF)		MBF	1893-97	Copy in unique red wrapper MBF; F72
34	The Voice of Toil [1884]	S213	F (T)			MBF	1893-97	Wrapper only; F138
35	Westminster Abbey (1893)	S213	C				1896-97	HBF acknowledged wrapper; F167
36	How I became a Socialist (1896)		C			MBF		

Sequel to *A Sequel*

Sequel/ Todd No.	Short Title & Putative Date	Dossiers	Status & Evidence	No./Location	Gorfin	Auction Record	Fabrication Date	Evidence of Responsibility or Dating, and Other Notes
				DANTE GABRIEL ROSSETTI (3)				
37 (192f)	Sister Helen (1857)	E215	F (PT)	Unique	1+C	10.6.03 (21)	1894+	TJW rev. Slater
38	Hand and Soul (1870)	S214	C (T)			HBF (Lot 589)	1886?	HBF title-page & wrappers
39 (193p)	Verses (1881)	E218	F (T)	BL 12.11.94	1+C	10.5.95 (10E+1S)	1887?	HBF:MS. endorsement; 3 vellum
				JOHN RUSKIN (8)				
40 (199c)	Turner Sketches in NG (1857)	E230/W25	BF (PT)	5-6 (TJW)	No.?	[12.5.97]	Jan 1890	TJW Ruskin Bibl. Pt. 3
41 (202f)	The Future of England (1870)	E238/D181	BF (PT)		30-40	12.5.97 (5)	May 1890	do, Pt. 5
(203c)	"Reprint" (1870)	E238/*D185	BF (PT)		2 bundles		do	Bundles destroyed by Gorfin & TJW?
42 (201f)	Leoni (1868)	E236/D170	F (P)	1 extant?	14	12.5.97 (5)	do	TJW Ruskin bibl. Pt. 5
43 (198f)	The National Gallery (1852)	E227/D171	F (PTC)	do	41	12.5.97 (12)	Nov 1889	do., Pt. 2
44 (205f)	The N&A of Miracle (1873)	E242/*D174	F (PT)	BL 16.6.90-R	36	14.6.97 (4+)	Oct 1890	do., Pt. 7
	["Reprint"?]			no copies	extant?		do	Bundle destroyed by Gorfin?
45 (200f)	The Queen's Gardens (1864)	E232/D178	F (TC)		7	30.7.94 (5E+1S)	Dec 1892	TJW Ruskin Bibl., Pt. 16 Omissions
46 (204f)	Samuel Prout (1870)	E240/D172	F (T)		27	12.5.97 (5)	May 1890	do., Pt. 5
47 (197f)	The Scythian Guest (1849)	E225/176	F (PT)		16	10.6.03 (5)	Dec 1892	TJW Ruskin Bibl., Pt. 16 Omissions
				PERCY BYSSHE SHELLEY (1)				
48 (252p)	Poems and Sonnets (1887)	S215	DP	30 (cert.)		29.11.05 (2)	1887	Letter Dowden:TJW (Aug 88, S133-4); ed. "Charles A. Seymour" (aka TJW)
				ROBERT LOUIS STEVENSON (7)				
49 (286d)	Familiar Epistle (1896)	S216	P	"a few" (cert.)	7	12.5.97 (16)	1896	Ashley Library device
50 (281f)	Some College Memories (1886)	E254	P		14	14.6.97 (14)	1894+	Athenaeum corresp. Jan-Feb 1898
51 (280f)	The Story of a Lie (1882)	E251/T39	S (N)		21	28.7.99 (25)	1899?	Suspicious imprint
52 (279f)	Thermal Influence (1873)	E247	F (PT)		27	12.5.97 (30+)	1897?	
53 (283f)	Thomas Stevenson (1887)	E265/379/*S217	F (N)		6?	26.1.99 (14E+4S)	1896?	
54 (283/4f)	Ticonderoga (1887)	E266/W77/*S218	F (1)	BL 9.5.91(B)	3(B)	27.6.98 (22 of B)	1891?	Letter Colvin:Gosse (S217)
55 (285p)	War In Samoa (1893)	E266/*S222	P/F? (N)		10?	21.3.98 (26)	1896?	3 states: A-25, B-50, C-4+ vellum

-3-

Sequel/ Todd No.	Short Title & Putative Date	Dossiers	Status & Evidence	No./Location	Gorfin	Auction Record	Fabrication Date	Evidence of Responsibility or Dating, and Other Notes
				ALGERNON CHARLES SWINBURNE (22)				
56 (294f)	An Appeal to England (1867)	E292/*S224	F (N)	BL 12.4.90-W	24	14.6.97 (22)	Dec 1890	BL; improbability of publication
57 (305p)	The Ballad of Bulgarie (1893)	S225	P	B 7.2.17-W	3/8*	23.2.09 (10)	1893	Piracy with connivance of Gosse
58	Ballad of Dead Men's Bay (1889)	S226	P/F?	BL 9.5.91	2*	26.1.99 (10)	1891	BL
59	The Bride's Tragedy (1889)	S227	P/F? (N)	BL 5.12.09-W	7*	10.10.99 (10)	1889-96	LA; HBF
60	The Brothers (1889)	S227	F (N)	BL 17.12.97		13.3.01 (4)	1892-96	do, BL
61 (292f)	Cleopatra (1866)	E278	S (N)	BL 13.5.90-R	6?	1.12.91 (12)	27.4.88	Letter ACS:TJW (S134); proofs:Wrenn
62 (291f)	Dead Love (1864)	E269	F (PTI)	BL 12.4.90-W	20?	9.5.98 (17E+1S)	1890	BL; a facsimile of DL exists
63 (297f)	The Devil's Due (1875)	E291/*W38/S228	F (P)	BL 19.4.19-W	5*	17.6.07 (12E, 25S)	16.2.97	Letter TJW:Gosse (S29)
64 (295f)	Dolores (1867)	E285	F (PT)	BL 14.6.19-W		9.5.98 (16)		
65	Dolorida (1883)	S230	P [RHS]	BL 3.2.90		13.5.92 (15)	1887	Shepherd's Bibl.; remainder stock
66 (302f)	Gathered Songs (1887)	*F/S232	F (I)	BL 1909-W	4/6*	10.10.99 (18)	8.87-5.91	4 vellum; proofs:Slater-Bodley
67 (306p)	Grace Darling (1893)	S233	"Changeling"			11.12.95 (32)	1893	Acknowledged TJW:30 paper, 3 vellum
68 (301f)	The Jubilee (1887)	*F/S234	F (I)	BL 9.5.91	5*	13.2.01 (6)	8.87-5.91	4 vellum; proofs:Wrenn
69 (293f)	Laus Veneris (1866)	E272	F (P)	BL 12.4.90-W	15?	13.11.90 (31E+1S)	1890	BL
70 (298d)	Note on Epipsychidion (1886)	S235	?"Embryo Piracy"	Unique proofs (Ashley Library)		28.3.99 (17)	15.7.86	Proofs corrected ACS and TJW
71 (300f)	The Question (1887)	*F/S235	F (I)	BL 1909-W	5*	10.10.99 (7)	2.10.96	4 vellum
72 (307p)	Robert Burns (1896)	S236	P/F?	Ashley	1/9*	25.1.99 (16)	May 1891	Burns Centenary Club (a fiction?)
73 (303p)	Sonnets on Browning (1890)	S237	F (PTI)	BL 9.5.91	13	[10.12.89] (22?)	Dec 1889	Challenged by Watts-Dunton in 1909
74 (296c)	Siena (1868)	E287	BF (T)	BL 9.12.93-W		13.5.92 (12)	1888	BL
75 (304p)	Unpublished Verses (1888)	E291/S239	P [RHS]	BL 10.4.94	15		13.3.89	Remainder stock:Shepherd piracy
76	Warning Note (1886)	S240	"Blind"	Unique copy (Ashley Library)				Letter "Frederic Avery":ACS
77 (299f)	A Word for the Navy (1887)	*F/S240	F (CI)	BL 1909	6*	4.12.89	8.87-5.91	4 vellum
				ALFRED LORD TENNYSON (18)				
78 (396f)	Becket (1879)	*B98/WP2/S245	F (PTC)	Ashley copy not received BL			1893+	4/6? copies brought to light by TJW
79 (403f)	Carmen Saeculare (1887)	E336	F (T)	BL 10.10.03	C	20.11.99 (14)	?	Type; 18/20? copies known
80 (398f)	Child-Songs (1880)	E379/S247	F (PTI)		C	HBF (Lot 867+2S)	1892-99?	Lack of imprint irregular
81 (399f)	The Cup (1881)	E327/*W36/WP2	F (PI)	BL 11.3.99-W	C	20.11.99 (11)	?	Absence from Macmillan records
82 (404f)	The Death of Clarence (1892)	E343/*S248	F (N)	BL 8.2.08	6?	HBF (Lot 1091)	1883+	Type
83 (394f)	England and America (1872)	E379/*P/*S249	F (PT)		C	none to 1920	1892-99?	Lack of imprint irregular
84 (397f)	The Falcon (1879)	*E323/*WP2	F (P)	BL 11.5.07-W	C	20.11.99 (12)	1888-90	Title-leaf only
85 (390f)	Idylls of the Hearth (1864)	*R584/S249	F (T)	BL 20.5.90-R		1.4.02 (7)	?	Presentation A. Strahan:TJW
86 (393f)	The Last Tournament (1871)	E315	F (PTC)	C 14.8.16-W	1+C	28.2.00 (19)	1897?	Forgery of R. H. Shepherd edition
87 (392c)	The Lover's Tale (1870)	E307/WP1	BF (PT)	50? (cert.)	23	non-evidential	1892-94	TJW rev. Slater; cloth casing
88 (391f)	Lucretius (1868)	E305	F (PT)	BL 13.9.92	1+C	3.6.98 (12)	1892-94	Death of T; LA
89 (387f)	Morte D'Arthur (1842)	E295	F (PT)		1+C	1.4.02 (8)	1892-96	

Sequel to *A Sequel*   287

-5-

Sequel/ Todd No.	Short Title & Putative Date	Dossiers	Status & Evidence	No./Location	Gorfin	Auction Record	Fabrication Date	Evidence of Responsibility or Dating, and Other Notes
				TENNYSON (Continued)				
90	The New Timon (1876)	*K111/WP1/S252	C (N)	15-18 (WP)		15.3.20 (6)	1888-91	From RHS Poems; Quaritch (9 HBF)
91 (389f)	International Ex Ode (1862)	E300	F (PTC)		1+C	18.4.04 (4)	1889+	Pres. A. Strahan:TJW
92 (402f)	Colonial & Indian Ex Ode (1886)	E342/*S257	F (I)		5?	16.2.17	1888-92	Printed by Clay not Clowes
93 (400f)	The Promise of May (1882)	E332/*WP2	F (P)	BL 10.10.03-W	C	7.5.01 (12)		Absence of imprint; cf. 81, 84
94 (388f)	The Sailor Boy (1861)	E298	F (P)	BL 11.3.99-W	C	1.4.02 (11)		Emily Faithfull & Victoria Regia
95 (395f)	Welcome to HRH Alex [8vo](1874)	E320/*W35	F (PT)	BL 8.7.99-W	C	27.11.05 (3)		TJW says 40 copies printed
				BL 9.1.04-W				
				WILLIAM MAKEPEACE THACKERAY (2)				
96 (408f)	An Interesting Event (1849)	E347	F (PT)	8.7.99-W	4?+C	27.2.99 (13)	29.6.90	Letter C.P. Johnson: Athenaeum
97 (409f)	Leaf out of a Sketch Bk (1861)	E350	F (P)		6?C	28.7.03 (8)		Emily Faithfull & Victoria Regia
				JAMES ("B.V.") THOMSON (1)				
98	George Meredith (1909)	S259	P?	50? (cert.)			1909	Unacknowledged MBF offprint
				WILLIAM WORDSWORTH (1)				
99 (422f)	To the Queen (1846)	E355	F (T)	6 (TJW)-2		26.4.15-HBF (2)	1889-93	Only pamphlet on pure rag paper
				EDMUND YATES (1)				
100 (425c)	Mr Thackeray &c. (1859)	E359	BF (PT)	15		[11.3.89]		2 issues distinguished by paper

Summary Notes

Status of 100 Titles: BF and F (63), P/F? (5), S (4), P (11), C (10), DP (3), "Changeling" (2), "Embryo Piracy" (1), and "Blind" (1)

Binary Editions (8): Arnold's Alaric at Rome (1), Cruikshank's The Artist and the Author (11); G. Eliot's Agatha (13), Ruskin's Catalogue of the Turner Sketches in the National Gallery (40) and The Future of England (41), Swinburne's Siena (74), Tennyson's The Lover's Tale (87), and Yates's Mr. Thackeray, Mr. Yates and the Garrick Club (100)

Three-Star Pamphlets: Convicted on Paper, Type, and Collation (5): G. Eliot's Brother and Sister (14), Ruskin's The National Gallery (43), and Tennyson's Becket (78), The Last Tournament (86), and Ode for the Opening of the International Exhibition (91)

Multiple Entries (5): Morris's Sir Galahad (28), The Socialist Platform (30), and Socialists at Play (31); Ruskin's The Future of England and The Nature and Authority of Miracle (44)

Notes

1. *TLS*, 21 May 1937, in *Books and Book-Collectors* (London: Rupert Hart-Davis, 1956), pp. 15-21.

2. By Thomas Wharton, Edward Malone, and N. E. S. A. Hamilton on, respectively, Thomas Rowley (1792), William Henry Ireland (1796), and John Payne Collier (1860).

3. It did—in 1938, but not as a gift. The purchase price of £66,000, payable to TJW's estate over 10 years, was, even then, and notwithstanding the more than 200 books in the *Catalogue of The Ashley Library* which proved to be missing, a great bargain and less by half than other offers made for the collection at the time. In 1924, TJW, in a letter to Francis Needham of the Bodleian Library, to which institution TJW was then favourably disposed, calculated the value of his library as "at least three times" his outlay, which he estimated as "barely £40,000" (quoted in *S*, p. 58 from the catalogue of the Sotheby Pariser sale [4-5 December 1967] Lot 423). TJW insinuated on a number of occasions his intention to bequeath the Ashley Library to the British Museum. Writing to WMR on 10 November 1905, he concludes a discussion of his Tennyson manuscript purchases from the Rowfant Library with the note, "Well, they'll never drift into the market again. They will remain in my Library whilst I live, and at my death they will pass to the British Museum with the rest of my books, where, as Dr. Garnett has assured me, they will be kept together as a separate collection."

4. A privately printed leaflet inserted in Michael Sadleir's copy of *E* in Sotheby Lot 373.

5. The two volumes are sold only as a set. A deluxe boxed edition is also available, bound in full dark blue morocco and limited to 80 sets, with a copy of the first edition of Robert and Elizabeth Barrett Browning's *Two Poems* (1854) and an essay on that pamphlet by Nicolas Barker in a matching folder. The original *Enquiry*, printed by letterpress on cream wove paper and cased in a quality maroon cloth, was a handsome example of contemporary book-making, beside which neither the ordinary nor deluxe editions of the *Sequel*—both printed by photo-offset on stark white paper, the one cased in bright red material, the other bound in uninspiring leather, with uneven lettering—compare favourably.

6. Some readers and reviewers apparently (and unreasonably) expected *S* to replicate the detailed documentation contained in C&P's *Footnote* (London: Hart-Davis, 1948), four *Working Papers* (Oxford: Blackwell's, 1967-70), *Centenary Studies* (Austin: Univ. of Texas Press, 1959), and numerous articles, as well as the information contained in publications by other scholars. See, for example, A. Ridge, "Following the *Sequel*,"*ABMR*, 11 (March 1984), 110. Such an expectation ignores the sizeable library of Wiseiana accumulated since 1934.

7. In 1934, the American bookseller Gabriel Wells defended TJW in a small pamphlet entitled *The Carter-Pollard Disclosures* (New York: Doubleday). In a postscript citing an error in *E*, he revealed that he had bought at the Forman sale in 1920 the manuscript of the chapter "The Building of the *Idylls*," printed in the second volume of *Literary Anecdotes,* and that HBF, not TJW (who with W. Robertson Nicoll edited the volumes in 1896), was the author of the article. This seemingly trivial disclosure caused William A. Jackson, Carl Pforzheimer's librarian, to recall that Pforzheimer had purchased the document from Wells. On examination, it proved to contain a written exchange between TJW and HBF that positively incriminated HBF as an accomplice in the forgeries. Although the document was shown to Carter in March 1935, Pforzheimer persisted in refusing to allow its publication until 1945, when it was edited as *Between the Lines* by Fannie Ratchford for the University of Texas Press. For the rather invidious history of this episode, see John Carter's February 1945 *Atlantic Monthly* (pp. 93-100) review of Fannie Ratchford's *Letters of Thomas J. Wise to John Henry Wrenn* (New York: Knopf, 1944), reprinted in *Books and Book-Collectors* (pp. 129-49); Ratchford's *Review of Reviews* (reprinted from the *University of Texas Literary Chronicle,* 1946); and Dwight MacDonald's "Annals of a Crime," *New Yorker,* 10 November 1962, pp. 168-205.

8. The most interesting account of the origins of the investigation into the forgeries is found in Percy Muir's autobiography, *Minding My Own Business* (London: Chatto & Windus, 1956), pp. 89-90, 94-100.

9. Edmund Gosse first retailed the romantic legend of the *Sonnets* in his introduction to the Dent edition of *Sonnets from the Portuguese* in November 1894; the forgery, however, was in existence at least as early as the middle of the previous year, and is first cited in W. G. Kingsland's *Poet Lore* article on "Browning Rarities" in March 1894 (6, 264-68). TJW first identified Dr. Bennett as the source of *Sonnets* in his privately printed *A Bibliography of Elizabeth Barrett Browning* (London, 1918), reserving for *A Browning Library* (London, 1929), issued for private circulation a decade later, the story of the acquisition of his own copies from Dr. Bennett.

10. Although he had responded peremptorily to earlier correspondence from the Enquirers relating to E.B.B.'s *Sonnets*, TJW probably had no real inkling of the scope of the Enquirers' project until Graham Pollard's appointed visit to 25 Heath Drive on 14 October 1933, the details of which are laid out in C&P's Epilogue, "Aftermath of 'An Enquiry,'" in *E2*. TJW had no way of knowing at the time either the extent or gravity of the evidence they had collected; neither did he know of their previous contact with Gorfin, to whom he wrote two days before Pollard's interview, presumably immediately on receipt of Pollard's request. His subsequent tactics to suborn Gorfin's testimony led the Enquirers to secure the two affidavits printed in WP4 (1970), which, together with the promised sworn statement from Cecil Clay, were their only legal protection against any suit that TJW might bring against the book,

the whole of which, in the opinion of Constable's counsel, James P. R. Lyell, also a book collector and founder of the Lyell lectures, "provides ample material for Wise to commence proceedings"; further, he continued, "it would be quite impossible for the authors to present their case . . . to the public without giving him that opportunity" (*E*2 , p. 23).

11. TJW's interview with the *Daily Herald* was printed on 30 June 1934; his only response after the publication of *E* was in a long letter in the *TLS* for 12 July, the bulk of which consisted of a letter by HBF's son, Maurice (later revealed to have been dictated by TJW), supporting TJW's assertion that HBF was the source of the pamphlets. TJW concluded by asserting, "When I have read the book with the care and attention it deserves I shall doubtless have something to say regarding its contents." For his *ABC* defence and its subsequent withdrawal, see William B. Todd, *Suppressed Commentaries on the Wiseian Forgeries* (Austin, Texas: Humanities Research Center, 1969). In a letter to the *TLS* on 23 August 1934, Lord Esher (Oliver Brett), epitomizing the frustrations of all English and American collectors, demanded that Wise clarify the status of the indicted pamphlets, but the last word the public had from TJW was through a letter from his wife announcing to the readers of the *TLS* that "her husband was now forbidden by his doctor to engage in 'controversy'" (*E*2, p. 19). Thoroughly disillusioned, Lord Esher later sold his books and abandoned book collecting altogether.

12. Shaw's "Notes," made in a copy of *Forging Ahead* (New York: Putnam, 1939), are printed in an annotated appendix to Wilfred Partington's revised English edition of his biography, *Thomas J. Wise in the Original Cloth* (London: Hale, 1946), pp. 315-21.

13. Foxon's first report was in the *TLS*, 19 October 1956, p. 624; his monograph was issued by the Bibliographical Society in 1959; in 1961, he and Todd collaborated on a supplement, published in Vol.16 of the *Library* (pp. 287-93). Freeman's article is in the *TLS* for 17 September 1982. Quaritch generously presented the new cache of stolen leaves to the British Library, "where they will be kept as a collection, so that the evidence of Wise's malpractice will be preserved" (*S*, p. 381).

14. Partington, Ratchford, and Todd have already been cited; Mr. Nowell Smith's address appeared in the *Library*, June 1969, pp. 129-41; the eleven-volume *Ashley Catalogue* was reprinted in 1971.

15. Quoted by Todd in *Wiseian Forgeries*, pp. 44-45. Pollard's comment was in response to an impassioned letter from Madan objecting to R. B. McKerrow's review of the *Enquiry* in the *Library* (December 1934, pp. 379-84). "You are the life and soul of the Bibliographical Society," Madan wrote: "Will it allow this signed review by its Secretary to pass without remark as a fair representation of the position?" (*E*2, p. 34). Interestingly, while C&P quote this portion of Madan's letter in their Epilogue, they omit Pollard's response.

16. See Edwin Wolf and John F. Fleming, *Rosenbach* (London: Weidenfeld and Nicolson, 1960), p. 397.

17. Quaritch, p. 2.

18. "Postscript" was published in Dwight Macdonald's "Annals of a Crime," pp. 202-3.

19. The proofs contained a heated marginalia exchange between TJW and HBF who complained of TJW's use of the words "a few" as opposed to giving the precise figure to describe the number printed of a privately issued pamphlet. TJW's angry retort convicted them both: "Quite so. And we print 'Last Tournament' in 1896, & want 'someone to think' it was printed in 1871! *The moral position is exactly the same!*" (See Ratchford, *Between the Lines*, Plate 22B.)

20. *Book Collector*, 21 (Winter 1972), 503-23.

21. Statistically, the combined *Enquiry* and *Sequel* present a number of problems. The summary given by B&C on p. 121 fails for several reasons to clarify the precise relationship between the two volumes, the most obvious of which is that at no point do the authors provide a synopsis of the status of the 100 pamphlets indicted in their List of Works. Beyond that, however, they conflate (and thereby confuse) both the total number in their List and the number of items considered by C&P, many of which were rejected in *E*, with the dossiers contained in each volume, when, in fact, the two must be kept separate if the works condemned in each are to be accounted for. Further, while the authors assert that *S* contains 59 dossiers, that figure is difficult to recreate by actual count. In fact, there are 53 separate titles listed in the Dossiers section (pp. 191-259); three Morris items which exist in two states bring the total to 56; adding to that number Carroll's *Some Popular Fallacies on Vivisection*, which, grouped with the Omitted Items in Appendix 3 (pp. 267-68), is puzzlingly included in the List of Works, the total is 57. Only if the other two omitted pamphlets are included is the total 59, but these are not canonical. If these are counted, then the three rejected pamphlets in the Swinburne Postscript are also dossiers, and they bring the total to 62. Though the numbering is complicated, the contradictions can be resolved.

In total, *E* contained dossiers on 54 works categorized as forgeries (29), suspects (18), piracies and dubious (7); other works were discussed but dismissed, either as genuine or for lack of evidence. B&C give this total as 76. Commentators (including even Pollard) have disagreed about the breakdown in each category, in part owing to the ambiguous status of Swinburne's *Cleopatra*, but primarily owing to the looseness of the Enquirers' use of the adjectives qualifying the terms "suspect" or "suspicion," which vary from "highly" to "considerable," to "a deal of," to "extremely," to "moral certainty." In general, however, the Enquirers reserved the term Forgery for those items which could be stigmatized by one of the three verifiable criteria —paper, type, and collation of text (the paper and text tests are inexplicably omitted from B&C's discussion on the opening page of their Prologue [p. 17], where only type and Herbert Gorfin are cited as evidential factors)—relegating to the category of "Suspect" those items for which there existed only an accumulation of negative evidence—based on provenance, dubious imprint, auction record, typographic similarity to pamphlets condemned on other grounds, the absence of presentation and association copies, and suspicious marketing procedures. They were later to include a confirmed falsified imprint as a fourth ground for positive censure in the case of the four Charles Ottley, Landon & Co. Swinburne pamphlets.

To the 29 works by 15 authors condemned unequivocally as forgeries in *E*, another 18 were subsequently added by various researchers, including C&P, singly or together, bringing the total of indicted works to 47 and introducing one new writer, Cruikshank. In order of their exposure, these are: Arnold's *Alaric* and Tennyson's *Becket* (Roland Baughman, 1936); Tennyson's *Idylls of the Hearth* (Fannie Ratchford, 1941); the four Ottley Swinburne pamphlets (C&P, 1948); the "2nd ed." of George Eliot's **Agatha* (Carter, 1957); Swinburne's *The Devil's Due* and Tennyson's **The Cup*, **The Falcon*, and **A Welcome to Alexandrovna* (Pollard 1959); Cruikshank's *The Artist and the Author* (K. I. Garrett, 1962); Morris' **Two Sides of the River* (Maurice Pariser, 1964); Tennyson's *The New Timon* (W. D. Paden, 1965) and **The Promise of May* (C&P WP2, 1967); and Ruskin's **The Nature and Authority of Miracle* (James Dearden, 1969); another Tennyson—**England and America*—was condemned by Pollard's researches on paper, and later by B&C on grounds of anachronistic type. (The eight asterisked items were suspect or doubtful in *E*.)

The Sequelers are noticeably less rigid in assigning the stigmata to the remaining works that comprise the total 100 in their List in Appendix 7, but they fall into four distinct groupings:

(1) 9 works by 5 new authors—Lewis Carroll, R. H. Horne, George Meredith, Shelley, and James ('B. V.') Thomson. Of these, Horne's *Galatea Secunda* is an HBF forgery condemned by watermark; those by Carroll, Meredith, and Thomson have little or no TJW-HBF connection, though four of them may be associated with Maurice Buxton Forman.

(2) 9 new works by *E* authors are indicted as either forgeries or possible forgeries/piracies, but only 3 are condemned on hard evidence: Morris' *The God of the Poor*, *Socialists at Play*, and *The Voice of Toil* on type—(Rossetti's *Hand and Soul* is typographically anachronous, but its uniqueness militates against labelling it a forgery); Stevenson's *Ticonderoga* on imprint; the others are cited on negative evidence: Swinburne's *The Brothers* (F) and *The Ballad of Dead Men's Bay*, *The Bride's Tragedy*, and *Robert Burns* (all P/F?).

(3) 10 suspected or doubtful items in *E* are identified by B&C as forgeries or possible forgeries: 5 on typographical evidence—Browning's *Gold Hair*, Rossetti's *Verses*, Ruskin's *Samuel Prout*, Swinburne's *Laus Veneris*, and Tennyson's *Carmen Saeculara*; one on imprint—Tennyson's *Ode on the Opening of the Colonial and Indian Exhibition*; another four are indicted on negative evidence—Stevenson's *Thomas Stevenson* (F) and *War in Samoa*

Sequel to *A Sequel*

(P/F?), Swinburne's *An Appeal to England* (F), and Tennyson's *Ode on the Death of the Duke of Clarence* (F). For 6 *E* pamphlets—two each by Arnold and Kipling, plus Stevenson's *Some College Memories* and Swinburne's *Cleopatra*—the assigned status remains unchanged.

(4) Of the remaining 18 items, principally by Morris and Swinburne (see the Master List, below)—2 are piracies: Stevenson's *Familiar Epistle* and Swinburne's *The Ballad of Bulgarie* ("with Gosse's connivance"); the rest are taxonomically unorthodox: 8 "Chimaeras" (fabrications falling outside the range of forgeries and simple piracies), and 2 DP's (deceptive productions: unauthorized editions intended to deceive)—all by Morris and identified with HBF; 2 Herne Shepherd piracies, 2 "Changelings" ("piratically manufactured though probably not falsely dated," S, p. 243), 1 probable "Embryo Piracy" (an intended piracy legitimized by the Shelley Society facsimile), and 1 "Blind" (a unique, abortive reprint)—all by Swinburne. There is even an unexecuted "Ghost" of one of the Morris chimaeras.

The Sequelers add 36 separate titles to the canon, nine of them by 5 new authors, and reclassify another ten—a total of 47 out of the 100 in the List of Works. Broken down by categories, the 54 title-dossiers (counting the Carroll in the "Omitted Items" section) consist of 6 repeated entries from *E* (not counting Morris' *Two Sides of the River* and Tennyson's *England and America* which are included in the next category); 12 (out of 18; no reason given for the exclusion of the others) works added between *E* and *S*; 9 works by 5 new authors; 9 additional works for authors included in *E*; and 18 new works, mainly unorthodox, by Morris and Swinburne. In sum, an impressive supplement to C&P's original gallery of faked editions.

22. Owing primarily to delays in issuing the *Sequel*, these three chapters were prepublished in three successive issues of the *Book Collector* (Spring-Fall 1983).

23. It would be a miracle if the *Sequel*, containing as it does such a wealth of detail, were error-free; and charter members of the F. S. S. R. (the Fly Speck School of Reviewing—an offshoot of the School of Bibliography founded by John Carter in the third edition of his *ABC for Book-Collectors*)—may be as interested as the authors (for different reasons) in some of the blemishes discovered. Always a nuisance, simple typos—such as the misdating of Swinburne's *Unpublished Verses* in the dossiers as 1866 for 1888 (p. 239) or the absence of boldface numbers for the four type styles of 1883 (Nos. 70-73 in the "List of Types") that indict Rossetti's *Verses* (No. 39) on anachronistic grounds—do not abound in the *Sequel*. There are, however, more substantive misprints, and these can be misleading, such as twice assigning an article (not included in the "Concise List of Sources") by W. B. Todd to Simon Nowell Smith (pp. 250n1, 252n3); identifying the "enlarged" English edition of Partington's *Forging Ahead* in the same list (p. 377) as a brief note in the *Book Collector*, which is repeated from an entry four items earlier under Mr. Nowell Smith's citations; and shifting the location of the manuscript letters of HBF to G. M. Bucke from the University of Western

Ontario (p. 41n3) to the University of Toronto (p. 377). Most of these the alert and informed reader will automatically adjust; he may, however, be unduly inconvenienced by the persistent confusion of *page* numbers with *item* numbers in all but two references to HBF's *The Books of William Morris* in the 14 Morris dossiers. It is also disconcerting not to have listed together (presumably for reasons of strict alphabetical arrangement) the four pamphlets identified by C&P in their *Footnote to An Enquiry* in the "Charles Ottley, Landon Group," subsection of the Swinburne dossiers. Finally (and oddly) the date of the 1972 Sotheby sale, catalogued by John Collins, is repeatedly cited as 12 rather than 10 April.

Inconsistencies and factual errors are more serious. Two affect the canon itself: why, for example, is Lewis Carroll's *Some Popular Fallacies About Vivisection*, for which "there is nothing to suggest that either Wise or Maurice Buxton Forman [Type 87 postdates HBF's death by three years] . . . had anything to do with it" (p. 268) and which is grouped with the omitted pamphlets in Appendix 3, included in the "List of Works" when HBF's unique copy of Christina Rossetti's privately printed *Verses* (now at Princeton), in wrappers, "apparently inserted by [HBF] himself" (p. 192) is not considered a chimaera of the same class as Dante Rossetti's *Hand and Soul* (p. 214)? Occasionally discussions in the text are not confirmed in the tabular sections of the book: Thackeray's *A Leaf out of a Sketch-Book*, for instance, was condemned by C&P on grounds of paper; B&C condemn it also on its type— a "combination rule border, intended, for some reason, to give the impression that both were printed at Emily Faithfull's Victoria Press" (p. 110); yet there is no anachronistic type indicated for this pamphlet in the "List of Works" (No. 97). Similarly, four pamphlets are identified as "changeling editions" in the Swinburne Postscript (pp. 243-44), but only two—*A Sequence of Sonnets on the Death of Robert Browning* and *Grace Darling*—are so denominated in the dossiers themselves. While the other two—*The Ballad of Bulgarie* ("a piracy produced by Wise, with Gosse's connivance," p. 226) and *Robert Burns* ("A piracy, and [as to its place of printing] probably a forgery," p. 237)— clearly fall within the author's definition of "changeling" ("piratically manufactured though probably not falsely dated" editions), the inconsistent use of nomenclature obfuscates unnecessarily the status of the fabrications. Finally, one major gaffe in the "Corrections and Notes" in *E2* should be pointed out. On p. 13, B&C provide a list of works condemned on the evidence of their paper subsequent to *E* by Pollard's researches into the date by which chemical wood was introduced into England. Three of the works itemized— Ruskin's *Leoni* and *The Future of England* and Stevenson's *On the Thermal Influence of Forests*—were, in fact, indicted on paper in *E*; but two pamphlets which now stand convicted on paper, but *not* so condemned in *E*—Tennyson's *Child-Songs* (S, p. 247) and *England and America* (S, p. 249)—are omitted.

24. Ratchford, *Letters to Wise*, p. 68.

25. *The Pilgrims of Hope* well illustrates the borderline status of some of the items added to the canon in the *Sequel*. B&C rightly condemn the

Sequel to *A Sequel*

pamphlet on the basis of what is, patently, an ambiguously dated title page, a deliberate attempt to obfuscate the relative dates of the original, serial publication (*Commonwealth*, 1886) and the date of the pamphlet (probably 1897). That HBF included it with the works of 1886 in his Morris bibliography (1897) confirms the intentional deception stigmatized by B&C. And yet *The Pilgrims of Hope* is trebly acknowledged by HBF as a piracy—in the prefatory note to the pamphlet, in his bibliography of Morris, and in a letter to Cockerell (*S*, p. 155)—which suggests either that HBF was insensitive (or indifferent) to the moral issues involved (which is hard to credit), or that, by comparison with the deception employed in the *bona fide* forgeries (if that irony is not too contradictory), the misrepresentation in *The Pilgrims of Hope* was simply too trivial to matter. The third possibility—that he was obsessed with "enriching" his bibliography of Morris's works and his own private collection with items of genuine or manufactured scarcity—may be the operative motive for HBF's complicity in the whole affair of the forgeries in the first instance.

26. TJW's spurious edition of Shelley edited by his alter ego, Charles Alfred Seymour (1886, dated 1887, *S*, p. 215), elicited from HBF the response (on 2 October 1886): "Those sonnets you sent me were 'a caution'!" (*S*, p. 272).

27. Quaritch, p. 3.

28. HBF's "Criticisms of Contemporaries" series, published anonymously, also included articles on CGR and WMR. In *Our Living Poets* (London: Tinsley, 1871), he reprinted a revised version of his two *Tinsley* articles on DGR (5 [September 1869], 142-51; 8 [March 1871], 150-60) and his article on CGR in a section entitled "The Preraphaelite Group." His "The Fleshly Scandal," also anonymous, appeared in *Tinsley's*, 10 (February 1872), 89-102.

29. The forgers' relationship with W. M. Rossetti will be examined in a forthcoming article in the *Book Collector*.

30. Wolf and Fleming, pp. 129-31.

31. Carter, *Books and Book-Collectors*, p. 149. In their Epilogue to Section 3, "The Course of the Crime," the Sequelers invite speculation on just this point with their question, "Was there a third conspirator?" (p. 187). Graham Pollard in the section "A Third Conspirator" in his introduction to Quaritch's catalogue raised a similar query about HBF's brother, Alfred, who was, among other things, a translator of Wagner and in its later stages Secretary of the Villon Society. By trade a paper manufacturer's agent, Alfred "supplied the paper, and probably did the layout, for some of the later Morris forgeries." He could not, Pollard concludes, "have done this without knowing what he was doing. He must therefore take his place—though a minor place—alongside the two more eminent forgers in this celebrated conspiracy to fabricate items for the rare book market" (p. 4).

Neither John Collins, in his most interesting "A Short Note on Alfred Forman" (*Book Collector*, 23 [Spring 1974], 69-76), nor the Sequelers pick up on Pollard's indictment, and Alfred receives only casual and occasional mention in the *Sequel*. The third man in the Sequeler's Epilogue is HBF's son, Maurice, from whose 1972 sale so much of the new Morris material derives, and with whom, almost exclusively, the pamphlets by Carroll, Meredith, and James Thomson introduced into the canon are associated. Given Barker and Collins' admission that "of his direct complicity in the major conspiracy there is no evidence either way" (p. 187), their decision to include these works tends to introduce red herrings into their search for the smaller fry among the forger's cache. MBF's position consequent on the exposure—his published comments on his father, his advisory service to TJW, and his role as middleman in the transfer of the Ashley Library to Bloomsbury—and his own tampering with texts form a fascinating footnote to the *Sequel*, but they should not be allowed to intrude—as they do—on the major task at hand.

Abbreviations

The following abbreviations are used consistently in the notes; abbreviations of other publications cited in the notes are provided in "Sources" in the Master List.

B&C	Nicolas Barker and John Collins
C&P	John Carter and Graham Pollard
HBF	H. Buxton Forman
TJW	Thomas J. Wise
DGR/WMR/CGR	The Rossettis: Dante Gabriel, William Michael, Christina
E	*An Enquiry* (1st ed.)
E2	*An Enquiry* (new material in the 2nd ed.)
S	*A Sequel*

How Substantial Was Robert Browning?

John Maynard

Jacob Korg. *Browning and Italy*. Athens: Ohio University Press, 1983. ix, 246 pp.

Clyde de L. Ryals. *Becoming Browning: The Poems and Plays of Robert Browning, 1833-1846*. Columbus: Ohio State University Press, 1983. x, 292 pp.

Over the years discussion of Robert Browning has tended to be dominated by biographical issues. As with the very different life of Keats, Browning's life seems to stand in a special kind of symbolic relation to his work. Coming from a sheltered, very self-involved family, he moves out, in both life and work, to embrace a rich world of men and women. He leads Elizabeth Barrett out of her far more sheltered, invalided, life; they find a brilliant life of love, high art, political engagement, and literary society in Italy. The loss of Elizabeth brings Robert to the dark tower but, from there, back to a more profound involvement with human life, in which he confronts, most magnificently in *The Ring and the Book*, the depths of depravity, the heights of selflessness and love, of humanity. Were there two Robert Brownings? Henry James initiated the question grandly and it has echoed ever since in biographies. Yet the diner-out and man of the world isn't so far as many would like to think from the central biographical-critical idea: the poet involved with his world, student of men and women, fierce metallurgist intent on smelting in his poems no less than the truth of human life.

The conception of Browning, man and poet, that emerges has attractive mass in our days when even nuclear particles wink and disappear into quarks and photons, and signifiers point only to other signifiers in the endless recessions of aesthetic theory. It is not surprising that while most attention in Browning studies recently has been turned to controversy over the substantiality of the various editions—Ohio, Penguin-Yale, and now Oxford English Text—there has been emerging a very real debate—sometimes explicit, sometimes only implicit—over the traditional vision of the substantiality of the poet and his works. Back in the sixties, W. David Shaw's *The Dialectical Temper* focused brilliantly on the process of argumentation in Browning that created not so much a solid vision of human life as Kierkegaardian levels of being in his characters. Hillis Miller's *The Disappearance of God* saw all Browning's characters confronting an essentially identical existential condition, swimming for very life in the rough waves of phenomena, yet driven by a spark of divinity within to find a way to transcend reality in its very apprehension. In biography, Park Honan uncovered the restless, disturbed side of the older Browning, showing lumps and faults, threatening to crack entirely under the pressure of the great potter's shaping blows. My own study of the young Browning disassembled simple fictions of the biographical Browning into a fluid diversity of family and cultural streams and personal potentialities. Following Betty Miller's excessive account of Browning's guilty abandonment of his subjective heritage in Shelley, critics such as Harold Bloom have seen Browning's work not so much as an engagement with real life as a prolonged encounter with his Romantic forebears.

More recently, Herbert Tucker produced *Browning's Beginnings,* an excellent first book with an ecletic theoretical background in Bloom, Derrida, and Barbara Herrnstein Smith that formulates the issue explicitly in terms of Post-Structuralist ideas. In Tucker's view, Browning creates a poetic discourse that avoids finality, whether of life or art. Browning puts off closure, avoids definitive meanings and conclusive dramatic statements. He is always beginning again, avoiding artistic closure and finality by a process of differing from his predecessors and from his own earlier work. It is modern poetry precisely because the mind must always act, again and again, in an endless process of finding what will suffice—and of course nothing really will, or the process would have ended long ago. Two even more recent studies, by Constance Hassett (*The Elusive Self in the*

Poetry of Robert Browning) and E. Warwick Slinn (*Browning and the Fictions of Identity*) come even closer to the issue of substantiality, though neither is as impressive an approach to Browning as Tucker's fine work. Slinn subjects Browning to a rigorous reading on a "dramatically based model of man as verbal artifice." Personality, substantial character, the Browningesque world of so many critics and biographers is dissolved into a "shifting series of dramatic hypotheses, unified only by a self-perpetuating consciousness."[1] The center of human character will not hold. *Uberhaupt* this Post-Structuralist vision of character *stammt aus Browning*. Hassett's work, very much on the same track, seems to me the better because it subjects this ideology to an historical vision of Browning's works within her special subject of conversion. Earlier Browning tends to work to a vision of conversion that creates a coherent personality for its subject; later Browning begins to deconstruct its own sense of stable, substantial character. Perhaps there is a moment in which the idea of coherent, stable character is created and another when it is destroyed: Browning presents those crises.

In the context of this larger discussion, two new full-length studies of Browning by senior scholars, Jacob Korg's *Browning and Italy* and Clyde de L. Ryals's *Becoming Browning: The Poems and Plays of Robert Browning, 1833-1846*, make rather opposing statements. Korg ignores the discussion itself, yet the premises and structure of his inquiry make a very decisive statement. He finds in Italy the essential real object on which Browning cuts his personal and poetic teeth. Browning's two trips to Italy as a young poet, in 1838 and 1844, and then his long life in Italy in his middle years until Elizabeth's death are crucial in his development into the objective dramatic poet that Korg admires. It is a settling, attractive idea which affords an irresistable research project for anyone who shares the Brownings' interest in Italy. Korg has been and seen, and he shows us how the real became the poetry. He accounts for Browning's swerve away from the intricacies of *Sordello*. Browning's own Italian research for that perplexed, inward-turned account of the way of a poet's soul brought him to a very different vision from that of the poem. In Venice,

Browning—later the narrator Browning of *Sordello*—sees and realizes the plight of poor suffering humanity; he adopts his muse from the poor women he observes there, thus making manifest the objective side of his poetic genius. "Direct experience of Italy and Italian life" rescues Browning from the abstractions of his excessively subjective heritage and lets him focus his art on the human scene. The varied human theater of Italian life opens Browning's eyes to the potentialities in a full display of the variety of human nature—men and women— as the great subject of his art. And, more interestingly, Browning's position in Italy—the keenly interested and sympathetic observer who nonetheless retains his critical stance as a representative of a different nation and set of values—sets up the characteristic relation of sympathy/judgment of the dramatic monologist to his subject.

Writing a book around a single theme is difficult. Browning doesn't in fact write all that much about human life in contemporary Italy as he would have experienced it, however much the realist-fantasy melodrama of *Pippa Passes* (following immediately on *Sordello*) suggests that Italy was a gateway to Browning's turn to the dramatic monologue as his central poetic form. Korg stresses that his is a critical study, but the organization is determined mostly by the connecting story of Browning's encounters with Italy—a pleasant story that Korg retells well. (He has consulted the Hall Griffin papers in the British Library and has seen Browning's brief records of his Italian journeys, but most of his account repeats previous biographies, with some new first-hand impressions of places Browning visited and art Browning saw.) On top of this account, the past Italy, which is the major use of Italy in Browning's work, comes in somewhat awkwardly. Korg wishes to move from the present Italy that Browning saw to the past Italy that Browning more often writes about as if they were both substantial realities confronted by the poet. But the past, especially for a poet so concerned with art history, is not so much reality as fictions of history (like the documents in *The Old Yellow Book*) and works of art. Korg's paradigm of poet-confronts-reality-creates-art is undermined by the more common one of poet-confronts-art-creates-art. Korg summarizes Browning's sources in history and art without adding much that is new, though he draws together conveniently a great deal of Browning scholars' collective digging among old pictures and places. His ideas of history in Browning, poetry as resuscitation of the past, seem somewhat naive as historiography and don't relate Browning sufficiently well to the many complicated strands of historical thinking in his time. The third subject implicit in the topic, that of Browning's relation to Italian literature, is dealt with least adequately. Korg's work is a convenient and generally reliable summary of what we know of Browning's poems of Italian life and art. Perhaps the most important critical point he raises comes up incidentally as the result of repeatedly comparing Browning's art to its sources in Italian artifacts or history: that Browning was always exercising his poet's right to lie. As Korg well puts it, Browning "was entirely capable of going to much trouble to learn small facts . . . and then altering them to suit the needs of his poem" (p. 187). The point is not highlighted, perhaps because it is somewhat subversive of Korg's general thesis. Browning put real toads in his imaginary gardens, as Marianne Moore might say, to make them even more powerful fictions.[2] Italy does not so much do the grinding as provide more grist for his imagination's mill.

Browning wrote, "Florence looks to us more beautiful than ever after Rome. I love the very stones of it, to say nothing of the cypresses and river" (p. 95). So spoke *Mrs.* Browning. Mr. Browning, despite the testimony of "De Gustibus," generally rather preferred France, especially as a contemporary social and intellectual reality with which he and his mind could interact. That was the subject of a fine study by Roy Gridley of two years ago (*The Brownings and France*), to which Korg's seems almost planned as a companion piece: tours with Browning— in France, in Italy. Browning's love for France, and the major influence of French literature and culture on his work, was to some extent news, especially in the accumulation of detail that Gridley presented. Browning's interest in Italy is, of course, not. Indeed both Gridley *and* Korg contribute to our overall vision of Browning by reminding the Italo-phile in most of us of the limits to Browning's immersion in Italy, especially in contrast to his enthusiasm for contemporary French culture. Korg correctly stresses how little contact Browning sought with contemporary Italians and Italian culture.

The bulk of Korg's work is a very competent job of compilation and collection. But its strength, the clear vision of what influence confrontation with Italian realities had on Browning, is also its weakness in the larger critical debate it ignores. We are essentially given a finely tuned version of the traditional Chestertonian vision of a hearty art made from the assured and manifest realities of the sunny South. That Chesterton built his own old ale and small human community vision as a bulwark against his more that Conradian fears of unreality and disintegration should give critics in his tradition at least some pause.

Clyde de L. Ryals, who has already published a good study of the late Browning, might seem a glutton for punishment. In *Becoming Browning*, he has moved back from the hard and unread late Browning to the hard and little read early Browning. Unlike Korg's, his work is very much aware of the broad critical controversies that have been developing around the definition of Browning and his art. In many ways his work attempts a broad mediation and conciliation of disparate views, much as Browning himself in his essay on Shelley sought to balance and credit both poetics from which he could see himself derived, the subjective (or Shelleyan), the objective (or Shakespearean). Although Ryals's book fills in the context for Browning's early poems, it is a work essentially of criticism as Korg's is one essentially of biography. Because it puts forward a general theoretical definition of Browning's art rather than a genetic account of source-into-work, it is bound to be more controversial and likely to be more influential.

If Korg's study of Browning and Italy has to undergo comparison with Gridley's of Browning and France, Ryals's more critically focused and theoretical work will necessarily have to withstand comparison with Tucker's fine and innovative *Browning's Beginnings*. It says a good deal for Ryals's *Becoming Browning* that it can withstand the comparison, even though it is neither quite so exciting in its readings nor so strong in its critical apparatus. Both critics cover essentially the same material, as their similar titles suggest. Whereas Tucker looked at the dynamics of Browning's art as an attempt to avoid artistic closure and finality, Ryals is more concerned with rhetoric than poetics, especially the way in which Browning creates an ironic structure in most of his work. Ryals identifies this with Romantic irony, especially as it was defined in German critical writing of the Romantic period. His aim is not to make a dubious point about Browning's debt to German culture (a third companion travel guide on Browning and Germany should not be written), but to define the peculiar art Browning develops most fully in *Sordello* and uses as a structure for his best monologues. If Browning, in Tucker's view of him, is always beginning over again, in Ryals's he is always becoming, moving to position himself at a higher level of being or consciousness but always aware of the ironic crosslights this creates: of the limitedness of everyday life and matters; of the insufficiency and mythic fabrication of one's becomings into higher intellectual and spiritual states. Ryals offers this as an approach that simultaneously constructs and deconstructs Browning along with Browning's own movements. As such, his view is close to Constance Hassett's vision of conversion and deconversion.

The critical conception of Browning as a master of a complicated double irony is a bold and quite convincing new framework for understanding Browning's achievement. Taking the young Browning through *Bells and Pomegranates,* Ryals offers impressive readings of Browning's ironic patterns, from the opening *Pauline* and *Paracelsus,* with the increasing self-division of the first and the full dramatic irony of aspiration, attainment, failure, aspiration in failure of *Paracelsus* to the complicated ironic relations of speaker and implied author in the famous early dramatic monologues. As with Tucker (to whose book, by the way, Ryals acknowledges some debt, though his thinking was essentially complete before Tucker's book came out), his finest work is on *Sordello.* Where Tucker dazzles, Ryals makes solid headway in rendering this poem comprehensible, especially by focusing on the radically shifting and strangely humorous motions of the narrator in his ironic presentation of Sordello's possibilities and failure. Such a critical strategy is sufficiently successful to help take even the least patient readers into the work: "Only believe me," as the narrator of *Sordello* futilely commanded.

Ryals's study, also like Tucker's, is weaker where it ought to be strongest: on the glories of early Browning in *Dramatic Lyrics* and *Dramatic Romances and Lyrics* (however, again like Tucker, his study of *Pippa Passes* is excellent). The book also suffers, as Korg's does, from DeVane-ism: a disease that drives Browning critics to cover *every* work by Browning in their purview and to retell all the well-known facts of publication and appearance. Inasmuch as Ryals covers early plays that he likes and dislikes alike, I would also recommend this as a good general study of the early works, though that is not its essential virtue.

Ryals fashions a new approach to Browning by borrowing equally from the insights of those who argue for the substantial, objective Browning and those who see his art as a fabric, or maze, of dialectic and fictive structures that unravels itself. Occasionally he seems to attempt to wash away controversy in compromise. But on the whole his study illuminates Browning precisely because it allows these diverse views of Browning's art to play their conflicting and often ironic patterns over his puzzling yet so manifest art. The quite conflicting visions of Browning presented by Korg and Ryals suggest that the broad issue of substantiality will continue to be a subject for debate in a variety of new arguments and critical structures. After all, what is more basic than the issue of substance: our own, our world's, our creations'?

Notes

1. E. Warwick Slinn, *Browning and the Fictions of Identity* (London: Macmillan, 1982), pp. 154, 156.

2. I borrow the nice application of Moore's conceit from Mary Louise Albrecht, "The Palace and Art Objects in 'The Statue and the Bust,'" *Studies in Browning and His Circle*, 11 (1983), 47-60, in a study that stresses Browning's high-handedness in reassembling history for his poetic aim. Allan C. Dooley, "Andrea, Raphael, and the Moment of 'Andrea del Sarto,'" *Modern Philology*, 81 (1983), 38-46, supplements Korg on another Italian old favorite.

The Message in the Novels: Walker Percy and the Critics

Veronica A. Makowsky

Martin Luschei. *The Sovereign Wayfarer: Walker Percy's Diagnosis of the Malaise*. Baton Rouge: Louisiana State University Press, 1972. viii, 261 pp.

Robert Coles. *Walker Percy: An American Search*. Boston: Little, Brown, 1978. xx, 250 pp.

Panthea Reid Broughton, ed. *The Art of Walker Percy: Stratagems for Being*. Baton Rouge: Louisiana State University Press, 1979. xix, 311 pp.

Jac Tharpe, ed. *Walker Percy: Art and Ethics*. Jackson: University Press of Mississippi, 1980. viii, 160 pp.

Jac Tharpe. *Walker Percy*. Boston: Twayne, 1983. 141 pp.

Lewis Baker. *The Percys of Mississippi: Politics and Literature in the New South*. Baton Rouge: Louisiana State University Press, 1983. 237 pp.

In 1962 a little-known philosopher and essayist named Walker Percy won the National Book Award for his first novel, *The Moviegoer*. Four more novels and two books of philosophical and cultural commentary followed.[1] Despite two decades of achievement, Percy's stature as a novelist remains problematic. His novels are praised more for their message than their art, an approach reinforced by Percy's willingness to discuss his beliefs and ideas in interviews, using examples from his novels. After we have boiled *The Moviegoer* down to Kierkegaardian rotation, repetition, and the leap of faith, with a good measure of Gabriel Marcel's intersubjectivity, do we still need the novel? Wouldn't we be better off if we directly confronted our fear and trembling with *Sickness unto Death*? Because Percy asserts that science's categories and generalizations abstract the individual from himself, his novels also attract a kind of personal criticism in which the writer avows his agreement with Percy's ideas about man and the postmodern world and cites his own supporting evidence from contemporary life and letters. Though Percy's ability to strike a sympathetic chord in many bosoms may make him a canny contemporary commentator, it still does not prove him an artist of the first rank.

Percy's novels and the type of praise they evoke reveal the postmodern critical confusion about what makes a novel good. In the heyday of the New Criticism, the answer was clear: ambiguity. The ingenious interlocking of symbols, images, and tones successfully eluded attempts at reduction to a single meaning, message, or — Brooks and Warren forbid! — moral. What *did* James mean by making Maggie bury her face on her husband's breast at the end of *The Golden Bowl*? Despite hundreds of preceding pages, labyrinthine in imagery and syntax, the answer is not at all evident, as the volume of almost Talmudic commentary on this and James's other masterpieces shows.

Since it is perfectly possible to know what Walker Percy believes and how his fiction illustrates some of these beliefs, are the novels less good because less puzzling? Although James himself said that everyone sees from his own window in the house of fiction, would he have pictured Percy's aperture as a stained glass window which depicts his Catholic existentialist beliefs and lets in some light, but obscures his view of life's richness and complexity? Or does the fault lie not with Percy but with his critics who fail to notice the medium in their haste to decipher the message and reject all that threateningly amoral modernist ambiguity? The books written to date about Percy raise these questions because they show good critics trying to prove Percy a good novelist without full recourse to formalist standards, but also without benefit of a new consensus on what makes fiction great.

Martin Luschei's *The Sovereign Wayfarer: Walker Percy's Diagnosis of the Malaise* (1972) was the first full-length study of Percy and set the pattern for the later criticism. Luschei asserts that "it is impossible to understand his novels fully without some knowledge of their sources in philosophical existentialism" (p. 18). In his second chapter, Luschei ably presents the views of the existentialists and defines important terms such as everydayness, inauthenticity, and abstraction. As Luschei himself states, he relies on many secondary sources for his interpretation of philosophers, but he has digested them well, and his explanations are clear and neatly directed toward Percy's brand of existentialism. He recognizes that Percy's early novels are not solely influenced by Kierkegaard. He stresses that Percy values Marcel's intersubjectivity, rather than solitude. This belief in the importance of "the other," Luschei demonstrates, leads directly to Percy's fascination with man's need for language, a trait uniquely human that Percy believes to be the key to man's peculiar nature.

Although Luschei is quite correct in stressing the importance of existentialism to Percy, he neglects two other important influences, Percy's southern heritage and his Catholicism. In interviews Percy tries to minimize the influence of the South on his work, and Luschei rightly asserts that "Percy is impatient with the notion that he was prompted to write by the oral tradition of Southern storytelling" (p. 11). Luschei does note, though, that when the omniscient narrator of *The Last Gentleman* (1966) "is dramatizing, the effect can be awesomely real; when he begins rhapsodizing on the same theme it can go hollow without advance notice. He seldom yields to this temptation that so often undoes Faulkner, and it could be that on occasion the looseness of his third person narration taps a vein of suppressed orotundity" (p. 143).

I would take Luschei's point about suppression even farther and argue that Percy's sources, characters, and style were formed in a vigorous reaction against the towering figures of the preceding generation, including the cousin who raised him, the Mississippi poet William Alexander Percy. Neither Walker Percy's voice nor the voices of his narrators are characterized by grand southern rhetoric, with the exception of Lancelot Lamar, who is mad. Percy uses place only to show that a fallen man can't go home again, in this life anyway, so each of the novels ends with the protagonist on the right spiritual path, not at his destination. He refuses to brood on the sins and burdens of guilt bequeathed by the past, but stresses man's position in the contemporary world or in the near future as in *Love in the Ruins* (1971) and the futuristic scenarios of *Lost in the Cosmos* (1983). Indeed, Percy thinks we are all lost in the cosmos, not just the vanquished of the Civil War, and he reverses every commonplace of southern fiction to demonstrate it.

Luschei's treatment of Percy's Catholicism is probably all that could have been expected in 1972. Only three of Percy's novels were published then and the last of these, *Love in the Ruins*, begins the more explicitly Catholic themes developed later in *Lancelot* (1977) and *The Second Coming* (1982). Little is known about Percy's actual conversion to Catholicism. Luschei speculates, "It appears to me that in embracing what amounts to a way of life after the troubled probings of three years of psychoanalysis and an anguished existentialist quest, Percy was not only being born again . . . but also consolidating his life, making a major synthetic move to reassemble the elements"(p. 12). As noted, in interviews Percy repeatedly stresses the Kierkegaardian patterns of his first three novels, and he never proselytizes.

My own guess is that Percy is highly conscious of writing for a secular audience for whom, as he suggests in his essay "Notes for a Novel about the End of the World," the words of Christianity have become worn out, repeated so often that modern man does not really hear them. Percy emphasizes existentialism, a trendier system, to which he hopes his audience will not close their ears, but he slips a message of Christian love into the final pages of each novel when the protagonist signals his improved condition by breaking out of his solipsism and caring about another person. As he indicates in "The Man on the Train," the novelist's strength is his ability to make the reader feel a unique situation, not merely deconstruct it with his intellect. I believe Percy wants the reader to experience the hero's progress toward God, but he avoids much explicitly religious discussion so that his secular readers will not automatically tune out.

Luschei's method is a combination of personal agreement with Percy's views and New Critical explication and close reading. His stance is usually unobtrusive, but occasionally there are passages such as this comment on Percy's tuberculosis at the beginning of World War II: "There is something fateful in the way Percy was put to trial at the outset of the war that marks such a turning point in American life. The postwar mood has been an almost steadily rising malaise, a malaise finally unaccounted for that threatens the psychic annihilation of us all. . . . In such times it is good to hear from a physician-philosopher-novelist who encountered the malaise early, in a highly personal form, and has been thinking it over" (p. 17). Note how Percy's stress on the individual over the abstract evokes the personal note from Luschei. In the last lines of his book, Luschei even suggests that Percy may be a contemporary prophet whose message we should heed: "His pilgrimage bears watching, for who else do we have in America who writes superlative novels out of a considered philosophical position and a professional knowledge of medicine? And what contemporary who *is* our contemporary speaks to our predicament from a sense of his own sovereignty as this man does? It looks as if we too will have to wait and watch and listen" (p. 243).

Although Luschei does occasionally interject a personal agreement or exhortation, most of the book is a standard and thorough exegesis. As noted, in his first chapter he expounds Percy's philosophical sources. In the remaining chapters, he explicates Percy's first three novels. Particularly fine are his close readings of Percy's extremely important opening paragraphs. Luschei then leads the reader through the novels chapter by chapter. This method makes for clarity for a reader new to Percy, but the seasoned reader sometimes is temporarily led to believe Luschei has missed the point when he has merely delayed it. For example, early in the chapter on *Love in the Ruins*, Luschei discusses Dr. Thomas More's lapsometer, a device which More believes will cure man's angelism-bestialism and restore him to wholeness: "Tom's invention is no technological miracle for which the science-worshipping public should hold its breath, but a focusing device introduced to dramatize the condition for which it is designed" (p. 178). The reader who has read *Love in the Ruins* wonders why Luschei doesn't say that the device is Faustian and that it tells us a great deal about Dr. More's sinful pride. The reason is that Luschei is discussing the novel in its order and so does not give us insight until late in his chapter when he explicates the end of the novel: "The aspiration symbolized by the lapsometer was one to 'practice more than heavenly power permits' " (p. 229).

This "diffusing" of points, characteristic of close reading, does not do justice to Luschei's insights—which can be remarkably fine—as in his comments on Will Barrett's vision of a New York street scene in *The Last Gentleman*. "What Will sees in his hallucination, I think, is a vision of *modern* life. What invests it with 'archaic sweetness and wholeness' is that he is viewing it from a *post*modern vantage point in time . . . . The view is backward in time to the period before the Western world view had been totally shattered. This modern world had a sweet wholeness about it, illusory or not, even if it was living off the diminishing capital of the Christian faith. . . . From a postmodern perspective . . . this world can only evoke the repetitive nostalgia of an old silent film" (p. 129). Because of such observations, its balance and thoroughness, its index, and its primary and secondary bibliography, Luschei's book remains the best introduction to Percy. I wish he would update it.

Robert Coles's *Walker Percy: An American Search* (1978) has a fuller biographical section than Luschei's *Sovereign Wayfarer* but beyond that contributes little to the interpretation of Percy's work. The book is difficult to use for a number of reasons. First, there are problems of organization. The first two chapters are entitled "Philosophical Roots" and "The Essays." In "Philosophical Roots," Coles considers the philosophers who influenced Percy but he does not relate them to Percy. For example, pages 8-11 offer a long discussion of Kierkegaard's differences with Hegel without any mention of Percy's position on these issues. In "The Essays," after a good but misplaced biographical sketch, Coles restates or paraphrases the arguments in Percy's essays without sufficient reference to the "philosophical roots" of the preceding chapter. Since Coles seems to expect his reader to integrate all the information, the book is frustrating. The first two chapters should have been combined into one, with parallels explicitly drawn between

Percy and his predecessors. Coles's interesting biographical sketch of Percy could have been the first chapter.

The faults of organization in Coles's book derive from a larger difficulty, his apparent inability to decide for what audience he is writing. His introduction suggests that the audience may be Coles himself. On the first page he demurs, "I have no distance, certainly, on Dr. Percy's writing; I have liked it intensely and consistently for many years." He compares himself to Percy: both were in psychoanalysis, and both are Catholics influenced by the same philosophers. Both men are also doctors, and although Percy has never practiced, Coles usually refers to him as "Dr. Percy" in the introduction. Coles credits Percy's philosophical essays and *The Moviegoer* with motivating him to initiate his groundbreaking *Children of Crisis* series. "Walker Percy's novel gave hope to me, helped me feel stronger at a critical time, when I was somewhat lost, confused, vulnerable, and it seemed, drifting badly" (p. xi). Coles's description of himself "at a critical time" also describes the Percy protagonist at the beginning of each novel.

A strong identification with a writer certainly does not disqualify someone from writing about him, but Coles forgets the needs of his readers and does not satisfy any particular group. The book is certainly not written for an academic audience since it has neither bibliography nor explanatory notes. Coles can discuss Gabriel Marcel for three pages without citing a single title by Marcel, never mind providing a footnote. In a discussion of alienation and rotation in Percy's essay "The Man on the Train," Coles notes, "Percy mentions Hemingway's story ...a fisherman leaves a train in the middle of the Minnesota woods and charts his course" (p. 29). Coles assumes his readers know or remember that the story is called "Big Two-Hearted River," so perhaps his audience is to consist of Hemingway fans. He mentions Luschei's book on page 55 but otherwise does not seem to cite him. I cannot be certain since there is no index.

Coles's intended audience cannot be Walker Percy enthusiasts because his chapter on the novels relies heavily on plot summaries, as if his readers had no knowledge of the novels. In his discussion of the novels, he also includes a number of philosophical digressions, such as disquisitions on Pascal and Descartes (pp. 200-2) in relation to Dr. Thomas More's theory of "angelism-bestialism" in *Love in the Ruins*. In his section on *Lancelot*, Coles seems most interested in vetting the novel as an accurate picture of contemporary life. He states disapprovingly, "When over half of America's families stay away from church, when 'swapping partners' and 'trying out relationships' are considered by millions not only permissible, but even desirable, then the word *adultery* becomes at the very least old-fashioned—a moralistic hand-me-down from another age" (pp. 227-28).

Interestingly enough, the intensely moral Coles does recognize the possibility that Percy's deep convictions might overwhelm his fictions, as in this comment on *The Moviegoer*: "At certain points in the novel Percy's didactic intentions appear, but never disruptively. The reader is free to glide through and beyond, simply enjoying a witty and charming Binx" (p. 154). Coles is sophisticated enough about literature to realize the dangers of the didactic, but only as threats to enjoyment, not to a balanced, well-integrated work of art. In short, Coles can deal with themes, but not technique.

I would speculate that Coles intends his book for a Catholic layman, with a considerable knowledge of existentialism, to whom he wishes to introduce Percy as a kindred spirit. This layman, though, ought to share Coles's strong sense of injustice and need for social activism, and therein lies the rub. Coles wants to defend Percy's novels from the potential charge that they are too concerned with upper-class rather than universal problems. If you're starving, you have more vital interests than Kierkegaard. Through long quotations from the less privileged, such as a woman in a Brazilian slum or an American migrant worker, Coles tries to show that they too wonder about life or ask "existential" questions: "Here is a factory worker saying in his own way, out of his own life, what Percy, through Binx, says: 'Twice, just twice have I stopped and thought to myself: who are you, mister, and what are you doing here, and what *should* you be doing—besides what you're told by your boss and your neighbors and everyone else? It was after my father died; and when my little boy fell sick and he had leukemia, they thought' " (p. 163). These interjected stories are quite compelling, but they do make the book a literary curiosity or hybrid. Percy's ability to evoke personal testimony, which appeared lightly in Luschei, emerges in full force in Coles and his supporting cast.

The Art of Walker Percy: Stratagems for Being (1979), a collection of essays edited by Panthea Reid Broughton, is a much more serious scholarly endeavor, but it too has tinges of personal testimony, directed not to the reader, but to Walker Percy. The book's dedication is "For Walker," and in her introduction Broughton states, "Implicit in the book is a desire that it will find an audience not only in Percy fans and Percy students but in Walker Percy himself" (p. xv). The collection, however, is by no means a festschrift of relentless praise for Percy; rather, some contributors seem unable to resist the professorial urge to offer Percy suggestions and criticism, presumably in the hope he will do better. Can one imagine the New Critics doing this to Joyce or Eliot?

In her introduction to the volume, Broughton faults Percy for a distrust of intellect, then criticizes him for rigid intellectual constructs in her essay "Gentlemen and Fornicators: *The Last Gentleman* and a Bisected Reality." In her introduction she refers to Percy's theory that modern man has turned into a complete consumer who allows supposed experts to control the way he sees reality and then validate his prepackaged perceptions. Broughton comments, "As Percy well knows, we cannot think without such complexes. But Percy rather too often hypothesizes as if he believes we should. That is one reason why there is such a curious ambiguity in his work. It is as if he so distrusts the intellect that he disclaims the fruits of his own labors. But so much distrust belies the character of Percy's own fine achievement. Neither art nor theory necessarily deflate experience; both art and theory and their creators can be at once in and of the world around them; thus they need not interfere with our access to being but instead may enhance it" (p. xviii). Of course, Broughton is justifying the need for a collection of essays on Percy, but she correctly characterizes Percy's attitude toward art, which arises from his beliefs about the paradox inherent in language and symbols. As he explains in *Lost in the Cosmos*, language as liberator becomes language as jailer when words become overused and worn out or when they dominate perception.

In her article on *The Last Gentleman*, Broughton maintains that Percy himself has become trapped in a cliche, the separation of men into gentlemen and fornicators. She relates this bifurcation to larger dualisms in his work, especially the dualism of mind and body: "Percy is committed to the idea that transcendence is mental; thus he aligns the spirit with the mind not the body" (p. 113). As a further consequence, he does not see sex as "a means for overcoming that split, since sex, even for a married gentleman, is still fornication" (p. 113). One could argue that Broughton is too closely identifying Will Barrett with his creator, but she correctly asserts that no character in *The Last Gentleman* unites mind and body or "transcends through love" (p. 113). At the conclusion of her essay, Broughton prescribes "not opposing poles or equilateral triangles, but a mandala which, as an emblem of integration and wholeness, cannot be bisected" (p. 114).

Perhaps Percy actually did profit from Broughton's advice. In *The Second Coming* (1980), published after this collection, Percy joins Will Barrett and Allison Huger in a love that unites body and spirit and does seem to offer a path to transcendence. In the last sentences of the novel, Barrett looks at an old priest and thinks of Allie: "What is it I want from her and him, he wondered, not only want but must have? Is she a gift and therefore a sign of the giver? Could it be that the Lord is here masquerading behind this simple silly holy face? Am I crazy to want both, her and Him? No, not want, must have. And will have." I must stress, however, that this love is a sign of future happiness, "And will have," not immediate gratification, for Percy is after all a Christian, and so does not believe that fallen man can recover complete happiness in this world.

Other critics in this collection also focus on the dualism they perceive in Percy's thought and art. In "The Sundered Self and the Riven World: *Love in the Ruins*," J. Gerald Kennedy traces the mind-body split, or what Dr. Thomas More calls "angelism-bestialism." Kennedy, unlike Broughton, finds this bifurcation inevitable for a Christian but shares her conviction that it damages Percy's fiction: "Though Percy disparages 'edifying' fiction, his commitment to Christian eschatology inevitably binds him to a didactic program and governs his representation of experience. . . . Although the technique [metaphor of the mind-body split] enables him to investigate, in clinical fashion, the peculiar relationship between spirit and flesh, it leads likewise to an oversimplification of human personality" (p. 135). Kennedy ends by diagnosing Percy's art as a case of angelism, "not as the confession of a fellow sufferer but as the clinical diagnosis of an angel orbiting the earth" (p. 136), a charge Percy at least partially confirms in *Lost in the Cosmos* when he writes of the artist that "Like the scientists, he transcends in his use of signs." Percy, however, adds an important qualification to his portrait of the abstracted artist: "Unlike the scientists, he speaks not merely to a small community of fellow artists but to the world of men who understand him" (p. 119). For Percy, Marcel's "intersubjectivity" can redeem abstraction.

William H. Poteat agrees with Kennedy's charge of angelism in his "Reflections on Walker Percy's Theory of Language," but only as applied to some of Percy's essays: "[Percy] himself becomes a victim of that same abstraction when in his philosophical essays he loses his grip upon himself" (p. 204), and slips into jargon. Poteat comments, "I know very well what it is like to speak a grammatical sentence in English about something in our mutual world; but what is it to 'couple semological and phonological elements' "? (p. 210). He finds "The Delta Factor" Percy's best essay because "Here, free of the self-set demand for a philosophical rigor which, cultivated in the 'old modern age,' has a built-in gravitational drift toward dualism, Percy willingly gives himself over to the power of his imagination to make an unfamiliar juxtaposition of images" (pp. 216-17). In "Homo Loquens, Homo Symbolificus, Homo Sapiens: Walker Percy on Language," Weldon Thornton also explores Percy's dualistic essays as he presents and explains Percy's theory of language. Thornton does not think that Percy solves the problem of meaning, the way signifier relates to signified: "All Percy offers is a more specific description of the problem, not an explanation of how it works" (p. 186).

Still another dualism, that of Christian versus Stoic, is presented in the collection's two essays on *Lancelot*. In an article full of allusions and images explicated, "The Fall of the House of Lamar," Lewis A. Lawson sees Harry, the Catholic priest, and Lance, the southern stoic, as two irreconcilable halves of Walker Percy: "The Stoic has not been vanquished. Walker Percy can no more stop being a southerner than he can stop being a Christian. As a southerner he will continue to despise the things that he as a Christian can live with" (p. 244). In *"Lancelot* and the Search for Sin," William J. Dowie also posits that through Lance, "Percy seems at once to be expressing his outrage [at the corruptions of contemporary life] and, at the same time, parodying it" (p. 249), particularly through Lance's search for, not maladjustment or mental illness, but *sin*, which he ironically does not seek in his own soul. Both these articles are valuable for the light they shed on Percy's southern heritage, which usually tends to be neglected in favor of his Christian existentialism.

The Art of Walker Percy is most valuable for essays like the ones I have discussed, those that explore the complexities and problems in Percy's view of man. The collection also contains essays which take a simpler approach, that of fitting Percy into a larger system. Janet Hobbs applies Kierkegaard to *The Moviegoer* in "Binx Bolling and the Stages of Life's Way." Max Webb's "Binx Bolling's New Orleans: Moviegoing, Southern Writing, and Father Abraham" applies Kierkegaard only in his last category and so earlier appears not to recognize that Binx's experience is a series of rotations. Webb is most refreshing, though, in conveying the idea behind rotation without philosophical jargon, as in his discussion of the opening paragraphs of *The Moviegoer*: "These fresh starts and false starts comment on each other and finally enact a major theme: the necessity of seeing one's life as a series of fresh beginnings and the corresponding dangers of lapsing into the everydayness of habit" (p. 10).

In contrast, Ted R. Spivey's "Walker Percy and the Archetypes" reduces Percy's novels to an incomplete Jungian quest. Spivey prescribes: "Percy must bring his fictional characters of the future into a profounder relationship with the shadow than he has already done if he is to continue his exploration of archetypal territory" (p. 291), although Spivey does not claim Percy knows Jung (p. 274). Cleanth Brooks does not assert that Percy is familiar with the works of Eric Voegelin, but in "Walker Percy and Modern Gnosticism," he demonstrates the way many of Percy's characters, particularly Lancelot Lamar, share the gnostic belief that man can save himself and found a perfect society, as opposed to Christian doctrines such as dependence on a savior and happiness only in the next world.

Two essays are written in rather dense jargon, but fortunately they do contain much of interest to reward the patient reader. Consider Richard Pindell's thesis statement in "Toward Home: Place, Language, and Death in *The Last Gentleman*": "Two rival arts of being-here, one essentially entropic or reductive, the other essentially news-making or creative, converge on the prime world-making *materia* of place, language, and death. Out of these three phenomena Percy bodies forth Will's inwardness and tracks his possibilities, and failures, of progress toward receptivity to news. Finally it is within an imagination of home that Percy advances and unifies the dialectic relationships within place, language, and death" (pp. 50-51). Under all this Pindell astutely delineates the relationship between Percy's Christianity and his theory of language with emphasis on death as the "transfiguring factor" (p. 62) which once more can make the language of Christianity meaningful, a notion I would compare to Wallace Stevens's "Death is the mother of beauty."

Simone Vauthier's jargon can be a bit pretentious in her "Narrative Triangulation in *The Last Gentleman*." She cites a passage from the novel about Will Barrett and speculates upon it.

"Yet it fell out, strange to say, that when he did find himself in a phone booth, he discovered he had spent all but nine cents! Oh damnable stupidity and fiendish bad luck, but what are you going to do"? (*The Last Gentleman*, p. 306). Is the narrator assuming his commentator's role, as "strange to say" suggests, and is he then addressing the hero—an intradiegetic narratee—in mock pity, or is he taking an extradiegetic narratee to witness? Is the narrator rather reporting the character's inner monologue, in which case Will is talking to himself alone, and the narratee is metadiegetic? Or is he thinking of himself and anyone in the same circumstances, which makes the narratee both meta- and intradiegetic"? [p. 91]

Beneath the terminology, Vauthier is asking who is speaking at various points in the passage, and she is also trying to determine the tone or tones. These are important questions which, as Vauthier asserts, contribute to the ambiguity of the novel, particularly the last chapter where the narrator largely drops out of the dialogue between Sutter Vaught and Will Barrett. The narrator reenters in the final paragraphs and supplies the highly ambiguous last line, "The Edsel waited for him."

The two essays I found most interesting treat Percy's attitude toward his art through consideration of the diabolic Art Immelmann of *Love in the Ruins*. In "Thomas More's Distorted Vision," William Leigh Godshalk provides much evidence of the unreliability of the narrator, Dr. More. He claims that More's vision of the present is warped by various myths or fictions from the past (p. 144), including the "myth of diabolical intervention" (p. 152) as personified in Art Immelmann. More wants to blame Art since he "does not want to be responsible for any misuse of the lapsometer" (p. 152), More's dangerous panacea for the existential predicament. Godshalk plays on Art's name to suggest Percy's ambiguity toward his art: "Art merely helps More do what he basically desires" (p. 153); "The rejection of Art becomes important for More as a rejection of his own pride and irresponsibility" (p. 154); and "By distorting reality, he [More] failed to live and love *in the real world* and was a soul divided from its body" (p. 155). I would carry the argument further by asserting that Percy believes art can help man transcend reality and understand it better, but false or merely escapist art is just another consumer anaesthetic.

In Walker Percy's Devil," Thomas Le Clair states, "Art Immelmann represents both Percy's philosophic allusiveness and the aesthetic inconsistency of the novel. Immelmann's temptation of Thomas More is the internal analogue of Percy's temptation by an old-fashioned art. Briefly put, Walker Percy's devil is the attempt to render existentialist material in an unexistentialist novel form" (p.158). Consequently, Le Clair considers *Love in the Ruins* "essentially an adventure story" (p. 165) and the "least successful of Percy's [first] four novels" (p. 158). Both LeClair and Godshalk are raising the question of didactic art. Godshalk wonders if Percy regards art as a distraction from the necessary confrontation of life's dilemmas, even if that art embodies a moral. LeClair feels that Percy's existentialist message should find a truly *novel* form. These kinds of problems do not arise in the case of artists without clearly defined philosophies and didactic intentions, and they suggest a further question: if the message is more important than the medium, does it need an elaborate package like a novel at all?

As its title would suggest, similar issues are addressed in some of the essays Jac Tharpe has collected in *Walker Percy: Art and Ethics* (1980). The articles divide rather neatly into three categories: those that consider Percy's art in terms of technique or literary allusions, one essay on Percy's ethics, and several on the relationship between Percy's art and his ethics. In my first category, that of art, I would place John Edward Hardy's "Percy and Place: Some Beginnings and Endings," a study of Percy's use of setting. Susan S. Kissel compares Percy's protagonists to those of two other contemporary Catholic novelists in "Voice in the Wilderness: The Prophets of O'Connor, Percy, and Powers." Corinne Dale traces allusions to clarify Percy's themes in *"Lancelot* and the Medieval Quests of Sir Lancelot and Dante." In *"Lancelot*: Sign for the Times," Jerome C. Christensen leads the reader through the novel by playing upon the implications of the fragment of a sign Lance can see from his window. And Kierkegaardian rotation emerges once again as Lewis A. Lawson explicates "Moviegoing in *The Moviegoer*." These articles are all mainstream New Critical explications, useful for the various facets of Percy they illuminate.

The political, or rather apolitical, facet of Percy's work is critized by Cecil L. Eubanks in "Walker Percy: Eschatology and the Politics of Grace." Eubanks, a professor of political science, attempts to deduce Percy's system of ethics from his essays and novels only to find that Percy's ethics preclude politics: "In a word, *politics is an abstraction, fundamentally incompatible with the searchings of a sovereign wayfarer.* Therein lie the dilemma and shortcomings of Percy's 'political philosophy' " (p. 126). Eubanks suggests a way that Percy's individualism could be considered a form of "political" action: "It may be that in these 'consciousness' novels Percy is preparing the way for a new and perhaps more socially based emphasis on love and the politics of community building" (pp. 130-31). But this rationalization transforms Percy's philosophy into Emersonian individualism: if every man remade himself and practiced self-reliance the world could be perfected; institutions cannot remake society, but each individual can. As Eubanks elsewhere rightly points out, Percy is not a latter-day transcendentalist but a Christian, so he "regards change in human nature or character as simply not possible" (p. 131).

Eubanks, however, charges that "the emphasis by Percy on *consciousness at the expense of experience,* on grace as 'Word' and not 'Word made Flesh' does a grave injustice to Christianity as well as to the notion of grace" (p. 131). Although Percy's protagonists make what Eubanks calls "small, insecure steps," not leaps of faith, I think they do move toward improving their world. Binx Bolling enters medical school and cares for the fragile Kate and his half brothers and sisters; Will Barrett joins Sutter Vaught and prevents his suicide in *The Last Gentleman,* and Will starts the literal building of a community by handicapped workers at the end of *The Second Coming*; Dr. Thomas More practices medicine and founds a new family, and Father John rejects Lancelot's way of the sword for life as a parish priest. Percy is suspicious of the pride inherent in grandiose schemes and so his characters' Christian love or charity must begin at home.

Percy's art could be considered his way of changing the world, a possibility suggested by the articles addressing the relation of Percy's art to his ethics. In "Walker Percy and the Resonance of the Word," as Charles P. Bigger places Percy's theory of language in a larger philosophical context, he also indicates where Percy might rank art. "Walker Percy is a colonial thinker. The territory he inhabits received its charter for exploration from the established order as it existed when he was in fact a student member of the academic community; and as a colonial he has explored his territory from this perspective. His medical and scientific training certainly disposed him to regard the sciences as eminently respectable. Indeed, I think that as a novelist he feels that he is dealing with a frivolous genre, with something slightly suspect which does not befit the concern of a serious and public-spirited Christian gentleman" (p. 46). Bigger does not treat the novels, but praises Percy's work on language, particularly the process of naming, "as a remarkable service towards our recovery of strangeness" (p. 53). We are left, then, with the question of what the novels are good for, if the essays illuminate Percy's ideas so well.

Three writers provide three complementary answers to this question, and Percy's *Lancelot* is crucial to their arguments. In "Art as Symbolic Action: Walker Percy's Aesthetic," Michael Pearson posits that the novels act upon the reader and make him act: "Novelist recaptures reality; reader re-experiences it . . . . Both are involved in naming, the novelist in creating new metaphors to re-present experience and the reader for devising new strategies for re-understanding the symbol and the world" (pp. 60-61). Pearson maintains that *Lancelot* is the obvious enactment of this strategy since the reader must evaluate and respond to a book-length monologue by the crazed title character. In "Charles Pierce and Walker Percy: From Semiotic to Narrative," J.P. Telotte moves from a consideration of Pierce and Percy's triadic theory of language—speaker, word, and object—to the importance Percy gives to language because it makes truly human relationships possible: "The novelist initiates a triad with himself as speaker to a listening public, and he functions through the symbolic value of his novel— a symbol writ large—which serves his public as a very vital 'message in the bottle' " (p. 74). Telotte also points to the triad of Lancelot, Father John, and the reader (p. 75).

Robert H. Brinkmeyer, Jr. believes Percy's readers not only re-see and re-name, but experience and profit from ordeals. In "Percy's Bludgeon: Message and Narrative Strategy," Brinkmeyer asserts that Percy's "primary fictional strategy [in *Love in the Ruins* and *Lancelot*] is to shock the complacent reader, jolt him, by putting him through an ordeal and impel him to look more critically at his world of 'everydayness' " (p. 83). In short, these three articles suggest that the novels do fully what a treatise could only do partially, make the reader feel as well as think since the fiction works on the whole person, not just his intellect. One might even posit that the novel's efficacy as a means toward change lies in its ability to affect man on many levels.

In general, Tharpe's *Art and Ethics* is less rich and varied a collection than Broughton's *Stratagems for Being*, which remains the better introduction to Percy's work. *Stratagems for Being*, however, contains neither an index nor a bibliography. Tharpe's *Art and Ethics* is not indexed but does include a bibliography by Joe Weixlmann and Daniel H. Gann, which provides chronological listings of Percy's books and the reviews of them, Percy's shorter works, interviews with Percy, and secondary works, all complete through 1979. Curiously, Tharpe's introduction mentions an essay which does not appear in the book: "Finally, Randolph Bates briefly discusses the three books that have studied Percy's work . . . " (p. viii).

Jac Tharpe is also responsible for the Twayne volume *Walker Percy* (1983). Tharpe posits that there is more to Percy than existentialism: "But for Percy man is alienated from God, not from society. Percy is primarily a Roman Catholic novelist attempting to recall the nation (not the irrevocably lost world) back to God, much as the American Puritans wished to do with more naive and sanguine hope. His main theme is man, and, along with man, love. Sex and religion are his interests in all his novels. And his interest in marriage includes a desire to prevent overindulgence in sex and the accompanying loss of compassion that treats people as objects of pleasure and substitutes flesh for God" (p. iii). In Tharpe's book the pendulum has swung completely in the other direction; instead of Percy as philosopher, we have Percy as Puritan.

Tharpe's moralistic interpretation can be as reductive as is the search for Kierkegaard's categories in every novel. Of Binx's failed intercourse with Kate in *The Moviegoer*, Tharpe states that "Percy's wish [is] to point to marriage as the prerequisite for sexual intercourse" (p. 58). He asserts that "the central question" of *Lancelot* is "what sex is" (p. 94). In order to stress the sexual morality of *The Last Gentleman,* Tharpe writes as if he believes Will Barrett will marry Kitty Vaught after the novel ends: "His return to faithful married life with Kitty is precisely what Percy thinks proper for a young man" (p. 77), an outcome disproved by *The Second Coming.* Although I agree that Percy is a profoundly moral novelist, I would distinguish Percy's humorous and sympathetic recognition of man's fallen nature from the obsessive hunt for sexual sin more characteristic of the maniacal Lancelot Lamar than Walker Percy himself.

Tharpe's book is somewhat choppy, probably because it is meant to suit the basic introductory level of the Twayne series. His first chapter, "Biography, Background, and Influences," is the best because it covers all these categories lucidly, concisely, and accurately. I would recommend it to anyone seeking information on Percy's literary, historical, and philosophical contexts. His second chapter, "Theory of Art," stresses Percy's didacticism and posits that it weakens his characterization: "Percy speaks literally of emphasizing what people do, not what individuals do, for he does not characterize brilliantly, despite his interest in the psychological and the grotesque" (p. 13). "Christendom," the third chapter, seems unnecessary. Tharpe considers various social groups, such as blacks and women, in Percy's novels, but in so brief a discussion can do little more than count and categorize. The points he makes here on Percy's view of society would be more effective if worked into his chapters on the novels. The fourth chapter, "Techniques," is quite disjointed since Tharpe tries to cover all the bases for his presumably undergraduate audience. For instance, in a single paragraph on pages 35-36, he ranges all over the map of American literature. Of Percy's characters he states, "They resemble Southern grotesques in sensational situations. The pact with the devil [in *Love in the Ruins*] could almost come from Poe and the comic setting for it from Mark Twain. Lancelot has sources in Hawthorne and Erskine Caldwell. An aspect of Will comes from any Southwestern humor column called riffraff and hayseed. Binx might almost appear as a Young Goodman Bolling, and Lancelot is any grotesque. From another point of view, all the characters are dreamy and romantic." After the moralistically reductive chapters on the novels, Tharpe's compendium concludes with a brief, annotated "Selected Bibliography" of primary and secondary sources. Strangely enough, it does not include Tharpe's own *Art and Ethics* (1980).

Lewis Baker ably delineates Percy's southern heritage in his *The Percys of Mississippi: Politics and Literature in the New South* (1983). Baker, a historian, traces the Percy family from its origins in New Spain to Walker Percy. He writes clearly and knows how to keep his narrative moving briskly. As his title indicates, he emphasizes the public aspects of the Percys' careers, so we learn little about their private lives, thoughts, and feelings. The Percy women get especially short shrift, which is disappointing considering the unusual women in Walker Percy's fiction. Although Baker's thesis is that the Percys' outlet for their noblesse oblige has shifted from politics to literature, he is plainly more comfortable discussing politics. He gives a fascinating account of William Alexander Percy's life and the themes of his poetry, but offers little on his techniques.

For those interested in Walker Percy, *The Percys of Mississippi* is most useful for showing the surprising extent to which Percy uses his family history in his novels, despite his frequent disclaimers of the "southern" qualities of his fiction. Aunt Emily's stoic monologue in *The Moviegoer* or Lancelot's diatribe against social corruption could have been delivered by any number of Percys. In *The Last Gentleman* and *The Second Coming*, Will Barrett's Ku-Klux-Klan-fighting ancestors are modelled on those of Walker Percy. More importantly, though, Baker demonstrates that Percy is the heir to a goodly portion of the family's impulse toward social reform, in spite of his Catholicism, existentialism, and very private way of life: "In one sense Walker has withdrawn behind the innermost wall of individuality. By recording the fruits of his search in his novels, however, he has preserved his family's influence and tradition of leadership in an increasingly democratic society that has little use for aristocrats" (pp. 176-77).

Unfortunately, though, Baker's chapter on Walker Percy is the weakest in the book, mainly because it contains nothing new. The preceding chapters use letters, diaries, and other sources to illuminate and reanimate Walker Percy's ancestors, but the chapter on the novelist is derived mainly from the novels, so we do not receive an equally vivid portrait of the artist. In his preface to *The Tragic Muse*, Henry James noted that the artist was so hard to portray because all one could see of him was his back as he wrote at his desk, and that is about all we get here. Baker's sources indicate no access to Walker Percy's papers or any interviews with him, so we do not even receive his reflections on his family. Walker Percy is actually a member of the Alabama Percys, a second cousin of the poet William Alexander Percy of Greenville, Mississippi. We learn practically nothing of Walker's immediate family or his life in Alabama before his father's suicide when Walker was eleven. Although Baker's shift in the last chapter from lively biography to literary explication is anticlimactic, I would still recommend the book as a well written account of the men of a fascinating and prominent southern family who were controversially involved in every aspect of the South's story from its founding to the New South.

Percy appears to listen to his critics. He responds thoughtfully to criticism in interviews, and his last two books, *The Second Coming* (1980) and *Lost in the Cosmos* (1983), seem to answer the concerns of his critics. *The Second Coming* is a full, rich novel. Although Kierkegaardian concepts such as rotation and repetition are represented in Allie's amnesia and Will's memories of his childhood, these categories are unobtrusive; the reader does not need to know anything about them to appreciate the novel. Percy retains his satirical touch, but his characters here are not caricatures and thus they are more credible than many characters in his earlier books. In Allison Huger, Percy for the first time uses a woman as a central consciousness, and uses her well, for Allie is one of the freshest and most appealing women in contemporary fiction. Because he has fully developed Allie's character, Percy can finally depict true "intersubjectivity"; a Percy protagonist at last has another completely human character to talk with, as in this diagolue between Allie and Will:

"What luck. Here we are. Hold me."
"I am."
"Oh, I think you have something for me."

"Yes."
"What?"
"Love. I love you," he said. "I love you now and until the day I die."
"Oh, hold me. And tell me."
"Tell you what?"
"Is what you're saying part and parcel of what you're doing?"
"Part and parcel." [p. 405]

Through love Will and Allie are learning to unite body and spirit, actions and words, "part and parcel." Their plans to start building houses and running a greenhouse with handicapped workers suggest that their love will not imprison them in romantic isolation, but join them with others in the Christian love evinced by the old priest, Father Weatherbee. In *The Second Coming*, Percy succeeds in embodying his philosophy and religion in his fiction, without swamping it with rigid abstractions.

In *Lost in the Cosmos*, Percy responds to the criticism that his early essays, many of them collected in *The Message in the Bottle*, are full of scientific and semiotic jargon, and consequently ineffective in conveying his ideas. Percy breaks out of the academic essay in *Lost in the Cosmos*, subtitled *The Last Self-Help Book*. Under the guise of this perenially popular American genre, Percy makes his usual points about contemporary life, philosophy, religion, and language. He posits various fictional situations to the reader and asks him to respond to them by answering multiple-choice questions; for example, Question 8: "Why is it that One's Self often does not Prefer Sex with one's Chosen Mate, Chosen for His or Her Attractiveness and Suitability, even when the Mate is a Person well known to one, knowing of one, loved by one, with a Life, Time, and Family in common, but rather prefers Sex with a New Person, even a Total Stranger, or even Vicariously through Pornography?" (p. 41). In terms of Percy's existentialism, the answer is that man is seeking another rotation to break out of the malaise of everydayness. Percy, however, eschews that vocabulary and makes the reader respond to a concrete situation, in this instance "The Last Donahue Show," a hilarious parody.

The reader is forced to think more than he is by the novels, but he does not lose a sense of the real world as he did in Percy's highly abstract early essays.

Lost in the Cosmos also provides some insight into Percy's response to the critics and the critics' response to Percy. The artist, to Percy, is not Joyce's god-like figure paring his nails; in fact, Percy believes that the artist's susceptibility to seeing himself as a god is his greatest flaw. In the section called "Why Writers Drink," Percy shows that the writer tends to live in a state of transcendence or abstraction, what Dr. More would diagnose as "angelism," and so he uses liquor to ease his reentry into the world (pp. 147-48). Percy's artist may have great gifts, but these gifts have concomitant perils. Since Percy rejects the god-like status of the high-modernist artist, he both listens to and acts upon criticism, and so evokes more suggestions. As an alternative to the dehumanized texts and deconstructing readers of some postmodern schools, the interaction between Percy and his readers offers a more humane and constructive model for the contemporary world of letters.

Note

1. The editions of Percy's books cited here are: *The Moviegoer* (New York: Avon, 1982); *The Last Gentleman* (New York: Avon, 1978); *Love in the Ruins* (New York: Avon, 1981); *Lancelot* (New York: Avon, 1980); *The Second Coming* (New York: Pocket Books, 1981); *The Message in the Bottle* (New York: Farrar, Straus, Giroux, 1981); and *Lost in the Cosmos* (New York: Farrar, Straus, Giroux, 1983). Original dates of publication are indicated parenthetically in the text.

Waste Land Indeed: Eliot in Our Time

Ruth Z. Temple

    Charles Tomlinson. *Poetry and Metamorphosis.* Cambridge: Cambridge University Press, 1983. xi, 97 pp.

    Ronald Bush. *T. S. Eliot: A Study in Character and Style.* New York: Oxford University Press, 1983. xiii, 287 pp.

    David Spurr. *Conflicts in Consciousness: T. S. Eliot's Poetry and Criticism.* Urbana: University of Illinois Press, 1984. xx, 136 pp.

    Caroline Behr. *T. S. Eliot: A Chronology of His Life and Works.* New York: St. Martin's Press, 1983. vii, 123 pp.

    Michael Grant, ed. *T. S. Eliot: The Critical Heritage.* London: Routledge and Kegan Paul, 1982. 2 vols.

    Robert H. Canary. *T. S. Eliot: The Poet and His Critics.* Chicago: American Library Association, 1982. xiii, 392 pp.

    David Ned Tobin. *The Presence of the Past: T. S. Eliot's Victorian Inheritance.* Ann Arbor, Michigan: UMI Research Press, 1983. Studies in Modern Literature, no. 8. x, 180 pp.

> Il y'a quelquechose de plus précieux
> que l'originalité: c'est l'universalité.
> Paul Valéry

When Eliot died in 1965, his poet friends testified: Robert Lowell, "Our American literature has had no greater poet or critic"; Allen Tate, "Mr. Eliot was the greatest poet in English of the 20th century;" Robert Penn Warren, "He is the key figure of our century" (*New York Times*, 5 Jan. 1965). Where does Eliot stand now? A mass of critical commentary has accumulated, so that guides to it are needed. (Two of them I shall discuss.) What is most worthy of comment, I suppose, is that a new wave of Eliot criticism is taking shape—if shape it may be said to have. New Criticism, the mode Eliot helped to form and on occasion illustrated, has been fashionably supplanted by newer modes. It is in the light of these that Eliot is now undergoing revision. I say *Eliot* advisedly: to the newer critics the poetry as poetry does not matter; it is an instrument for dissecting the poet's unconscious or a provocation to the free exercise of the critic's imagination.

Those of us who grew up academically with Eliot's developing career were most of us insurgents in the battle to replace biographical criticism with New. Close reading of texts was the means to the end of discovering meaning. Biographical facts were largely irrelevant, but, as Eliot had instructed us, the tradition was not, and literary allusions must be pursued to their source, for the context of such allusions formed the connotation of images. Evaluating poetry grew out of interpretation. I recall this (vanishing) discipline for two reasons. First, to establish that this is the way I think poetry should be read and judged. Second, to remind newcomers to the literary scene of how Eliot looked at poetry and criticism and their connections, including, of course, his own poetry. There are still critical voices that enrich his poetry and critics alive to his excellence and to traditional standards of criticism. Charles Tomlinson represents the first class; Robert Canary the second. Two of the authors under review here, Ronald Bush and David Spurr, illustrate the new wave.

What shape this takes varies from critic to critic, but two of the fashionable methods are called criticism of consciousness and deconstruction, both borrowed from France, where since World War II a succession of new critical modes has exercised the minds and pens of a number of gifted and now famous men. The French, as is their wont, have passed lightheartedly from one to another of the modes, shifting ground as they engaged new adversaries in debate on such topics as *Nouvelle Critique ou Nouvelle Imposture*. American disciples tend to be rather Puritanically earnest as they embrace these borrowed doctrines, taking each in turn as the way, the truth, and the light. The essence of "criticism of consciousness" is just what the phrase suggests. The poem is strictly a means to the end of unveiling the poet's consciousness or, more probably, unconscious. The essence of deconstruction is the assumption that the literary text is up for grabs. For both "schools," what the poetry seems to say, or what it probably says in the light of what the poet said he was doing or usually tried to do—all this is quite beside the point. There are no controls, and the laws of evidence are suspended. These remarks are not intended as an adequate account of such serious new doctrines and methods. They are simply a preface to the kind of consideration I shall be obliged to give specimens of this approach to poetry. By definition, of course, such books are undefined, and evaluation of their conclusions is inappropriate. It may be noted, however, that, whatever their protestations of scientific objectivity, their analyses are pursued in a spirit of detraction. Valéry's aphorism, which Eliot quotes with approval and which I have used as epigraph, should, I think, serve as a warning and a guide to critics. It would surely be endorsed by Tomlinson, who provides an explicit corrective to Bush and Spurr. "For Eliot, inviolable song must somehow be possible despite violation, and despite the self-violation that preyed on him at the time of *The Waste Land*" (p. 46).

In a series of four Clark lectures at Cambridge, Charles Tomlinson explored the themes of "metamorphosis, recreation, translation—these and their meaning for poetry," led to the subject by his re-reading of Ovid as editor of *The Oxford Book of Verse in English Translation* (p. xi). Like Eliot in his Clark lectures (1926, a series left unpublished), he traces an idea through generations of poets. Only one of the lectures is on Eliot. (The others are on Pound and various translators of Ovid.) In it Tomlinson explores Eliot's preoccupation in his early poems with the affliction of tonguelessness so daunting to poets, modulating from the temptation to silence, through the distraction of social chatter, to the comfort of "subhuman noises and bird-sounds,"—all the elements of what he calls the "soundscape" of Eliot's poetry. (We shall find another critic denying all but visual images to Eliot's poems through *The Waste Land*.) In *The Waste Land* Eliot has metamorphosed, as had so many earlier poets, the fear of silence into the myth of Tereus and Philomena, using both Ovid and the *Pervigilium Veneris*. And Tomlinson provides an insight that might profitably have been used by two critics we are about to discuss when he observes how in "a fragmented art form . . . psychic wholeness can yet be hinted at by the use of myth and metamorphosis" (p. 13). Tomlinson's treatment of his subject is today rare indeed. We shall look in vain for other instances of his kind of close reading, informed by knowledge of the European literary tradition, by disciplined imagination and tact, sustained by an appropriate critical theory.[1]

The current new wave was suitably described a long time ago by a poet who had suffered from the critics. Pope has Dulnes give the call to battle:

> Let standard authors, thus, like trophies borne,
> Appear more glorious as more hacked and torn.
> And you, my Critics! in the chequered shade,
> Admire new light through holes yourselves have made.

Though not expressly framed as exercises in detraction—they protest their admiration—the studies of Ronald Bush and David Spurr contrive to leave their poetical subject in tatters. For Bush, Eliot is "the finest poet of his generation." The declaration appears on page 8. If by chance one returns to it after reading the book, one can only say—What a generation. And one may make the further reflection that a generation is fifteen years. The *Waste Land* poet? Bush substitles his book *A Study in Character and Style*. "Style," he says, "is a habitual mode of bringing our preconscious impulses into harmony. And just as it is impossible to recognize a man's character unless we understand the internal pressures he lives with, so it is impossible to understand his style unless we first recognize the impulses it serves to repress, channel and adapt" (p. xiii). This is a far cry from *"Le style c'est l'homme même."* Style, far from being the expression of character in the proper sense of that word, is the cloak of the subconscious. One suspects that this ambitious book aspires to the condition of critical biography, an aspiration one can only deplore, for the emphasis throughout falls not on the poetry as poetry but on the poetry as evidence of conflicts within—destructive conflicts that result in flawed poetry. Furthermore, the author is unsympathetic to Eliot's conversion, so that he misreads the later poems. Bush is, in fact, writing a psychoanalytical study absent the patient on the couch. Though dealing with the subconscious might seem to be properly the role of the psychoanalyst, it is currently practiced in literary criticism by amateurs whose claim is only to literary expertise. In a scientific age, this is odd.

The portrait drawn of the poet Eliot is that of a psychological mess. The wonder is that it could write poetry. As Bush proceeds to "analyze" Eliot's states of mind, his procedure is that of unsupported assertion. (One of the features of the *nouvelle vague* is its suppression of the rules of evidence.) "Brought up short after five years of false tranquility, Eliot awakes to find himself alive and raw. Suddenly it comes to him that 'Burnt Norton' solved nothing, that all the old desires and all the old scars still hurt" (p. 214). (This, like much of the book, reads like fiction. It is.) In the course of writing *East Coker*, "Eliot responds with black elation. His way clear, there is nothing now for him to do but, in Conrad's words, 'into [sic—poor Conrad] the destructive element immerse.' And so he dares the flood" (pp. 214-15). Here is how Eliot writes *The Dry Salvages*: "Still angry, still intent on puncturing the mood of 'Burnt Norton' (and on punishing himself for having believed in it), he turns his anger toward a celebration of death and eternal judgment" (p. 215). Thus, using the documented facts painstakingly gathered by Helen Gardner about the composition of *Four Quartets*, Bush weaves a tissue of speculation—presented, however, as fact—as to how Eliot worked out the connections of the last three with *Burnt Norton* and with each other, deriving from those speculations his assessments of all three as poetically lamentable. (He fully endorses Donald Davie's annihilation of *The Dry Salvages*.)

When Bush is dealing with the elements of style, such as images, he betrays an insensitivity that no critic can afford. To say that the figure and function of Arjuna (hero of the *Bhagavad Gita*) in *The Dry Salvages* is *derived* from Eliot's "political journalism *entre deux guerres*," specifically an essay of 1937, is to betray ignorance of how a poet's mind works. Arjuna inhabited Eliot's mind, to be called on when needed, and the prose passages bear no resemblance whatever to the poetic. The fact of the derivation from "political journalism" is used to explain "the poem's awkwardness" (p. 223). Failure to analyze images and their function in a poem leads Bush to juxtapose four water images as referring to the same setting: the water-dripping image from *The Waste Land* he assigns to the "emotional terrain of Eliot's childhood, the place where 'the wind blows the water white and black' ('Prufrock'), the place where one can hear 'The cry of quail and the whirling plover' (*Ash Wednesday*) and the place where one knows the 'scent of pine and the woodthrush singing through the fog' ('Marina')" (p. 75). Not only are these four totally different in connotation; they do not even designate the same kind of scene. The spring dreamed of in the desert is a woodland spring; the others evoke variously meadow or seashore.[2]

Not to be capable of close reading disqualifies a critic from creating theories about the composition of poetry. Bush is so careless a reader that he endorses J. Hillis Miller's astonishing view: "Because Eliot's hold on the world outside him is so slack, there is little recognition in Eliot's early poetry 'that men have other senses beside eyesight' " (p. 166). Anyone familiar with the early poems will readily call up images of sound, smell, and taste, both positive and negative, not to mention touch and motion. Bush is insensitive, too, to the poem as unity. The use he makes of cancellation (which he has, to his credit, studied wherever possible) is to deduce the poet's need to hide something or other—never in the interest of constructing a better poem.[2] Bush has produced a well nourished book: he has read Eliot's uncollected essays and what he could of manuscript material. Although he provides no bibliography, the abundant notes testify to broad acquaintance with Eliot studies. He writes gracefully and his volume (Oxford University Press) is of course well made. It is a pity that so much effort was expended in so dubious a cause.

David Spurr's book, his first, is instructively entitled *Conflicts in Consciousness*. Eliot figures only in the subtitle, which is quite proper since Eliot's poetry and criticism are merely data used in the demonstration of a thesis. By comparison with Bush's study, Spurr's is slight, both in extent (127 pages, including one short chapter on the criticism) and in documentation and mastery of the materials. Spurr's book is written with an energetic acerbity quite different from Bush's bland grace. Spurr *seems* to lead a charge against Eliot's poetry and psyche. Both men, however, leave their subject "hacked and torn." I shall let the author proclaim his own subversion and line up his team. The tone of his pronouncement will prepare us for his argument:

> This relatively new critical attitude attempts to identify the submerged conflicts of Eliot's language and generally sees his poetry, like his critical writings and even his personality, as divided against itself in various ways. The contributions of critics like C. K. Stead, Bernard Bergonzi, and George Bornstein create at least two favorable contributions for a systematic study of Eliot's consciousness in all its complexity: first, they point to an essential polarity in Eliot's work that can be identified with both formal and thematic elements in his poems; and, second, they free the critic from traditional explanations of a poem based on searches for narrative sequence, allegorical meaning, or literary allusion and allow him to focus on the nature of poetic language as arising from the poet's own "obscure creative impulse."[3] Even if the unconscious motivation of such language can never be known in the historical or biographical sense, its hypothetical nature can enrich our experience of the text by allowing us to see the poem as a stage or field for the enactment of conflicts whose origins lie in the poet's mind.
>
> The reading of Eliot that I am proposing, then, shares with psychoanalytic approaches to literature the attempt to establish connections between the text and the author's unconscious, while it also follows certain deconstructive procedures in its refusal to take for granted the textual coherence of any poem. [p. xii]

Spurr begins by assuming, needless to say without evidence, that Eliot's impetus to creation is "Romantic," a view that he shares with Bush and expresses in Wallace Stevens's words: "Poetry is a cure of the mind." He announces his own special "formulation" of the problem of "a divided sensibility in Eliot's poetry." He sees "Eliot's poems as enacting a dramatic rivalry between the two kinds of order, one rational and a product of the poet's intellectual power, the other intuitive and a product of the more primitive and spontaneous aspect of the poet's imagination" (p. xii). Scarcely novel. The creative process has normally been so described, and was by Eliot. But here Spurr confuses the issue—and logic—by intruding a third term—a middle ground of disorder. "The poetic persona remains for a time passive in the face of his chaotic universe" (p. xv). To switch from processes of the poet's mind to a condition of the persona—a creation of that mind—is to give the case away. And it is this unfortunate invention of Spurr's that permits his judgment that Eliot's poems remain divided, whereas his models, Dante, Baudelaire, Yeats, manage a rational framework for theirs. A thoroughly surprising conclusion. Baudelaire and Yeats were scarcely Eliot's models, though perhaps Baudelaire reinforces for Eliot the notion of modern man as *homo duplex*, and both were by general agreement closer to Romanticism than was Eliot. We have not yet heard the last contradiction in Spurr's short preface: the tensions experienced by Eliot were "ruinous" to the poet and he could not go on with poetry—or effective criticism—after *Four Quartets*. Nevertheless, the strength of his poetry "derives from an awareness of its own inner divisions," and his determination to preserve them (pp. xix-xx). How the "division" was understood by Eliot, how it relates to the problem of belief in poetry that he explored repeatedly in differentiating metaphysical from philosophical poets, how he saw it affecting the poetry of modern man in a fragmented age (the waste land)— all these familiar aspects of Eliot studies Spurr ignores. His critical stance, of course, permits him this lacuna—and indeed all those lacunae exhibited in his readings of the poems— readings which occupy much of the book.

Paraphrase of Eliot's poems is an impossible enterprise at best but at its worst as engineered by a reductive and revisionist reader. Spurr ignores Eliot's technique of allusion, the enrichment of meaning through the context of a quoted phrase. As he has warned us that by virtue of his critical method he is freed from any constraints of considering unity in a poem, we should not be surprised at the *disjecta membra* he substitutes for the dramatic monologue "Prufrock." One illustration must serve to show Spurr's poetic insensitivity. Extremely diverse images of the sea, serving, as they occur, totally diverse purposes, are assimilated thus: "The speaker [in *The Dry Salvages*] looks down into a pool to behold 'The more delicate algae and the sea anemone,' *companions* [my emphasis] of the 'ragged claws' in *Prufrock*, and the 'current under sea' in *The Waste Land*" (p. 95). Of *Four Quartets* Spurr says: "The poet assaults language in his attempt to reconcile the conflicting ideas of order that govern his consciousness" (p. 100). (The critic assaults language when he describes the Holy Spirit as "bolting from heaven.")

Mistaking for failure of control what is artistic intent (how is it possible so to misread the very essence of Modernism?), Spurr finds in the early poems only "a disordered consciousness represented by images of fragmentation and impurity" (p. 13). Of such an image as "some infinitely gentle/Infinitely suffering thing" he observes, "This octopus or angel proves too much to handle" (p. 13).

The critic is indeed emancipated. He is dealing with an unknown (the author's unconscious) in the light (if that is the word) of a text that is in effect his own creation. (Eliot has provided at best the raw materials—a sort of inkblot to which the reader responds as he will.) What can one say about the results of such an enterprise? Merely that any correspondence to the original (the poet and his text) are, as in fiction, coincidental. Criticism this is not.

Representative of another mode of modern criticism is David Tobin's *The Presence of the Past: T. S. Eliot's Victorian Inheritance*, a Princeton dissertation published in the UMI series Studies in Modern Literature, of which the general editor is A. Walton Litz and the editor for Eliot Ronald Bush. The title is so vague as to permit wide ranging and almost to preclude positive results. Wide ranging is sure to be unproductive except for a mature scholar who has read widely and meditated long. The unformed judgment cannot pronounce persuasively and Tobin does not. Moreover, he wants positive results: parallels and even influences. A passage of Kipling's is juxtaposed with one of Eliot's. They have in common the word *housemaids* (p. 107). The influence search is pursued under the aegis of Harold Bloom and this allows the critic to have it both ways. If one poet praises another, influence can safely be assumed.

If he does not, one may assume "a strategy of defense," and the chase is on. Tobin builds his case for influence with the use of such phrases as "must have had their effect" or "obviously struck him quite deeply." Sometimes mere assertion serves: "Taine's influence on Eliot is clear in *The Sacred Wood*, with its manner of scientific scrupulousness and objectivity." "The 'contrapuntal arrangement of subject matter' in *In Memoriam* [the phrase is Eliot's but Eliot did not apply it to *In Memoriam*] provided Eliot with an important model for the building of long poems" (pp. 112, 151). Claiming the lyric "O that 'twere possible" in *Maud* as an unacknowledged source for Eliot at several points, Tobin writes, "Reverting to Harold Bloom's terms, one would say that Eliot had no choice but to ignore it, for the lyric encroaches far too much into his own poetic territory—to confront it would be to admit that he was Tennyson's successor" (p. 131). Wimsatt, to whom Tobin refers, had, one would have supposed, said the final word on Eliot's connection with this lyric.

Tobin must be commended for diligent exploration. What he has found by way of analogy is interesting but not much more. The analogy quest is a diversion usually harmless and sometimes suggestive. The pursuit of influences is a difficult discipline that must follow (*pace* Harold Bloom) strict rules and requires wide and exact knowledge together with a high degree of literary tact. This book is not an adequate example of the influence study.

A refreshing corrective to psychological portraiture and anxiety of influence is provided by Caroline Behr's *T. S. Eliot: A Chronology of the Life and Works*, one of a series which has the rather unusual aim of supplying for major literary figures a day by day chronicle of life and work. No general editor for the St. Martin's Press series is named and indeed insufficient editorial guidance has been afforded this author—described as "a free-lance writer" but obviously neither Eliot expert nor academic—to spare her such avoidable errors as inconsistent handling of titles, inaccurate terminology, occasional omission of sources, lapses in grammar, imprecision of detail where precision would have been possible, and innumerable typos. Owning to—perhaps directed by—no editorial principles, Behr has produced a highly individual work that is likely to satisfy no one. Nevertheless, the book supplies a kind of intellectual history together with a convincing portrait of Eliot. Both owe their character to the variety of sources consulted, and these, of course, include published letters and reminiscences of Eliot's friends—and enemies. Neglected facets of Eliot's career and personality emerge as we read summaries of his (uncollected) contributions to the *Dial*, the *Criterion*, the *Listener*, and *TLS*, and note which authors (when) he published in the *Criterion* (McNeice [sic], Oct. 1932; Auden, Jan. 1930) or selected for Faber editions (Auden, 1930). The listing of (partial) contents of the *Criterion* issues Eliot edited gives a clue to his changing interests. (And how many people know—need to know?—that on 29 Nov. 1936 the *Times* published Eliot's letter on Stilton cheese, recommending the formation of a Society for the Preservation of Ancient Cheeses?)

The extent of Eliot's labors for literature is documented in its diversity and overwhelming quantity: introductions and prefaces to books, manifold lectures and lecture series—in America, Sweden, Germany, as well as all over England, broadcasts (e.g., a BBC German series, 1946). Sometimes Behr excerpts unlikely prefaces to throw light on the poetry (e.g., that to Edgar Mowrer's *This American World*, 1928). Even Eliot's reading for various years is chronicled, as published in *Horizon* (1948) or the *Sunday Times* (1950, a Simenon *Maigret* included). And his growing reputation is traced in (occasional) summaries of contemporary reviews of his works, not forgetting productions of his plays. The portrait drawn is that of a man of letters, actively involved in the life of his time, not merely literary life but religious (his Church chores are duly noted) and political. The breed is rare in England and America though common on the Continent. And as man of letters Eliot's concern was always to encourage by example as well as precept the notion of culture as international. (He contributes to *La Nouvelle Revue française* and *La France libre*; writes on Machiavelli in *TLS*, writes the preface to Valéry's *Le Serpent* in Mark Wardle's translation.) We hear so much of Eliot the tortured spirit that it is delightful to find little entries like this one for July 1944 (from Harold Nicolson's *Diaries*, 1966) on a dinner party at

Sybil Colefax's where Eliot, a guest along with Spender and the Duchess of Devonshire, was "in a charming mood."

One disquieting note. The account of Eliot's contribution to *Horizon* (May 1941) on Virginia Woolf is thoroughly misleading—one wonders whether Behr read it. Where so much ground has been covered in cursory fashion, errors in fact as well as proportion are probably inevitable and one must use the *Chronology* with caution. Nevertheless, though eccentric, this book is a good read. And to give form and substance to the public figure here outlined one need seek no further than Donald Hall's modest account in *Remembering Poets* (1977).[4]

The two Eliot volumes edited by Michael Grant for the Critical Heritage series are, of course, indispensable to the scholar; even for the common reader they will be enlightening. Objections first. The format of this series has long since been set, so perhaps there is no point in finding fault, but it does seem unfortunate that so useful a concept should present itself in so disagreeable a dress. The photo-offset text is unpleasant to read (margins unresolved and exclusion of italics so that titles of books and articles are indistinguishable). The two volumes are paged continuously and table of contents and index (repeated, fortunately, in each volume) make no distinction between volumes. There are no running heads on pages for orientation as to which book is under review by whom. The omission of quotations in the articles is both inconsistent and inconvenient—though the reason for omission (cost containment) is clear. There is no explicit statement of limits and principles. Actually the book includes criticism (usually, of course, reviews) of Eliot's works as they appeared and up to (this I deduce—we are not told) the publication of the next book. Since the various editions of collected poems are included, this takes us through 1963. The subject is not the critical heritage of *Eliot* but of Eliot the poet and playwright. This should have been clearly specified, and, alas, the omission of Eliot the critic leads to a basic falsification that is in no way compensated for in Grant's introduction. Like the *apparatus criticus* of the volumes, that essay takes insufficient account of the hypothetical audience. The uninitiate, who are presumably addressed here, need more guidance on *The Waste Land* Notes than the phrase, not even attributed to Eliot, "that remarkable exposition of bogus scholarship" (p. 18), and on *The Waste Land* facsimile. And surely British should be distinguished from American periodicals when the title does not specify.

The very long and badly written introduction is a guide to the book, pointing out the highs and lows of Eliot's reputation and usefully extending the book with a section on Eliot's posthumous reputation as traceable in recent scholarship. On the whole, the selections have been sensibly made so that one does not very often ask: Why this? (Why the eight-page essay by Gorham B. Munson—who he? Why only one review—to be sure it is a superb one by Marianne Moore—of *Marina*?) Or why not that? (Why not a review of the Broadway *Cocktail Party* with Alec Guinness?) One is glad to find the distinguished essay by James Johnson Sweeney (1941) and Edmund Wilson's perceptive essay in *The Dial* (December 1922). What a fine critic Edmund Wilson was—acutely aware at that early date of the novelty of *The Waste Land*. Morton D. Zabel's assessment (1936) is worth returning to, as are, toward the end of Eliot's publication, such general appraisals as Donald Davies's (1963) and Frank Kermode's (1963), though Kermode is here not up to his usual standard. One is in the presence not only of a reputation forming and undergoing adjustment, but also of a host of authors, most of them well known, practicing with some distinction their critical craft. The early lot is the most star-studded, though when they wrote on Eliot they were not yet stars. Eliot scholars are not well represented (Helen Gardner is there), owing to the inclusion only of journal articles immediately responsive to a new publication, but academic critics are (Leavis, Bateson, Kermode). The outline is discernible here of Eliot's reputation as a special case—that of the expatriate American rejected by his countrymen as a deserter and never altogether assimilated into the culture of his adopted country, one traditionally suspicious of the French heritage Eliot acknowledged. On the whole the collection cannot fail to impress us with the body of judicious criticism that has taken shape over the past sixty-odd years.

The Critical Heritage includes only one review of *Practical Cats*—only one, but Spender's. It is a pity that owing to the cut-off date no word could be said of Eliot's latest theatrical triumph. (Behr does include *Cats*.) Having through a special dispensation of Fate found collaborators (Andrew Lloyd Webber and Trevor Nunn) who made of Eliot's superior amusement an even more superior amusement—and lots of money—Eliot has achieved the great splash on Shaftesbury Avenue and Broadway he had always vainly aspired to. Indeed all over America Old Possum may now be known as Eliot never was. Some of the audience at the Boston production I saw had come all the way from the Cape to see *Cats*—for the second time, bringing the children. They were singing the hit songs along with the performers. What a pleasure for Eliot to know— somewhere in the Empyrean he may—that his career in the theater ended not with the whimper of *The Elder Statesman* but with a very big bang.

The Critical Heritage gives us an overview of Eliot's reputation in his own time. For Eliot's reputation today we have Robert Canary's *T. S. Eliot: The Poet and His Critics*, an indispensable book. Nothing is more needed in our time, when publishing proceeds by geometric progression and editorial standards are to say the least mysterious, than a guide through the highways and byways of Eliot terrain. This Canary provides, writing with good sense and literary tact, with learning and balanced judgement; writing, moreover, in a lucid and graceful style. This is no mere annotated bibliography. The summaries Canary provides are generous enough to indicate tone and point of view as well as content, and he engages his authors in dialogue, indicating at comfortable length how the argument is developed and whether or not it holds up. He unravels the complicated tissues of fabrication woven by his subjects—quite without outrage even when common sense shows them to be outrageous. Not intimidated by names, he finds useful insights in the work of unknown writers and builds a convincing case against, for example, the contentions of J. Hillis Miller (*Poets of Reality*), demonstrating Miller's confusion of Eliot's philosophical position as derived from Bradley with Prufrock's state of mind. (Actually, Miller in his account of Eliot's dissertation on Bradley frequently makes Eliot responsible for what, according to Eliot, Bradley is saying.)

The book is organized by topics: The Personal Poet, The Impersonal Poet, The Social Critic, The Religious Poet, The Traditional Poet, The Modern Poet. This arrangement allows the author to direct his attention to the *loci critici* of Eliot criticism, e.g., the objective correlative, dissociation of sensibility, Eliot's "Romanticism." (No longer should it be possible for an author to "discover" in 1970 a "source" for the perplexing term *objective correlative* mentioned not only by Eliot in 1960 [to dispose of it] but by Robert Stallman in 1950.) The book is a pleasure to use—well printed, well indexed, the pages agreeably presented. Long lists of references at the ends of chapters both document and supplement the text. The American Library Association should be commended for this series, The Poet and his Critics, as should its general editor, Charles Sanders of the University of Illinois, Urbana.

I think I can best indicate the quality of Canary's book by quotation. On the accusation (especially by Bernard Bergonzi and Ian Hamilton) that Eliot lacked "loving warmth and other good things": "Most assertions about Eliot's ability to love are not serious biographical statements but value judgements, based on personal reactions to the poetry, simplistic theories of poetic creation, and, quite often, sympathy—or lack of it—for Eliot's religious position" (p. 29). On the perennial question, was Eliot Romantic? "It may seem paradoxical to label as Romantic a critic who proclaimed himself a Classicist and was sharply critical of his Romantic predecessors, but there is evidence that Eliot felt the intellectual and aesthetic attractions of the subjectivism and Romanticism he criticized. Difficulties arise, however, when Eliot's intellectual position is distorted, either by the 'discovery' of implausible sources for his criticism or by exaggerating the extent to which he shared the critical assumptions of Romanticism." (p. 74). "Although criticism cannot advance beyond impressionism without employing general notions about structure, the failure of our concepts of unity to account for our experience of a work should not be charged against the work; great works should alter our view of the nature of art" (pp.101-02). This last is on the method of Stephen Kirk and Ann Bolgan, who, having severally dissolved the unity of *The Waste Land,* judge the work a failure. On the original of the hyacinth girl: " 'Eliot might have repudiated the interpretations here advanced,' admits [G. Wilson] Knight, 'having perhaps forgotten the meanings, which came only under poetic inspiration. Or through caution. But this is not to say that he would repudiate them now. What appears necessary on this plane may assume different proportions on the next. Granted this key of the seraphic, Eliot becomes a great poet wrestling with the ultimates of human culture.' It is this sort of confidence in his interpretations that has made Knight a major critic. How few of us would think, lacking earthly evidence, to call in a dead poet's ghost to ratify our reading!" (p. 31). Implied in Canary's exposition and evaluation of all these divergent views, is Canary's own interpretation, for a critic can scarcely be a persuasive critic of critics, himself lacking a critical position. Thus this substantial and judicial book provides not only a portrait of Eliot a figure in the carpet of criticism but, beyond that, of Eliot the poet and critic who is still there to tempt critics—and to reward readers.

Notes

1. I should like to mention here another exemplar of old-fashioned critical reading: Barbara Everett's, who in 1975 published in the Spring issue of *Critical Quarterly* an admirably lucid and persuasive commentary on *The Waste Land* in which she distinguished Eliot's earlier style of "travesty" from his later style of "sincerity" and made the wise observation: "Style differentiates men, ideas assimilate them" (p. 7). This was Eliot's own view, e.g., "Not our feelings, but the pattern which we may make of our feelings is the center of value" (Foreword to Mark Wardle's translation of Valéry's *Le Serpent* [London: Cobden-Sanderson, 1924], p. 13).

2. One of Bush's errors in judgment and reading is to overplay Mallarmé's influence on Eliot. As we all know, Eliot said that immature poets borrow and mature poets steal. His theft from Mallarmé in *Burnt Norton* has long been recognized. His "Note sur Mallarmé et Poe," tr. Ramon Fernandez, *Nouvelle Revue française* 14, no. 58 (1 Nov. 1926), actually part of the re-exploration of the term *metaphysical* in poetry that formed the subject of the 1926 Clark lectures, makes his relationship to Mallarmé pretty clear. I have discussed this "influence" in "Eliot: An English Symbolist?" in *The Symbolist Movement in the Literature of European Languages*, ed. Anna Balakian (Budapest: Akadémiai Kiadó, 1982), pp. 295-310.

3. Bernard Bergonzi, *T. S. Eliot*(New York: Collier Books, 1972), p. 92. By what legislative mandate or supernatural edict were the triad invoked by

Spurr as *dei ex machina* empowered to "free the critic" from the conventional limitations of the genre? To pose the question is to answer it.

4. Behr includes an ostensibly complete list of Eliot's publications, books and pamphlets in one chronological list, periodical contributions in another. The bibliography (called "Source Books") is very short indeed on Eliot studies byt lists the diaries, reminiscences, and other collections drawn on.

Contributors

WILLIAM H. ALLISON is Professor of Theatre Arts and Associate Director of the Institute for the Arts and Humanistic Studies at Pennsylvania State University.

FRED D. CRAWFORD is Instructor of English at the University of Oregon.

LEOPOLD DAMROSCH, JR. is Professor of English at the University of Maryland.

DAVID J. DELAURA is Avalon Foundation Professor of Humanities and Professor of English at the University of Pennsylvania.

L. S. DEMBO is Professor of English at the University of Wisconsin.

RICHARD J. FINNERAN is Professor of English at Newcomb College.

BARBARA M. FISHER is Adjunct Assistant Professor of English at City College, CUNY.

ARNOLD B. FOX is Professor of English at Northern Illinois University.

WILLIAM E. FREDEMAN is Professor of English at the University of British Columbia.

FRED HOBSON is Professor of English at the University of Alabama.

RICHARD S. IDE is Associate Professor of English at the University of Southern California.

JEROME LOVING is Professor of English at Texas A&M University.

ROBERT F. LUCID is Professor of English at the University of Pennsylvania.

VERONICA MAKOWSKY is Assistant Professor of English at Louisiana State University.

JOHN MAYNARD is Professor of English at New York University.

MELVYN NEW is Professor of English at the University of Florida.

JEFFREY C. ROBINSON is Associate Professor of English at the University of Colorado.

MARY BETH ROSE is Director of the Center for Renaissance Studies at the Newberry Library.

RODGER L. TARR is Professor of English at Illinois State University.

RUTH Z. TEMPLE is Professor of English Emeritus, Brooklyn College, CUNY.

RUTH BERNARD YEAZELL is Professor of English at the University of California at Los Angeles.